Grassroots at the Gateway

CLASS : CULTURE

Grassroots at the Gateway

Class Politics and Black Freedom Struggle in St. Louis, 1936–75

Clarence Lang

THE UNIVERSITY OF MICHIGAN PRESS

Ann Arbor

2012   2011   2010   2009   4   3   2   1

A CIP catalog record for this book is available from the British Library.

Library of Congress Cataloging-in-Publication Data

Lang, Clarence.
    Grassroots at the gateway : class politics and Black freedom
struggle in St. Louis, 1936-75 / Clarence Lang.
        p.   cm. — (Class: culture)
    Includes index.
    ISBN 978-0-472-07065-7 (cloth : alk. paper) — ISBN 978-0-472-
05065-9 (pbk. : alk. paper)
    1. African Americans—Missouri—Saint Louis—History—20th
century.   2. African Americans—Missouri—Saint Louis—Social
conditions—20th century.   3. African Americans—Civil rights—
Missouri—Saint Louis—History—20th century.   4. Saint Louis (Mo.)—
History—20th century.   5. Saint Louis (Mo.)—Social conditions—
20th century.   6. Saint Louis (Mo.)—Race relations.   I. Title.
F474.S29N46   2009
305.5'6208996073077866—dc22   2009018644

ISBN-13 978-0-472-02654-8 (electronic)

In memory of
Annie Louise Eastman,
Marsha Jordan, and Doris Wesley

Preface

IN THE MID–1990s, when I was an M.A. student at Southern Illinois University at Edwardsville, I became a member of a grassroots organization in nearby St. Louis, Missouri. In conversations with activists of various stripes, I encountered the frequent complaint that the city was a cultural backwater and its black community politically timid. As I became more familiar with the local landscape, however, I was struck by what appeared to be vibrant and deeply rooted traditions of black resistance. Yet, aside from George Lipsitz's groundbreaking book on Ivory Perry, there were precious few published works on St. Louis's black freedom struggle, especially in the post–World War II period. I wanted to learn more about the local movement that had given me many formative experiences, as well as discover more about the peculiarities of a city that was curiously both midwestern and southern.

Consistent with my broader concerns, I also wanted to explore further the role of class in defining relationships and political interests among black movement organizers, their would-be constituencies, and African Americans more generally. Indeed, on a range of issues including police violence, criminal sentencing, the death penalty, school reform, living wages, and urban redevelopment and economic policy, I found time and again that the battle lines literally were not drawn in black and white. A stark illustration of these complexities of race and class occurred in 1997, when St. Louis experienced one of the most polarizing Democratic mayoral primary races in its history. The incumbent, Freeman Bosley Jr., had been elected the city's first black mayor in 1993. His opponent, Clarence Harmon, was the former police chief and the first African American to hold the position. Although they were both black middle-class professionals, they were the surrogates of distinctly different and competing racial-class alliances in this formerly Jim Crow city. While Bosley drew his support largely from the city's predominantly black north side, Harmon was overwhelmingly favored by downtown corporate leaders and white politicians and residents of the South St. Louis wards, who were unwilling to betray an explicitly racial agenda by running a white candidate. Harmon handily won the primary and subsequent general election, allowing conservative white St. Louisans to claim that race had nothing to do with Bosley's ouster. But after serving four undistinguished years in office, Harmon, too, became a one-term black mayor. Tellingly, the same white voters who had put him in City Hall abandoned him just as dramatically to elect white Democrat Francis Slay in 2001. With the effects of the 2005 Hurricane Katrina crisis still unfolding, the energies unleashed by the 2008 Barack Obama presidential candidacy still percolating, white racist ideologies, practices, and institutions still regnant, and internal cleavages among African Americans widening, the need to historicize the racial and class politics of black freedom struggle looms far beyond St. Louis.

I have amassed more than my share of debts over the course of bringing this book to fruition. I have benefited from the guidance, patience, wisdom, selfless assistance, and continuing advice of Sundiata Keita Cha-Jua, Juliet E. K. Walker, James R. Barrett, Mark Leff, and David Roediger. Shirley Portwood, Ellen Nore, Norman Nordhauser, Wayne Santoni, Anthony Cheeseboro, Anne Valk, Steve Tamari, Leslie Brown, and Katharine Douglass have also been invaluable sources of professional and personal encouragement. In the earliest stages of this project, I was fortunate to receive a summer research fellowship at the Missouri Historical Society (MHS) in St. Louis. My deepest gratitude goes to the MHS Library and Research Center's helpful archivists, librarians, and staff, especially Jacqueline Dace, John Wolford, Dina Young, Dennis Northcott, Edna Banner Smith, Jason Stratman, Carol Verble, Ellen Thomasson, Amanda Claunch, and the late Marsha Jordan. I am indebted, further, to the wonderful staff at the Western Historical Manuscript Collection in St. Louis: Zelli Fischetti, Linda Belford, Kenneth Thomas, and the late Doris Wesley. As well, Miranda Rectenwald, of the Department of Special Collections at Washington University in St. Louis, and Deborah Cribbs, curator of Special Collections at the St. Louis Mercantile Library, gave vital last-minute research assistance. The research librarians at the Chicago Historical Society, and at the Archives of Labor and Urban Affairs at Wayne State University, were equally giving of their time, insights, and expertise. The College of Liberal Arts at Wayne State, and the Department of History, extended every courtesy during my tenure in Detroit as a research associate, including vitally needed resources, office space, and more importantly, the time to write.

I am fortunate to have belonged to a community of scholars and activists that has kept me grounded in the view that scholarship is never separate from concrete political interests. I still wrestle with how to resolve the tension between sustaining a meaningful commitment to social change while also meeting the sometimes isolating demands of the tenure track, but I am nonetheless thankful to Jamala Rogers, Kalimu Endesha, the entire OBS (Organization for Black Struggle) "Family," Percy Green, Minkah Makalani, Jung Hee Choi, Monica White, Steve Hollis, John Pappademos, Kim Jayne, Janey Archey, Jim Wilkerson, Anyango Asantewaa, Maneesha Bidani, Dianne Riley, Reynaldo Anderson, Tonya Hutchinson, Audrey Collins, Myrna Fichtenbaum, Jeff Williams, David Crockett, Theodore Koditschek, Stephen Ferguson, John McClendon, Bill Fletcher, Grace Lee Boggs, Scott Kurashige, Robbie Lieberman, Dianne Feeley and the staff of *Against the Current,* Stephen Ward, Imani Bazzell, Melodye Rosales, Sam Smith, Carol and Aaron Ammons, Ricky Jones, Will Patterson, Jimmie Briggs, Jabari Asim, Rebecca Ginsburg, Bill Sullivan, Tony Tyeeme Clark, Lena Roberson-Joshua, and the board members of the Davis-Putter Scholarship Fund.

Revisions of this book were made possible by a Beckman Fellowship, which I received from the Center for Advanced Study at the University of Illinois at Urbana-Champaign. The university also provided a subvention payment for this project. As a faculty member, I could not ask for better colleagues than the ones I have found during my joint appointment in the Department of African American Studies and the Department of History. Helen Neville, John Jennings, Christopher Span, Adlai Murdoch, Robin Jarrett, Ray Muhammad, Thomas Weissinger, Brendesha Tynes, Peter Fritzsche, Antoinette Burton, Adrian Burgos, Dianne Harris, and Vernon Burton are notable among the many who have given me their unflagging friendship and support. My special appreciation goes to my colleagues Christopher Benson, Pedro Cabán, Abdul Alkalimat, Lou Turner, Ruby Mendenhall, Rayvon Fouche, and Marc Perry for their comments on early manifestations of this work; Chris and Pedro also gave me indispensable advice at several moments of uncertainty. During his residence here as a postdoctoral fellow in African American Studies, David Goldberg became one of my most trusted interlocutors on the subject of black freedom politics and labor, and freely shared his observations, sources, and deadpan humor. This work is a thousand times stronger because of his interventions. In addition, Emanuel Rota, of the Department of Spanish, Italian, and Portuguese, generously allowed me to bother him with questions about Gramscian thought. I have also been fortunate to work with some of the most serious and generous graduate students one could ever wish to teach: Ashley Howard, Kerry Pimblott (who also provided crucial research assistance), Marty Smith, Ed Onaci, Dave Bates, Nick Gaffney, Stephanie Seawell, Jay Jordan, Heidi Dodson, Valene Whittaker, Jon Hale, Kwame Holmes, Richard Benson, Elisabeth Corl, Ellen Tillman, Trey Davis, and Michael

Burns. I hope that they have received from me a modicum of the knowledge that I have gained from them.

Many thanks go to Steve Wrinn, Steven Lawson, Robert Devens, and Janet Francendese for their enthusiasm and wise counsel, as well as to Gerald Horne and George Lipsitz for good-naturedly answering my last-minute request to read several chapters of this manuscript. Lipsitz also shared valuable insights about Teamsters politics in St. Louis during the early 1970s. Trevor Griffey shared important FBI documents, while Julie Gay gave needed direction on how to turn an appallingly long manuscript into something approaching manageable length. I have had the extremely good fortune, as well, of working with the staff of the University of Michigan Press, including my generous and skillful editor LeAnn Fields, Scott Ham, Bill V. Mullen, Amy Schrager Lang, Marcia LaBrenz, Mary Hashman, and the Press's anonymous manuscript reviewers. Equally vital to this project has been the emotional sustenance from my family, especially my mother, Delores Lang-Patton; my cousins, Sheri and Samuel Temple; my grandmother, Mary Lang; my uncles and aunts, DeEdward, Carol, Smiley, Darcel, Yvonne, Bill, and Annie; Elsie and Johnnie Hamer, and my bountiful harvest of in-laws in Texas and Illinois; and my children, Nile and Zoe. My final and greatest debt is to Jenny Hamer, who has been my best friend, confidante, parenting coach, therapist, comrade, and spouse. Amid her own grueling schedule and research agenda, and the shared tasks of child rearing, she accommodated my writing schedule, which frequently removed me from household responsibilities. She did so, further, with love, understanding, and astonishing ease. She truly holds up my sky; this project would not be without her. Any mistakes have been mine alone.

Contents

Abbreviations

ABC	Association of Black Collegians
ACLU	American Civil Liberties Union
ACTION	Action Council (Committee) to Improve Opportunities for Negroes
AFL	American Federation of Labor
AWU	American Workers Union
ANLC	American Negro Labor Council
BAG	Black Artists Group
BSCP	Brotherhood of Sleeping Car Porters and Maids
CBC	Congressional Black Caucus
CBTU	Coalition of Black Trade Unionists
CCRC	Citizens Civil Rights Committee
CIO	Congress of Industrial Organizations
CNP	Christian Nationalist Party
COINTELPRO	Counterintelligence Program
CORE	Committee (Congress) of Race Equality
CRC	Civil Rights Congress
EEOC	Equal Employment Opportunity Commission
EHE	Experiment in Higher Education
FBI	Federal Bureau of Investigation
FEPC	Fair Employment Practice Committee
FOR	Fellowship of Reconciliation
FWIU	Food Workers Industrial Union
HDC	Human Development Corporation
HUAC	House Un-American Activities Committee
ICBO	Interracial Council for Business Opportunity
IUE	International United Electrical Workers
JOC	Job Opportunities Council
JVL	Jeff-Vander-Lou Community Action Group

LAW	League of Adequate Welfare
LCRA	Land Clearance for Redevelopment Authority
LSNR	League of Struggle for Negro Rights
MCC	Mid-City Congress
MOKAN	Missouri-Kansas Construction Contractors Association
MOWM	March on Washington Movement
NAACP	National Association for the Advancement of Colored People
NALC	Negro American Labor Council
NBPA	National Black Political Assembly
NNC	National Negro Congress
NNLC	National Negro Labor Council
NOI	Nation of Islam
NRA	National Recovery Administration
OMBE	Office of Minority Business Enterprise
PMEW	Pacific Movement of the Eastern World
PWA	Public Works Administration
SBA	Small Business Administration
SCAN	Student Committee for the Admission of Negroes
SCLC	Southern Christian Leadership Conference
SDS	Students for a Democratic Society
SNCC	Student Nonviolent Coordinating Committee
TAC	Tandy Area Council
TUUL	Trade Union Unity League
UE	United Electrical, Radio & Machine Workers of America
USES	United States Employment Service
WEC	Women's Economic Council
WPA	Works Progress (Project) Administration
YWCA	Young Women's Christian Association

Introduction

IN THE MIDSUMMER OF 1964, St. Louis's Congress of Racial Equality (CORE) picketed the construction site of the Gateway Arch monument, protesting the exclusion of African Americans from the skilled building trades involved in the publicly supported Jefferson National Expansion Memorial. Demanding a fair share of jobs for black workers, two activists scaled one of the Arch legs, where they effectively shut down the site for several hours. The demonstration was part of a series of events that later led to a settlement creating apprenticeship and outreach programs for working-class African Americans. In July 1999, thirty-five years later, nine hundred people converged in North St. Louis, near the ramps to and from Interstate 70. A contingent of three hundred marched onto the highway and poured across its five lanes, halting traffic for an hour. Unlike before, the guiding nucleus of this protest was the Missouri-Kansas Construction Contractors Association (MOKAN), a consortium of minority-owned firms; the demonstration itself stemmed from a dispute with the Missouri Department of Transportation about the lack of state highway construction contracts to black-owned businesses. Subsequent negotiations with state officials produced a settlement directly with the MOKAN members. Occurring on the anniversary of the 1964 Arch protest, and involving mass direct action reminiscent of this earlier period, the I-70 demonstration invited obvious comparisons. However, the 1999 protest was in many respects a retreat from the black freedom struggles of the previous decades. Thus, while MOKAN organizers used the demand for better-paying jobs to mobilize the many who participated in the highway disruption, the resulting concessions were focused on a small cohort of entrepreneurs.[1]

The wide historical dissonances between the Gateway Arch shutdown and the I-70 drama in 1999 symbolize the decline of working-class agendas in shaping black social movement activity, even as the working class has become ubiquitous in contemporary black social histories. Labor historians have turned their attention to independent working-class agency, both inside the workplace and in the larger urban "home sphere." They also have gone beyond simply chronicling black participation in trade unions to documenting black workers' self-organization outside organized labor. Theorists of the "New Black Urban History," moreover, have offered a finer grained sense of black working-class experience and culture, while historians and social scientists in the area of "Black Freedom Studies" have continued the recovery of working-class, or "grassroots," origins, aims, character, and constituencies of twentieth-century African American social movements.[2]

But while scholars in these overlapping fields have conjured the visage of the African American working class, this book contends that the historical role of this class in urban and social movements is less clear. Some historians have argued that most black working-class resistance has been unorganized, evasive "hidden transcripts" falling between the margins of both white labor unions and black protest organizations. Others, in contrast, have highlighted the overt, decidedly "unhidden transcripts" of black working-class agency, as evident in the episodic street battles between individual black workers and whites. Both lines of argument, however, have tended to efface the institutional and collective nature of black workers' self-organization, in the form of all-black unions; local, indigenous political and civic groupings; grassroots chapters of Black Nationalist organizations; and even local branches of ostensibly black middle-class organizations. Some historians have even tended to blur the lines between working-class and middle-class endeavors and aspirations. Thus, despite the "historic role that the black working class has played in the development and survival of the black community," its activities remain in need of greater theorization.[3]

Indeed, middle-class professionals have been making a vigorous "comeback" in black social and cultural histories. Whereas an emphasis on black "proletarianization" dominated the 1980s, a current scholarly trend has reasserted middle-class stewardship in black community life and social movements. This has been possible, ironically, because scholars like Richard W. Thomas and Joe William Trotter, who did the most to advance the proletarianization thesis, foregrounded black cross-class unity in a manner that ultimately minimized class-based fissures. Trotter, for instance, argued that black laborers "responded to their urban experience through both class and racial unity, though mainly through the latter." Urban historian Earl Lewis similarly averred that white racial hostility was a "great leveler" that forged black cooperation and community across class lines. While arguing for the catalytic role of the industrial working class in the African American urban experience, Thomas even refuted the proletarianization model in favor of a "more holistic" thesis of "community build-ing," including the key role of the "traditional" black middle-class leader-ship, and an emphasis on African Americans' "organic, communal ties." Yet, because middle-class professionals already were so thoroughly con-spicuous in earlier histories, reifying the idea of black community cohesion has, in the long run, only buttressed the centrality of black professionals to the community-building process. It has been easy, therefore, to characterize black working-class strivings as indistinguishable from, or collateral to, middle-class professionals' pursuit of peaceable reform through elite inter-racial cooperation, upward occupational mobility limited by class, and moral "respectability."[4]

A Historic Bloc and the Making of Black Freedom

Yet, working-class people historically constituted the most crucial segment of black America. They have not only been more numerous, but as Trotter and others documented, they also provided the economic bedrock for modern black middle-class formation, and facilitated the building of a black "home sphere" more generally. "Clearly," Lewis argues, "what bene-fited the worker paid dividends to the community." Resituating working-class politics at the center, this work argues that the growth and develop-ment of a black working-class community of interest propelled, and shaped the goals of, the major African American social movements be-tween the 1930s and 1970s, including the modern civil rights (1955–66) and Black Power (1966–75) phases of the Black Freedom Movement. "Someone needs to debunk the notion that the movement's goals and results were merely improvements in the lives of middle-class blacks," admonished vet-eran activist Julian Bond. Echoes scholar Manning Marable: "Most histori-ans fail to observe that the massive efforts waged for desegregation and, to a lesser extent, for Black Power, were basically black workers' movements." Indeed, civil rights, Black Power, and their interwar antecedents, repre-sented the racial-class agendas of black working people for fair and full employment, better wages, union protection and the overall desegregation of the U.S. labor movement, racial fairness under the law, political repre-sentation, fair housing, education, health care and other social wages, equi-table access to parks and similar public amenities, and urban development policies geared toward black communal preservation—in short, a mini-mum program for full citizenship and self-determination.[5]

These struggles, however, caused sharp class tensions among African Americans, principally about methods, means, and decorum, but increas-ingly about goals. Thus, while black professionals and workers shared overarching concerns about racial inclusion and equality, they did not agree on whether the full exercise of rights and freedoms hinged primarily on stable blue-collar jobs or advancement in salaried professions and business enterprise, the revitalization of existing black ghettoes or the selective integration of white middle-class suburbs, downtown redevelopment or black economic opportunity, "breadwinner wages" for unemployed men or "autonomous households" for poor women, formal electoral politics or community organizing, mass grassroots mobilization or black middle-class stewardship, a focus on disruptive grassroots protests or faith in white elite paternalism and interracial "civility," or immediate concession or long-term negotiation. Certainly, the black working and middle classes collaborated politically, but the terms of that cooperation were mightily contested. In reality, the idea of a "black community" was a tangle of mutuality, self-interest, and stratification—as sociologist Mary Pattillo argues, a collective endeavor more than a static phenomenon. Long before the post–World War II period, middle-class professionals and workers vied for influence within shared organizations. Disagreeing about everything from gender norms to protest politics, they also created their own separate institutions. The politics of black middle-class "respectability," often contingent on the white gaze, collided with a black working-class politics of "self-respect" autonomous from both white approval and black middle-class assent. Moreover, in their efforts to act as "representative Negroes" on behalf of the race, middle-class African Americans frequently sought to simultaneously distance themselves from their working-class counterparts, administer to their many social needs, and dictate to workers norms, behavior, and their "best interests" through ideologies and practices of "racial uplift."[6]

Nonetheless, the mass nature of black popular struggles favored the laboring majority, allowing it the principal role even in popular upsurges nominally led by middle-class people. Workers' agendas, then, formed the core of a "historic bloc" of forces within the black community. Briefly defined, a historic bloc is an ensemble of contradictory and discordant relationships (economic, ideological, and political) in which a dominant class rules not only through coercion, but also through active consent and participation of the subordinate class—or rather, hegemony. More narrowly, it refers to a complex, internally combative amalgam of social forces that unifies around a sweeping, "universalizing" agenda, but that centers on the leadership of a distinct class grouping. This concept, though typically employed to describe the hegemony of dominant classes, is also pertinent to identifying the counterhegemonic politics of subaltern groups, which speaks to the fact that neither dominant nor dominated classes act singly, or simply in their own name. Rather, projecting themselves as representatives of the popular will, members of a given class function within diverse coalitions, even as they pursue their own specific interests. This was the case for black freedom struggles between the 1930s and 1970s when, on behalf of an African American public, black workers decisively led, forming the nucleus of a black cross-class coalition of resistance.[7]

Generally speaking, class comprises not just occupational prestige and status, income, education, "lifestyle," or even wealth. It is also the place one occupies in the production and distribution of goods and services, and the degree of authority and autonomy one exercises in determining the content and pace of work. This is, further, intertwined with the levels of power individuals exert in the broader society. Modern U.S. society has contained three major classes. The first is the capitalist elite, which owns and controls the major means of production, distribution, and finance. Attendant to these circumstances, this class holds disproportionate power in setting policy, law, social knowledge, and cultural norms, both through coercive and ideological means. The second grouping is the working class, whose existence hinges on skilled, semiskilled, and unskilled wage-labor, or in its absence, income subsidies. Thus, it consists of both manual and mental laborers, who perform any number of routinized, regimented tasks under the supervision of a manager or "boss." It also encompasses those in casual, informal labor markets, as well as the unemployed. As a whole, workers create social wealth through their labor, paid or otherwise.[8]

Third in this schema is the middle class, composed of trained professionals, civil servants, small business owners, and various administrative officials, managers, executives, and supervisors. Relative to their working-class counterparts, members of the middle class characteristically enjoy greater flexibility and autonomy in the content of their work, decision-making responsibility, and managerial control over others. Although sharing in the exercise of authority over working classes, members of the middle class are themselves subordinated to capital. Depending on a range of circumstances, segments of the middle class may either oppose capitalist prerogatives, or form alliances with this elite against working-class interests. Of course, the lines separating classes are not neat, nor are classes internally monolithic. Not only do they overlap at the edges, but those ostensibly within the same class may also differ economically, politically, ideologically, and culturally. Although class has an objective historical and social reality, it nonetheless includes one's self-identification. Thus, it constitutes an identity rooted simultaneously in individual and collective experience, consciousness, and practice. Class is an uneven, constantly evolving process, and what constitutes a particular social class during one period is not the same as at others. Classes are, in fact, always in a state of historical formation—coming into being, developing, and acting in multiple ways. Moreover, because classes are fundamentally relationships, they only exist in reference to each other. Ultimately, these are relationships of power.[9]

Class is a slippery concept by itself, but racial identity makes it even more elusive. As a racially oppressed and unassimilated people within the U.S. polity, African Americans historically have lacked a fully formed internal class structure. Given the realities of racial exclusion, black people have been overrepresented in the working class, the black middle class has been underdeveloped and weak, and black capitalists, until very recently, have been virtually nonexistent outside of small banks, real estate, insurance companies, and newspapers. Consequently, the ways in which African Americans have identified and located class have been shaped by internal communal standards—ranging from perceptions of stable employment to purely "nonmaterial" phenomena such as personal character, behavior, skin color, comportment, Christian morality, and similar markers of "respectability." Because U.S. racial apartheid fostered the development of a separate black public sphere, African Americans have viewed their interests through the lens of a shared history and culture, and have often determined their individual welfare through perceptions of common group interests and a "linked fate" superseding class.[10]

Yet, despite the amorphous lines of demarcation between black elites and laborers, African Americans have not existed as a unified racial community. To say that the black experience has not conformed to prevailing patterns of class formation is not to conclude, then, that class is inapplicable to the black experience. To the contrary, African Americans have been quite class conscious—often more than whites, especially in perceiving the distinctions between managers and workers, and mental and manual labor. Rather, the point is that class formation has had its own particular historical trajectories among African Americans. While these conditions may have led African Americans to regard themselves as a people sharing a common fate, the ways in which they have interpreted these linkages have been multivocal. This has especially been the case with regard to identifying the proper battles to be waged by the black community, who is qualified to lead, and through which means.[11]

Along these lines, this project asks: What social forces conditioned the emergence of a black urban working-class political bloc, and how did it evolve? How did black working-class formation, politics, and consciousness remain consistent, as well as alter, over of time? How did this black working-class coalition of resistance decline? Or rather, how and why did these early, and subsequent, democratic mass movements surrender to an emphasis on the personal advancement of black entrepreneurs by the end of the 1970s? "When and how," Julian Bond asked, "were 'jobs and freedom' replaced by 'joint ventures and set-asides'?"[12] More pointedly, how did these processes precipitate the discursive transformation of a black working class into a contemporary black "underclass"? I conclude that by the mid-1970s, a new historic bloc led by the black middle class emerged. Black electoral politics, and appeals for greater access to business capital, contracts, and corporate franchises shifted the class-based meanings of black citizenship and self-determination away from the distinct laboring interests that had been rooted in demands for expanded social wages.[13]

St. Louis, Missouri, and the Middle Border Region

This shift speaks directly to the historical importance of class in conceptualizing black freedom struggles. This book examines the role of black working-class formation in St. Louis, Missouri, in guiding African American politics between the late 1930s and the mid-1970s. These years encompassed the Great Depression and World War II, which created preconditions for a relatively stable black working-class bloc of forces; and the twilight of the Great Society, when the effects of long-standing urban quandaries and political realignments eroded black working-class activism. The period encompassing the interregnum between world wars, and the end of the War on Poverty, was also a moment of heightened black mass movement struggle. I situate black St. Louis's working-class formation and popular protest within five major contexts. The first is the changing economy, which included transitions from commercial to industrial, and then postindustrial, capitalism. These transitions affected patterns of black employment, income, and quality of life, and other class relations. The second context is national and local governmental policy, including the federally sanctioned land-use initiatives that made, and remade, St. Louis's black spatial communities. Third are black people's varied interactions with white workers, professionals, and capitalists over time, which formed the matrices in which African Americans experienced a collective racial identity. The fourth context grounding this study is black social cleavage along axes of gender, class, and markers of status, and schisms of political ideology. The final context is local black social movement activity, which provides an index to working-class agency, consciousness, and intraracial conflict.[14]

A specific focus on St. Louis is timely in that it coheres with an emergent "Black Freedom Studies" emphasis on local grassroots movements north of the Mason-Dixon Line—including border state communities, which historian Peter B. Levy argues "were neither northern nor southern but a combination of both." A geographically interstitial city like St. Louis further illustrates that North-South distinctions, though not absolute, were real in shaping black freedom struggles. This project is therefore part of a growing conversation about black popular movements outside the South.[15]

St. Louis also has relevance to trends in the field of black urban history. Earlier narratives centered on the Midwest and Northeast. In contrast, this book reflects a developing prominence of black community studies rooted in the South, the West, and the spaces between. Like its midwestern industrial neighbors, St. Louis had been a magnet for European immigrants, especially skilled German mechanics and unskilled Irish laborers, and later for waves of black southern migrants. Food and tobacco processing, flour milling, shoes, lead paints, bricks and tiles, brewing, clothing manufacturing, and iron and steel production were economic mainstays, though no one sector predominated. Located across the banks of the Mississippi River from East St. Louis, Illinois, St. Louis was in fact part of a regional metropolitan economy. Similar to Chicago and Detroit, St. Louis boasted an active black working class by the early twentieth century, and a labor movement with pronounced "social unionist" strains. Characteristic of other Rust Belt capitals, moreover, the Gateway City suffered fiscal crisis, industrial relocation, and population loss, and became overwhelmingly black. At the same time that St. Louis was a quintessential urban metropolis, however, it was a unique bellwether of urban trends. Adopting the nation's first home rule municipal charter in 1876, residents freed themselves from state and county government, yet shackled themselves to fixed city boundaries that prevented future growth and fragmented metropolitan government. The eventual result, by the late 1970s, was the nation's most severe urban crisis, making St. Louis "a telling (and understudied) setting for understanding the broader patterns of modern urban history."[16]

Bustling along the Mississippi River, near the joining of the Missouri River, the "Gateway City" was, moreover, a regional crossroads. From the building of a continental American empire and national market economy, through the secession crisis over slavery, it was a pivotal site in determining the nation's path of development. Historically, the city had been a cultural, political, and economic midpoint between the centers of eastern capital and the West. With the advent of steamboat technology, it had emerged in the 1830s as a key transshipping hub, and by the 1840s had become the first major urban center of the trans-Mississippi region. The completion of the Eads Bridge in 1874, unifying rail transportation between Illinois and Missouri across the Mississippi, ensured St. Louis's reinscription as a midcontinental link. When a major strike spread west along the rails in 1877, consequently, the city became the focal point of the nation's first pitched battle between industrial labor and capital.[17]

Situated along the railroad lines joining the North and the South, the city was also a site of political convergence and contradiction between the two regions. Since entering the United States through the controversial 1820 Missouri Compromise, the city had existed uncomfortably on the fault line between hostile proslavery and free-labor forces. Despite the presence of the "peculiar institution" in St. Louis, and in the hemp-, tobacco- and cotton-growing settlements east along the Missouri River, central Missouri had not fully developed the plantation slave system that became a taproot of southern distinctiveness. Neither had the state depended on a single agricultural product, as was the case with Dixie's reliance on cotton. The smaller scale of plantation agriculture meant both that African Americans had comprised a much smaller proportion of Missouri's population than in the Deep South, and that slaveholding interests had never dominated the state's economy or General Assembly. Nonetheless, the U.S. Supreme Court's ruling in *Dred Scott v. Sandford*, and the Missouri Supreme Court's ruling in *State v. Celia, a Slave*, fed the flames of North-South animosity. Bloody skirmishes along the Missouri–Kansas Territory border between "bushwhackers" and free-soil "jayhawkers" were another portent of a full-scale national civil war. Yet, Missouri occupied the center of an emergent "middle border" region of slave states—Kentucky, West Virginia, Delaware, and Maryland—whose citizens rejected secession. St. Louis became the state's Unionist stronghold, though such partisans were an uneasy bloc of Republican free-soilers, skilled tradesmen, abolitionists, and conservative Democrats.[18]

Possessing the commercial might of a southern riverfront city, postwar St. Louis remained "southern" in its overall civic temperament. The city's white native-born stock, drawn from rural areas of Missouri, Arkansas, and southern Illinois, was comparable in background to their southern counterparts. They enjoyed a long history of associationalism, in the form of "citizens' committees" that maintained social cohesion and public consensus around the values and authority of the local white economic-political elite. Given their common French, Spanish, and Catholic origins, and close trade relations with New Orleans via the Mississippi, St. Louisans also shared cultural affinities with Orleanos. The Veiled Prophet parade and ball, begun in 1878, was a yearly reminder of St. Louis's French-Creole past that combined Mardi Gras carnival, city boosterism, secret society rite, and debutante soiree. Following directly on the heels of the 1877 railroad strike, it was also a manifestation of St. Louis's associational culture that symbolically asserted capital's hegemony over the working-class "rabble." The Mystic Order of the Veiled Prophet of the Enchanted Realm, the society that coordinated the gala, further consolidated the dense relations among the city's business elite.[19]

Black Community in a Border State Crucible

ɒ

Because the Gateway City was the first major metropolis southerners encountered north up the Mississippi, it also functioned as an intermediate point between black communities in the Deep South and the Midwest proper. St. Louis had been a way station, in 1879, for more than six thousand ex-slave "Exodusters" migrating to Kansas in search of homesteads. With large increases in black migration during the Great War, racial segregation became a pervasive, though not a total, feature of the city's social life. Typical of other border state communities, Jim Crow apartheid was more uneven in its proscriptions than in the former slave territories of the Deep South. Public libraries and conveyances did not observe segregation, though swimming pools, ballparks, theaters, hotels, churches, restaurants, and hospitals did. Missouri's constitution enforced segregated public schooling and prohibited interracial marriage. In both the city and state, few opportunities existed for African Americans to receive a higher education. St. Louis's black workers were thoroughly excluded from most trades, especially skilled work in the competitive construction crafts. Historically, far fewer occupations had been open to free blacks than in many northern cities or even southern locales like Charleston, South Carolina, where European immigrants were scarce and African Americans had long been employed in numerous classifications. Indeed, resistance to black workers had been rampant in such border cities as Baltimore, Maryland, and Louisville, Kentucky, where large numbers of free black mechanics had come into conflict with an overwhelmingly German- and Irish-derived white working class. At the same time, more black St. Louisans were involved in professional and clerical work than in most southern cities. Still, African Americans in both the southern and border states were less occupationally diverse than black northerners.[20]

Such differences were indicative of the traits that made border state communities atypically southern. Their relatively small black populations, given the absence of plantation slavery, contrasted with the much larger numbers of African Americans occupying the Lower South; Missouri had the second lowest black-white ratio among the former slave states. This blunted the prospects for the full-scale disfranchisement campaigns that occurred in the former Confederacy. The ethno-religious diversity of white border-state residents, tied to massive European immigration, departed significantly from the greater homogeneity characteristic of an almost solidly Protestant white southern populace. Given this, the Republican Party remained politically viable in former slave states like Missouri, and shared power with the Democrats. While not necessarily dependent on black votes statewide, white Republican politicos nonetheless maintained an interest in continued black support. This state of affairs in the border region deviated sharply from the "Solid South," where the Democrats achieved an almost total hegemony through the white primary system. Finally, border state Democrats were internally split in a manner reflecting the turmoil of the national party. That is, they were factionalized by schisms between their rural "Bourbon" and urban "populist" wings, both of which, despite deep conflicts, were forced to inhabit the same state parties. Illustrative of these tensions between both St. Louisans and rural Missourians, and Republicans and Democrats, the Missouri General Assembly offered the city home rule as part of a special constitutional amendment, allowing its residents in 1876 to legally sever St. Louis City from the surrounding St. Louis County.[21]

It is notable, moreover, that while African Americans were stripped of the franchise in the post-Reconstruction South, black Missourians remained voting members of the polity throughout the period of segregation. Holding a status peculiar to other border state communities, black St. Louisans belonged to the sort of patronage networks typical of northern, big-city politics, and despite their small numbers enjoyed an uncommon degree of formal electoral influence. They proved to be "one of the most politically advanced groups among urban black communities in the first half of the twentieth century," allowing them to secure minor appointments and municipal jobs. While assenting to segregated schools and hospitals as a preferable alternative to outright exclusion, black St. Louisans used clientage, racial pragmatism, and interracial negotiation to stake claims on a continuing share of educational and health care resources—a strategy that historian Priscilla A. Dowden defines as "the manipulation of public culture." Opening in 1875, St. Louis's High School for Colored Students (later renamed Charles Sumner High School in honor of the Radical Republican senator from Massachusetts) was the first black secondary school west of the Mississippi. By 1900, the state also had the highest percentage of black elementary school attendance among the southern states.[22]

Black voters' growing presence in the city's central riverfront wards also allowed them to leverage spoils from white officials in exchange for critical ballots. The city's decentralized, weak-mayor system of government, moreover, enabled black ward politicians to exercise greater power than was possible in hierarchical, machine-run cities like Chicago. Some historians have alleged that one of the South's defining features was its citizens' marked tendency toward ritualistic violence—the result of the region's distinct economic and racial traits. To the extent that this was true, the white St. Louis government and citizenry eschewed the brutal excesses of the Lower South to maintain Jim Crow, preferring instead "polite racism." Notwithstanding police violence against African Americans, white civic leaders in St. Louis and other border state communities tended to prefer the politics of interracial "civility," which reinforced black subordination under the guise of cooperation, goodwill, and public voluntarism among black and white professionals and elites. The assumption was that racial conflict stemmed from the dissolute habits of "common" blacks and the unrestrained bigotry of "uncouth" white laborers. Indeed, City Hall often acted proactively to "manage" race relations and suppress racial resentments, often with the assistance of St. Louis's Catholic archdiocese, ecumenical civic institutions, and elite academic institutions such as Washington University. Paradoxically, the diversity of the city's religious communities had a liberalizing effect on its racial politics, even as whites preserved their racial hegemony.[23]

A "northern city with a southern exposure," in the words of lifelong resident and activist Margaret Bush Wilson, St. Louis demands attention because it embodied the essential facets of U.S. urban racial stratification prior to 1964–65. "For a full understanding of how white America dealt with its 'Negro problem,'" historian George C. Wright maintains, "it is extremely important to discuss the circumstances of blacks in border cities." Forms of African American resistance in St. Louis, likewise, represented a merger of both the insurgent politics of southern black struggle, and the electoral politics of the North. Combining the formally articulated racial segregation of the South with the more de facto patterns of northern racial control, the political landscape of such border region cities often prefigured shifts in the rest of the nation. Liberal Republicanism, an opening salvo in the retreat from Reconstruction, emerged first in Missouri, then other border states. In 1916, St. Louis City became the first to pass a housing segregation ordinance through initiative petition and direct vote. The law was nullified a year later when the U.S. Supreme Court struck down a similar ordinance in Louisville, but by the early 1920s private restrictive covenants, realtor practices, and in some cases house bombings, accomplished the racialized, spatial containment of St. Louis's growing black populace.[24]

However, Missouri and other border states were equally noteworthy as the first former slave territories to begin dismantling legal racial apartheid, and numerous test cases had their beginnings in St. Louis. The Supreme Court's 1938 ruling in *Missouri ex rel Gaines v. Canada* was a pivotal step on the road to the celebrated 1954 *Brown* decision. Three of the nation's key fair-housing cases—*Shelley v. Kraemer* (1948), *Jones v. Mayer* (1968), and *United States v. City of Black Jack* (1974)—originated in or near St. Louis City, and two were decided by the U.S. Supreme Court. With the building of the city's Gateway Arch in the mid-1960s, St. Louis was also the place where the federal state was forced into its first major showdown in enforcing nondiscrimination clauses in government construction contracts. Another case of local origin, *Green v. McDonnell Douglas* (1973), produced a landmark Supreme Court decision on employment discrimination. Border-state politics and culture lent black working-class St. Louisans' freedom struggles a "Dixie-Yankee" duality that condensed the regionally diverse experiences of black working people in the United States.[25]

I develop the themes of black working-class formation and St. Louis freedom politics over the course of eight chapters. Chapter 1 focuses on the varied forms of black worker activity and self-organization during the later 1930s, when economic crisis and a rising tide of grassroots militancy and radicalism forced a major realignment of the federal state and its policies, and broadened the constituency of the national Democratic Party through the New Deal. Black St. Louisans, who entered Democratic ranks through a reorganization of local black ward politics, staged consumer boycotts, organized independent trade unions through a radicalized Urban League, provided a bedrock of support for building the Congress of Industrial Organizations (CIO), fought for access to newly created federal relief and work programs through the National Negro Congress (NNC), turned to Black Nationalist movements, and pressed for greater services for African Americans within the parameters of Jim Crow.[26] By far the city's most far-reaching, if short-lived, black working-class project of the 1930s was a militant strike wave inaugurated by women in the food-processing industry. Indeed, black women's activism brought a renewal of industrial union organizing in St. Louis. Overall, the depression period weakened the black middle class, broke its dominance as the purveyor of "racial uplift" in the black community, and heralded the emergence of a new black historic bloc led by a maturing working-class public.

Chapter 2 considers the broad-based "Double V" campaign, and especially the protests led by the St. Louis unit of the March on Washington Movement (MOWM) to expand the hiring and upgrading of black defense industry workers. Of the branches that formed around the nation, St. Louis's MOWM unit was consistently the most combative, and among the most successful. St. Louis also became a site of more loosely organized black working-class activism at work and intransigence in public spaces, and provided the locus of some of the nation's earliest lunch counter sit-in demonstrations. Staged by an interracial group of middle-class women activists, these sit-ins creatively married the trappings of interracial elite "civility" with the demands for immediate reform favored by working-class organizers. Despite their diversity, these wartime activities further consolidated the black grassroots bloc, and foreshadowed many of the political demands for fair employment and an end to segregation that black working-class activists would continue to raise after the war.

For a short period after the MOWM's demise, the local chapter of the National Association for the Advancement of Colored People (NAACP) served as a hub of black working-class organization. Yet, as Chapter 3 discusses, the early Cold War had a dampening effect on this militancy, ultimately shifting the association from grassroots mobilization to legal action directed toward black professional advance and public accommodations. The NAACP and a newly formed local branch of CORE fought segregation at swimming pools, schools, restaurants, and movie theaters, which were not inconsistent with working-class interests but nonetheless resonated more with a biracial, middle-class professional base. Fewer activists, in contrast, were willing to risk accusations of "communist subversion" by raising demands for fair employment. Exceptions to the rule included a local committee of the left-wing Civil Rights Congress, and the St. Louis branch of the National Negro Labor Council, which launched several job campaigns. Although both were drummed out of existence, they nonetheless helped transmit a clear "jobs and justice" agenda into the postwar period.

A black working-class political renaissance occurred in the late 1950s. Chapters 4, 5, and 6 explore this "heroic" moment of civil rights struggle in St. Louis, which culminated in the 1963–64 Jefferson Bank Boycott. I situate the stirrings of this phase in the intense battle around a proposed new city charter in the late 1950s, which renewed the mass movement for fair employment, and set in motion a grassroots campaign for meaningful black electoral power, equitable education and housing, and the complete end to segregated accommodations. The St. Louis NAACP, revitalized by the presidency of a labor-based activist and intellectual belonging to the powerful Local 688 of the International Brotherhood of Teamsters, led this fight, as did local branches of the Negro American Labor Council, and CORE, whose own membership was transformed by black working-class sympathizers attracted by CORE's newfound national prominence and changing program of action. During the early 1960s, St. Louis's black political bloc waged freedom struggles against the onset of automation, the de facto "re-segregation" of public schooling, the uprooting of black working-class communities through urban renewal, and police abuse. Embittered by ineffectual fair employment legislation, activists began abandoning demands for "fair employment" and adopting more systematic mobilizations for "full employment." A rising generation of black working-class youth rediscovered Black Nationalism, and became the arrowhead of postwar black urban rebellion. The movement's growth amid these conditions brought deepening political and class divisions among black St. Louisans, exacerbating internal differences over tactics, strategies, and goals. It also contributed to a widening rift among the city's growing community of black elected officials, who were split between older party functionaries and a better-educated, more professional group of challengers.

Chapters 7 and 8 address further the reemergent Black Nationalist thrust of the late 1960s, popularly identified as "Black Power." The key local organization in the transition from "civil rights" to "Black Power" was the Action Council (Committee) to Improve Opportunities for Negroes (ACTION), formed by militant dissidents from St. Louis CORE. Interracial, politically eclectic, wide-ranging in its activities, yet rooted in an agenda for more and better job opportunities, the group best illustrated the expansive character of the black working-class bloc. ACTION and several other local organizations gave direction to a resurgent Black Nationalist politics chiefly through a series of protests tied to a national black working-class reparations campaign. Another high point of local Black Power mobilization occurred in 1969, when black female public housing tenants waged the nation's first, and largest citywide public rent strike. Implicitly challenging a black working-class program to win "more and better jobs for black men," they added to the city's black grassroots agenda the demand for households autonomous from male breadwinners. Yet, while workers were a critical component in its formation and development, Black Power had both an ambiguous class content and social base. Not only did it encompass "hard core" unemployed youth, welfare mothers, workers, antipoverty organizers, revolutionary Black Nationalists, and militant high school students, but it also appealed to electoral politicians and would-be small capitalists.

Several factors boosted the fortunes of the latter group. State-sponsored repression suppressed the most radical and social-democratic sectors of the movement. This occurred in simultaneity with the development of an antiurban, anti-social welfare, racially conservative coalition under the banner of the "New Right." White northern Democratic workers were part of this cross-class political bloc, and they came to symbolize President Richard M. Nixon's disaffected "Silent Majority" who rejected New Deal liberal "elitism" in favor of a new Republican-style populism. But while Nixon cultivated a white "blue collar" constituency, his administration also endorsed Black Power in the form of "Black Capitalism," and in concert with corporate capitalists promoted a new stratum of black professionals in the salaried and self-employed professions. Electoral politics also became a dominant mode of black freedom activity by the early 1970s, supplanting working-class insurgency with a reconfigured historic bloc led by a middle class nurtured in the bosom of Black Power. The cumulative result was an updated version of middle-class "racial uplift" in which black professionals were invested with the trusteeship of the African American community, in terms of policing their working-class counterparts, moderating their demands, and setting a political agenda privileging elected officials, trained professionals, corporate officers, and business entrepreneurs. St. Louis, thus, serves as a case study of the key irony of the post–civil rights/Black Power period: the existence of an economically fragile, relatively small black middle class, and a larger poor black working class, both with intertwined yet conflicting interests.

CHAPTER ONE

A Black Working-Class Public, 1932–39

DISEMBARKING AT St. Louis's teeming Union Station, black migrants from Arkansas, Louisiana, Alabama, and rural Missouri encountered a stable black community that had developed remarkably during slavery and matured rapidly after its demise. Waves of newcomers in the second and third decades of the twentieth century had also dramatically remade the city's black social, institutional, and cultural life. Community growth had also more clearly distinguished and stratified African Americans along the axis of class. The Urban League of Metropolitan St. Louis, formed in 1918 by black clubwomen and businessmen, and white industrial philanthropists, not only coordinated employment, housing, education, and health care services for black working-class migrants, but also committed itself to training black social workers. St. Louis's Phyllis Wheatley Young Women's Christian Association (YWCA), another progeny of black middle-class women reformers, reflected concern about the lack of leisure and "upright example" to black girls from the laboring class. Staffers at the Pine Street YMCA took similar initiative in providing recreational facilities and moral guidance to black youth living on the outskirts of the central business district. The *St. Louis Argus,* published by Joseph E. Mitchell, was the city's major mass-circulation black newspaper, and editorially was a combination of Booker T. Washington–style "racial uplift" ideology and "New Negro" militancy. The city also had local branches of the National Negro Business League and the National Association for the Advancement of Colored People (NAACP), both of which were heavily composed of struggling black capitalists and trained professionals.[1]

Despite these signs of internal differentiation, black St. Louisans were largely excluded from the growing sector of professional occupations and white-collar clerical work. They comprised a "laboring laity" of common laborers restricted to hauling, mopping, sweeping, and digging, and performing other dirty, mean, and unskilled work. The Laclede Gas Company employed a substantially small number of black workers, as did the Emerson, Wagner, and Century electrical plants. Another handful worked in the shoe and clothing industries, and in the local General Motors factories. Circa 1930, about 1,751 African Americans worked in the iron and steel industries, over half of them as laborers. Most longshoremen on both the St. Louis and East St. Louis sides of the Mississippi riverfront were black, though the majority of black men were in construction—typically as hod carriers, but occasionally as bricklayers, plasterers, and other "trowel tradesmen" at the bottom of the industry. In 1930, close to 14,000 black women were servants, housekeepers, waitresses, elevator operators, hairdressers, and laundresses. Almost 2,300 were employed in manufacturing, including rag making and industrial laundries. Some 1,100 African American women worked in food processing.[2]

Previous to this period, the black elite had chiefly determined the African American political agenda, shaping its focus on "racial uplift." But the widespread crises of the Great Depression stimulated a seismic shift in St. Louis's black politics that swung the pendulum toward the black laboring majority. With wage earners' newfound centrality in determining the direction of protest, the popular, grassroots character of black struggle advanced more strongly to the forefront. During the 1930s, black St. Louisans waged community campaigns for more recreational space, schools, and relief and employment. The dramatic realignment of the national Democratic Party and U.S. social welfare policy, and the popular upsurge that drove it, also affected the city's electoral politics, with African Americans defecting in overwhelming numbers to the party of the federal New Deal. Overall, the black freedom struggles of the 1930s brought into being a new political bloc rooted in an evolving working-class standpoint and agenda.

St. Louis's "Black Archipelago"

*

By the 1920s, St. Louis was home to the nation's eighth largest black urban community. Like similar cities that had attracted black migrants during the Great War, it belonged to the "Black Archipelago"—"islands of vibrant black social life surrounded by seas of white racism and hostility."[3] The trend of residential segregation, in fact, rose earlier in St. Louis than in the nation overall. Alongside Chicago, Milwaukee, and Cleveland, the Gateway City experienced a dramatic spike in spatial apartheid between 1910 and 1930. St. Louis's major island of black settlement was Mill Creek Valley, a congested railroad thoroughfare in the Central Corridor lined with foundries, warehouses, and manufacturing. Chestnut Valley, located near the city's downtown business district, was the area's lively black honky-tonk center that had produced ragtime music.[4]

Another outcropping in St. Louis's black archipelago lay several miles west of downtown in the more prominent community of Elleardsville, known as the "Ville." Racially restrictive housing covenants, imposed by white neighborhood associations in the second decade of the century, had long since limited the area's black residence to less than a square mile. By the end of the 1920s, however, the Ville possessed the dense core of black St. Louis's institutional life, including many of its elementary schools and oldest houses of religious worship. The five-acre Charleton Tandy Field, named after a notable St. Louis "race man" of the Reconstruction era, hosted an amateur baseball league organized by the local Negro Business League. The Charles H. Turner Open Air School, nearby on Kennerly Avenue, was the nation's first school for disabled black youth. Black leaders pressured the board of education to relocate Charles Sumner High School, the nation's first black high school west of the Mississippi, to the area, as well. In 1910, the school had reopened in a brand-new Georgian-style building on Cottage Avenue and Pendleton Street. Nearby, the stately PORO College of Beauty Culture, owned by the wealthy Annie Turnbo Malone, provided training in black hair and skin care, ran one of the city's largest mail-order businesses, and boasted its own state-of-the-art switchboard, dormitory rooms, bakery, dining hall, federal Post Office, barbershop, and ice cream parlor.[5]

Another group of African Americans had found their oasis in South Kinloch Park, five miles northwest of the city in St. Louis County. The subdivision's idyllic, semirural environment was redolent of the open spaces of southeastern Missouri and Arkansas, where many of the settler families had their origins. In the aftermath of the bloody 1917 East St. Louis race riots, migration to the suburb also provided many survivors with a psychic balm and respite from lingering white malice. A local branch of Marcus Garvey's Universal Negro Improvement Association, formed in the late 1920s, moreover spoke to the Black Nationalism underlying early black working-class suburbanization.[6]

Black Class Relations and Power on the Eve of the Depression

The very presence of Mill Creek Valley, the Ville, and South Kinloch Park spoke to the rivulets of class fragmenting black St. Louis. Certainly, a clear black economic elite existed at this historical moment, though most black "capitalists" were, in fact, small commodity producers, while only about 3 percent of black St. Louisans were in the professions. The bulk of the black middle class were of a historically new segment that supplied paid services to an expanding African American clientele—schoolteachers, undertakers, lawyers, beauticians, barbers, physicians, nurses, and dentists. At the same time, this class included the remnants of a previous black "elite" that had served white patrons. Despite the intraclass fissures these differences elicited, the common denominator was service-oriented work. Given the elusive nature of steady, year-round employment for most black St. Louisans, the membrane separating the black middle class and proletariat was often a porous one. In 1933, the largest category of black business enterprise in St. Louis, aside from barber and beauty shops, was ice and coal, which vendors hawked door to door. Indeed, the vast majority of ostensibly middle-class or elite black families occupied "contradictory class locations," falling somewhere between the laboring majority made of casual and common wage earners, and a more stable black laboring elite.[7]

Other, fluid traits designated certain African Americans as middle class or "elite." Education, as well as nativity to the city, entitled one to membership among the "better element of Negroes." Control over one's conditions of labor could be a mark of distinction. Wearing a crisp uniform to work, instead of dungarees, also qualified one as a professional. Black postal workers were a rarified group, too, given the clerical nature of their job. The ability to travel widely made the Pullman porter a cosmopolitan in his community. Outfitted in stylish blue, porters were even more select because obtaining these jobs depended on their composure, "gentility" and "good character." Harkening back to St. Louis's antebellum "colored aristocracy," skin color and hair texture further augmented black class differences, for the lighter skinned tended to occupy the most "prestigious" jobs as porters, elevator operators, and upscale maids and cooks. Black people's interactions with educated, influential white political and civic leaders mattered in defining their class status, as did the voluntary activities they pursued outside of paid work. Some cooks, headwaiters, and chauffeurs ran their own small candy stores and shops, allowing them to be part-time petty capitalists. Other laborers were members of the distinguished Knights of Pythias, or the Prince Hall Freemasons, two popular black lodges—though the Greater St. Louis Lodge of Colored Elks was more forthrightly working-class in membership. Affiliations with the exclusive Twentieth Century Club, the Royal Vagabonds, or the Informal Dames also conferred social distinction. Families revealed much about their regional provenance, community standing, and overall class affinities, by whether they attended a southern-style evangelical church or the more reserved, older congregations of Episcopalians and Methodists. Given the city's French-Spanish history, many status-conscious black St. Louisans embraced Catholicism through either dint of upbringing or conversion.[8]

Black clubwomen, many of whom were modestly paid teachers or wage workers, measured their status by "ladyhood," as demonstrated in personal appearance, comportment, and "moral virtue," and conspicuous adherence to patriarchal family norms. Ironically, behind many "successful" black businessmen, doctors, or attorneys were the wage-earning wives who actually supported them. Yet, cleaving to prevalent ideals of bourgeois respectability, black women might completely obscure their waged identities, identifying themselves instead by civic associations, the physical maintenance of their households, or some combination thereof. The Elleardsville Social Settlement Club, which sponsored public lectures on hygiene and child-rearing, asserted a place for "the better sort" of women in domestic management. Homeownership was a trait that particularly distinguished the Ville's symbolic elite from the laboring majority who rented housing in the ramshackle Central Corridor. The one- and two-story homes in the Ville were often small brick cottages nestled among unpaved, tree-lined streets. Still, residents took active pride in these single-family dwellings, with the Elleardsville Civic League awarding prizes for the best-kept yard.[9]

The most contradictory aspect of black class relations was that African Americans across ranks constituted a racially oppressed minority, even if they experienced this oppression in dissimilar ways. Their interactions with whites were framed against previous patterns of European immigration. Although laborers from southern and eastern Europe had continued to arrive until World War I, St. Louis had largely ceased to be an immigrant metropolis by 1880. By then, larger, older populations of German and Irish immigrants had made deep impressions on civic culture. The Germans—responsible for St. Louis's sturdy brick architecture and numerous breweries—had become beneficiaries of a white U.S. republic through free-labor agitation. The poorer, less skilled "famine Irish," on the other hand, had taken advantage of the city's weak-mayor, ward-based municipal system to develop centers of Democratic power in North St. Louis. Possessing the franchise, yet caught between white Republican and Democratic competitors who were similarly ambivalent toward African Americans, black political elites had helped to forge a politics of biracial cooperation, racial pragmatism, and white electoral paternalism. Especially after race riots in East St. Louis (1917) and Chicago (1919) raised fears of a similar conflagration in St. Louis, black leadership was willing to accept the path of moderation. White elites' tacit expectation, in exchange for their benevolence, was that the "better Negroes" would assume responsibility for managing the behavior of the black laboring majority. As a result, a tenuous interracial "civility" remained the chief means of black subjugation.[10]

Paradoxically, black St. Louisans were able to insist on many of the terms of their subordination. Since Reconstruction, black political insiders had mastered the "manipulation of public culture," and used it to assert their interests. As formal racial apartheid had descended in the early twentieth century, moreover, St. Louis's black leadership had perfected the ability to negotiate a broad array of public resources. Public education for African Americans in the border states, though legally segregated, was well developed within the parameters of Jim Crow. Compared to most southern cities, and many northern ones, St. Louis's public school system exhibited an uncommon degree of racial parity: By 1910, the Gateway City had become comparable to Philadelphia, New York, New Orleans, and Washington, D.C., in the large number of black children enrolled.[11]

Nonetheless, black life in the Jim Crow city was far from halcyon. The maturation of black business and professional strata remained stunted by unequal commercial and employment markets. The Ville, moreover, may have been an "institutionally complete" community where children could grow to confident adulthood sheltered from white racism, but its schoolhouses burst at the seams from overcrowding. Segregated black playgrounds were the first to close in the fall and the last to open in the summer and were poorly maintained. Health facilities were equally scarce. The city's public hospital segregated African Americans by placing them at the rear of the building's second and third floors, while white physicians and medical students were known to perform "experiments" on black patients. City Hospital No. 2, which had opened in 1919 through demands from black physicians, businessmen, and lawyers, was housed in an old building previously belonging to a private hospital. Designed to accommodate three hundred people, it held twice its capacity, with some patients occupying the hallways. And while the ballot empowered black St. Louisans to bargain for some of the spoils of municipal politics, they were not the determining factor in the outcome of city elections. In the end, racial clientage did not amount to racial equality.[12]

New Deal A-Coming

*

At the outset of the nation's depression in late 1929 and early 1930, neither St. Louis mayor Victor Miller nor the Board of Aldermen commanded a public relief system. Reflecting the city's history of private voluntarism and associationalism, authorities during previous recessions had disbursed funds through a miserly relief structure of private welfare agencies. Thus, as local unemployment soared above the national average, it strained services past the breaking point. In makeshift homes along the riverfront, fifteen hundred evicted and penniless people of diverse racial backgrounds formed the nation's largest "Hooverville." Disaster hit African Americans earliest and hardest, as black stores, mutual aid societies, and other communal institutions folded. The PORO complex in St. Louis kept its doors open, but it ceased to function as the vibrant cultural center it had been. The People's Finance Building, a hub of black business and professional activity, and the headquarters of St. Louis's NAACP, Brotherhood of Sleeping Car Porters and Maids (BSCP), and the weekly *St. Louis American,* also fell on hard times. In the meatpacking industry and rolling mills, managers reduced their workforces mainly by cutting black employees, in some cases by over half. Of the 35,089 unemployed St. Louisans in 1930, 8.4 percent were white and 13.2 percent were black.[13]

By 1933, 70 percent of black St. Louisans were jobless, and another 20 percent employed only part-time. In eight areas with high black concentration, more than half the families received some form of aid by 1934, while the highest number of workhouse cases were recorded in the heavily black downtown districts. Because most black workers made their living in personal and domestic service, many lost their jobs through employers' forced retrenchment. A related factor in the inordinate numbers of unemployed African Americans was their continuing exclusion from craft unions in a strongly unionized city. Most construction had ground to a halt, though federal funds would allow several unfinished municipal projects to resume. As had been the case before the Depression, building contractors, as well as city and federal authorities, turned a blind eye to white control of the skilled building trades. By far the greatest inequality between black and white unemployment rates affected African American women in the laundry plants, where their rate of joblessness stood 48 percent higher than white operatives.[14]

Resonant with an expanding national Democratic Party constituency, President Franklin Delano Roosevelt's administration emerged as both friend and foe to African Americans, becoming an unwitting political vehicle of black working-class formation while simultaneously blunting black workers' demands. At different moments since the late nineteenth century, black St. Louis political functionaries had traded votes for patronage in competing local Democratic factions. For good reason, many African Americans had considered black Democrats unscrupulous for aligning with the party of white southern reaction. Within St. Louis's black public, Democrats were generally known as "rough Negroes," "ward-heeling hustlers," and "macks" who sold illegal liquor or ran crap games and call houses on the riverfront. The recruitment of more "respectable" black Democrats like George Vashon, Oral S. McClellan, Joseph McLemore, and David Marshall Grant began to transform this image. Born in the working-class Mill Creek Valley area, Grant had graduated from Sumner High School. After years of ambling among a number of jobs, he had graduated from Howard University's School of Law. Tall, dignified, and with a relaxed sense of humor, Grant rose to leadership within the Young Negro Democrats committee, becoming its most visible representative.[15]

A competing faction, the Civic Cooperative Association, was the creation of Jordan W. Chambers, a black Republican leader. A former railway car cleaner and an undertaker, Chambers had gained a formidable reputation through his ability to muster black votes for Mayor Miller. Dubbed by the white press as the "Negro Mayor of St. Louis," he had built an extensive base of grassroots power in the densely black populated Nineteenth Ward of the Central Corridor. While Roosevelt won both Missouri and St. Louis by lopsided majorities, Chambers, and the majority of black people in the city's Fifth, Sixth, Twentieth, and Twenty-third wards, voted the Republican ticket. But they had done so by exceedingly small margins, indicating a rising skepticism with the party.[16]

Bernard F. Dickmann, St. Louis's Democratic mayoral candidate in 1933, reaped this harvest of discontent when he courted black support through a pledge to replace the dilapidated City Hospital No. 2 with a new black-staffed medical facility. The matter remained the only major item from an $87 million bond issue that the city's Republican leadership had not implemented. Chambers backed Dickmann, and the city's emerging black Democratic bloc urged other African Americans to do the same. These overtures were most successful among disaffected Republican insiders like Chambers, as well as younger black St. Louisans like Grant, who lacked their elders' memories of the party of Lincoln. Democratic entreaties also beckoned the growing numbers of black working-class itinerants who had gained little, if anything, from Republican patronage, and for whom Republican identity held no attachment as a totem of middle-class respectability. Many African Americans perceived the truth in Grant's wry observation that "Negroes had all the mops, brooms and garbage cans" and little else by way of local Republican patronage. The *Argus,* a longtime Republican stalwart, also endorsed Dickmann. Publisher Joseph Mitchell, then president of the St. Louis NAACP, added the weight of this office to support the Democratic challenger, as well.[17]

On election day, 18,000 of the city's 43,000 African Americans switched parties. The upset made Dickmann the city's first Democratic mayor since 1909. The new regime rewarded Grant with an appointment as assistant city counselor, while the impressive numbers Dickmann polled in the

Nineteenth Ward also brought Chambers to the attention of local white Democrats. By 1937, 60 percent of St. Louis's 50,000 African American voters had defected to the party of the New Deal, sweeping Democrats into other offices, including the Board of Aldermen. "[T]he importance of the Negro vote in St. Louis to both parties is possibly greater than in any other city in the country," reporter Earl Brown rhapsodized. When Dickmann was reelected, the city's black wards were in the advance guard of the shift to Democratic hegemony.[18]

St. Louis's small-ward system also began to produce results in the election of black officials. In 1938, Chambers won the offices of constable and Nineteenth Ward Democratic committeeman, becoming the city's first African American to join St. Louis's Democratic Central Committee. The election inaugurated his ascent as the city's black political boss, which had concrete results for his working-class constituents. Because of St. Louis City's home rule charter, municipal government was responsible for fulfilling both city and "county" functions; yet, "county" offices such as sheriff, license collector, constable, and recorder of deeds were independent of the direct influence of the Mayor's Office, as were the thousands of associated jobs. "County" positions were, instead, the preserve of the ward committeemen. Not only did committeemen hire polling judges, clerks, and watchers and dictate the names printed on ballots, but at a more intimate neighborhood level they could delay evictions when families fell behind in their rent, help them relocate, provide them with sustenance and work, and provide bail money when individuals had run-ins with the law. Given St. Louis's fragmented system of government, where the mayor's reach was limited and each ward boss was a virtual fiefdom unto himself, Chambers was able to intervene on behalf of black grassroots supporters with a great deal of power. Using his party ties, patronage, and connections to firms like St. Louis's Scullin Steel, he dispensed employment, food, coal, cash loans, and favors among ward residents in exchange for their loyalty at the polls and cash tributes to his organization. In a city famously condemned for its official corruption, men like Chambers necessarily had disparate ties to a range of unsavory actors, including those who ran policy rackets, gambling dens, taverns, and brothels. An undertaker, he also operated in a field known for associations with organized crime. With his large bankroll, expensive cigars, and diamond ring, Chambers was a throwback to the riverfront "macks" of the nineteenth century who had functioned within the realpolitik of urban politics.[19]

Initially, however, the new Democratic regime did little to retain African Americans' trust. Because municipal government proved unable to deliver even the paltry forms of patronage black people had come to expect, the early Depression years weakened African Americans' overall linkages to the city's institutional politics. In the meantime, the newfound activism of the federal state, especially in the creation of direct relief programs, energized black working-class people. The Public Works Administration (PWA) established nondiscrimination rules, though its successor, the Works Progress (Projects) Administration (WPA), had a better record at deploying black construction workers across skill levels. Many New Deal laws and agencies tacitly supported black economic subordination. The Agricultural Adjustment program, for example, benefited large-scale white farmers to the detriment of black tenants and sharecroppers, many of whom lost their livelihood when land was removed from cultivation, or were cheated by landlords out of their share of federal payments. This certainly became the case in the southeast Missouri "Bootheel," the northernmost tip of the cotton-producing Mississippi Delta region. The National Industrial Recovery Act was another case in point. Section 7a of the law rekindled industrial unionism by recognizing workers' right to collective bargaining, but the act contained no safeguards against black workers being locked out of closed shops. Under the National Recovery Administration (NRA), jobs performed mainly by black men and women received the lowest wage scales, or were exempted from the NRA minimum wage codes altogether. Enforcement of NRA-level wages sometimes even exacerbated black layoffs. Rather than pay them the fourteen dollars the NRA required, managers at St. Louis's Conferro Paint and Varnish Company laid off eighteen black women in the filing and labeling department, and replaced them with whites. At another St. Louis company, managers flatly informed black workers that NRA wage guidelines did not apply to them. Other bosses fired black laborers when they demanded their wage increases—or when white workers, chafing at the prospect of black workers receiving a semblance of equal pay, petitioned for their removal.[20]

"Third Period" Rebellion in the Central Corridor

The emergence of a self-conscious black working-class public found its most insurgent expression in the political radicalism of the period. During the 1920s, black Socialists and left-wing Garveyites had been drawn to the Communist Left by Russia's Bolshevik Revolution, and its condemnation of all forms of national oppression and colonialism. At the Sixth Congress of the Communist International (Comintern), convened in 1928, members had formally supported African Americans' right to full equality in the United States, and their right to self-determination as a landless, oppressed "Black Belt" nation in the South. The thesis of black self-determination was part and parcel of the Comintern's revolutionary "Third Period," prompted by the crisis of capitalism and the seeming imminence of socialist revolution in the global North. Communist parties were directed to create their own independent organizations and unions, as with the formation of the Trade Union Unity League (TUUL).[21]

African Americans, especially southerners, were regarded as key to igniting a revolutionary workers' movement, and Communists gained credibility among black constituencies through their willingness to physically resist evictions, demand public relief and social insurance, and combat racial segregation and white police violence. From neighborhood meetings and rallies to hunger marches to the state capital of Jefferson City, black St. Louisans were an especially visible and militant core of the party's Unemployed Councils. Hershel Walker, a recent migrant from Memphis, had been living in the city for only two months when he enlisted in the burgeoning unemployed movement. "It was building itself pretty strong, more and more people were joining, because unemployment was rising all the time," he recalled. "Among the black men I would say it was better than half were unemployed." Being part of the council meant "fighting back and getting help. See at that time you could get no help. There was no social security, no unemployment [insurance]. They did have some minor soup lines, which you could hardly get into. People were really desperate. And so we just fought back against it all." Sometime during 1930, Walker joined the Young Communist League, beginning an odyssey that would place him in the middle of several local and national campaigns, including the International Labor Defense committee's campaign to defend the "Scottsboro boys."[22]

Between January 1930 and January 1931, when the council led numerous demonstrations in the corridors of City Hall downtown, the crowds were mostly black. African Americans were equally active in crafting the council's demands, which included a $1 million relief fund, free use of city streetcars and vacant buildings, and the passage of a minimum weekly wage law. Yet aspects of the city's border-state culture kept the unemployed movement from developing as rapidly as it did in nearby Chicago, Milwaukee, and Detroit, where rallies drew tens of thousands of participants. Foremost, despite the party's stance on black-white working-class unity, the racial segregation of residential space meant that the Unemployed Councils functioned essentially as two separate entities: The membership and officers of the North St. Louis neighborhood branches were black, while in South St. Louis they were white. Ironically, "the very success of the movement in incorporating the black unemployed was a major factor working against the involvement of the masses of white unemployed in the movement." But while St. Louis's Unemployed Council functioned on a smaller scale than in many other cities, the indifference, and growing hostility, of the Board of Aldermen and Mayor Miller to the economic catastrophe guaranteed its expansion.[23]

Unemployed protests reached their zenith in July 1932, when the city's semiprivate relief system cut fifteen thousand families from the rolls. The possibility of an additional eight thousand family cutbacks also loomed. On July 8, the council coordinated four concurrent marches from different corners of the Central Corridor, with all of them converging on City Hall. Initially involving five hundred people, the demonstration gained over one thousand other spontaneous participants. Addressing the crowd, one black speaker simultaneously spoke to the mood of interracial class unity joining the marchers, and evoked a fierce tradition of black working-class "self-respect" within which violence figured centrally. "There is only one way left for the working class, and that's the militant way," he stated. "I am speaking for the Negro workers who know how to fight and will fight. We will not continue to starve peacefully." On Monday, July 11, five thousand more unemployed demonstrators, half of them black, gathered on the City Hall lawn. Again, the numbers swelled as other protesters gravitated to the scene, joining the chant, "We want bread. We want milk."[24]

Heretofore, police had responded to unemployed civil disobedience with some restraint. But the scale of the July 8 demonstrations—nearly two thousand people—had placed the Mayor's Office, the Board of Aldermen, the police department, and the city's banking, industrial, real estate, and civic elite on notice that they could no longer ignore the protests. As a group of black women, backed by several ex-servicemen, surged toward the doors of City Hall, police pitched a tear gas canister. The crowd receded, but one protester picked up the missile and volleyed it back, forcing police to retreat into the building's rotunda. As the police regrouped, lobbing more tear gas bombs and firing their revolvers above the crowd, the main body of demonstrators fled across Market Street, escaping through alleyways and vacant lots. Pockets of unemployed workers grabbed debris from a nearby demolition site and hurled brickbats as the authorities waded in. Others, at closer range, swung their pickets at club-wielding officers. A police phalanx pursued a throng up Twelfth Street and down Chestnut, shooting four men and hitting several automobiles. When the melee subsided, forty-five people had been arrested on charges of rioting, while others had been beaten or trampled. One person was fatally wounded.[25]

Press coverage of the "July Riot" defended police conduct and took great pains to highlight the active role of black workers in the clash. Previously, racial conflict had been managed through negotiation among interracial elites. The black workers who gathered at City Hall, however, were not of the "better sort of Negroes," and their actions were far removed from the expected rituals of "civility" and deference. In every way, they were "out of their place." Their angry presence, in such awesome numbers and with a Communist imprimatur, was key to triggering the police rampage. In the "July Riot," thus, antiradicalism had collided with white supremacy, and with explosive results. In the aftermath, the president of the Board of Police Commissioners directed authorities not to permit another public rally organized by Communists. The Unemployed Council, in defiance, telegrammed Mayor Miller demanding the release of all those arrested in connection with the melee. The party, in the meantime, experienced a surge in membership. Organizers sponsored a visit by Communist leader William Z. Foster, who gave a rousing address to an audience of six hundred people. In the context of the creation of a national welfare state, the street battle with police stimulated the appropriation of $2 million in city funds for relief, and helped goad City Hall into erecting the public welfare structure it had lacked for so long.[26]

"We Demand Ten and Four": Nutpickers and the TUUL

Communists like Foster applauded the July street fight so enthusiastically because it conformed to a model of "manly" struggle the party often celebrated. The emphasis on industrial strongmen in Communist iconography not only implicitly devalued black women's particular issues around work and living conditions, but it also ignored their involvement in the presumably masculine arena of street battles—as in the case of the black women whose charge at the doors of City Hall had ignited the July skirmish. It also ignored their pivotal role in the imagined male preserve of union organizing. Drawn to the council's neighborhood-level mobilizations, where they came into contact with radical labor organizers, black women became especially active in renewed unionization drives. Indeed, the most significant black Communist-oriented labor insurgency in St. Louis was "manned" not by the thickly muscled, square-jawed heroes idealized in proletarian art and literature, but rather by black women employed in the marginal sweatshops of the city's food-processing industry.[27]

Pecan nut-shelling was St. Louis's major food-processing enterprise, and one of the rare industries that the Depression seemingly had not affected. St. Louis and East St. Louis housed sixteen shops, seven of them owned by the R. E. Funsten Company. The unskilled work of shelling, organized on a piece-rate basis, was a naked case of sexual and racial divisions of labor, and the superexploitation of black labor. Nearly 90 percent of the industry's workforce was female and black, while company foremen were typically white males. While black and white women both earned starvation wages, the latter enjoyed several privileges. African American women logged fifty-two hours a week; white women, in contrast, arrived fifteen minutes later to work each day, had fifteen minutes longer for lunch, and quit fifteen minutes earlier. White women performed the "cleaner" work of sorting and weighing, while black women were assigned the harder task of separating the meats from their shells. When they did perform the same job as white women, black nutpickers received three cents per pound for nut halves and two cents for pieces, while their white coworkers received four to six cents. On average, white women earned $2.75 a week, with black women receiving $1.80. These racial differentials, combined with a series of wage cuts between 1931 and 1933, meant that some older workers—who could not work as quickly—took home less than one dollar a week. Between 40 and 60 percent of the employees were on relief.[28]

Amid the unemployed insurgency and the implementation of Section 7a, such grievances produced a mounting restlessness among the nutpickers. Through a black Communist who had relatives at Funsten's Easton Avenue plant, a group of women began conducting secret meetings. Joining them were Ralph Shaw, William Sentner, and Mat Pelman, white organizers of the Food Workers Industrial Union (FWIU), an affiliate of the Communists' Trade Union Unity League. Of the two hundred workers at the Easton Avenue plant, half signed up for the union. An FWIU organizing committee, composed overwhelmingly of black women, produced a set of demands issued to the Funsten Company headquarters in April 1933: "ten and four," or rather an increase of ten cents for nut halves and four cents for pieces; equal pay for black and white employees; and union recognition. Organizers, in the meantime, extended their efforts to other Funsten factories. When the company rejected FWIU demands, approximately nine hundred nutpickers went on strike. Traveling from one plant to another, the women called out to their coworkers to follow suit. Having been prepared for the walkout through earlier contact, many workers spontaneously put down their shelling knives and joined the march.[29]

The action quickly spread to eight other plants, as well as two shops run by the Liberty Nut and Central Pecan companies. Between 1,200 and 1,400 people were suddenly on strike, bringing four factories to a standstill. More significantly, the conflict assumed the form of a community movement as husbands, children, and family pastors joined the mass pickets at Funsten's Delmar Boulevard headquarters, as did an estimated six hundred supporters from the Unemployed Council. The Communist Party, whose offices became the strike headquarters, lent the FWIU seasoned picketers, as well as action strategies and tactics. A relief committee coordinated the collection of food and other sustenance, much of it donated from sympathetic clothing and bakery workers, butchers, a few local business-men, and the Chicago-based Workers International Relief. White female nutpickers, many of them of Polish background, had been leery of the FWIU's "Russian" ties, though on the second day of the strike two hundred of them had joined the picket lines. More typical among the strike leader-ship, however, were black women like Cora Lewis, a mother of four who had supported her family on a weekly salary of three dollars. So, too, was Carrie Smith, a middle-aged black woman who had worked in the indus-try for nearly twenty years. Smith coined the slogan that powerfully sum-marized the strikers' main objective in reference to company piece rates: "We Demand Ten and Four." Drawing from this black leadership's work-ing-class tradition of emotive religious worship, many gatherings assumed a church revival atmosphere, with speakers freely employing biblical refer-ences, songs and chants, and call-and-response political homilies.[30]

The pronounced religiosity of the strikers, in fact, was a source of pri-vate consternation among the Communists' nominally atheist leaders, who feared it might dull the strike's revolutionary edge. But as was the case among Alabama's heavily black Communists during the same period, reli-gion, protest, and even revolution were not incompatible. At a crucial mo-ment during the May 13 meeting when the nutpickers had delivered the strike vote, Smith had lifted a Bible in one hand and hefted a brick in the other. "Girls," she had said, "we can't lose." The gesture avowed the women's faith, even as it asserted their determination to wage war for union recognition, a fundamental change in their material conditions, and respect. The women subsequently rejected two offers from the company. Managers began importing strikebreakers from outside the city, with St. Louis police ferrying them to and from the plants in patrol wagons and taxicabs. The unionists assembled a brigade of women who physically re-sisted their entry with bricks and bats, and attacked their male protectors as well. "There were some fights," one female observer later recounted. "They were trying to keep some of them from going back in. One lady went in and she worked all day and her husband came that evening for her and they beat him terrible. He was trying to keep them from hurting his wife." The strike brigade even took on police, who arrested nearly one hundred of them.[31]

While refusing to retreat from their militancy, the strikers took advan-tage of the city's heritage of ecumenical liberalism and interracial negotia-tion. Accompanied by an American Civil Liberties Union (ACLU) attorney, a delegation met at Temple Israel with the St. Louis Commission for Social Justice, an interdenominational coalition of religious clergy and university professors. Although sympathizing with the strikers' goals, the commis-sion refused to intervene pending action from City Hall. Strikers had already left their demands at the office of newly installed Mayor Dickmann. On May 22, they returned. About one thousand strikers waving union and Communist placards paraded from the party's Garrison Avenue headquarters to the steps of City Hall, where they began a thunderous chant for living wages. Although a police detail was on hand, Dickmann departed dramatically from Mayor Miller's response to the unemployed the previous year. Emerging on the building steps to cheers, he agreed to speak with strike representatives. In dissimulating language, he expressed a desire to see the workers get "just pay," yet declared that the strike was not a municipal matter. Sentner, one of the FWIU's representatives, publicly countered that because so many nut workers received relief through St. Louis's semipublic Provident Association, the city was in fact guilty of subsidizing the Funsten Company. Therefore, he insisted, the Mayor's Office had an obligation to assist in ending the strike, as well as withdrawing police protection of strikebreakers.[32]

Pulled reluctantly into the fray, Dickmann salvaged the city's reputation for "civility" by appointing a citizen's inquiry committee that included Rabbi Ferdinand Isserman of Temple Israel, Father William Markoe of the predominantly black St. Elizabeth's Catholic Church, John T. Clark of the Urban League, and black Democrat Joseph McLemore. Mediating between the Funsten workers' negotiators and company representatives, the inquiry committee helped reach a tentative consensus granting the nutpickers a "nine and four" piece rate, and the end to racial pay differentials. Although the agreement did not include formal recognition of the union, the company agreed that managers would receive complaints from shop committees. In another symbolic break from the preceding administration, Dickmann and David Grant, assistant city counselor, accompanied a parade of strikers to the Communists' headquarters, where Grant thanked the party for its role in fighting to alleviate the nutpickers' dismal working conditions. Addressing an audience of seven hundred from atop a bench, he summarized the settlement to enthusiastic applause. The strikers voted unanimously to accept the agreement, eliciting the unqualified praise of even the antiradical *Argus,* whose editors saw the defeat of racial pay differentials as a broad victory for African Americans across class lines.[33]

Within days, other smaller nut companies met similar strike demands. Over the eight days the strike lasted, moreover, eleven FWIU locals had formed in the St. Louis and East St. Louis, totaling about fourteen hundred members. Like many other African Americans who had gained political consciousness in the unemployed movement, an estimated one hundred nutpickers joined the Communist Party. By 1933, about a third of the party's local membership was black. The strike also inspired a larger wave of unionization in other poorly paid, female-dominated sectors of black industrial labor. A month after the Funsten strike ended, St. Louis bag factory workers also struck for better wages and working conditions, with the International Ladies Garment Workers tripling its membership. Buoyed by the success of the Funsten struggle, the national Communist Party headquarters also urged affiliates around the nation to use it as a model. In Chicago, sixteen hundred black garment workers, inspired by the nutpickers' example and similarly aligned with Communist organizers, went on strike in protest against racial divisions of pay. They too won wage increases, a shorter workweek, and equal wages.[34]

Black women's labor militancy also engulfed labor sectors dominated by black men. African American levee workers in St. Louis and East St. Louis walked out in reaction to a chain of abuses such as pay cuts and irregular and long hours. TUUL organizers aided them under the auspices of the Marine Workers Industrial Union. But in a significant departure from the response to the nutpickers' and the bag workers' strikes, U.S. secretary of labor Frances Perkins, Leo Wolman of the National Labor Board, NRA administrator Hugh Johnson, the St. Louis Urban League, and the AFL intervened in the drama almost immediately, supplanting TUUL involvement. This more attentive response stemmed from a number of circumstances, including the vital role of the St. Louis riverfront in the nation's commercial distribution; the "male" character of levee work, which appealed to many black Urban Leaguers' emphasis on family breadwinner wages; and for the AFL, but certainly across the board, a common interest in countering Communist influence among the city's increasingly restive working class.[35]

Yet, if the TUUL was thwarted in its efforts to build a base among black longshoremen, black women in and around the FWIU were expanding their sphere of activity beyond the workplace. In concert with the Unemployed Councils, they participated in ongoing protests around public relief, beginning a campaign for national unemployment insurance. They also became "the core group of a nascent working-class based civil rights movement in St. Louis," activating a general offensive against Jim Crow. The Communist-sponsored American Negro Labor Council (ANLC) had sponsored an antilynching conference in St. Louis in 1930. The conference had marked the ANLC's dissolution, and its succession by the League of Struggle for Negro Rights (LSNR). In 1934, the FWIU's black working-class female leadership, in conjunction with the LSNR, spearheaded the demand for a city ordinance—a "Bill of Rights for Negroes"—barring all forms of Jim Crow in housing and public accommodations, as well as employment.[36]

Ultimately, though, TUUL union and community organizing ran aground. First, Communist organizers had regarded the food-processing workers as a foothold in the ranks of black industrial workers and a stepping-stone to a white native-born working class base. They remained frustrated by their inability to achieve either. Second, the Funsten Company undermined its agreement with the FWIU through a rearguard campaign of mechanized nut shelling, selective layoffs of labor militants, nonunion white women replacements, work speedups, and the parceling of labor to the South. By the summer of 1934, the union was at best on the defensive, and at worst in a state of decline. Third, despite Mayor Dickmann's peaceable expressions toward the striking nutpickers, his appointment of an inquiry committee was, according to Grant, a voluntarist ploy to "get the heat off and stymie the communists who were making great headway with these issues." City officials, the Urban League, Washington, D.C., and the AFL were thoroughly committed to curbing the party's role in workers' and union affairs. When meatpacking workers went on strike in 1934, the AFL took the lead, reaching out to black workers to an unusual degree. Black workers were certainly critical to organizing the packinghouses, but the strategy was also a preemptive strike against the more racially egalitarian TUUL. This outreach, as well as violent opposition to FWIU organizers, effectively shut Communist affiliates out of the industry.[37]

Finally, the TUUL's demise was tied to the Comintern's shift, by the mid-1930s, from its "Third Period" to the advocacy of a left-liberal "Popular Front" against fascism. The party dismantled the TUUL in January 1935. Jettisoning the focus on building radical black alternatives to the NAACP, it disbanded the LSNR a year later. The Communists' return to "boring from within" the AFL effectively lessened attention to the black particularity that had characterized the party's union organizing.[38]

"Independent" Radicalism and Worker Self-Organization

Long before the Communists' emergence, Missouri had been a hotbed of Socialist Party activity, and home to one of the nation's strongest statewide chapters. German socialists had formed the leadership of St. Louis's working-class uprising in 1877, and had been instrumental in building the local AFL in the 1880s. The city also had had one of the few black sections of the Socialist Labor Party. Peter Humphries Clark, an activist in the National Colored Labor Union and a former principal of Sumner High School, had been a well-known black Socialist. By the early twentieth century, however, several leading black radicals had grown tired of the party's racial myopia and single-minded focus on trade unionism. Some black Socialists had voted with their feet, joining the Communists. Others, like Asa Philip Randolph, had become militant anticommunists. While retaining his Socialist affinities, he had nonetheless committed himself to building black worker formations like the BSCP. In St. Louis, an important locale in the nation's rail network, the union had been built largely through the efforts of E. J. Bradley, a former porter. His organizing activities, however, had been handicapped by bribery, beatings, and an elaborate company spy system. The porters also contended with the editorial opposition of the *Argus,* the nation's most explicitly anti-BSCP black newspaper. Organizing had been not only arduous for Bradley, but also financially ruinous, leaving him "flat broke" and separated from his wife by 1933. Many members had scattered, with St. Louis's branch losing over half of its two hundred members.[39]

Despite these many setbacks, the porters had established a cohesive community of interest on the rails. Just as they had been traveling emissaries of black cultural knowledge, the porters had also become mediators of an expanding black working-class public, identifying better wages, and better working conditions and opportunities, as the portals of full black citizenship. For Randolph, they remained the perfect group to spread the message of unionism among the black laboring class: Because of their mobility along the rails, the porters' home was "everywhere." Of course, the porters' community was almost exclusively male. Black maids had been effectively marginalized in 1928, when the union had pursued affiliation with the AFL. The BSCP had convened nationally to draft a new constitution corresponding more closely to the white railroad brotherhoods, and dropped "Maids" from its name and removed from its documents any specific references to them. The porters' casual practice of neglecting women members in union affairs and agendas was reified in policy, buttressing the idea that women's ideal role was as porters' wives, or members of BSCP auxiliaries. This was an insult added to injury particularly because black women had been central to sustaining the union since its inception. This continued base building paved the way for the porters' eventual victory after 1934, when amendments to existing railroad legislation provided the right to bargain collectively. When, in 1935, a national mediation board sponsored an election to determine legitimate representation between the BSCP and a company union, the Brotherhood won overwhelmingly. Of the 386 porters eligible to vote in St. Louis, 271 of them voted for the BSCP. The AFL subsequently approved the union's application for an international charter, and the Pullman Company—finally forced to recognize the BSCP—signed an agreement in August 1937 after two years of arduous negotiations.[40]

By then, separate black working-class initiatives had given rise to the broad federation of organizations that became the National Negro Congress (NNC). Emanating from widespread dissatisfaction with the racism embedded in New Deal recovery policies, the NNC platform called for full relief, social security and unemployment insurance, living wage jobs, and full union membership for African Americans. In the period leading up to its first convention in February 1936, sponsoring committees had formed in Los Angeles, Milwaukee, Chicago, Memphis, Cleveland, New York, and other locales. Prominent in St. Louis's efforts to organize the congress were David Grant, James McLemore, and Langston Harrison, all of them connected to the Democrats' emerging black working-class base. Also active were Sidney R. Williams, the St. Louis Urban League's assistant industrial secretary, St. Louis NAACP president Henry D. Espy, and Leyton Weston, an organizer of the Missouri-Pacific Dining Car Cooks and Waiters, Local 354, who was elected to the NNC's national executive council. The NNC platform, and the range of forces drawn to it, thus solidified a working-class agenda at the "mainstream" center of black activism. This was exemplified most clearly in the selection of Randolph as NNC president. Haloed with the publicity surrounding the BSCP's recognition by the Pullman Company, he became a titular leader who gave the NNC legitimacy in the growing black working-class public sphere.[41]

In St. Louis, it was the Urban League's Industrial Department that became the nerve center of local NNC work. Assistant secretary Williams had been directly involved as a member of the NNC presiding committee, while industrial secretary Charles Collier became an NNC advisor. Not known nationally for protest politics, the Urban League in St. Louis had mainly stood aloof from the nutpickers' strike. As the Urban League's role in the longshoremen's strike attested, however, it was integrally involved in areas largely inhabited by male labor insurgents. The NNC–Urban League relationship in St. Louis suggested a new synergy created by the political radicalism of the period. Among the many resolutions adopted at its founding congress, the NNC had issued support for the National Urban League's involvement in black workers' mobilizations outside organized labor. The Urban League, in fact, had provided a template for this activity nationally. Staffers had vehemently opposed Section 7a of the NIRA, fearing that black workers would be excluded from unionization efforts. In 1934, a group of black bricklayers had contacted John T. Clark, the St. Louis Urban League's executive secretary, about the possibility of using the NIRA provision to organize outside the AFL. Sensing a unique opportunity to challenge local white control of skilled labor, Collier and Williams had lent the black workers eager administrative support. Black construction craftsmen had formed the International Laborers and Builders Corporation and the Allied Building Crafts Union. A merger with other groups of black workers had given birth to the St. Louis Negro Workers' Council, attracting national attention. "Negro labor in St. Louis, Missouri," announced National Urban League spokesman Lester B. Granger in the journal *Opportunity*, "has shown the way for colored workers throughout the country to make an aggressive attack against prejudice and discriminatory policies on the part of certain sections of the American labor movement." Indeed, Clark was drafted by the New York headquarters to create a national Negro Workers' Council modeled in the Gateway City's likeness, spawning councils in cities such as Chicago, Baltimore, Seattle, Memphis, Louisville, Cincinnati, Newark, and Jackson, Mississippi.[42]

St. Louis's council brought under its aegis a broad swath of the black working-class public: hotel and levee workers, carpenters, janitors, bricklayers, domestics, quarry workers, motion picture operators, milk drivers, electricians, packinghouse and steel workers, and AFL-affiliated dining car employees and Pullman porters. Given the BSCP's recognition by the Pullman Company, and its membership in the AFL, E. J. Bradley and Theodore D. McNeal, both BSCP leaders, were especially potent allies in opening the House of Labor. By 1936, with some two thousand members, it was one of the nation's two largest councils. That February, in collaboration with the founding meeting of the NNC, the Urban League had convened a National Conference of Negro Workers' Councils in Chicago. That June, Clark was part of a delegation of representing Negro Workers' Councils from around the nation that met with federal officials in D.C. to discuss recommendations for ending discrimination against black building tradesmen in public works projects.[43]

Locally, the black workers' council had achieved early success when activists pressed the St. Louis Board of Education into hiring African Americans in the heating plants of its black schools. The council had also led a popular, community-wide campaign in 1935 to employ black motion picture operators and ticket takers at black neighborhood movie theaters. Picketers, organizing independently of the Motion Picture Operators' Union after being denied entry, had faced gunmen dispatched by the AFL, prompting the Mayor's Office to intervene. A piecemeal settlement had granted black theater workers a Jim Crow local, and higher wages. By 1937, however, the city's white union leadership had moved swiftly to subvert the burgeoning black labor coalition. Bradley, elected president of the Negro Workers' Council in 1936, resigned amid intense pressure from the AFL. With the sleeping car porters withdrawing their formal support, the council floundered. A successor, the Negro Trade Union League, formed in 1938, though again the AFL Central Trades and Labor Union blocked its development.[44]

Yet, its dissolution also came as the result of black labor militants' growing investment in the percolating industrial union movement, which the Negro Workers' Council, the Urban League, and NNC had all encouraged. The 1935 National Labor Relations (Wagner) Act, asserting workers' right to form unions and bargain with their bosses, had been celebrated as a U.S.

working-class "Magna Carta." To the chagrin of black intellectuals and organizers, it had not included a hoped-for amendment denying federal protection to exclusionary white unions. Nonetheless, many NNC activists fought to defend the law from amendments designed to cripple it. A similar commitment to industrial organization, along with prior involvement in the unemployed movement and the Popular Front, propelled African American workers into the AFL's organizing drive in the meatpacking industry. More significantly, black freedom workers helped build the local Congress of Industrial Organizations (CIO), whose activities had grown organically from the foundation laid by the nutpickers strike. A cohort of black St. Louis social workers, many of them grouped around the Urban League and NNC, formed the Social Service Employees Union–CIO, Local 83. Another critical site of black CIO activity occurred in the steel industry, where the numbers of African American mass-production workers gave them their most strategic foothold. Sentner, meanwhile, became the key leader in the local drive to establish the CIO's United Electrical, Radio and Machine Workers of America (UE). The electrical workers union would grow rapidly, becoming St. Louis's largest CIO affiliate, and Sentner would become president of UE District 8. Deeply inspired by the Funsten struggle, he remained a purveyor of community-oriented "civic unionism."[45]

Black Neighborhood Upsurge

These activities overlapped heavily with ongoing black grassroots neighborhood initiatives. This spirit of neighborhood insurgency had been manifest in a "Don't Buy Where You Can't Work" mobilization earlier that decade. The campaign had become a national phenomenon in 1932, with protesters demanding that white-owned retail stores in black residential communities hire black workers in sales, clerical, and labor positions, or face disruptive boycotts. In St. Louis, the campaign had its genesis in the Colored Clerks' Circle, which was created in cooperation with the Urban League by David Grant, Nathaniel Sweets, Nathan Young of the black-owned *St. Louis American,* and jobless youth. An alliance formed with the Housewives League, a local affiliate of the Detroit-based organization. Led by Edwina Wright, a Sumner High School teacher, St. Louis league members followed the premise that since mothers and wives spent 80 percent of their families' income, they were best situated to issue demands to local businesses for a fair share of employment for black workers. They joined the clerks in a campaign to place black men and "girls" at several white-owned department stores, theaters, and bakeries. The local dairy companies became the Housewives League's central target since milk, from a maternalist standpoint, was the family's most vital commodity—and one that mothers spent a hefty amount of their budget purchasing.[46]

Financially unable to expand beyond a black consumer base, local white business owners had to make concessions. The St. Louis Dairy Company became the first business to hire black delivery drivers along routes heavily populated by African Americans. One bakery also hired black driver-salesmen. Boycotts even forced major chain stores to accede to reform. Woolworth's made an agreement with the Colored Clerks' Circle to hire black workers in each of its two dime stores located in black neighborhoods, including a new store on Franklin Avenue near the business district. That the protests were actively supported by the BSCP, the *American,* and the *Argus* was particularly indicative of the new social atmosphere, for the *Argus* had been an ardent foe of the BSCP, and the *American* had begun in explicit competition with the older newspaper. Grassroots employment campaigns may not have created black political unanimity, but the protests were cementing a new kind of working unity driven by a laboring majority.[47]

The lack of city services also elicited an organized black response. In 1931, George Boyer Vashon Elementary School, located in the Carr Square area, became a high school to deal with the growing volume of black students at Sumner. When the city's school superintendent announced in January 1937 that the Board of Education would build a new elementary school on the Vashon grounds, activists protested that the campus already was too small and cramped, and questioned the ethics of placing young children in such close contact with much older students. Enlisting the financial backing of Nineteenth Ward leader Jordan Chambers, attorney George Vaughn filed suit. He argued in court against the plan alongside other NAACP lawyers Robert L. Witherspoon and the Harvard-trained Sidney Revels Redmond (who was a grandson of the Reconstruction-era U.S. senator from Mississippi, Hiram Revels). A circuit court ruling, with support from the *Argus,* the NAACP, the NNC, the National Alliance of Postal Employees, and the Vashon Parent-Teacher Association, forced the board to shelve the plan. A parallel struggle created the city's only black trade school, the Booker T. Washington Vocational Training School for Negroes. The Urban League, likewise, coordinated the development of neighborhood organizations. Under the direction of Patty Cox Hall, the St. Louis Federation of Block Units promoted community gardens, regular garbage collection, and the expansion of segregated playground space in the black community.[48]

The 1930s had also witnessed an upsurge in black working-class religious millenarianism, with the Midwest providing fertile ground for a flowering of prophetic Black Nationalist movements. They were, further, characteristically pro-Japan, reflecting many African Americans' regard of the Japanese as the "champion of the darker races." The Lost-Found Nation of Islam (NOI), formed in Detroit, was emblematic of this sentiment. The most important of these groups, however, was the Pacific Movement of the Eastern World (PMEW), founded in 1932 by Satokata Takahashi, a Japanese national organizing among African Americans in Detroit, Chicago, and St. Louis. Led nationally by the Reverend David Erwin, the minister of an East St. Louis Holiness church, the group espoused the worldwide unity of black and other people of color, and advocated a Japanese military invasion of the United States, from which would follow black emigration to Japan, Brazil, or the African continent. Spirited PMEW meetings took place at the Pythian Hall, the People's Finance Building, and along Market Street, where pro-Japanese black militants vied against Communist-affiliated black unionists for the same Central Corridor audiences. From St. Louis, the group expanded to the "Bootheel" region of southeast Missouri, where its doctrines appealed to the black sharecroppers and day laborers suffering economic and physical displacement.[49]

For St. Louis's black laboring majority, of whatever political persuasion, the most crucial unresolved issue was the building of the new black public hospital promised by Mayor Dickmann. Merging the issues of health care, and the Negro Workers' Council's demand for skilled paid labor, the campaign was one of the period's most contentious affairs. Construction of the new $3,160,000 facility had begun in 1933 in the Ville. Partly funded by federal monies, the hospital had become a PWA project, and its building contract had come under Section 7a of the NIRA, which did not require unions to accept African Americans. It remained a continuing source of outrage among black workers that they could not get skilled jobs building and repairing the very institutions created to serve their own communities. City officials turned down work applications by a reported twenty black plasterers, thirty-one carpenters, thirty-five electricians, and forty-four painters, all with union cards from other cities. "It seems strange to us," Williams commented archly, speaking for the Urban League, "that a Negro qualified for membership in Cleveland, say, or Detroit is held not qualified in St. Louis." When the General Tile and Marble Company hired a black tilesetter, AFL tradesmen went on strike. They returned only after he was fired, and the city agreed not to contract with any other companies employing skilled black labor. Black workers responded with public demonstrations at the construction site, but while a few additional common laborers were hired, the overall restrictions on skilled African Americans remained intact.[50]

On February 22, 1937, thousands of people packed the area around Goode, Kennerly, Whittier, and Cottage avenues for the dedication of

Homer G. Phillips Hospital, named in honor of a well-known black attorney-activist who had been slain years earlier. A massive art deco complex of five buildings with 670 beds, the facility improved the quality of life for many black working-class St. Louisans, while providing a training facility for black middle-class professionals and adding to the Ville's importance in the city's black institutional life. Through these experiences, a self-conscious African American working-class public sphere had emerged, led and peopled by unskilled industrial laborers and skilled craftsmen; educators and social workers; dining car cooks, sleeping car porters and maids; housewives and the homeless; educators, attorneys, and the unemployed; the middle-aged and the young; the secular and the religious; and millenarian Black Nationalists, Communists, Socialists, and independent radicals. Formal organizations like the Communist and Socialist parties, the Urban League, the National Negro Congress, the Pacific Movement of the Eastern World, the Colored Clerks' Circle, the St. Louis Housewives League, even the AFL, were vessels for an ideologically diverse and autonomous black working-class politics. In many instances, black worker-activists acted in accordance with the expectations of their organizational sponsors. In other cases—as in the nutpickers' abiding religious faith in defiance of Communist orthodoxy—they followed their own prerogatives. And in the case of the Urban League's Negro Workers' Council, the initiative for its formation came entirely from unorganized black craftsmen.[51]

While their energies veered in multiple directions, St. Louis's black laboring class shared a common "platform" of jobs, trade union organizing, social security expenditures, housing, neighborhood amenities like trash collection, street repair and recreational space, public health care and education, consumer cooperatives and rights, and the abolition of Jim Crow in all its manifestations—in essence, full citizenship, self-determination, and "respect." These demands profited African Americans across class, just as black workers' activities benefited the working class across racial lines. Popular clamor for playgrounds, regular garbage pickups, and other public infrastructure may have sprung most directly from black workers' interests, but they contributed generally to improving the quality of life in the African American community.

Location of birth, area of residence, education, conditions of work, and notions of "moral virtue" continued to foster real internal schisms among black St. Louisans. Yet the conditions of the Depression both enlarged and politically awakened an African American working class. Although savaged by economic upheaval, this racial class was paradoxically strengthened, becoming the center of an emerging new historic bloc of black freedom forces. The small size of St. Louis's African American community, and the even smaller size of its black activist community, gave added continuity and multiplicity to the individuals and organizations holding it together. As depression gave way to a new global war and industrial regeneration, the consciousness that black working people had gained of themselves during the 1930s was further consolidated, largely in the form of the March on Washington Movement.

CHAPTER TWO

The St. Louis March on Washington and the Historic Bloc for "Double Victory," 1942–45

THE BLACK WORKING-CLASS political bloc that had arisen during the Depression was further reified in the new wartime crisis raging in Europe. As the United States joined the campaign against the Axis powers of Fascist Italy, Nazi Germany, and Imperial Japan, an industrial renaissance occurred on the domestic front. Many aspects of the local economy allowed the St. Louis metropolitan area to benefit from this resurgence. It housed a pool of skilled workers, and its diverse manufacturing base was the largest west of the Mississippi. Further, the city's strategic location below the confluence of the Mississippi and the Missouri rivers made it an inland waterway hub. As the nucleus of national railroad links, St. Louis was also an easy destination point for migrant workers, and the largest industrial center west of the Big Muddy. For decades, moreover, it had been a laboratory for the developing aviation industry, which now brought numerous federal war contracts to the city.[1]

Just as they had been the first fired during the Depression, African Americans now found themselves the last hired as the economy tilted toward full employment. As the 1940s began, 20 percent of St. Louis's black workers were unemployed, and another 11 percent were on WPA projects. However, wartime tumult created new opportunities for black working-class struggle. Britain, the United States, "Free France," and the Soviet Union gave African Americans new discourses with which to fight for full citizenship and self-determination on the U.S. home front. Whereas variants of left-wing radicalism had been pervasive during the Depression, black freedom workers now largely adopted a critical American patriotism. Likening Hitler, Hirohito, and Mussolini to southern segregationists and northern white racists, they highlighted how Jim Crow undermined the moral credibility of the United States in defending the "Four Freedoms" abroad. The Brotherhood of Sleeping Car Porters, acting through the broad working-class front of the March on Washington Movement (MOWM), formed the cutting edge in a fight for victory over Nazism overseas and racial apartheid at home.[2]

This chapter discusses the activities of the St. Louis Unit of the MOWM, specifically its campaigns around the hiring and upgrading of black workers in defense plants and public utilities. While confronting a qualitatively different set of circumstances than during the Depression, the St. Louis MOWM continued patterns of black worker self-organization from the 1930s, and thus contributed politically to the ongoing processes of black working-class formation. The St. Louis division was also notable as the MOWM's most active and militant branch, and among the most successful in achieving defense industry work for African Americans. But while the MOWM occupied the center of black St. Louis militancy during the war, other patterns of resistance thrived. Because they revolved around the interests of a defined—and self-defined—black working class, these developments helped further recreate African American civil society and its evolving class structure. These experiences contributed to heightening a black racial-class consciousness, which not only propelled the black freedom struggles of the 1940s, but also seeded the soil for a subsequent period of black grassroots insurgency.[3]

"We Fight for the Right to Work as Well as Die for Victory for the United Nations"

Wartime St. Louis remained one of the nation's most segregated cities. Most downtown hotels, restaurants, and theaters continued to bar African Americans. While athletes Jesse Owens and Joe Louis personified America's rejection of the Nazi "master race" doctrine, African Americans could not sit in the grandstand at Sportsman's Park, home of the St. Louis Cardinals and Browns baseball clubs. Local dime and drug stores prohibited black patrons from dining at their lunch counters. The central business district's three major department stores—the Famous-Barr Company, Stix, Baer & Fuller, and Scruggs, Vandervoort, Barney—did not serve black shoppers at their popular eating facilities. These patterns spilled over into the lucrative new war production industries, as black workers were virtually nonexistent in the new job boom. In 1940, the Curtiss-Wright aircraft plant received a $16 million contract for training and cargo planes, while a $14 million facility run by the Atlas Powder Company became the nation's largest maker of TNT. The American Car and St. Louis Car companies both received hefty contracts for tanks, and in December 1940 the federal government approved plans to build a small-arms ordnance plant. Opening the following year, the U.S. Cartridge Small Arms/Ordnance plant became the largest of its kind in the world. By November 1941, the federal state had awarded some sixty thousand defense contracts in the city, and after the United States formally entered the war, government war spending in St. Louis leapt from $3 million per month to over $3 million per week.[4]

In early 1941, the BSCP organized the "Negro March on Washington Committee" for a mass protest in D.C. against racial discrimination in war production industries, the United States Employment Service (USES), and the armed forces. The momentum illustrated how far the BSCP had traveled since joining the AFL. Attacks, leveled by black newspapers like St. Louis's *Argus*, had subsided in the 1930s, while the porters had wrested higher wages and other concessions from the Pullman Company in the first collective bargaining agreement between a major company and a black labor organization. BSCP head A. Philip Randolph had become "the most widely known spokesman for black working-class interests in the country," and NNC delegates had given him additional status when they named him their president. Yet Randolph had become disturbed by the more open relationship the NNC had developed with active Communists. Amid public scrutiny by U.S. congressman Martin Dies's House Committee on Un-American Activities (HUAC), Randolph, an ardent anticommunist, had not sought reelection to the post at the NNC's 1940 convention. Lacking Randolph's imprimatur, the coalition was stigmatized as a Communist "front" at a moment when shifts in Comintern policy, including the 1939 Nazi-Soviet Nonaggression Pact, had tarnished the party's reputation among many black antifascists. The D.C. march committee's "Negro-only" stance, in contrast, and its refusal to sacrifice black demands for the sake of "national unity," catapulted it to the center of a burgeoning black working-class public sphere.[5]

The Roosevelt administration averted the threat of one hundred thousand black protesters converging on the nation's capital by conceding to BSCP-led demands for an executive order against racial discrimination in government and defense industry employment. The executive order created the Fair Employment Practice Committee (FEPC) to monitor both employers and labor unions involved in war production, or otherwise engaged in business with the federal state. Critics heaped scorn on Randolph for autocratically calling off the protest, prompting him to claim he was merely "postponing" rather than canceling the demonstration. Other contemporaries, however, hailed the executive order as the most significant decree since the Emancipation Proclamation. The immediate challenge, however, was to actually enforce the order's provisions. Clauses prohibiting discrimination appeared in all defense contracts, but the FEPC, aside from being meagerly funded and understaffed, lacked subpoena and enforcement powers. Reliant on individual complaints, public exposure, embarrassment, and moral persuasion, the agency was most successful in appealing to war industrialists in places where labor markets were tightest, and where it had active local support. St. Louis confronted the FEPC with some of its toughest cases, for such cities were closer in social temperament and policies to the South than they were to the North. Indeed, many St. Louis firms engaged in war production easily flouted the executive order. This also had partly to do with the fact that the city did not experience severe labor shortages, though when pressed for labor, employers frequently chose to meet demand by recruiting white men from rural Missouri and the South, and white women.[6]

A few major St. Louis defense firms, including Curtiss-Wright and U.S. Cartridge, began hiring small numbers of black workers in the spring of 1942. Of the Gateway City's 816,000 residents, 110,000 were African American; among the 50,000 black people in the labor force, a negligible number were employed in the war industries. Black women suffered worse, for the president's executive order was mute on the question of gender discrimination. In St. Louis, USES ran two segregated offices—one for whites, who were steered into skilled and semiskilled work, and the second for African Americans, who were referred to low-skilled and unskilled work. Although union-minded black workers readily joined the UE, many white coworkers were at best ambivalent about their presence. Industrial personnel managers, moreover, segregated bathrooms, canteens, and other plant facilities.[7]

Still, the latent promises of the FEPC and the creation of the MOWM opened new vistas of black working-class consciousness and activism in St. Louis. In May 1942, twenty-two local leaders met with Randolph and Chicago BSCP leader Milton P. Webster at the Wheatley YWCA to discuss forming an MOWM unit. The gathering represented a cross-section of St. Louis's black public sphere, and threads of previous working-class struggle. BSCP field organizer Theodore D. McNeal, and Leyton Weston, a leader of the Dining Car Employees, Local 354, were both veterans of the defunct Negro Workers' Council. Weston, moreover, had been a member of the NNC's national executive council, while McNeal had been involved in the activities of the Colored Clerks' Circle. David Grant, also in attendance, was similarly a veteran of the clerks' "Don't Buy Where You Can't Work" campaigns of the early Depression, and a key actor in black St. Louisans' electoral shift to the Democratic Party in 1933. Attorney-activist George Vaughn, further, had given legal leadership to several community upsurges, while the new NAACP branch president, Sidney Redmond, had helped argue *Missouri ex rel. Gaines v. Canada* before the U.S. Supreme Court, whose 1938 ruling had undermined segregated professional and graduate schools.[8]

Subsequent meetings resulted in the formation of a St. Louis MOWM unit headquartered at BSCP office's in the People's Finance Building. Mc-Neal was named chairman of the committee, and Weston assistant chairman. Grant took charge of the complaints committee, while Chambers, likely at the behest of his close associates Vaughn and Grant, became the unit's treasurer. Thelma Grant, who was married to the Democratic attorney-activist, took on the duties of secretary. St. Louis BSCP president E. J. Bradley was also actively involved in the new committee, but held no formal title. By early June, meetings occurred every Wednesday evening at the Pine Street YMCA, while volunteers staffed the office every day from morning until evening. Among their stated goals, organizers planned to gather complaints of racial discrimination at the city's defense plants, and wage mass protest. They sought, as well, to expand the number of classes in skilled defense industry jobs at the Booker T. Washington Vocational High School for Negroes. In the short term, the goal was to bring the president's FEPC to St. Louis for hearings on racism in the war industries. More broadly, the unit's executive committee envisioned itself as part of a campaign to rid the city of "all economic discrimination against Negroes."[9]

As in other cities, the black press was a leader in this "Double Victory" campaign against authoritarianism at home and overseas. The *American* and the *Argus* aided the local MOWM's outreach efforts by granting its activities favorable coverage, and allowing its leaders to make their case directly to black St. Louis. In a three-part statement that ran in the *Argus,* Mc-Neal underscored the importance of the war to African Americans by appealing to the sentiments of the laboring majority. "The chief crisis of the Negro people is the crisis of the Negro worker, for in the main, the Negro workers are the Negro people," he argued, asserting a central premise of the black working-class bloc. "Therefore, if the Negro workers are harmed, the Negro people are harmed." Evoking an expansive black public rooted in a gendered working-class culture, he declared, "We intend to organize the Negro in the poolroom, on the street corner, in the church and every place else he is found."[10]

The unit's first opportunity to do so came in May and early June when U.S. Cartridge's Small Arms plant dismissed nearly two hundred black workers, including black Communist Party veteran Hershel Walker. The company, at the time, was hiring upwards of one thousand new production workers a week. Certainly, racial discrimination at the North St. Louis factory had been a catalyst in forming the local MOWM unit in the first place, and had remained a principal target of organizers' attention. With a federal contract worth $200 million, the ammunition plant was the city's major wartime employer. But of its 20,500 employees, only 600 were African American, all of them hired as lower-paid laborers and porters. No black women at all were among the plant's 8,000 female employees. McNeal telegrammed the FEPC in Washington, D.C., objecting to the dismissals and urging an investigation. Building on a tide of public outrage, the MOWM unit ran a series of advertisements in the daily press exhorting black St. Louisans to register at its office to "Join the effort to win your RIGHTFUL JOBS in the local War Industries." Walker, and many of the other fired black workers, called for demonstrations. In a meeting with R. V. Rickard, the U.S. Cartridge Company's industrial relations manager, MOWM officers outlined several demands, including the immediate employment of black women in production jobs, in-plant training and upgrading, and a halt to the recruitment of "outside labor" from the South until the company's hiring agency had exhausted local labor pools. Stepping beyond the immediate issue of employment and promotion, MOWM negotiators demanded the abolition of segregated accommodations at the ordnance plant. U.S. Cartridge officials disputed claims about a mass expulsion of African Americans, and refused the committee's proposals. They assured that at most, the firm would hire one hundred black women as "plant matrons" to clean the lavatories used by white female employees. Following the rancorous summit, McNeal announced plans for a "peaceable demonstration" on the Small Arms plant.[11]

An unlikely source of opposition to the planned march, however, came from local Communist Party leadership. Under its "Popular Front" strategy, the Comintern's chief priority had become defending the Soviet Union against Nazi aggression, which led local party leaders to regard the impending demonstration as an "ill-advised procedure." American Communists had not only urged "no strike pledges" between workers and industrial employers—with individuals like Sentner even volunteering his union for wage cuts—but they had also opposed the idea of black militant protests that would disrupt the U.S. war effort. At a more fundamental level, too, Communist organizers objected to the MOWM's "chauvinistic" tone. Indeed, Randolph had conceived the march as an all-black affair mainly as a way of blocking the involvement of white Communists, whom he blamed for ruining the NNC. But neither Communists nor U.S. Cartridge officials could slow the momentum toward a march. Between two hundred and four hundred protesters gathered at midday in front of Goodfellow and Bircher boulevards with placards condemning Jim Crow at the plant. "We'll Grind AXES 'Gainst the AXIS in Europe or Japan And Also Grind Them At the Small Arms Plants!" read one sign. "We Fight For The Right To Work As Well As Die For Victory For the United Nations" vowed another. Led by a man carrying an American flag, the retinue of unemployed workers, housewives, teachers, railroad men, and laborers walked silently, and in single file, around the plant's eight buildings for nearly two hours.[12]

Locally and nationally, the black press celebrated the protest parade as an unqualified victory. In a popular social affairs column published in the *American* by "Mel and Thel," Thelma Dickerson and Melba Sweets, wife of publisher Nathaniel Sweets, dispelled any doubts about the new organization's abilities. "We're happy in the assurance that at last colored St. Louis has in this committee a hound-dog with big teeth to guard its meager existing bone and to snap at the cuffs of the well-tailered [*sic*] trousers of the trustees of the meatier pieces that are its due," they crowed. The white daily press seemed equally sympathetic to the MOWM committee's appeal for fair play. The St. Louis CIO Industrial Union Council joined the chorus of those demanding the immediate reinstatement of the black workers discharged by U.S. Cartridge. This stance mirrored the UE's strong influence within the council, and its links to the Communist Left. Even as the party had opposed the Small Arms march, and the MOWM itself, Communists like Sentner, the UE's leading figure in St. Louis, remained committed to defending black workers' rights, even in contravention of official party positions.[13]

This mobilization of opinion elicited immediate response from U.S. Cartridge officials. Within days, management raised its black laborers' wages—white workers already had been receiving automatic pay raises. By early July, the company had rehired three hundred black men and seventy-two matrons. Personnel managers also began inducting several hundred male trainees for skilled work, though they had yet to hire black female production workers at any skill level. Seventy-five percent of St. Louis's defense plants, meanwhile, had absolutely no African Americans.[14]

"Winning Democracy for the Negro Is Winning the War for Democracy"

To expand their campaign, and sharpen the potent threat of a march, national MOWM leaders planned mass rallies in several major cities in the summer of 1942. With the White House paying close attention, eighteen thousand people packed New York's Madison Square Garden for a "monster rally" on June 16. Another twelve thousand converged at Chicago's Coliseum on June 26. The last of these rallies occurred in St. Louis, where local organizers adopted as their theme the March on Washington Movement's national slogan: "Winning Democracy for the Negro is Winning the War for Democracy." Several women active in the unit led the financial drive to fund the event, and helped recruit a range of cosponsors, including the Interdenominational Ministerial Alliance of St. Louis, a coalition of black ministers. On Friday evening, August 14, over nine thousand people packed the downtown Municipal Auditorium Convention Hall for five hours of speeches and entertainment, including a reading of Langston Hughes's "Freedom Suite" accompanied by music. James Cook, executive secretary of the Pine Street YMCA, coordinated a collection of funds from the sizable audience. Featured guests included Randolph, Webster, and other MOWM leaders from Chicago, and national NAACP executive secretary Walter White.[15]

The stirring speeches, punctuated by standing ovations, were a summary of the current state of the "Double V" campaign against fascism and Jim Crow. Pressured by southern congressmen, the Roosevelt administration in July had transferred the FEPC from the president's direct control to the War Manpower Commission under Paul V. McNutt, where the agency was now dependent on congressional funding. The transfer had occurred over the vigorous protest of black leaders, and Randolph intimated that a national march to D.C. was still on the organization's agenda. White took specific aim at Theodore Bilbo and other segregationist senators and governors of the "Fascist South," whom he condemned for choosing to lose the war rather than give black people an equal chance to work. Sally Parham, a member of the local MOWM committee, asserted the need for women to stand behind the coalition as wives and mothers. In this emphasis, she highlighted the male-centered nature of the MOWM's goals, for if women were naturalized as keepers of the domestic sphere, surely the men were, by implication, "workers."[16]

Grant, the St. Louis MOWM's most forceful personality, asserted that the Depression and the New Deal had imbued many black people with a sense of entitlement to federal protection and largesse. The underlying premises of the war, additionally, had given antiracist efforts official legitimacy. Linking their own situation to those of other peoples nationally oppressed by Allied nations, the audience passed a resolution defending Indian independence from Britain, and supported a cablegram to Mohandas Gandhi pledging solidarity. The gesture reflected a respect for the Gandhian techniques of nonviolence that informed the MOWM's own tactics.[17]

Soon after its first mass meeting, the St. Louis MOWM committee set its sights on Carter Carburetor, which manufactured bomb and artillery fuses, and army vehicle parts. The company, which had over $1 million in government war contracts, employed no African Americans among its roughly three thousand workers. The company's vice president and general manager, H. C. Weed, conceded that none were presently employed at the plant, but contended the firm had no policy barring them. But when Carter Carburetor management refused to come to the negotiating table, militant race leaders took to the streets. "This Plant Ignored Our Request For A Conference Hence It ASKED FOR A MARCH!" blared an organizing flyer addressed to black St. Louisans. "HELP FIGHT For Jobs!! Freedom!! Equal Opportunities!! Full Citizenship!!" On the afternoon of August 29, between two hundred and five hundred protesters responded to the call. Assembling in the Ville at the Charleton H. Tandy Park, the men, women, and children marched the ten blocks to the Carter plant on Spring Avenue, winding through white residential areas and passing large crowds of bystanders, all without incident.[18]

The march yielded no immediate concessions from Carter Carburetor. Yet attendance skyrocketed at the MOWM unit's weekly Pine Street Y meetings, at times numbering three hundred people. In October, as the MOWM and the Interdenominational Ministerial Alliance organized for a mass prayer meeting in Memorial Plaza, the committee's membership stood at fifteen hundred. Broadcast by radio, the open-air service drew three thousand people, who prayed for an Allied victory, fair play for black Americans, and global peace. Resolutions by the local CIO Industrial Council, coverage by the white-owned press, and encouragement from individual citizens illustrated white sympathies for this budding "march for jobs" campaign in St. Louis. At the same time, many whites viewed such black agitation with rage and uncertainty about what African American demands for full citizenship would mean socially. Housing shortages, overcrowding, work fatigue, rationing, and high consumer prices sharpened these racial tensions. Fights were common on streetcars and shop floors and in schoolyards, frequently fed by rumors of impending race war. Rural areas felt these tremors, too. In early 1942, a white mob in Sikeston, Missouri, lynched Cleo Wright, a black mill worker accused of butchering a white woman during a rape attempt. Because it was the first lynching after the 1941 bombing of Pearl Harbor, the incident drew instant national attention. Outcry among liberal whites and race leaders, and international embarrassment, prompted a state investigation and even the entry of the U.S. Justice Department. No indictments followed, though the case marked the first convening of a federal grand jury in a lynching.[19]

Meanwhile, at southern military training bases, black troops reared in the North chafed under the humiliations of Jim Crow imposed by white officers and local residents. St. Louis's Jefferson Barracks was typical in its segregated policies, and black enlisted personnel traveling through the Gateway City could not visit the city's United Service Organizations club at the Municipal Auditorium. These resentments frequently exploded in pitched battles involving black soldiers, white trainees, military police, and townspeople at camps around the nation. Driven by the same sentiments that had led to executive-ordered relocation and detention of Japanese Americans, many whites assumed latent disloyalty among African Americans. Randolph's reticence to lead a D.C. march therefore reflected the legitimate fear of the MOWM being labeled not only unpatriotic, but also treasonous—thus, the conspicuousness of U.S. flags at MOWM events. Indeed, some young black men, angered by segregation in the army and navy, refused induction through either dissemblance or outright resistance. Many authorities feared their collusion with the Japanese. When, in early 1943, authorities indicted two East St. Louis leaders of the pro-Japanese PMEW on charges of espionage and sedition, many white observers took this as evidence of a black threat to the body politic.[20]

"We Are Americans, Too"

But the real saboteur, race leaders insisted, was Jim Crow. As 1943 began, St. Louis's MOWM leadership outlined plans for greater outreach among other black political, civic, and religious organizations. Porters, maids, and dining car workers provided the MOWM's financial base, though support from such organizations as the St. Louis Negro Grade Teachers Association and the Booklovers Club indicated the broad communal support the unit had cemented. Sweets and black Democrat Joseph McLemore were named chairmen of MOWM subcommittees, and James Cook of the Pine Street YMCA was added to the unit's executive board. Since its first march, the local unit had made important strides in the campaign for jobs and justice. McNeal boasted that protest efforts had yielded eight thousand African American defense industry jobs, notably in skilled and semiskilled positions. The sprawling Small Arms plant alone employed more than seventeen hundred black workers, and by spring, the number had risen to over three thousand. Grant bragged that at Building 202, the all-black unit created at the plant, absenteeism and tardiness were the lowest in the entire factory, while production was higher than in similar units. At Curtiss-Wright, twenty-four black women had joined their black male counterparts in skilled work on military planes. One group of women had received in-plant training, while another had graduated from classes at Washington Vocational High School. Other African Americans were engaged in skilled defense work at a handful of firms, including the Wagner and Emerson electric companies, and Scullin Steel, which had long employed skilled black labor.[21]

Many of these workers became MOWM members, and sent warm letters and money to the organization's Jefferson Avenue headquarters. "I am a girl you helped get placed at the Small Arms Plant," one woman wrote to Grant. "I am very grateful to you and in token of my gratitude am enclosing five dollars to be used as you see fit in the 'March-on Washington' Movement." Writing to McNeal, another Small Arms worker enthused, "I received [m]y certificate for Membership, and the little peace of paper gave me grate pleasure." Pointedly referring to himself as "a member of the working class," he imagined, "[I]t may be good if a little [window] sticker with the march sign, could be in thousands of [windows], so the slow to act people, may be aroused." As this letter implied, the St. Louis MOWM's successes, though real, had been relatively modest. For each black worker hired, more than five were not. By MOWM leaders' own estimate, three-fourths of the 325 defense plants in the area still barred or segregated black workers. Like the General Chemical Company, other local defense factories, both large and small, still had no black employees in any job classification. In March 1943, as the federal government cut relief appropriations, some twenty thousand African Americans were still without work.[22]

A summary sent to the FEPC had detailed dismally discriminatory practices by McDonnell Aircraft Corporation, McQuay-Norris, and other St. Louis–area plants. Black laborers had supplied Grant and McNeal with the bulk of these complaints, and actively invited the movement's intervention. "We have about hundred [black] men out to this plant and we all are doing porter work but just a few men they put on Production line," wrote Herman Hester, a rank-and-file MOWM member employed at the Amertorp Corporation, a producer of torpedoes. No black women worked at the plant in any capacity. Hester noted, "I has been there 10 1/2 months my self and I has been sweeping every since I been there. . . . We as Amertorp Workers are looking forward for you all to march on this place just as soon as you can." Following a meeting with these black employees at the Wheatley YWCA, Weston sent correspondence to the company's industrial relations manager for a meeting. Complaints from workers at the Atlas Powder Company prompted McNeal to write the company's general manager for a similar conference on hiring, upgrading, and segregated work conditions.[23]

Curiously, however, the MOWM had avoided a showdown with the construction trades involved in building the new war production facilities. In late 1941, the federal Office of Production Management had entered a "stabilization agreement" with the AFL Building and Construction Trades, granting them a closed shop in exchange for no-strike pledges. Like the government-labor pacts of the early New Deal, this arrangement implicitly sanctioned the well-entrenched patterns of white privilege and black exclusion. On purely pragmatic grounds, MOWM leaders may have calculated they stood a better chance of winning defense jobs in the mass-production industries, where labor guilds could not determine the complexion of the workforce through a monopoly on skills. Second, it was harder to identify discrimination at building construction sites, since the workplace was temporary, general contractors and subcontractors could shift blame to unions, and the hiring bosses themselves were affiliated with different unions. The BSCP's central role in the MOWM may have been another factor guiding it away from direct confrontation with the construction unions. In the past, Randolph and other national BSCP leaders had shown a willingness to defy racism within the AFL, though they had consistently done so within boundaries that did not jeopardize their seats within the federation. During the 1930s, certainly, local BSCP leaders had dealt the St. Louis Negro Workers' Council a mortal blow when they withdrew from the coalition at the AFL's behest. Viewed in this light, the MOWM's silence on the construction trades served the interests of maintaining the porters' volatile relationship with organized craft labor.[24]

Although timid on the matter of wartime construction contracts, MOWM officers expanded the scope of their grievances to include the Laclede Gas Light Company, Union Electric Company, Southwestern Bell Telephone Company, and the St. Louis Public Service Company, which ran the city's buses and streetcars. Protest leaders and FEPC members contended that these public utilities constituted essential war industries, and therefore fell under the president's executive order. The MOWM committee particularly singled out the phone and transportation companies. Some twenty-five thousand black St. Louisans paid bills to the phone company, but fewer than fifty held jobs among its four thousand employees, and all of them were janitors and cleaning women. Black working-class women, in particular, were excluded from the ideal of demure white ladyhood that the Bell System promoted in its hiring of telephone operators, and that white women employees themselves defended. Under the MOWM's direction, many highly trained young women filed applications for positions as telephone operators at the company's employment office. Despite labor shortages and daily newspaper advertisements clamoring for applicants, none were hired. Among the Public Service Company's 4,200 employees, only 250 were African American. Except for one mechanic, all of them either cleaned buses and cars, or worked on track gangs. None of the company's 2,670 streetcar and bus operators were black. In March, the MOWM committee sent letters to both the phone and transportation companies seeking conferences. It appears that Southwestern Bell officials flatly refused to discuss the matter at all, though the Public Service Company's personnel director agreed to a meeting with McNeal, Grant, and Weston. In the end, nonetheless, the company only hired twenty-five black women as bus cleaners.[25]

It was no surprise, then, that a straw poll conducted by the *Pittsburgh Courier* had revealed a great deal of popular support for a national march, with black respondents in St. Louis, Chicago, Detroit, New York, and Los Angeles registering overwhelming majorities. In November 1942, the FEPC had announced tentative plans for public hearings in the Gateway City, principally on the strength of complaints gathered by the St. Louis MOWM. But in early January 1943, the agency's budget was cut as the Roosevelt administration bowed to pressure from the Democrats' powerful southern wing. McNutt, head of the War Manpower Commission, indefinitely postponed upcoming FEPC hearings in Cleveland, Detroit, Philadelphia, and St. Louis, as well as highly anticipated hearings on racism in the railroad industry. In February 1941, several southeastern railroads, the Brotherhood of Locomotive Firemen and Enginemen, and officials from the National Mediation Board had signed the Southeastern Carriers' Conference ("Washington") Agreement, protecting white control of railway crafts. Now the future of the FEPC seemed uncertain as many committee members, including chairman Malcolm S. MacLean, resigned.[26]

In the absence of a functioning FEPC, black freedom workers relied on themselves even more to keep public attention on continuing violations of the president's executive order. Newly announced hiring and wage freezes intensified the sense of alarm, as many assumed that black St. Louisans stood to lose the most. On May 9, the St. Louis MOWM sponsored another mass meeting at the recently renamed Henry W. Kiel Auditorium. Calling for "Victory at Home," the congregants passed a resolution urging resumption of the canceled railroad hearings. Randolph, the meeting's featured guest, exhorted black workers to continue pressing for the breakdown of racial barriers in the trade union movement. Despite the obvious exigencies of the moment, only fifteen hundred people attended the meeting, dismal in comparison to the nearly ten thousand who had participated in the previous mass gathering in 1942. Editorials in the black press indicated a rising impatience with the MOWM organization, which had staged rallies but so far had not made good on the threat to lead a march to Roosevelt's doorstep.[27]

Initially, the St. Louis MOWM had set an agenda for African American workers. But as labor unrest spread among all defense workers in St. Louis, McNeal and his officers scrambled to respond to spontaneous upsurges on the plant floor. A chain of events, begun a day after the May 9 rally, confirmed black workers' eagerness to act independently, especially in response to the white "hate strikes" that swept the nation during the spring and summer of 1943. By mid-1943, the U.S. Cartridge Small Arms plant employed thirty-four thousand people, thirty-six hundred of them black. In the segregated Building 202, they had been able to advance to skilled positions at higher pay. This tense equilibrium was disrupted when management abruptly transferred a work gang from the lily-white Building 103, replacing them with fifty black employees. On Monday morning, May 10, thirty white female machine operators responded with a sit-down strike at the building that spread to the afternoon shift. Work resumed the next day only after the company removed the black workers. The leadership of UE Local 825, facing a National Labor Relations Board election in a few days, interpreted the transfer as a cynical ploy to thwart the union by inflaming racial tensions. In a public statement, the company agreed in the future "not to utilize Negro production workers in all units but to expand to the fullest extent the capacity" the plant's all-black production unit. Ironically, the hate strike led to the hiring of more workers for a third shift at Building 202, which Grant helped negotiate. This did little, however, to soothe the black employees' feelings of injury. In the early morning hours of May 12, black workers from all three shifts called a meeting, where they debated staging a work stoppage of their own. Proponents envisioned a strike most immediately as a protest against the refusal of whites in Building 103 to accept black workers, and the company's humiliating capitulation. At the same time, the strike would repudiate management's own opposition to upgrading competent black employees to supervisory positions.[28]

Grant, invited to the assembly as chairman of the MOWM's Complaints Committee, argued against the strike proposal, perhaps out of concern that a production halt at a moment of national emergency would shift attention away from racial injustices and strengthen antiblack demagoguery. He characterized the withdrawal from Building 103 as a "temporary retreat" made necessary by the abrupt and clumsy way in which black workers had been introduced. Yet Grant reminded the congregants of the advances they had already made in production jobs, and highlighted the assurances company representatives had made to integrate them throughout the plant. This latter point disingenuously ignored the company's recently expressed intention *not* to fully integrate African Americans. In a detailed report to U.S. Cartridge Company officials, he described how, as a result of his involvement in the meeting, "the motion to continue work, won over-whelmingly." Significantly, he also noted that despite their grievances, the assembled employees had an "entirely pro-CIO" outlook. This served notice that black workers were squarely aligned with the UE in the plant's pending union elections, and would not be pawns in company antiunion schemes.[29]

Grant undoubtedly made these disclosures to company officials without the knowledge of anyone at the black workers' secret meeting. As an act of intrigue, his letter affirmed the MOWM's willingness to cooperate with U.S. Cartridge, though at the same time it confronted the managers with the reality of a union victory, and the potential consequences of their deferred promises. "It is our sincere hope and belief that we have not been misled or deceived, and thus induced to advise a course of action disadvantageous to those seeking our counsel," Grant wrote, referring to the company's agreements. "We do not want to see the war effort impeded in any manner, but at the same time, we are duty bound to break clean and square with those whose confidence we enjoy." However, his efforts to prevent black rank-and-file militancy proved short-lived. On June 2, the afternoon shift at Building 202 struck when the company hired a white foreman to fill a vacancy. Whites had supervised the black production unit since it began in July 1942; now, emboldened by the events of May 10, black workers clamored for opportunities in supervisory jobs. In a hastily written circular distributed at the plant, Grant, McNeal, and Weston condemned the strike as "unwise, ill-timed, *hasty* and without outside support of the Negro people." Despite their entreaties, and orders from the UE, which had won the plant's May 13–14 elections, the midnight shift refused to report for work. When members of the 8:00 a.m. shift joined the work stoppage, all thirty-six hundred black ordnance workers were engaged in the wildcat strike. A committee composed of Grant, McNeal, UE Local 825 president Otto Maschoff, and other union representatives arranged an emergency conference with the management, who agreed to immediately assign black employees to foremanship training. Informed that the first class would begin on June 7, twelve hundred men and women heeded the call to return to work that afternoon, and the strike in Building 202 was effectively over. By the end of the month, management appointed thirty-two black foremen at the building.[30]

While the drama at St. Louis Ordnance/Small Arms reached its denouement, the MOWM steadied troops for a march on Southwestern Bell. In the midmorning of June 12, black men, women, and children assembled at Memorial Plaza, then trekked to the company headquarters nearby on Pine Street. Estimated at one hundred people by the white dailies, and three hundred by the black press, the demonstrators encircled the building in a picket line and distributed "fact sheets" to passersby and spectators. "NEGRO OPERATORS WORKING IN OTHER CITIES, WHY NOT IN ST. LOUIS?" one placard asked, calling attention to employment precedents set in border cities like Baltimore and Washington, D.C. Praising the peaceful parade, Henry Winfield Wheeler—a black postal clerk and founder of the National Association of Postal Employees, and a well-known *American* columnist—echoed the race- and working class-conscious sentiments that had become conventional wisdom: "No Negro teacher or preacher or doctor or business man has economic security so long as the efficient and educated and even the humblest menial laborer is denied the right to work where he is needed and to use his initiative to the best advantage of his country."[31]

At the same time, the Bell demonstration was an important departure for the MOWM, and particularly the BSCP. To obtain its contract with the

Pullman Company in the 1930s, the union had bargained away the rights of its train maids and relegated them to membership in the porters' Ladies Auxiliary. While most of the day-to-day tasks of leafleting and answering phones for the MOWM were "women's work," the porters' long-standing focus on winning "manhood" had straitjacketed women into domestic identities as wives and mothers, displacing their lived realities as wage-workers. Winning defense industry employment for black women was certainly part of the MOWM's overall campaign, but few of its leaders expected that women would still be welding and operating machines after the war. In seeking nonmanufacturing jobs for "Negro girls," however, MOWM leaders signaled support for black women's postwar employment outside domestic labor, even as they accepted a gendered division of work. Around the same time as the telephone company protest, the *American* reported with fanfare that Washington Technical High School had placed four women typists at the Missouri Printing Company and Aetna Finance, white-collar working-class jobs many would have considered suitable for young, unmarried women.[32]

In mid-1943, when St. Louis delegates arrived in Chicago for a national MOWM conference organized around the claim "We Are Americans, Too," they were preceded by a reputation as one of the nation's most combative units. Attended by 110 representatives, the gathering further consolidated the MOWM as a national organization. Affirming policies already in place, the assembly formally restricted membership to African Americans, and a Resolutions Committee recommended uniform opposition to any cooperation with the Communist Party and its "front" organizations. Both measures effectively severed the organization from radical forces that had been vital to black insurgency just a decade earlier. At the last minute, the convention also voted for a national march on D.C. "If present conditions continue," McNeal argued, "we will have to march on Washington whether we like it or not."[33]

The possibility of this occurring, however, appeared ever remote. Responding to rank-and-file demands for greater involvement in decision-making, Randolph had convened a national MOWM conference a year earlier in Detroit. Then, the matter of whether to march had been tabled for a future convention. Now, as the embers of the recent Detroit race riot still smoldered, Grant—backed by militant Detroit delegates—argued for setting a specific date for the march. As he had often done within the BSCP, Randolph maneuvered to satisfy the MOWM's militant flank without relinquishing his control. The MOWM chief supported a general endorsement, with Grant named national chairman of the march. Yet authority to call the gathering rested solely with the New York City national headquarters. Many critics, thus, had ample reason to believe that the national

MOWM would continue to threaten white authority with mass black working-class insurgency, while actively working to forestall actual grassroots disruptions. On the other hand, hopeful signs may have convinced Randolph that a national march was unnecessary. Pressed by the National Alliance of Postal Employees, the U.S. Postmaster General had issued a bulletin in early June banning racial discrimination against all Post Office personnel. Wheeler and other members of the *American* staff began lobbying for the placement of black postal workers on window assignments, and in supervisory jobs on the Post Office's main floor downtown. On May 27, a few days before the bulletin, Roosevelt had issued Executive Order 9346 establishing a new FEPC, which was placed under the jurisdiction of the Office of Production Management.[34]

Further, the railroad hearings, long delayed, had been rescheduled. In December 1943, after hearing testimonies, the FEPC would issue a directive instructing twenty railroads and seven unions to "cease and desist" their discriminatory practices, and ordering the nullification of the "Washington Agreement." Moreover, racial rioting around the nation had prompted several city and state governments to establish race relations committees to ease tensions. In the Gateway City, early impetus came from the Industrial Union Council, whose Communist-centered leadership in the UE presented Mayor William D. Becker with an eight-point program that included an interracial citizens' committee. Fearful of a "Detroit" exploding in St. Louis, the black press and liberal-left whites readily supported the platform. The mayor, concerned about black working-class militancy affecting war production, gave his assent. Following Becker's death in a glider accident, his successor, Aloys P. Kaufmann, continued plans to assemble the race relations committee. By September, he had named sixty-five people to the body, including twenty-five African Americans. McNeal, Grant, Sweets, and *Argus* publisher Joseph Mitchell were among them, as were John T. Clark of the Urban League, NAACP president Sidney Redmond, and representatives from the Pine Street YMCA, the Wheatley YWCA, St. Paul's AME Church, and Sumner High School. Newspapermen like *Post-Dispatch* publisher Joseph Pulitzer, Jr. and prominent unionists like Sentner were also appointed to the commission, alongside officials from firms like U.S. Cartridge, Scullin Steel, and the public utilities. Significantly, Mayor Kaufmann named as the commission's temporary chairman Edwin B. Meissner, president of the St. Louis Car Company, one of the many companies criticized by the MOWM.[35]

Like its counterparts in Detroit and Chicago, the committee took shape within an emerging sociological model embodied by Gunnar Myrdal's *An American Dilemma.* This perspective refuted scientific arguments for black inferiority, and regarded racial progress as the result of education and changing cultural norms, principally among a white citizenry exercising its innate capacity for reform. From this standpoint, the United States would gradually fulfill the promises of the "American Creed" through greater interaction among "responsible," and implicitly middle-class, white and black leadership. At a practical level, this liberal interracialism sought to dampen black insurgent impulses, reinforcing previous local patterns of dependency on white paternalism and black accommodation. Lacking any legal powers, such committees gave the appearance of activity while doing little to change the city's social landscape. Maintaining "racial peace" took precedence over immediate demands for racial justice. As McNeal protested futilely to the Mayor's Office, Meissner chaired the commission despite the fact his company was "one of the worst offenders" against Executive Orders 8802 and 9346, as were other business representatives on the committee.[36]

St. Louis race leaders, thus, looked to other primary means to shepherd change. In August 1943, the MOWM had redoubled efforts against Southwestern Bell. Members distributed stickers to be placed on supporters' telephone bill stubs. "Discrimination in Employment is Undemocratic—I Protest It!" the small notices read. "Hire Negroes Now!" On the morning of September 18, demonstrators staged a mass payment of telephone bills at the building, slowing collection lines by paying with pennies. Answering the St. Louis unit's demands, the War Manpower Commission arranged a November conference between telephone company officials and MOWM leaders. But McNeal, borrowing a tactic from protesters at the Chesapeake and Potomac Telephone Company in Baltimore, vowed to maintain daily picket lines at the company pending the outcome of negotiations. Resistance at Southwestern Bell eventually folded, and in early December the St. Louis unit announced plans for a branch office on Vandeventer Avenue to be staffed entirely by black employees. The branch opened in July 1944 with a staff of thirty female "Negro white collar workers." The agreement, however, was silent about employing black telephone operators. Although willing to consider the settlement a "step forward" within the context of racial segregation, MOWM leaders envisioned, at some future date, "the complete integration of Negro workers into all phases of this public utility's employment."[37]

"What Will Negro Workers Do After the War?"

Yet, a spiral of layoffs, caused by cutbacks in production schedules, undercut such progress. In July 1943, U.S. Cartridge eliminated the third shift at Building 202, and in November announced that one thousand other black workers would lose work. Curtiss-Wright, the city's other major defense operation, also planned to cut half its 598 African American employees. The layoffs were certainly not restricted to black workers; given their late entry into many plants, they were just hit hardest. Sentner, attempting to mobilize UE leadership against the layoffs at Building 202, viewed the cutbacks as retaliation against black worker agitation, and part of an overall strategy to subvert the union. In an atmosphere of scarce defense work, dramatic resistance to fair employment flared again. In March 1944, several hundred white workers at the General Cable Corporation staged a walkout to protest the hiring of black employees. That May, white workers at the St. Louis Car Company went on strike when the local United Auto Workers local proposed a nondiscriminatory contract clause.[38]

Among African American defense workers, females continued to suffer the least protection. By May 1944, the MOWM was sounding desperate alarms about an estimated seventeen thousand jobless black women. By June, according to Grant, the estimate had risen to twenty-five thousand. With the elimination of many New Deal programs, no immediate relief was in sight. "What Will Negro Workers Do After the War?" a headline in the *Chicago Defender* asked at the time, and many searched for answers. In a written complaint against St. Louis's International Shoe Company, Christine Berry Morgan turned to the MOWM for advice on how she and other black coworkers might confront job and wage disparities. "The girls are desirous of starting a union and plan to strike," she wrote. "Do you agree we should have a union? Would a strike be the best possible . . . for results?"[39]

Locally, the MOWM had finally succeeded in arranging FEPC hearings in St. Louis. Seven firms faced charges of refusing to hire black women and upgrade black men: Amertorp, Bussman Manufacturing Company, Wagner Electric, Carter Carburetor, St. Louis Shipbuilding and Steel Company, McDonnell Aircraft, and McQuay-Norris. An eighth, U.S. Cartridge, faced allegations of laying off black workers before whites with less seniority, and hiring them back last. "They promise automatic raises & a chance for advancement when they hire you, but these never come," a male employee at the company explained in one affidavit. "You do anything from shoveling coal to moving supplies, and don't even have a decent place to wash your face & hands. No locker, or anywhere to keep your clothes." Another statement urged the MOWM to add the General Cable Corporation to the FEPC docket. "There is no jobs open for negro's there but janitors maids kitchen help," the employee described. "Small Arms and 'Tnt' [Atlas Powder] or any other defense plants cannot be any worst then General Cable."[40]

In early August, when the FEPC convened in a crowded federal courtroom in downtown St. Louis, nearly one hundred individuals exposed many of the conditions the MOWM had been stockpiling for two years. While most denied guilt, company representatives attributed their practices to "community patterns" that made segregation necessary for productivity. Sentner, on behalf of the UE, attacked this assertion and its underlying suppositions. "The policy seems to be based solely on the premise that the main course of resistance to the employment and integration of Negroes in industry comes from white workers," he said. "Of course, this is not true. . . . The main objection to the integration and full utilization of Negro labor springs from industry. This was prior to the war and it still exists." Without question, many defense employers had concealed their own hiring preferences behind arguments that white workers would not accept black personnel on the plant floor, especially in production jobs. Sentner may have underestimated the level of white rank-and-file worker resistance, but white workers' enmity toward fair employment was not as dyed-in-the-wool as it appeared. In its review, the FEPC similarly concluded that local manufacturers bore the weight of blame for racial discrimination in their plants. The agency called for the eight firms to take several steps toward "affirmative action," including hiring the black men and women who had filed complaints, educating white workers about Executive Order 9346, and publicly announcing a nondiscriminatory employment and promotions policy.[41]

The FEPC would later establish a subregional office in St. Louis, where it fielded one of the heaviest caseloads in the country—attributable to St. Louis's location as an unstable "borderline" between the North and the South. But beyond the new office's symbolic importance, the St. Louis hearings had little impact. In the period preceding and immediately following the two-day inquiry, ironically, black wildcat rebellions reignited. In March 1944, over three hundred African Americans at the Monsanto Chemical Company had struck against the plant's segregationist practices. Ignoring the wishes of the AFL Tobacco Workers' union, four hundred workers demanding a wage increase staged a walkout at the Liggett & Myers Tobacco Company warehouse. At the National Lead Company's titanium plant, black workers complained of being barred from four departments, and denied upgrades in the three segregated departments they occupied. On Thursday, July 27, between 160 and 180 of them went on strike, ignoring orders from the United Gas, Coke and Chemical Workers Union–CIO. Ten white workers observed the picket, but most of the plant's five hundred whites crossed the line. The strikers returned to work that Monday at the request of federal mediators.[42]

The CIO's lack of support for such strikes highlighted black workers' uneven relationship with industrial unionism. In the 1930s, Negro Workers' Council members, NNC organizers, and the Urban League's Industrial Department had all helped build the CIO. Because of their efforts, the Steel Workers Organizing Committee had led "the most extensive effort to organize black industrial workers that had ever occurred in St. Louis" between 1936 and 1939. Relative to the AFL, the CIO—especially its Left-led unions—had supported the FEPC's aims. Of all the industrial unions, UE Local 825 remained most emblematic of an antiracist labor agenda. The organization had employed African Americans and women in its unionization drive, and sponsored interracial social activities with an eye toward transforming white workers' racial attitudes. Despite the objections of some white workers, the local had also rid the St. Louis Ordnance / Small Arms plant of segregated bathrooms. In November 1943, further, the UE had assembled an Interracial Victory Council, leading a delegation to Jefferson City to testify in support of civil rights for black Missourians.[43]

Still, the liberal-left coalition that had propelled the unionization drives among steel and electrical workers was dissolving amid bureaucratization. Nationally, the CIO had agreed to a no-strike pledge for the duration of the war, and many radical organizers were summarily dismissed as their unions entered partnerships with management. The union movement's "no discrimination" policy apparently did not apply to endorsing black grievances against the racism of employers. Even in the UE, where left-wing, antiracist influences were evident, the Communist Party's own win-the-war agenda increasingly required African Americans to postpone demands for serious reform. Even Sentner, who steadfastly supported black rights, ran afoul of the MOWM and Urban League when he blamed them for the black wildcat strikes in nearby Granite City, Illinois. Hence, the growing conservative tendencies of the CIO converged with the conformist drift of the Communists' "Popular Front" strategy.[44]

"Democracy Can Work in St. Louis"

Elsewhere, efforts against Jim Crow yielded more dramatic results. By the fall of 1943, the city's main Post Office had desegregated its cafeteria. In January 1944, the city's first black alderman, Jasper C. Caston, of the Sixth Ward, put forth a bill outlawing Jim Crow eating facilities at City Hall and the Municipal Courts Building. The proposal came at a time when delegates were meeting in Jefferson City to revise the state constitution. Early the previous year, Edwin F. Kenswil of St. Louis—the only black member of the 163-member Missouri House of Representatives—had introduced legislation to end racial discrimination in all public places. The measure, sponsored by the St. Louis NAACP, had been roundly defeated, though advocates found new hope when two St. Louis delegates submitted a resolution to the Bill of Rights committee guaranteeing civil rights for black Missourians. A subcommittee undercut the recommendation by substituting a watered-down version that left the issue of public accommodations open-ended. By the same token, the Missouri Constitutional Convention eventually adopted a proposal by the St. Louis delegates to end inequalities in black teachers' pay, reinforcing a recent court decision won by Grant and NAACP attorney Thurgood Marshall.[45]

The matter of educational opportunity, however, was uncertain terrain. After high school, no further instruction existed for black St. Louisans, except at Stowe Teachers College (formerly the Sumner Normal School). Missouri's historically black Lincoln University, in Jefferson City, was the only other option. State law barred them from the University of Missouri, and since 1921, officials had paid full tuition for black high-school graduates to attend professional schools in other states—a policy adopted most prominently in West Virginia, Maryland, and Tennessee. The maneuver avoided equalizing in-state graduate institutions while maintaining the facade of a "separate but equal" public higher education system. St. Louis's private institutions, like Washington and St. Louis universities, observed segregation, as well. Reflecting the liberal judicial activism of Roosevelt-era appointments, the Supreme Court had ruled in *Gaines* that the University of Missouri either had to admit black students to graduate training programs at its flagship university, or create separate black programs of equal quality. State officials had circumvented the decision by creating segregated law and journalism schools at Lincoln University, but the case had nonetheless legitimized a full-scale judicial assault on legal racial apartheid in education.[46]

St. Louis's Race Relations Commission therefore recommended that the Missouri Constitutional Convention remove legal requirements for separate black schools. The commission also proposed that St. Louis University, a Catholic institution, admit black students. Some 60 percent of the city's residents were Catholic, and commission members wagered the university could influence change through prestige and example. Father Claude Heithaus, an outspoken assistant professor, and Father William Markoe, the priest at the largely black St. Elizabeth's Parish, had joined black Catholics in prodding university president Father Patrick Holloran to desegregate the institution. In the spring, the Jesuit school quietly enrolled two black undergraduates and three graduate students, making it the first school in Missouri, and the first university in a former slave state, to desegregate. In the meantime, Caston's bill to end segregated municipal lunchrooms came before the Board of Aldermen. A large crowd of black ministers, civic leaders, and students from Sumner High School were present when the board passed the measure. The vote came only days after the Supreme Court handed down the watershed *Smith v. Allwright* decision outlawing Texas's all-white Democratic primary election.[47]

In many respects, unorganized black responses to Jim Crow outpaced legislative and judicial reform. The situation on St. Louis streetcars and buses was especially combustible. Black areas of the city were already the poorest served by public transport, and with gas rationing, these routes further contracted. Yet bus and streetcar routes expanded in predominantly white areas, a development duly noted in the black press. Already slighted by the absence of black motormen, African American workers bristled at the behavior by white conductors, who cursed, expelled, and physically assaulted patrons. Violence between black and white passengers also became commonplace, sparked by minor inconveniences that brought deep-seated resentments roiling to the surface. One black woman was shot to death on a crowded streetcar, and over the span of three days in August 1944 a series of altercations erupted. During one streetcar incident, a black woman, enraged that all the seats had been taken before she boarded, "upbraided the occupants about the treatment accorded Negroes." A brawl ensued, and she cut a soldier with a knife. Following another fight on this same route, police arrested two whites and four black women. In a separate melee on a Hodiamont streetcar, a black man beat a white passenger to death after complaints about his smoking. With fears of a race riot mounting, the Race Relations Commission battled rumors about a sudden black demand for ice picks, and a plot to harass white pedestrians on a designated "Push Day."[48]

If streetcar battles were evidence of internecine warfare between black and white workers, the opening of the Post Office cafeteria, municipal buildings, and St. Louis University convinced members of a growing liberal community that no natural "community preference" existed for Jim Crow. A number of black and white St. Louisans argued that desegregating the downtown soda fountains, restaurants, and movie theaters would provide another step toward "racial good will and unity." By this time, an NAACP committee chaired by Pearl Maddox had sent correspondence to the Famous, Stix, and Scruggs department stores about employment discrimination and segregated lunch counters, but had received no reply. A subsequent coalition of black civic organizations had initiated a mass letter-writing campaign, again without response.[49]

Continuing silence in May 1944 led to the creation of the Citizens Civil Rights Committee (CCRC), formed under the general leadership of Maddox, Thelma Grant, and Ruth Mattie Wheeler, daughter of the outspoken and respected news columnist and postal worker. Largely female, the CCRC brought together a cross-class grouping of more than twenty women from the NAACP, MOWM, the ladies' auxiliaries of the black postal employees union and BSCP, and a variety of backgrounds. The

CCRC's gender character was more than coincidental. Denied membership in organizations like the BSCP and formal leadership roles in political vehicles such as the MOWM, largely absent from war production, and unprotected by the FEPC, black women resolved to create a wartime venue of struggle. It was one specific to their roles as neither "soldier," "worker," nor "race spokesman," but rather as the wives and mothers who had given their men and boys to the war effort on its multiple fronts, and as the consumers on whom retailers and other downtown businesses depended for their receipts. Though the new organization was overwhelmingly black and working class, several white middle-class women from Eden Seminary, St. Louis University, and the Fellowship of Reconciliation, an interracial, religious pacifist organization, also joined. Nonviolence was the committee's guiding principle, borrowed from Chicago's Committee of Racial Equality, a FOR-related project that had staged peaceful sit-in protests two years earlier. CCRC members were eager to incorporate this method into their own program against the local department stores, though they worried their protests would violate trespassing laws. They solicited legal advice first from NAACP president Redmond, who attempted to dissuade them. They then approached Grant, who was more attuned to popular protest: In May 1942 he had been fired as St. Louis's assistant circuit attorney for traveling to Sikeston to protest the Cleo Wright lynching. The bold MOWM leader enthusiastically urged the women to proceed, and promised that Chambers would arrange their prompt bail if they were taken into custody, and that Grant would represent them in any ensuing courtroom struggle.[50]

On the evening of May 15, five demonstrators staged an interracial sit-in at the Stix lunch counter, where they sat until closing. Throughout May and June, an emboldened CCRC executed weekly sit-ins at all three department stores, as well as the downtown-area Katz Drug Store. Flustered attendants refused to serve the seated African Americans, but white activists undermined the snub by purchasing their food. As involvement snowballed, demonstrators added small signs and handbills composed, printed, and paid for by the St. Louis MOWM. Few white patrons, the demonstrators learned, reacted with hostility, which demonstrated the conditional, "civil" quality of white racism in St. Louis. On July 8, forty black women and fifteen whites launched a massive wave of sit-ins that forced the closure of several lunch counters and soda fountains. In one vein, the protests approximated the conventions of liberal, interracial middle-class "civility" and decorum, and resonated with African American professionals' aspirations for equitable treatment as consumers in public space. Yet the demand for equal access to public accommodations was also meaningful to black workers, who often relied on public amenities more than their middle-class cousins. Similarly, the demonstrations' sublimely disruptive features were consistent with a querulous working-class ethos that favored "self-respect" by any means over polite, "respectable" appeals to racial paternalism absent any force. Reflecting its cross-class base, the CCRC bridged both approaches, while effectively revising the latter.[51]

Moving quickly to quell the protests, other members of Mayor Kaufmann's Race Relations Commission convinced the organization to halt demonstrations long enough to negotiate a settlement. After several meetings, department store representatives in August offered a clandestine deal that would permit African Americans to eat only in their basement cafeterias. "It is a disgrace to the principles for which the boys both black and white are being maimed and crippled and blinded and lying in foxholes dying for democracy," Wheeler scoffed in his news column. "And they want it kept secret, yes, all of the damn liars and hypocrites in the world want secrecy. Well, this column is shouting from the housetop, 'Cafeteria service like all other human beings or nothing.'" Maddox was similarly adamant that the CCRC would accept no partial concessions, and in September the organization refused the offer. While Scruggs opened its basement lunch counter to African Americans anyway, committee members refused to applaud the "separate but equal" arrangement that denied them their self-respect.[52]

As she lamented this setback, CCRC member Thelma Grant was nonetheless encouraged by several events. Following the desegregation of St. Louis University, a Union Station restaurant and the grandstand at Sportsman's Park had both desegregated. Such rapid, though piecemeal changes, Grant wrote in the *American,* gave her hope that "*Democracy Can Work in St. Louis.*" But as the war began to wind down, her affirmative statement became more of a question. Locally, the MOWM had gained an estimated fifteen thousand industrial jobs for black men and women in the defense industries. With forty-five hundred African Americans in 1944, the U.S. Cartridge Ordnance Plant was the largest employer of black production workers, who earned an average of seventy-five dollars a week. For a moment during the spring of 1945, Emerson Electric, Century Electric, and a few other firms opened their doors to black male and female employees. Even the General Cable Company, where over a thousand white women had staged a hate strike in January against a plan to train black women workers, had successfully integrated its production lines by April. But from late May 1944 until the war's end, St. Louis's labor markets remained slack, undercutting defense work for African Americans. With military demobilization, the window of opportunity created in war production closed as U.S. Cartridge's ordnance plant closed its doors, and other firms heaved toward reconversion.[53]

Antagonists in Congress killed the FEPC in 1946, and conservative foes of the New Deal blocked legislation to create a permanent fair employment agency. The CCRC, too, fell into inactivity, but its fleeting sit-in crusade signified an emergent new model of political agency built around the creative methods of nonviolent direct action. Besides Chicago, St. Louis was the only city where black and white activists had experimented with the tactic of lunch counter sit-ins. The St. Louis MOWM, which had extended critical resources and personnel to these activities, disbanded in early 1945. At the time of its dissolution, MOWM membership in St. Louis numbered four thousand people. By then, most MOWM branches had long since fizzled, though the end of the war was only partly to blame. It mainly floundered, argued *Pittsburgh Courier* columnist Horace R. Cayton, because neither a D.C. march nor a larger campaign of passive resistance ever materialized. While articulating a protest strategy of militant reformism, national MOWM leaders shunned the tactics of civil disruption necessary to realize their goals. Aside from the St. Louis unit, moreover, most branches never energized supporters around local action.[54]

Notwithstanding such criticisms, the MOWM had thrust black civil rights to the forefront of the national agenda, creating a framework for black struggle and federal activity long after the war. The NAACP was a beneficiary of both the MOWM's success and decline, in its immediate aftermath growing prodigiously from 50,000 to 450,000 members nationally. In St. Louis, the numbers increased from 5,500 to 8,000, with the bulk of these new recruits hailing from the working class. The war years remade St. Louis's black workers in other ways. Although many African Americans lost industrial jobs as white veterans returned, they did not return to the exact same prewar patterns of work. Coupled with organizing efforts in several CIO unions, black workers achieved a greater presence in organized labor, with the UE and the United Steelworkers among those notable for large black memberships. The ranks of black skilled workers more than doubled, and the gains in semiskilled jobs were even greater. Thus, the 1940s marked the beginnings of a more occupationally diverse, and stratified, black community born through wrenching struggle. In St. Louis, the wartime job advancements proved too brief and shallow to affect the overall structure of African American work opportunities, or black St. Louis's class structure. Nonetheless, political activism solidified a broad black racial and working-class consciousness. Battles for African American citizenship, self-determination, and "respect" would continue, unfolding within the coerced consensus of a society committed to vanquishing a postwar "communist menace."[55]

CHAPTER THREE

Black Working-Class Demobilization and Liberal Interracialism, 1946–54

By 1946, following british prime minister Winston Churchill's "Iron Curtain" speech in Fulton, Missouri, the United States and Soviet Union had emerged as rival world powers. Under the administration of Missourian Harry S. Truman, this simmering Cold War generated an American security state to contain the spread of Communism. Mass U.S. labor unrest in 1945–46, conflict in Europe and the Mediterranean, revolution in China, and war in Korea also spawned a domestic crusade against suspected Communist subversives. The antilabor and anticommunist Taft-Hartley Act, passed in 1947, inspired similar legislation at the state level, including Missouri's King-Thompson Act, enacted that same year. Organized labor largely began to shun broader demands for social welfare beyond its membership. In exchange for contracts offering high wages and benefits, union leaders restrained their rank and files, accepted owners' control of the workplace, and conceded their power to strike. The CIO, never stable in its defense of black equality in the first place, almost totally retreated from racial justice.[1]

In this climate, the black militant reformism present during the war was no longer possible, at least not without greater risk. Democratic segregationists and Republican conservatives now had "Communism" as a shibboleth to attack the gains of the New Deal and arrest other initiatives for social reform. The very recognition of class, to say nothing of class relations and inequalities, became tantamount to treason, and Cold War southerners handily equated black civil rights and economic justice with Communism. Not only actual Communist members, but also any activists with expansive visions of social change were isolated and harassed.[2]

The prevailing Cold War environment threw into disarray the black working-class political bloc that had emerged during the Depression and consolidated during the war. But while anticommunist politics disrupted the pace of racial reform in St. Louis during the late 1940s and early 1950s, it did not entirely halt it. With the MOWM gone, the Urban League eschewing its earlier flirtation with labor radicalism, and the NNC in decline, the NAACP emerged briefly as an organized center of black working-class activity. As the national leadership accommodated itself to the emerging anticommunist consensus, however, the association tacked away from both mass mobilization and agendas that spoke immediately to grassroots constituents. Newer groups stepped forward to fill the void, including the National Negro Labor Council (NNLC) and the Committee of Racial Equality (CORE). Although greatly concerned with the matter of black employment, the NAACP and CORE both focused on ending Jim Crow in public accommodations and education. These were by no means trifling grievances, nor were they easier battles to wage. But they were relatively "safer" issues that fit comfortably within a developing postwar liberal, middle-class interracial framework, one preoccupied with changing white attitudes rather than challenging economic inequalities. The NNLC's efforts, in contrast, were more directly tied to black working-class interests in the work sphere and in organized labor. The NAACP and CORE were not unresponsive to the black working-class majority's striving for full citizenship and self-determination, but the NNLC was the most consistent in an activist agenda derived from a conscious black working-class standpoint.

Because of the strictures imposed on working-class black militancy, most protest campaigns during the early Cold War occurred amid a steep decline in mass participation. Consequently, St. Louis CORE's efforts became the most influential. Lacking a mass base, CORE had a biracial, largely professional membership typical of the liberal race relations committees created during the war. Unlike most committees of this stripe, however, CORE did more than offer recommendations to elected officials and issue moral appeals. Instead, similar to the wartime activities of the CCRC, CORE combined these methods with strategies of nonviolent protest, and in the process expanded the discourse of liberal interracialism. The tasks undertaken by the NAACP, NNLC, and CORE in the late 1940s and early 1950s lacked sizable black constituencies, but they provided a bridge to a revival of mass insurgency rooted in an interwoven black racial and working-class consciousness.

Metropolitan St. Louis after the War

In postwar St. Louis, downtown was the hub of city life, teeming with dime stores, drugstores, specialty shops, hotels, restaurants, and first-run movie houses and theaters. To stabilize the real estate value of the downtown area, city officials in 1935 had promoted the construction of the Jefferson

National Expansion Memorial as a monument to Thomas Jefferson's Louisiana Purchase, the Lewis and Clark expedition, and St. Louis's role as the gateway to the western U.S. empire. For its centerpiece, a panel of architects selected design plans for a stainless steel arch rising from the banks of the Mississippi. Mayor Dickmann had obtained federal funds for the project, and St. Louis voters had approved a $47.5 million bond issue to cover the city's share of the venture. Federal authorities had taken possession of the decaying central waterfront area and razed its structures, sparing only the Old Cathedral and the Old Courthouse.[3]

World War II had also transformed St. Louis's economy. The area was becoming fertile ground for emerging industries in electronics, chemicals, aerospace defense, and research and development, particularly as the nation veered toward greater military spending. Emerson Electric, Mallinckrodt, Monsanto Chemical, and McDonnell Aircraft all became regional juggernauts. Circa 1950, St. Louis was the nation's eighth largest city, its population peaking at 856,769—a 5 percent increase from 1940. Yet substantial migration continued to St. Louis County, where the population had leapt from 274,230 to 406,349 between 1940 and 1950.[4]

Wealthy white communities remained in St. Louis City, principally in the exclusive West End near Forest Park. Many poor white workers who had migrated during the war for defense work lived along the north riverfront, and overall the city was still a cluster of working-class enclaves. Mill Creek Valley, a center of black working-class settlement, continued to occupy the shadows of the Central Corridor skyscrapers and warehouses. It had, however, become a target of city officials and realtors, who regarded the ghetto community as ripe for federally assisted demolition and redevelopment. Although more stable than Mill Creek Valley, the Ville had also become an increasingly crowded black district. Circumscribed by the city's long history of restrictive housing covenants, community residents had also been thwarted in attempts to expand the array of social opportunities available within its segregated boundaries. In 1944, when they had sought to convert the Cote Brilliante Junior High School into a black schoolhouse, Ville residents had encountered resistance from a group of more than seven hundred white homeowners. Located in a densely populated black area, the school had only been partially used by its five hundred white students, while more than a thousand black children in the school district had suffered overcrowding.[5]

A similar school dispute had had a more far-reaching impact on the neighboring black community of Kinloch Park, in northwest St. Louis County. After several failed efforts to form a school district away from the growing black majority, white residents had filed a petition to incorporate as a separate municipality, and with county approval established the city of

Berkeley. Most of the community's tax base, and many tracts of farmland, went with them, leaving their former black neighbors with little more than the original settlement's name. The unincorporated remains of the split had formed a black wedge between Berkeley on the east and Ferguson, a predominantly white community, to the west. Incorporated in late August 1948, Kinloch became the state's first all-black city, and Willie Head, a construction foreman, was sworn in as its first mayor. Bereft of most municipal services, the black working-class suburb of twenty-four hundred depended on an antagonistic St. Louis County government for fire protection and law enforcement, creating a quasi-colonial relationship that mocked the aspirations that earlier had drawn African Americans.[6]

New Dynamics in Black Class Formation

Nonetheless, black workers from Mississippi, southeast Missouri, Tennessee, Alabama, and eastern Arkansas continued to arrive in St. Louis area. Between 1940 and 1950, 38,000 migrants came, expanding the number of African Americans to 153,766, or 18 percent, of the city's populace. In the short period between 1950 and 1954, the figure rose to approximately 177,000. Most resided in the Fourth, Fifth, Sixth, Sixteenth, Eighteenth, Nineteenth, and Twentieth wards, all of them in or near the Central Corridor and its riverfront. The boom contributed to additional black representation on the Board of Aldermen. Walter Lowe beat Democrat David Grant to become Nineteenth Ward alderman in 1945. Sidney Redmond, a former NAACP president, was elected in the Eighteenth Ward in 1947. Sixth Ward alderman Jasper Caston, who had become the board's first black member during the war, also retained his seat until 1950.[7]

Despite the fact that Lowe, Redmond, and Caston were Republicans, political weight had shifted decisively to the Democrats. As alderman, Lowe may have been the nominal leader of the Nineteenth Ward, but Democratic committeeman Jordan Chambers remained its boss. His new nightclub, Club Riviera, functioned after hours as an unofficial ward committee headquarters where, flanked by his deputies, he convened late-night meetings. Chambers had, moreover, consolidated substantial power far beyond the ward's gerrymandered borders by using patronage to cultivate legions of campaign workers and supporters at the precinct level.[8]

But the population density that gave black politicians their strength in the Central Corridor had a steep price. In the area around Jefferson, Cass, Carr, and Twentieth Street, black families were three times as crowded per block as were whites. More than 75 percent of them occupied dilapidated dwellings without indoor plumbing. Two federally sponsored public housing projects, begun in the late 1930s—Carr Square Village, located on the near north side, and Clinton-Peabody Terrace, just southwest of downtown—both had opened in 1942. A third housing development, Cochran Gardens, opened in 1953. While public housing offered many black working-class families an escape from ramshackle flats, black families remained in dire need of low-rent housing. The Clinton-Peabody projects, as a prime example, were restricted to white tenants, which the St. Louis Housing Authority justified through claims of a natural aversion between the races. Public policies reconstituted segregated housing patterns in other ways. The Federal Housing and Veterans administrations, which subsidized homeownership at low interest rates, favored detached, single-family dwellings in newer, "racially homogeneous" white communities west of the central city. Private lenders, realtors, and the federal Home Owners' Loan Corporation also institutionalized neighborhood ratings systems that excluded black loan applicants, and facilitated the decay of older communities. These programs, at the same time, fostered the close identification between "whiteness" and homeownership. Thus, the fact that a development like Carr Square Village was located in the business district's declining northern fringe only compounded black residents' lack of opportunities for independent homeownership and decent surroundings.[9]

Housing deficiencies were also the result of continuing racial disparities in income and wealth. Black employment since the war had contracted after the MOWM's dissolution. With civil rights agitation assailed as a Trojan Horse for "communist subversion," national efforts to make the FEPC permanent were rebuffed by congressmen from both political parties. In Missouri, legislative attempts to create state and local FEPC agencies reached a similar standstill, limiting the fight against Jim Crow hiring practices. Still, black workers held their gains in certain sectors, and even enjoyed some modest improvement as St. Louis emerged from a postwar recession in April 1950. Inflationary pressures created by the Korean War accelerated employment for both whites and African Americans. Although they still vastly outnumbered whites as janitors and porters (6,779 to 3,895), the number of black men in managerial and clerical occupations grew after 1950. An expanding federal state figured heavily in this growth. During the war, the Post Office had responded to demands for ending discriminatory practices, while President Truman, pressed by black workers and the exigencies of the Cold War, signed an executive order prohibiting racial discrimination in federal employment. By 1949, over one thousand mostly black St. Louis men worked in the postal service and federal public administration. But while 63 percent of white St. Louis males had professional, managerial, clerical, sales, and craft occupations, only 19 percent of black men were similarly situated. Black women's opportunities for paid labor were not appreciably different. By virtue of their greater levels of high school and college education, they continued to advance in white-collar work, though these advances were offset by their growing presence in service and labor positions. Of the 27,000 black women performing paid labor around 1950, the largest cluster (13,197) fell into the category of "personal service," especially private household labor and hotel work.[10]

Even when classified as professionals, black men and women were likely to be present in health, welfare, and education—helping professions they had occupied for decades in segregated St. Louis—rather than fields like accounting, engineering, and architecture. Indeed, most black managers and clerical workers generally were, according to a St. Louis Urban League report, "confined to small Negro owned service establishments located in the Negro community." Many black clerical workers had little autonomy on the job, and exercised no oversight over other employees, which often made their position more working class than professional. Clerical jobs were beginning to open to black women at this historical moment, in fact, precisely because these occupations were becoming "proletarianized, routinized, deskilled, and devalued." Clearly, U.S. census-derived job classifications and industrial categories could obscure the actual tasks black workers performed. Substantial numbers of black St. Louisans were also underemployed. In one 1953 expose, the *Argus* profiled a young woman, trained as an IBM operator, file clerk, and typist, who was engaged in a fruitless search for work at her skill level. More than likely, she settled for a job below her qualifications, or left town to seek better opportunities. Black craftsmen suffered underemployment most acutely: Seven out of ten of them were employed in common labor and other classifications well below their skills.[11]

On the one hand, then, black St. Louis remained on the occupational and economic fringes. Aside from government administration, most black employment gains were occurring in manufacturing. Aside from the 1920s and 1940s, however, commerce, finance, and utilities—not heavy industry—had dominated the local economy. Outside janitorial positions, African Americans were negligibly employed in banks, retail stores, and major grocery chains. Soft drink, dairy, bread, and brewing companies hired them neither as plant workers nor as driver-salesmen. Southwestern Bell, Laclede Gas, and the city's public transit company followed similar hiring policies. The result was a high rate of black joblessness, particularly among men. Thus, while they comprised 17 percent of the total civilian labor force around 1950, black St. Louisans were 37.6 percent of the unemployed. Circa 1950, black median income in the St. Louis metropolitan area was $1,417, in contrast to $2,333 for whites. Average black income did grow over the next few years, but as the St. Louis Urban League reported in 1954,

"The much greater labor force participation of non-white married females, attributed to necessity arising out of much lower earnings by the male breadwinner" attested to a continuing pattern of lagging black income.[12]

On the other hand, the black freedom struggles spawned by depression and war had stimulated the development of a slightly more diverse black class structure. Once employed almost singularly as laborers, black St. Louisans were now present across a number of job categories, however minimally. Pullman porters were still envied for their well-paying jobs, and were among the few African Americans belonging to autonomous black trade unions. Yet the CIO organizing campaigns of the 1930s and 1940s had given other black workers new opportunities in industrial work. Black attendants who served white elites still had social standing in the African American home sphere, only now they vied for communal prestige with the expanding ranks of federal employees. Likewise, the select number of black women who had operated elevators at downtown department stores shared the spotlight with another small cohort of black females employed at the phone company.[13]

Such transformations heightened difference and deepened stratification, even as African Americans across class lines shared a similar racial marginality. Homer G. Phillips Hospital remained the only local facility training black medical professionals, and the only public institution admitting black indigent patients. But even in the enforced commonality of Jim Crow, doctors might nevertheless treat their patients with contempt. At a high school like Sumner, the children of physicians and professionals attended classes with the children of common laborers. Yet, as the St. Louis–bred comedian Dick Gregory recounted in his memoirs, interactions between the two groups reflected visible hierarchies of class. The private balls, cotillions, and parties frequented by the young black middle class were a world removed from the street corners and back porches inhabited by their laboring-class counterparts. Both strata, ironically, were subject to harassment by the "downtown niggers," manifest in the ongoing rivalry between Sumner and Vashon high schools. Pep rallies at the Pine Street YMCA could turn rowdy as the "downtowners" fought those who resided "across town," illustrating the sharp line of social distinction that existed between African Americans living in Ville and the more transient Central Corridor area east of Sarah and Grand avenues.[14]

Working-Class Militancy in the NAACP

Notwithstanding black St. Louisans' internal social-cultural schisms, black civil rights assumed increasing national and international importance. The

United States' asserted new role as the leader of the free world against Communism collided with the realities of racial segregation, just as Jim Crow during the war had contradicted America's self-image as the "arsenal of democracy." Exposing this Achilles' heel in 1947, A. Philip Randolph's Committee Against Jim Crow in Military Service and Training revived the demand for desegregating the U.S. armed forces, with Theodore McNeal coordinating the committee's efforts in St. Louis. Black voters, meanwhile, were exerting their presence in national electoral politics. The outlawing of all-white primary elections had augmented their voice, and it was widely forecast they would play a decisive role in Truman's success or defeat in the 1948 presidential elections. Truman may not have been a racial liberal, but conditions forced him to establish the President's Committee on Civil Rights in 1946 and ban Jim Crow in federal employment and the armed forces, both through executive order.[15]

These gestures, long overdue, precipitated southern Democratic revolt. By the time of the Democratic National Convention in Philadelphia, southern delegates had announced a readiness to bolt. When the convention eventually nominated Truman on a civil rights platform, the Democrats were split into three rival camps: the Progressive Party, formed by Roosevelt's former vice president, Henry Wallace; Truman's "Regulars"; and the States' Rights Party—the "Dixiecrats" led by South Carolina governor J. Strom Thurmond. A longtime supporter of Truman in Missouri politics, Chambers threw his ward organization's political and fund-raising support behind the president's campaign. Usually a behind-the-scenes player, Chambers took the uncharacteristic step of appearing on stage with Truman during a campaign stop at St. Louis's Kiel Auditorium. The gambit further consolidated the city's black wards behind the sitting president.[16]

While the 1948 elections turned out large numbers of black voters, the NAACP was retreating into the developing Cold War liberal consensus. Executive secretary Walter White, who openly endorsed Truman, engineered W. E. B. DuBois's dismissal, and forbade NAACP members from endorsing Wallace. But while White's control over the various NAACP branches may have been pervasive, it was hardly complete. St. Louisan Margaret Bush Wilson, a young Lincoln University Law School graduate and onetime legal clerk for David Grant, ran for Congress under the Progressive Party banner—the first black woman from Missouri to do so under any party. Part of a prominent Ville family active in the local NAACP, she also belonged to the national board of the Progressive Citizens of America.[17]

"[T]he floodgates of revolt from below have been pushed ajar, permitting the increased initiative of the local [NAACP] branches," averred the black Communist theorist Harry Haywood. "These branches, led by a locally elected leadership, in which the voice of Negro labor has been increasingly represented, especially in many places in the South, have initiated and led significant struggles and campaigns around local and national issues, and constitute a continuous militant pressure upon the national leadership." The Midwest, similarly, was a hub of NAACP militancy. David Grant, a visible MOWM leader, had become president of the St. Louis NAACP in November 1944. His election had been a coup of sorts led by militant reformists like the aged *American* columnist and postal worker, Henry Winfield Wheeler. Using his considerable clout as a charter member of the St. Louis branch, Wheeler had changed the location of the election meeting from the Pine Street YMCA, where most NAACP meetings were held, to a meeting hall in the newly opened Carr Square Village, where Grant enjoyed wide support among the working-class residents. That an officer of the MOWM, an organization oriented toward the black working class, became local president of the nation's oldest civil rights organization illustrates how workers' interests had come to define the overall black political agenda. Grant, too, embodied a new kind of NAACP leadership. He was the branch's first Democratic president; hailing originally from the Mill Creek Valley district, he was also the first local NAACP president born and raised in St. Louis. His administration also began at a time of rising NAACP membership, when St. Louis's branch was among the nation's largest and most active. The new constituency that gravitated toward the organization was self-consciously working-class, and geared toward a style of protest the NAACP had typically rejected. This precipitated internal disputes between militants, who pushed the branch to expand its program and engage in more demonstrations, and older conservative trends insisting that the NAACP concentrate on court action.[18]

Even with this infighting, the branch was able to launch unified strikes against Jim Crow. When World War II veteran William Howard, a black auto garage worker, was shot and killed by an off-duty St. Louis policeman under suspicious circumstances in 1946, NAACP leaders were part of an interracial coalition of political, civic, and religious groups that organized massive public meetings and marches. Vocal and organized dissatisfaction with the inquest into the shooting, including a coroner's ruling of justifiable homicide, led to a subsequent federal investigation but no indictment. Concomitant NAACP efforts targeted public accommodations. When a production of the all-black musical *Carmen Jones* came to the American Theatre downtown in late 1946, it inadvertently highlighted the venue's policy of not admitting African Americans to the main floor or box seats. The NAACP participated in a series of picketings that included a rejuvenated local NNC and the St. Louis branch of the Civil Rights Congress (CRC).

Formed nationally in 1946, the CRC, like the NNC, with which it merged in 1948, was a coalition of Communists and progressive liberals. The CRC's most active members, like Hershel Walker and its early chairman, William Massingale, were black left-wing veterans of the unemployed movement and industrial union radicalism. The small interracial band of picketers received an unexpected boost when the internationally acclaimed concert singer and actor Paul Robeson joined the protest while in town to perform at the Kiel Auditorium. Leading thirty marchers and carrying a placard that read "Actor and Athlete Denounces Jim Crow at American Theater," he announced that he was suspending his career for the next two years to "talk up and down the nation against hatred and prejudice." "The next two years will be critical and important years for our country," Robeson told the press. "Some of us will have to speak up and appeal to the people to respect the common rights of others. I just can't understand things like this happening in a great city like St. Louis. It seems that I must raise my voice, but not by singing pretty songs."[19]

While some NAACP projects, such as the picket line at the American, struggled to attract wide participation, and even passed into the hands of more radical black freedom activists, the association's main thrust was toward a heavier reliance on a skilled minority. Attorney George Vaughn, for instance, had become deeply immersed in a case involving the sale of a house on Labadie Avenue to J. D. and Ethel Shelley, a black family. The home, just west of the Ville, was covered by a restrictive covenant, and while the Shelleys had won the right in circuit court to keep their house, the Missouri Supreme Court had reversed the decision. In April 1947, Vaughn filed the case before the U.S. Supreme Court, and the St. Louis NAACP, though deeply fissured, rallied in strong support. In the 1948 *Shelley v. Kraemer* decision, the nation's High Court ruled that racially restrictive housing covenants were legally unenforceable. Private racial covenants still persisted, but the ruling was a powerful rebuttal to the real estate policies that had spatially contained black St. Louisans since the 1920s.[20]

St. Louis's NAACP leadership had also maintained its legal gaze on the state's institutions of higher learning. In the spring of 1945, Vaughn, Grant, and fellow attorney Robert Witherspoon filed suit against Washington University, arguing that the school did not deserve tax-exempt status as long as it refused to admit black applicants for professional training. In 1948, Washington University's George Warren Brown School of Social Work changed its admissions policy, and other graduate programs followed. It was not until May 1952, when the administration and trustees formally desegregated the undergraduate divisions, that the plaintiffs dropped their suit. Despite considerable protest among white parishioners, St. Louis's

Catholic high schools desegregated by 1948, and Catholic elementary schools ended Jim Crow in the early 1950s. In the fall of 1950, continuing legal action on the part of the St. Louis NAACP led the University of Missouri to finally admit its first black students, ending a long legal sojourn begun with the *Gaines* ruling.[21]

While these cases had far-reaching implications, their immediate stakes were limited to a small black minority eligible for professional training. Guy S. Ruffin, a public schoolteacher and Grant's successor as NAACP president, envisaged the state's public elementary and high schools following the example set in higher education. When a vacancy on the school board suddenly opened, Ruffin and other advocates lobbied Mayor Kaufmann for a black replacement to fill the unexpired term. The mayor's indifference provoked an NAACP picket of City Hall in August 1948, and when another vacancy became available in 1950, Kaufmann's successor, Democrat Joseph M. Darst, appointed Edward Grant the school board's first black member. The Citizens Protest Committee on Overcrowding in Negro Public Schools, organized in the early 1950s, for a short period embodied a black working-class program against unequal education. As 1951 came to a close, however, advocates revisited the idea of filing a lawsuit against the public school system. In separate circuit court cases in 1949, NAACP lawyers had won decisions desegregating the all-white Herbert Hadley Technical High School and Harris Teachers College. The timing seemed good for a massive legal offensive, but plans came to a halt when a dispute over legal strategy erupted between Grant and Redmond, the NAACP's two leading attorneys. The acrimony spilled over into a general membership meeting, which further divided the chapter between competing class politics that emphasized legal action, or alternatively, popular grassroots mobilization.[22]

Increasingly distracted by rank-and-file factionalism, the NAACP became ineffectual as a membership organization. The branch experienced a steep decline among its working-class constituents, falling from a peak of seventy-five hundred members in 1948 to three thousand a scant two years later. Rising dues and black layoffs were also to blame, though the changing direction of the NAACP national office also took its toll, as White and NAACP assistant secretary Roy Wilkins sharply curtailed local branch activities. The policy was part of a general attack on progressive, anti-Truman activists, but this red-baiting campaign drove the NAACP away from all but the most timorous, legalistic objections to segregation. For national leaders, being able to claim thousands of members assumed precedence over their actual mobilization. Courtroom action, which depended on small numbers of trained lawyers, was the main order of the day. Although this strategy was not blind to the needs of the black working-class majority for social wages, neighborhood amenities, and civil liberties and rights, they were clearly subordinate.[23]

The Emergence of St. Louis CORE

At the same time that the St. Louis NAACP's grassroots was demobilizing, a white liberal community of interest was developing around "human rights," a concept growing out of the war and the creation of the United Nations in 1945. The episcopal bishop of Missouri, William Scarlett, had supported ending Jim Crow as early as 1943. The Metropolitan Church Federation of St. Louis had also begun working toward the goal of integrated congregations across the city. Myron Schwartz, director of the Jewish Community Relations Council, and Virgil Border, of the National Conference of Christians and Jews, were both involved in forming the Intergroup Youth Organization to promote interracial goodwill among the city's high school students. Other forces, rooted in secular humanism, also committed themselves to social democratic causes. Harold J. Gibbons, a former Socialist and a gifted white CIO organizer who had studied at the Wisconsin School for Workers, had been tapped during the war to lead local affiliates of the United Retail, Wholesale and Department Store Employees of America. An ardent anticommunist, he nonetheless shared much of the vision promoted by Communist-led unions like the UE. Thus, at a time when many unionists were disengaging from community-wide activism, Gibbons regarded labor organizations as vehicles for social change beyond the workplace, including the area of race relations. By 1947, the union had grown to sixty-five hundred members, auguring Gibbons's growing influence in labor and political circles. At Washington University, meanwhile, white students had demonstrated against the exclusion of black applicants, some even risking expulsion. Many war veterans attending classes at the university had been involved in the American Veterans Committee, formed to realize the "Four Freedoms" in the United States. Several of them joined social work students, and members of the campus YMCA and YWCA, to form the Student Committee for the Admission of Negroes (SCAN) in 1947.[24]

These trends all found a way station in the home of Irvin Dagen, a small businessman, and his wife Margaret, a high school teacher. Their apartment, in the all-white suburb of University City, served as a salon where unionists, professors, civic activists, student protesters, ecumenical leaders, and other liberal and progressive cognoscenti participated in Humanity, Inc., a regular discussion group. Bernice Fisher, a union organizer who worked with Gibbons, was one of the Dagens' featured speakers. Newly relocated from Chicago, she had been a founding member of that city's Committee of Racial Equality (CORE) in 1942, which sought to translate the ideas of peaceful cooperation and interracial harmony into creative action. Fisher now became the catalyst for St. Louis's own loosely affiliated Committee of Racial Equality, which drew its integrated membership from Humanity, Inc. Although many of its earliest members hailed from the labor movement, most were middle-class professionals with high educational and occupational status. Norman Seay, a student at Vashon High School, was involved with the Intergroup Youth Organization. Charles Oldham, Joseph Ames, and Steve Best had all been in the armed forces during World War II, and were active in SCAN with another St. Louis CORE founder, Marvin Rich. Walter Hayes, a black war veteran and postal worker, was emblematic of the many returning soldiers who, having fought European fascism and Japanese militarism abroad, were determined to vanquish Jim Crow at home. Another founding member, Marian O'Fallon, was a graduate of Stowe Teachers College and a kindergarten teacher who had participated in CCRC sit-ins at the Stix, Baer & Fuller department store, walked the NAACP's picket line at the American Theatre, and typed legal briefs for the *Shelley* case (She and Oldham would later marry, flouting the state's prohibition against interracial marriage.)[25]

One of the organization's first major activities involved a new public accommodations bill that had been introduced in the Board of Aldermen during the spring of 1948. One of its authors, Alderman Caston, had been responsible for the passage four years earlier of an ordinance prohibiting Jim Crow in municipal buildings. Along with aldermen Redmond and Lowe, he proposed a more comprehensive measure applying to all public establishments. CORE began a leaflet campaign on behalf of the bill, which mobilized as much antagonism as support. The Democratic aldermen of the South St. Louis wards, known as the "Dixiecrat" wing because of their racial conservatism, emerged as the main wedge against civil rights legislation, and suppressed the bill. The St. Louis Hotel Association and the Missouri Restaurant Owners Association were equally hostile, arguing the measure would discourage white patronage and hurt business. An emergent Racial Purity Committee also undertook a counterinitiative to make segregation compulsory in all public indoor and outdoor places. Sponsoring the committee was the recently formed Christian Nationalist Party (CNP), which embodied a uniquely American fascism adhering to antilabor white supremacy, xenophobia, anticommunism, and evangelical Christianity. Its founder, the proto-fascist populist Gerald L. K. Smith, had been an organizer for Louisiana governor Huey P. Long's Share Our Wealth Society, a member of the pro-Nazi Silver Legion, and a paid strikebreaker.[26]

Working closely with Gibbons's union, of which Marvin Rich was a staff advisor, CORE was also involved in drafting a 1951 report, "Planning for An Integrated School System in St. Louis," that strongly favored school desegregation. Although CORE's support for the public accommodations bill, and school desegregation, illustrated broad concern with the conditions of black St. Louisans, the group opted to focus its energies on fighting the closed-door policies at downtown-area restaurants and drugstore soda fountains. Lacking a sizable membership or deep black communal roots, the committee needed a narrowly tailored and manageable project, and since the CCRC's decline the terrain of segregated lunch counters had remained largely untouched. Indicative of St. Louis's uneven patterns of segregation, no city ordinances mandated such eating arrangements. To a group of young idealists living in a crossroads city like St. Louis, the malleable nature of this situation suggested a likelihood of success, particularly since other local institutions were abandoning Jim Crow. This strategic perspective, geared toward the middle-class-oriented politics of racial goodwill and patient negotiation, did not depart fundamentally from the conventional wisdom of liberal gradualism. Personified during the war by the Mayor's Race Relations Commission, this outlook assumed that change would come from sustained dialogue among the "better sort" of black and white St. Louisans typified by CORE's membership. Racial deference was typical in these relations, with African Americans expected to play the part of humble supplicants. Yet in their willingness to use direct action protest and "nonviolent noncooperation" to usher along reform, CORE's members implicitly challenged the dominant model of liberal interracial politics, which aimed mainly to bureaucratically "manage," rather than fundamentally transform, race relations.[27]

Stix, Baer & Fuller became CORE's first test case. Talks with Stix officials to desegregate its spacious first-floor lunch counter reached an early impasse, and CORE workers began distributing circulars to patrons and passersby outside the store, urging them to boycott. In early 1949, the organization added weekly lunch counter sit-ins on the first floor. Denied coffee and meals, the smartly dressed demonstrators often sat quietly the length of the day, occupying the silences with knitting, academic studies, or the Bible. These quiet hobbies and pursuits, much like the crisp, elegant clothes they wore, were part of a carefully orchestrated pageantry that asserted the demonstrators' middle-class "respectability" and cleverly aimed to shame white patrons. The silent protests attracted onlookers from the shopping floor, and made the pages of the *American* and the *Argus,* where Irvin Dagen had become a regular columnist. As they had done initially during the CCRC sit-ins several years earlier, the white-owned *Post-Dispatch, Star-Times,* and *Globe-Democrat* studiously avoided coverage. Darst, who had recently been elected mayor, reinforced this pattern through his administration's own silence.[28]

Race Riot at Fairgrounds Park

While CORE flailed at one facade of Jim Crow, another suddenly collapsed. St. Louis's public recreational facilities had long been inadequate for a city its size, while segregation made black play areas even scarcer. The local Division of Parks and Recreation supervised forty-nine city playgrounds, with only nine open to African Americans. Of the seven indoor municipal swimming pools the division operated, four barred black citizens from use. The outdoor swimming pools at Fairgrounds and Marquette parks, the only two such public facilities in the city, similarly prohibited black swimmers. The opulent, resort-style Fairgrounds Pool had in fact been, at its opening in 1913, the first outside the South to officially mandate racial segregation, typifying the city's border-state culture. Since then, staff had maintained a pattern of denying entry to the small groups of black people who had approached the pool gates every summer. As the summer of 1949 neared, however, park commissioner Palmer Baumes approached John J. O'Toole, Mayor Darst's new director of public welfare, about deciding a policy on the public pools. O'Toole informed Baumes that no legal basis existed for barring black swimmers, and that pool staff should let them enter upon request. On June 20, a day before the start of the swimming season, reporters learned of the order. Radio stations broadcast the news that evening, and the *Globe-Democrat* ran a front-page story in its late edition.[29]

On Tuesday, June 21, most swimming facilities opened without incident, including the outdoor pool at South St. Louis's Marquette Park. A different climate prevailed that afternoon in North St. Louis, where racial transition was occurring in the neighborhood around Fairgrounds Park. It was common knowledge among black St. Louisans that traveling north of the park could result in physical attacks by white gangs, and over the past six months vandals had targeted black-purchased homes in the area. When about thirty black boys entered the Fairgrounds Park pool, a crowd of two hundred white teenagers and young men gathered outside the enclosure, brandishing weapons and shouting epithets. Police escorted the black children from the pool and out of the park, barely containing the white youth who darted in and out of the small phalanx to strike them. Extra uniformed police had been assigned to the park that day, but their numbers proved inadequate to deal with the crisis that slowly erupted. A shifting nucleus of white teenagers began attacking black youth in and around the 129-acre park. As the rumor spread that a large number of African Americans were assembling at the west end of the park to retaliate, police began turning away black teenagers and confiscating weapons from roving bands of white youth.[30]

As night fell, some five thousand people crowded in and around the park, many of them exiting streetcars en route to a Cardinals baseball game at nearby Sportsman's Park. Two white men began to exhort the crowd to violence. "You want to know how to take care of them niggers?" one of them challenged a crowd of younger whites. "Get bricks and smash their heads." Clusters of white teenagers and men attacked several black park visitors with lead pipes, baseball bats, and in a few instances, knives. Traffic stalled on Natural Bridge Road and Grand Avenue as the violence spilled outside the park, and one black man, alighting from a streetcar, was assaulted. The relatively small numbers of African Americans in the park, and in the surrounding area, prevented more widespread rioting by whites, but by any measure the situation had become deadly. Authorities issued a belated riot call, and 150 police officers arrived to turn away traffic and scatter congregants. By the end of the evening, authorities had arrested three whites and four African Americans for peace disturbance and inciting to riot. Five black people, and one white youth, had been seriously injured, though others had been brutalized. Mayor Darst hastily rescinded O'Toole's desegregation order, and closed both outdoor pools.[31]

A week after the incident, Darst appointed a Council on Human Relations. Continuing in the vein of the city's former Race Relations Committee, several members from this body, including committee chairman Edwin B. Meissner, became participants in the new advisory group. The members' first act was to commission George Schermer, who had gained a national profile as director of Detroit's Interracial Committee, to produce a report assessing the riot's causes. With similar racial clashes occurring in Baltimore and Washington, D.C., that summer and fall, the study assumed added significance. Like St. Louis, both were border cities, and thus places where "northern and southern attitudes combine to form uncertain boundaries around the races," a *Post-Dispatch* writer stated, calling attention to the Gateway City's particular politics of place. Closer in geography to Dixie than the realm of the Yankee, he noted, St. Louis always had exhibited a social schizophrenia on matters of race, and with the same volatility.[32]

The Schermer report, issued in late July, assigned fault for the debacle to a general pattern of negligence in local race relations. "St. Louis is psychologically unprepared to undertake the adjustments which changing population, economic, and social conditions are forcing upon the community," the study concluded. "It is not a case of some people wanting to move too fast, but a larger majority wanting to move too slowly." For so long authorities had done little to promote integrated spaces of recreation and leisure, the report reasoned, then suddenly attempted too much too quickly without adequately preparing the public or fully mobilizing civic leaders and law enforcement. The absence of a larger program to expand the number of recreational areas in the city had not helped, either. Against the backdrop of pervasive Jim Crow, and black ghettoization, the abrupt order to open all municipal pools to African Americans had made a combustible situation unavoidable.[33]

The report advocated, among other measures, that the city administration reopen the pools on a nonsegregated basis, backed by "the full force of the law." In written correspondence to Darst, CORE president Joseph Ames concurred with the decision to keep the pools closed for the duration of the summer, but similar to Schermer he urged the Mayor's Office to reopen them next summer on an integrated basis. At the behest of the Council on Human Relations, which became an official arm of municipal government in January 1950, the Board of Aldermen approved money to build a pool at the Vashon Community Center, located in a black neighborhood. The offer might have mollified St. Louis's black activist community during an earlier period in its political maturation, when the preeminent goal was to extract as many social amenities from Jim Crow as possible. But with the legitimacy of segregation now under growing public scrutiny, and given the fact that black recreational spaces were bursting at the seams, black spokespersons rejected the proposal as a ploy to avoid integrating the city's recreational facilities. A biracial coalition including the NAACP, Urban League, the St. Louis Association of Colored Women's Clubs, and the St. Louis Rabbinical Association formed in opposition to the decision to postpone desegregating the pools, and in June 1950 the NAACP filed a federal suit against the City of St. Louis. In July, Judge Ruby Hulen, who had earlier ruled against racial differentials in schoolteachers' pay, ordered the city to end its pool restrictions, effective within two days. When a legal motion for a stay of execution failed, a reluctant Darst administration observed the order. White mobs again gathered when black NAACP-affiliated youth tested the policy at Fairgrounds Park, but uniformed police, backed by a strong public decree issued from the city counselor's office, prevented renewed rioting. Many whites residing in the vicinity of the Marquette and Fairgrounds parks, rather than defy police, simply abandoned the pools.[34]

The desegregation of Fairgrounds Pool had not involved black working-class mobilization, and indeed had been accomplished through NAACP legal action and liberal interracial networks. Yet the issue of municipal playgrounds and recreation was nonetheless pertinent to black working-class youth and families, who relied on public amenities just as much as, if not more than, their middle-class counterparts. Because the rioting at Fairgrounds Park was uncharacteristic of St. Louis race relations, moreover, it begs the question of how such a conflagration could occur in a city boastful of its interracial "civility." Certainly, this reputation had always been more image than reality, but posed against the unique backdrop of the early Cold War, the violence also seems to have been specific to an emerging white anticommunist civic mind-set that equated domestic racial reform with foreign "subversion." There is reason to believe, too, that members of the CNP, an overtly white supremacist and rabidly anticommunist group new to the city, played an active role in organizing the rioters, which would further explain the anomalous character of the rampage.

Working-Class Radicalism and Fair Employment

Far less conspicuously than in the events at Fairgrounds Park, members of CORE had quietly continued their campaign against Jim Crow at downtown eateries, along the way enduring harassment and violence from CNP foot soldiers. By April 1952, however, numerous downtown stores were "conducting CORE-arranged experiments in integrated eating, with a view toward a complete opening of their facilities." St. Louis CORE's new president, Charles Oldham, and other members authored a four-point proposal for "Establishing Equal Restaurant Service in St. Louis Department Stores," offering timetables for prearranged "eating tests" by small, integrated groups. Notwithstanding support from members of the Council on Human Relations, the Urban League, NAACP, and a number of white and black clergy, the document languished among department store executives.[35]

While demanding full service at department store lunch counters, remarkably few activists clamored about the absence of black sales workers. Several branches of CORE around the nation were involved in employment campaigns during the 1940s, but local organizers had become convinced through experience that a similar strategy in St. Louis would flounder. In July 1952, during a furtive protest against employment racism, St. Louis CORE activists initiated a small picket line outside one of the city's Reed Ice Cream stores. Deflecting attention from complaints about the lack of black clerks, shop managers affixed a sign in the store window announcing that owners would not be "intimidated by or associated with any Communist front organization in their attempt to arouse race hatred." The ease with which management levied the charge of subversion was indicative of how demonstrations for racial and economic justice could be dismissed through cynical appeals to anticommunism, patriotic loyalty, and the unspoken prerogatives of whiteness. Eating accommodations, therefore, remained St. Louis CORE's immediate target.[36]

The crusade for jobs fell to groups like Civil Rights Congress (CRC), which locally organized a series of rallies against black unemployment. Yet this focus was tied to other issues immediately relevant to black working-class St. Louisans. Under the chairmanship of the Reverend Obadiah Jones, pastor of Mount Tabor Baptist Church, the CRC had organized assemblies and street demonstrations against a spate of police brutality cases in 1949 and 1950. The most egregious case had involved James Perry, a forty-one-year-old unemployed war veteran. In August 1949, Perry was embroiled in an altercation with four policemen, who accused him of stealing from a vendor wagon in a park. Officers took him to Homer G. Phillips Hospital, where he died of a brain hemorrhage—the result, his companion reported to the CRC, of a vicious beating by police. Combining issues of unemployment and police violence had led to dramatic CRC growth: By 1952, when many other chapters were in decline, St. Louis's had grown to nearly two hundred members.[37]

The NNC, revived in 1946 under Communist leadership, was also part of this postwar spurt in black radicalism, and attracted about one hundred members. Working closely with the CRC, with which it shared an office at the People's Finance Building, the organization had similarly participated in the angry rallies and parades following the earlier police shooting of William Howard. In early 1947, the NNC had also organized a two-hundred-person delegation to attend the opening session of the Missouri General Assembly in Jefferson City, where William Massingale, a CRC activist, had been installed as a new Democratic representative from St. Louis. He had, in fact, been one of four black state representatives elected—the first group of African Americans since the adoption of Missouri's new state constitution. Pursuing a legislative platform consistent with Popular Front policies, he had promoted the elimination of the state's dual school system, the ending of Jim Crow in all public places, and the passage of a minimum wage. With another legislator, additionally, he had introduced a state FEP bill to the assembly.[38]

Of the mainline liberal black service, civic, and political organizations, the St. Louis Urban League was the most consistent on the employment front, but its return to conference-room negotiation, quiet lobbying, and gradualism since the 1930s fell far short of actual resistance. In 1948 and 1949, the Urban League, coordinated by industrial secretary Chester E. Stovall, documented the racial discrimination practiced at local Ford and General Motors assembly plants, where black workers were absent from production lines and concentrated in custodial service. Joining forces with the NAACP and the St. Louis Catholic Interracial Council, Urban League staffers held a series of conferences with Ford and UAW officials, confident the company would "accept Negro applicants for employment on the basis of qualification." In August 1952, the *Argus* and the Urban League–affiliated Federation of Block Units began a "campaign of exposure" against hiring practices at the Quality Dairy Company. The firm had recently purchased a competitor and rehired all of the company's driver-salesmen, except for three black drivers. Angry citizens called for a boycott, but without an organization to mobilize and sustain their energies, the outrage subsided with anxious Quality officials promising to hire a black route driver in the near future.[39]

In the noxious environment of the early 1950s, condemnations of job discrimination could invite unwanted attention from anticommunist zealots. Granted, President Truman had issued a decree against racial discrimination in government employment, and in 1951 created the Committee on Government Contracts. But critics had dismissed the agency as a barely functional substitute for a "real FEP," whose limited powers the president himself had helped strip. Truman had also begun subjecting government workers to wide-ranging loyalty tests that left black employees painfully vulnerable to charges of "disloyalty" for their involvement in protest activities. Calvin Houston Stevely, a black St. Louis postal clerk, was but one individual who ran afoul of the new policy. Active in the National Alliance of Postal Employees and the NAACP, and involved in complaints against continuing forms of segregation at the Post Office, he was charged with disloyalty in 1948. "I have learned by experience," he wrote bitterly in an affidavit, "to fight against Race Prejudice makes a Colored Clerk a subversive person." A twenty-year veteran of the Post Office, Stevely disputed the claim of disloyalty, and received support from the NAACP and other black postal workers—though the special counsel for the NAACP national headquarters, cautious about what might emerge from his background, advised the branch not to "act on the question of whether or not Mr. Stevely was a Communist."[40]

St. Louis's CRC, on the other hand, fought against such firings of black government workers accused of subversion on the basis of civil liberties. Like a number of organizations accused of being "red," the NAACP and CORE had sought to assuage suspicion by demonstrating their willingness to "clean house." While David Grant, for instance, had interacted with Communists during the 1930s, one of his boasts as local NAACP president had been preventing a Communist "takeover" of the branch. In 1950, members of the St. Louis branch had also refused to approve a nominee to the executive board when they learned she was an official in the United Office and Professional Workers, a union the CIO expelled for "subversion." Even CORE, founded on a platform of "nonviolent goodwill action," had passed a resolution in 1948 forbidding cooperation with so-called Communist-controlled groups.[41]

Such policies had antecedents before and during World War II. The national NAACP had long rejected alliances with the Communist Party, while the MOWM had mandated noncooperation with Communists in its by-laws. Randolph had long been a virulently anticommunist labor socialist, much like UAW president Walter Reuther and Gibbons. In an attempt to uproot suspected Communist influence in 1949, St. Louis's Retail, Wholesale and Department Store Employees had left the CIO and merged with Local 688 of the AFL's International Brotherhood of Teamsters. As Local 688 president, Gibbons had continued his assault on the local leadership of the powerful UE. William Sentner, facing mounting opposition within UE District 8, had been forced to stand down for reelection to the presidency in 1948. A new rival union, the International United Electrical Workers (IUE) had made steady inroads into the UE's rank-and-file majority, and in 1949 the UE had bolted the CIO convention rather than be expelled for Communist infiltration. Ten other "Communist-dominated" unions were purged in the following months, totaling over one million members. The expelled organizations had typically been the most vigorous in recruiting African Americans, women, and the emerging ranks of white-collar workers, and were the most progressively oriented in their civic politics.[42]

Nonetheless, strains of black working-class radicalism persisted. Surveying the rise of the CIO, postwar economic crises, and the "tremendous battle for the minds of the Negro people and for the minds of the population in the US as a whole over the Negro question," the Trinidadian-born Trotskyist C. L. R. James had concluded in 1948 that "the independent Negro struggle" was headed inexorably toward proletarian militancy. As if by prophecy, a postwar black union caucus movement, spurred by continuing racism in organized labor, emerged. In June 1950, nearly one thousand people convened in Chicago for the National Trade Union Conference for Negro Rights. The delegates represented NNC veterans, former Progressive Party campaigners, and activists from the UE, the Food, Tobacco, Agricultural, and Allied Workers, and the other left-led industrial unions expelled by the CIO.[43]

Detroit representatives, led by labor organizers Ernest Thompson, William R. Hood, and Coleman A. Young, raised the call for a new permanent organization to fight for full employment, upgrading, "an end to lily-white shops," the abolition of Jim Crow auxiliaries, and fair employment practice legislation. In October 1951, eleven hundred people reconvened in Cincinnati to consolidate the National Negro Labor Council (NNLC). They named as their president Hood, who was recording secretary of Detroit's massive UAW Local 600. Young, an official of the Amalgamated Clothing Workers–CIO, and former director of the Michigan Progressive Party, was elected executive secretary and national organizer. Octavia Hawkins, influential in Chicago's UAW Local 453, became the new organization's national secretary-treasurer. The "Bill of Particulars," the NNLC's working program of action, was a broadside against industrial employers, white organized labor, and government, who formed a "three-party conspiracy" of discrimination. Calling for greater formal union leadership, members also vowed to agitate for "model FEPC clauses" in all union contracts. Reminiscent of the early NNC, the new council's platform also addressed the particular rights of black working-class women, and advocated the labor organization of domestic workers. Conscious of the occupations that wartime militancy had made possible, rank-and-file participants, a third of them female, adopted a resolution supporting the expansion of black women's job opportunities in industry, department stores, and public utilities.[44]

Evoking the mass movements of the 1930s, NNLC founders also elaborated the goal of building interracial working-class unity, rekindling solidarity between black workers and trade unionism, and completing "the great unfinished task of organizing the South." As had been true of the NNC and the MOWM, embedded in the NNLC's platform for jobs and full union membership was a broader agenda to dismantle Jim Crow beyond the workplace. By the end of 1951 the national body oversaw the activities of approximately thirty-five chapters. Fresh from the national founding convention, Hershel Walker—a veteran Communist, and a janitor at Wagner Electric—had become chairman of the new St. Louis NNLC chapter. His cofounder, W. E. "Red" Davis, was a white Communist recently relocated from Memphis who had found work at the Emerson Electric Company. Other members of the council, similarly, were electrical workers affiliated with the expelled UE.[45]

The NNLC's first major national campaign began in March 1953, when the organization challenged Sears, Roebuck and Company for clerical positions, mainly for black women. The nation's largest retailer, Sears was strongly antiunion, and maintained an "ironclad policy" of barring African Americans from sales and clerical positions. As NNLC branches in Cleveland, Detroit, San Francisco, Newark, and Indianapolis launched boycotts, the St. Louis NNLC set its sights on the main Sears store at 1408 North Kingshighway Boulevard, where the company housed its district office. Announcing its campaign in the *Argus,* the NNLC appealed to all "fair-minded citizens" to boycott Sears until the store conceded to demands to hire black office and sales workers. Both black and white protesters walked a picket line six nights a week outside the store. Walker, who routinely led the picketing, also cultivated support within St. Louis's black community, bringing into the fold members of the Interdenominational Ministerial Alliance (including the local CRC chairman, Reverend Jones), Sumner High School students, and even Mayor Willie Head of Kinloch.[46]

The Nadir of Black Radicalism

◢

Even with the diverse communities of interests represented at the demonstrations, only thirty people were actually involved, a far cry from the hundreds that the MOWM had mobilized ten years earlier. The foremost reason for this lack of mass participation was that federal officials had declared the NNLC Communist-dominated, and by 1953 had named it to the U.S. attorney general's List of Subversive Organizations. This was a virtual death sentence that drove away many potential supporters, particularly government employees subject to investigation and dismissal for associating with such groups. The city's liberal protest organizations predictably also refused any involvement with the demonstrators on North Kingshighway. Henry Wheeler, then president of the St. Louis NAACP, rebuffed an offer by NNLC representatives to join the boycott, citing the national NAACP's prohibitions. Negro Labor Council leaders also approached members of St. Louis CORE, whose downtown demonstrations had impressed labor radicals. This appeal, too, was rejected by a unanimous vote. The National Urban League was equally antagonistic. At the CIO's 1951 national meeting, Urban League executive Lester Granger attacked the NNLC from the convention podium. As the venue for his speech suggested, leading representatives of organized labor had closed ranks behind the White House and the State Department to fight the Communist threat abroad, and "internal subversives." Several CIO affiliates sought to preempt the NNLC by establishing their own "citizens committees for the FEPC" and endorsing the integration of public accommodations. In March 1952, Randolph and other well-known trade unionists had also formed the National Negro Labor Committee in a blatant attempt to undermine its adversary. The recent elections of George Meany and Reuther as presidents of the AFL and CIO, respectively, and talk of a merger, exemplified the consolidation of a conservative labor leadership, leaving meager hope for cooperation with the NNLC.[47]

Deprived of broad cooperation and organizational support, the Sears boycotters were vulnerable to numerous forms of repression. Federal agents had been present at the NNLC's founding convention, and surveillance continued in St. Louis. An unmarked police van became a fixture at the picket site, piquing the curiosity of protesters. While marching one day, Davis pounded on the roof of the vehicle. "These guys come running out, they thought a bomb had hit 'em!" he later recalled. "So I looked in the back window and they had a camera on a tripod sitting in there, making pictures of everybody on the picket line." Lacking any further motive to remain hidden, police photographers placed their cameras and tripods on the open sidewalk across the street. The demonstrators also weathered physical harassment. In one incident, an altercation occurred when police accosted two youths walking the picket line. One fifteen-year-old was beaten, and in the commotion that followed, authorities arrested Walker and another demonstrator on charges of attacking a police officer. Ministers involved in the boycott organized a telephone corps, who complained to the St. Louis chief of police and Mayor's Office until Walker was released that evening.[48]

The aplomb with which demonstrators handled police revealed a strong morale, even with the lack of widespread encouragement and the stigma of being "subversive." The district superintendent and other Sears company representatives had been holding tentative meetings with protest leaders since the beginning of the boycott; embarrassed by negative publicity and visible police surveillance, they began negotiating an end to the strike. Negotiations took a more serious turn as the demonstrations stretched into their ninth month. Sensing that the company was close to offering concessions, Walker made another appeal to CORE and the NAACP to become partners in the Sears struggle, in the hope that their involvement would legitimize any hiring agreement. When both organizations again turned down proposals to collaborate, the local NNLC alone negotiated the hiring of the store's first black women in white-collar jobs—though local Urban League officials, who had surreptitiously approached the NNLC about negotiating a settlement, took the final credit for securing the jobs.[49]

By the end of 1953, virtually all Sears stores outside the South had come to terms with NNLC organizers. The success of the St. Louis boycott propelled the NNLC into a subsequent campaign against the local Public Service Company, which similarly ended in an agreement between company officials and the Urban League to hire black streetcar operators and bus drivers. "Our organization never did get a name, not more than some radical group," Walker admitted. "We never did get the respect that the NAACP, the Urban League and these people got." It is nonetheless remarkable that St. Louis's NNLC was able to sustain even its modest level of communal support among ministers and other "respectable" black civic leaders. But given the anticommunist assault, the ripples the organization created were faint indeed. While the NNLC was able to expand the range of work available to black workers, its efforts created jobs in only a few areas. Red-baiting, and accusations of "dual unionism" severed many NNLC activities from genuine mass support as the council's members were expelled from unions, fired from their jobs, or summoned before congressional committees. Despite the Interdenominational Ministerial Alliance's support for the Sears boycott, even its members expelled Jones in 1953 for his alleged Communist affiliation.[50]

At the beginning of President Dwight Eisenhower's administration, too, broader changes in the U.S. political economy were undermining the prospects for black economic equality envisioned by labor radicals and militants. Between 1947 and 1952, African American household family income had risen nationally from $3,563 to $4,344. After 1952, however, black income began to decline in relation to whites for the first time since the Depression. The Committee on Government Contracts, established by Eisenhower through executive order in 1953, strengthened federal antidiscrimination measures against government contractors in hiring, placement, training, and promotion. Nonetheless, the emerging industrial phenomenon of automation was symptomatic of a new period of black working-class formation characterized by declining job opportunities. The push toward automated production stemmed from political objectives, chiefly the desire to discipline a labor movement that had gained strength during the 1930s and 1940s. With the introduction of new labor-saving and union-busting technology, black workers began experiencing an unemployment that was "both more frequent and longer-lasting." Organized labor, concerned with a narrowing membership base, was indifferent to this economic displacement. Indeed, one of the consequences of the CIO's march into the Cold War consensus was that its leadership ceased organizing the unorganized.[51]

Black working people who paid attention could hardly have been encouraged when the AFL and CIO consummated their merger in late 1955, bringing together some 15 million members. The presidency of the new organization, and 75 percent of the positions on the executive council, went to the AFL, long known for its racial exclusivity. Some decisions, however, seemed to herald better relations between organized labor and black workers. Two African Americans—Randolph, and Willard S. Townsend of the United Transport Service Employees—were appointed to the executive council. The new federation's constitution promised to "encourage all workers without regard to race, creed, color or national origin to share in the full benefits of union organization," and provided for the creation of a Committee on Civil Rights. In a strategy designed, in part, to preempt the influence of radical trade unionists, the AFL-CIO also endorsed passage of an enforceable fair employment practices act, encouraged affiliates to seek nondiscrimination clauses in collective-bargaining agreements, and urged Congress to abolish the poll tax and pass antilynching legislation. But these gestures poorly compensated for the number of AFL-CIO affiliates that continued to exclude black labor. In "An Open Letter to the AFL and CIO," NNLC activists argued the confederation had not gone far enough in guaranteeing the end of racist practices. While unions were liable for expulsion for Communism and racketeering, racial discrimination carried no such penalties. Critics on the left insisted that what the AFL-CIO constitution needed were not statements that simply disregarded race in union organization, but to the contrary, provisions that consciously asserted the full membership of workers of color. Given the present constitution, craft unions could maintain segregated black auxiliaries under the pretext they shared "equal"—albeit separate—benefits. NNLC leaders argued that the welfare of all organized labor pivoted on the "Negro Question," and hence black workers. Particularly with many runaway industries departing to the South, strengthening trade unionism in this region would require full African American participation.[52]

Yet the National Negro Labor Council lay in shambles by the spring of 1956. Rather than dissipate resources fighting the Subversive Activities Control Board's charges of Communist domination, NNLC members voted to dissolve. A similar fate befell the CRC. Despite the organization's warm relations with *American* publisher Nathaniel Sweets and other black editors, St. Louis media largely repressed the CRC's exploits. While former NAACP presidents Witherspoon and Redmond gave legal support, others like Grant refused to aid the group for fear of being colored "red." In 1956, a HUAC subcommittee chaired by Missouri congressman Morgan Moulder began hearings in St. Louis to probe Communist activity and investigate the accusations of undercover FBI agents who had infiltrated the party. HUAC was especially interested in party activities among black St. Louisans. Four African Americans—Brockman Schumacher, Ella Mae Posey Pappademos, Romey Hudson, and former St. Louis NNLC chairman Hershel Walker—were subpoenaed to appear during the hearings. Notwithstanding the NAACP's aversion to alleged Communists, Witherspoon represented them as counsel. To their shock and dismay, one of the witnesses against them was none other than the chairman of the St. Louis CRC himself, Reverend Jones, who testified that he was a paid informant who, at the FBI's behest, had joined the Communist Party in 1946. Schumacher, Pappademos, Hudson, and Walker all invoked the Fifth Amendment when the committee queried them about their Communist ties.[53]

Between 1948 and 1951, several national Communist Party leaders had been indicted under the Smith Act, charged with the crime of teaching and advocating the violent overthrow of the U.S. government. Sentner and four other St. Louis party leaders had been indicted in 1952. Although the convictions were later overturned, Sentner, weakened by the ordeal, died of heart failure in 1958. Notwithstanding the involvement of an increasingly isolated U.S. Communist Left, organizations such as the NNLC had not been mere party "fronts." Consistent with their general retreat from building mass radical politics among African Americans, many Communists in fact had attacked the NNLC as too "narrow," favoring greater support to the NAACP, the AFL-CIO, and the Democratic Party. The party had been drifting from its "Black Belt Nation" thesis since the 1930s, and by the end of the 1950s had refuted it altogether. Its most vocal militant black members were expelled for the crime of "nationalism."[54]

Black America paid a heavy price for the repression of its left political flank. As NAACP leadership soon discovered, rapprochement with Cold War forces did not shield liberals from charges of Soviet domination. Following the landmark *Brown v. Board of Education of Topeka, Kansas* Supreme Court ruling, federal authorities lobbied to include the NAACP among groups covered by the 1954 Communist Control Act. It is hardly surprising, then, that with some exceptions, black protest in St. Louis during the late 1940s and early 1950s involved small numbers of people, in stark contrast to the World War II years. Even the St. Louis NAACP, which had grown in the immediate wake of the war, had suffered. Job layoffs, along with rising dues, decimated its ranks. Many of those who departed had formed the branch's growing working-class constituency, drawn to the NAACP by the momentum of the MOWM. Yet a conservative national leadership severely curtailed the activities of NAACP branches, breeding a reluctance to fight around the issue of job discrimination or even engage in struggles beyond the courtroom. The absence of a strong black protest movement arguably renewed the defense of segregation among St. Louis's white officials. Once the high tide of black agitation had subsided after the war, the Board of Aldermen, whose members had earlier passed ordinances in favor of integration, repeatedly resisted efforts to continue dismantling Jim Crow. A comprehensive public accommodations bill, introduced in 1948, had died in the board's legislative committee. Over the next six years, advocates made twenty-five motions to bring a civil rights bill to the floor, and each time they were defeated. When advocates reintroduced the bill in 1954, legislators overwhelmingly rejected it.[55]

Further, a lack of mass black mobilization enabled white-owned media to suppress coverage of CORE's sit-in demonstrations, as well as protests by the CRC and other groups. Ironically, the daily newspapers were helpful in one respect: For the most part, editors did not attempt to incite white anger through race-baiting headlines and articles, which spoke to the culture of "civility" that persisted among the city's white elite. Aside from coordinated assaults by Christian Nationalist Party members, sit-in demonstrators encountered relatively little physical violence. The reasons for black demobilization were internal as well as external, and involved more than simply a capitulation to the red scare. Although some of its participants were black, St. Louis CORE's rigid membership requirements, especially its strict emphasis on nonviolence, hampered the committee in its efforts to attract new recruits and establish strong black communal links. Although CORE had a far more protest-oriented bent than the Council on Human Relations and other liberal interracial committees, its philosophy and strategy of nonviolence proceeded from the same gradualist assumption that racial discrimination could be overcome through prolonged interaction and moral appeals. Many black working people knew better. However, the actions of the local NAACP, CORE, CRC, and NNLC formed a crucial link between the period between the militancy of World War II, and the rebirth of mass-based insurgency heralded by the Montgomery Bus Boycott. A full-blown resurgence, more securely rooted in the energies of black working class people, would not occur in the Gateway City until the late 1950s. The St. Louis NAACP, heretofore sharply divided, formed the cutting edge of this renaissance.[56]

CHAPTER FOUR

Grassroots Renewal and the
"Heroic" Period, 1956–61

IN JUNE 1954, following the U.S. Supreme Court's ruling in *Brown v. Board of Education of Topeka*, the St. Louis Board of Education voted to integrate its schools, and a number of historically black institutions, including the Booker T. Washington Vocational School, closed. By June 1953, CORE could boast of thirty-four previously all-white eateries that had ended Jim Crow arrangements. Earlier that year, the American Theatre also desegregated, largely in response to constant picketing. Without formal announcement, the Stix department store opened its eating facilities to all customers, with the exception of its exclusive upstairs tea room. With many professional associations also integrating their memberships, segregated lodging had become a potential obstacle to drawing conferences to the city; beginning in December 1954, many white downtown hotels relaxed their Jim Crow policies.[1]

At the same time, the ruling precipitated a full-scale white "massive resistance" rooted in race-conscious appeals to "states rights." The NAACP, an erstwhile ally against communism, also came under attack, with its operations halted in many southern states. Paradoxically, the association's repression set into motion both a renewal of black working-class mass action, and a new phase of black social movement activity. In Alabama, it created the space for the Montgomery Bus Boycott, one of the first major community mobilizations following *Brown*, and a clear departure from the national NAACP's strategy of legalistic reform. "[W]hen one considers that 75 percent of the passengers in Montgomery were black men and women who rode the buses to and from work," writes scholar William H. Harris, "then the picture becomes clearer" that Montgomery's was a working-class struggle, though not avowedly. To the extent that the Montgomery struggle marked the beginning of a new postwar black mass movement—the "heroic" civil rights period—it also represented a renaissance in the black working-class mass politics initially thwarted by the early Cold War.[2]

This was evident in the reorganization and revival of the St. Louis NAACP in 1956, and the opposition it led against a proposed new city charter in the spring and summer of 1957. The tangle of municipal issues underlying the charter struggle—downtown redevelopment, the black vote, and an ongoing effort to clear Mill Creek Valley—set in motion a local black renaissance in mass-based activity against racial apartheid in employment, public accommodations, housing, and electoral representation. Politically, "jobs" reemerged as the key discourse, and although this activism was cross-class in character, it emanated primarily from the interests of, and derived its leadership and base from, a resurgent historic bloc of working-class interests. Leading the NAACP was a member of the powerful Teamsters Local 688 who brought to the organization's ranks greater numbers of black trade unionists. But the charter fight, and the black communal struggles that immediately followed it, simultaneously heightened the class-based schisms within St. Louis's black leadership and constituencies, auguring the growing political salience of class among African Americans in the postwar period.[3]

Jim Crow in St. Louis circa *Brown*

Black-white race relations had become the nation's foremost moral issue by the mid-1950s. By September 1957, President Eisenhower would sign into law the first federal civil rights legislation since Reconstruction, creating the U.S. Commission on Civil Rights. Still, changes were barely perceptible in many areas of St. Louis's public life. The downtown YMCA accepted its first black full-fledged members in 1956, but to the chagrin of black parents and YMCA officials, the owners of the steamship *Admiral* barred African American youth from an all-day river excursion. Some Jim Crow policies presented halfhearted and idiosyncratic steps toward integration. Management at the Forest Park Highlands Amusement Park, for instance, only partially lowered its color bar by admitting black patrons to all rides and restaurants, yet restricting them from the park's dance pavilion and swimming pool. Several eating establishments had even backpedaled from earlier open-door policies, quietly reinstituting segregationist practices. Harry Pope, the owner of Pope's Cafeteria chain, a member of the Mayor's Council on Human Relations, and a self-styled "gradualist" and "moderate," resigned from the council under fire from the *Argus* and black activists who pointed out his two large cafeterias continued Jim Crow. As the *Argus*'s editors reminded members of the council, "moderation" and "gradualism" too often meant inaction.[4]

The *Argus*'s expose led to the appointment of Chester E. Stovall, the St.

Louis Urban League's director of industrial relations, as executive secretary of the Council on Human Relations—the first to integrate the council's previously all-white administrative staff. The council soon drafted a municipal fair employment practice bill covering all public works projects funded through municipal revenues or bond issue monies, and lent its weight to the ordinance's passage. The St. Louis Board of Aldermen passed the law unanimously that same year. St. Louis's seven-person FEPC was empowered to investigate and adjust complaints, but only through "education, persuasion and conciliation." In the event these strategies failed, the FEPC was to refer cases to the City Counselor's Office, where violators could receive, at most, a one-hundred-dollar fine. Most municipal and state FEPC laws, in fact, lacked enforcement powers and substantive budgets, and typically did not govern private job markets and trade unions. St. Louis's commission was no exception. "Any bill supposedly for our [black St. Louisans'] good that will pass in the Board of Aldermen as easily as that one did, will not accomplish much," former Eighteenth Ward alderman and ex-NAACP president Sidney Redmond chided in an *Argus* legal column. He noted that the same board had refused to enact a comprehensive civil rights ordinance since 1948.[5]

Redmond's skepticism about black progress could have applied to public housing as well. Since the opening of the Clinton-Peabody, Carr Square Village, and Cochran Gardens public housing projects, the federal government had sponsored the construction of the Pruitt-Igoe homes on the near north side, completed in 1955. Nationally recognized as one of the largest housing projects, it was a sprawling settlement of thirty-three eleven-story buildings. As had been the case with the city's other existing projects, the St. Louis Housing Authority imposed segregation. Policies reserved the thirteen Igoe apartments for white tenants, and the twenty Pruitt apartments for black occupants. St. Louis NAACP activist Frankie Muse Freeman, a young Howard University Law School graduate who in the late 1940s had been part of a campaign to equalize the curriculum of St. Louis's segregated technical high schools, was lead counsel in a lawsuit against the housing authority, and she argued the case with national NAACP attorney Constance Baker Motley. In a December 1955 ruling, a federal judge ordered the end of segregation in all St. Louis public housing. By 1957, the Housing Authority had instituted an open-occupancy policy and hired Freeman as its associate general counsel; she was also named associate general counsel of St. Louis's new Land Clearance for Redevelopment Authority (LCRA), which was combined with the housing authority and charged with overseeing local slum clearance and renewal. Yet with black working-class St. Louisans denied homeowner subsidies, a two-tiered federal housing policy already had developed: mortgage and loan assistance programs for white would-be homeowners, and public rentals for African Americans.[6]

In a continuing contradiction, however, housing discrimination solidified a racial voting bloc, strengthening the possibility of black electoral influence. Eighty thousand African Americans had migrated to St. Louis between 1950 and 1955; in 1956 approximately 180,000 black people lived in the city, well over 20 percent of the total number of residents. Although African Americans had helped the Democrats wrest control of the Board of Aldermen, Irish politicians maintained their dominance of the party, especially in the North St. Louis wards. They also maintained a tight grip on St. Louis's twelve citywide county offices, including sheriff, city treasurer, and collector of revenue. The demise of white-run "plantation wards," however, had been evident since 1952, when Frederick N. Weathers—a real estate broker, owner of the Marcella Cab Company, and a protégé of Jordan Chambers—beat Charles Reardon in the Eighteenth Ward to become the city's second black Democratic committeeman. Even the septuagenarian Henry Winfield Wheeler turned his movement bona fides into electoral success, winning a seat in the Missouri House of Representatives in 1956. By then, four African Americans sat on the Board of Aldermen: Archie Blaine from the Sixth Ward, T. H. Mayberry from the Fourth, DeWitte Lawson from the Nineteenth, and Wayman F. Smith Jr., who had defeated Redmond in the Eighteenth. But this was only roughly half the aldermanic power black politicians could possess, given that African Americans comprised a majority in seven of the city's wards.[7]

The NAACP, Local 688, and a Black Grassroots Revival

Like other African American communities around the nation, black St. Louisans had also followed the Montgomery boycott, and parallel struggles in Tallahassee, Florida, and other areas of Dixie. Thousands of black St. Louisans, in fact, contributed money to the *Argus*'s "$1s for Montgomery" fund-raising drive. The lynching of Emmett Till, a fourteen-year-old black Chicago youth visiting relatives in Money, Mississippi, also shocked and angered the city's black community into greater militancy. In his doctoral dissertation, published that same year, the local black educator Herman Dreer found that most black St. Louisans viewed their leadership as too moderate in their resistance to racial segregation. Occurring independently of the national NAACP, emerging postwar community struggles against U.S. apartheid spurred many local chapters of the association toward renewed grassroots action. Despite financial hardship and a continuing lack of internal cohesion, the St. Louis NAACP had shown signs of stabilizing.

For the first time in its history, the branch was able to employ a full-time executive secretary. Another group of activists chartered a branch of the NAACP Youth Council in 1955. Its key organizer, William L. Clay, was a young army veteran and graduate of St. Louis University raised in Mill Creek Valley. An insurance salesman and former bus driver, he had become active in Weathers's Eighteenth Ward organization.[8]

As the worst excesses of domestic anticommunism began to subside in the late 1950s, other energetic new local leaders reasserted a black working-class agenda of jobs and justice. Nominated for the NAACP presidency in November 1955, Ernest "Cab" Calloway, an official in Teamsters Local 688, ran against attorney George W. Draper, a former assistant circuit attorney and a plaintiff in the NAACP's 1950 federal suit to desegregate the Fairgrounds Pool. The forty-six-year-old Calloway, a self-described socialist, had embarked on a campaign calling for the association to adopt an aggressive community mobilization strategy. White antilabor forces hostile to the Teamsters' growing influence affixed themselves to Draper's candidacy, but the black press condemned the encroachment, and Draper himself publicly disavowed any connection with the backlash against his opponent. Calloway's radicalism was "acceptable," moreover, because as an A. Philip Randolph–style Cold War socialist, he had solid anticommunist credentials. He handily won the race, carrying his entire slate with him.[9]

The new president promptly began a reorganization of the branch. Given recent Supreme Court rulings, he argued, the NAACP's role at the local level had to be dramatically revised. "[T]he greatest tactical error that can be committed by the Negro community and liberal white elements," he warned during his inaugural speech, "is to permit these high court pronouncements to lull us into a false security." The Supreme Court, in short, had only given black freedom workers new tools with which to continue fighting. A trained labor intellectual and seasoned union organizer, Calloway had been a founder of the United Transport Service Employees, an experience that had given him a working relationship with Randolph. During a Chicago taxi drivers' strike, he had befriended Harold Gibbons, with whom he had much in common. The sons of trade-union-conscious miners, both had been propelled into activism through formative proletarian experiences, received training at workers' schools, honed political skills in the labor movement during the Depression, and shared a similar social democratic worldview. At Gibbons's invitation, Calloway had relocated to St. Louis to establish a special research department for Teamsters Local 688 and Joint Council 13.[10]

The new research director and his spouse, DeVerne Calloway, had quickly immersed themselves in progressive activism. Through Local 688's Democratic Rights Committee, Calloway had participated in drafting the proposal for desegregating the local public school system. By 1952, further, he had become the local NAACP vice president. The Calloways' Finney Avenue home, in the Ville area, became an intellectual hub where black and white students, trade unionists, and activists met to debate the state of the Black Freedom Movement. To be sure, Calloway's association with the Teamsters was central to the political weight he was able to exert in St. Louis's tight-knit black community, despite being a relative newcomer. Nationally, the Teamsters had become the most powerful organization in the AFL, touching virtually every industry dependent on transportation. With over ten thousand members, 20 percent of whom were African American, Local 688 was Missouri's single largest trade union. Teamsters Joint Council 13, representing sixteen organizations in the metropolitan area and four in eastern Missouri, encompassed forty thousand members, most of them in warehousing and distribution, food and beverage delivery, clerical work, and taxicab and chauffeur service. As president of Local 688, and trustee of Joint Council 13, Gibbons was the city's single most influential labor leader, and had used the city's strategic location as a warehousing and transport center to bargain for his members' high wages and generous pensions. Local 688 had built one of the nation's best union education programs, and under Calloway's direction developed a premier labor research department. The local had also gained international attention for its active rank-and-file participation and wide-ranging social democratic programs. A preeminent symbol of social unionism, Local 688 was, like most Teamsters locals, "unusually autonomous," which allowed it to function free from the interference of a proudly illiberal national leadership.[11]

As Gibbons's administrative assistant, advisor, and confidante, Calloway promoted a strategy skillfully merging issues of racial and economic justice in both the NAACP and the Teamsters. Gibbons was one of the few labor leaders during the 1950s to appoint African Americans and white women to leadership posts. The Teamsters' Labor Health Institute contained a nondiscriminatory passage in its by-laws, and 60 percent of the local's collective bargaining agreements contained antibias clauses. During Calloway's first year as NAACP president, the Teamsters reached an accord with the city's white-owned taxicab companies ending discriminatory hiring. In close succession, Local 688, the NAACP's Industry Committee, and the St. Louis Urban League jointly negotiated with the Coca-Cola Company to hire the firm's first black driver-salesmen. Mindful of the potential black St. Louisans possessed to transform the city's electoral politics, including the passage of a civil rights ordinance, the NAACP also launched an aggressive voter registration campaign that added nine thousand black voters to the precinct rolls in its first month.[12]

These efforts were tethered to the NAACP's relentless organization-building campaign. Exceeding even branch leaders' expectations, a recruit-ment drive attracted over fifty-five hundred new members, the highest peak in six years. Many of the recruits belonged to the social clubs and pro-fessional associations that had been the NAACP's traditional bulwark, and black women networks remained its most critical base. The Beauticians Volunteer Corps, entirely female in composition, was one major actor in this widening "Freedom Circle" of local members and supporters. Mar-garet Bush Wilson, a former Progressive Party worker, was among the most active and vocal members of the St. Louis NAACP—as were women like Kitty Hall, a leader of the St. Louis Housewives' League, and Ida Harris, who had become an influential figure in the Democratic politics of the Twenty-sixth Ward. DeVerne Calloway, likewise, was more than simply a dutiful spouse to the NAACP president. A former schoolteacher, she had worked with the Southern Tenant Farmers Union during the 1930s. Em-ployed with the American Red Cross in India during World War II, she had also led a protest against the agency's segregationist policies. In Chicago, moreover, she had participated in demonstrations sponsored by CORE. However, typical of many married black women of her generation, even those wed to left-leaning labor leaders, she minimized her public activism in deference to prevailing gendered ideals of female domesticity.[13]

Over 80 percent of the branch's new recruits, however, were first-time members with no previous ties to the NAACP. A large share of them hailed from organized labor. Urban League officials estimated that thir-teen of every twenty black St. Louis men belonged to trade unions. Few, in their estimation, possessed any deep loyalty to their locals, though they proved receptive to appeals to their combined racial-class identities. One hundred Consolidated Service car drivers, all members of Teamsters Local 688, joined the NAACP en masse, as did the employees of the Belva cos-metics manufacturing company. Ora Lee Malone, a union organizer in the city's garment industry, also became an anchor for the NAACP's organiz-ing projects, though the number of black female unionists was substan-tially less than that of men. Significantly, the NAACP branch's trade union division ranked second in the number of members it recruited, while the professional, business, and church divisions all languished. This had to do not only with Calloway's own orientation, but also with the efforts of other trade union organizers drawn to the NAACP, including former MOWM leader Theodore D. McNeal, who had become a BSCP interna-tional vice-president following E. J. Bradley's death in 1955; Fannie Pitts, another former MOWM activist who represented the Dining Car Employ-ees Local 354; and Herbert Taylor of the National Alliance of Postal Em-ployees. In this context, the St. Louis NAACP's overlapping voter regis-tration and recruitment drives mirrored general black racial concerns while echoing specific working-class sensibilities rooted in a desire to aid the "common Negro."[14]

"Massive Redevelopment": Civic Progress, Inc., and a New Proposed City Charter

The Gateway City, in Calloway's view, would be central in the coming national struggle for black citizenship, for it was an amalgam of northern and southern systems of racial control. While basically midwestern in its "civic psychology," he observed, it was by "tradition and social reflexes" a conservative southern community. Given St. Louis's particular history of interracial "civility," and its unique history as a way station between the North and South, backlash to the NAACP-led mass momentum did not take the form of southern "massive resistance." Rather, white opposition was manifested in a progrowth, urban planning and reform movement of "massive redevelopment" coordinated by local corporate leaders and City Hall. On a national scale, municipal reform, and "urban renewal" and "downtown revitalization," had become hegemonic in the thinking of many big-city Democratic mayors, central district businessmen, federal officials, and urban planners. In 1947, St. Louis's City Plan Commission had issued an influential report declaring the city virtually "unlivable" due to the blight covering half of its residential area, and calling for the destruction of properties surrounding the downtown business area. By the mid-1950s, St. Louis had suffered the loss of more than eleven thousand industrial jobs, due in large part to westward suburban growth and capital flight to the outlying St. Louis County. Under Missouri law, private investors were empowered to form redevelopment corporations to renew blighted sites, supported by generous tax breaks and the public authority of eminent domain. St. Louis's LCRA thus assumed oversight of land acquisition, relocation, demolition, and the sale of cleared inner-city properties to developers. The agency also cooperated with the St. Louis Housing Authority in the planning and construction of federally subsidized housing projects.[15]

Reflecting "a revival of corporate sway over public affairs" in the postwar period, many urban regimes also formed business-government alliances modeled after Pittsburgh's Allegheny Conference for Community Development. This strategy was apropos to St. Louis, where the city's history of private voluntarism and ward factionalism, and the relative weakness of the mayoralty, encouraged the formation of a bloc to oversee a broad citywide agenda. In 1952, St. Louis mayor Joseph M. Darst had assembled an informal body of chief executive officers from the largest St. Louis–based corporations to lend coherence to the central business district's resurrection. The result was the creation of Civic Progress, Incorporated. The consortium's initial eight appointed members included David Calhoun of the St. Louis Union Trust Company; Sidney R. Baer of the Stix, Baer & Fuller department store; and ex-mayor Aloys P. Kaufmann, who had since become president of the St. Louis Chamber of Commerce. Darst's handpicked Democratic successor, Raymond Tucker, consolidated and expanded this organized bloc. He appointed, among others, Edwin M. Clark, president of the Southwestern Bell Telephone Company; Morton May of the May Company, owner of the Famous-Barr department store; William A. McDonnell, head of the McDonnell Aircraft Company; and August A. Busch Jr., president of the Anheuser-Busch brewing empire, who became Civic Progress's first chairman. Tucker, a civil engineer and Washington University professor elected to the Mayor's Office in 1953, embodied the professionalism and technocratic expertise many viewed as the solution to the urban doldrums. Winning the Mayor's Office by a record fifty-thousand-vote margin, he had developed a reputation as a reformer free from ward-centered patronage.[16]

Despite this nimbus of reform, the Civic Progress leadership with which Tucker was allied constituted a policymaking fiefdom unto itself. There was, similarly, heavy overlap between Civic Progress participants, membership in the secretive Veiled Prophet Organization and exclusive Missouri Athletic Club, and seats on interlocking corporate and civic boards of directors. The extent to which Civic Progress functioned as a capitalist-led bloc directing the city's economic and physical development became clear over the next two years as the group crafted a far-reaching agenda for stabilizing municipal finances, promoting a series of bond issue development projects, and mobilizing popular approval through massive public education. Leaders organized and financed a successful campaign to adopt the city's first earnings tax, which voters adopted as an amendment to the St. Louis charter. In 1953, a citizens committee chaired by Clark had sponsored a $1.5 million bond issue proposal to clear a patch of the downtown slum area. As a centerpiece of this "Plaza Square" project, the private Urban Redevelopment Corporation—of which Clark was a member—planned to build seven middle-class apartment buildings, with the LCRA applying for federal matching funds. The NAACP had campaigned against the bond proposal, for neither the citizens committee nor developers would give assurances that black workers would share equally in the construction work, or that black residents would be able to rent the finished apartments. The predominantly black Fourth, Sixth, Eighteenth, and Nineteenth wards had voted against the proposal in a special election, though not in sufficient numbers to defeat it.[17]

In 1954, Congress had appropriated $5 million for the Jefferson National Expansion Memorial project, which was slowly continuing along the riverfront. That same year, a Citizens Bond Issue Campaign Committee had led an ambitious drive to pass twenty-three other proposals for civic improvement, including the construction of three highways, more playgrounds, and riverfront development. Civic Progress members Clark, Calhoun, Baer, McDonnell, and May all notably served as officers on the committee. Marshaling the support of several prominent churches and unions, the St. Louis League of Women Voters, civic boosters, and the press, St. Louis's capitalist patriarchs wrapped themselves in appeals to city spirit and public interest. Approving the bonds, committee brochures assured, would attract commerce and prevent further population loss. "The choice is simple," declared one widely distributed endorsement letter. "If you vote yes [on the bond proposals], you vote for a progressive and prosperous St. Louis. If you vote no, you vote for stagnation and decay." To energize the public around the bond measures, the coalition sponsored a lavish fifteen-mile parade with twenty-three floats, sixty-two cars, and several bands. In May 1955, St. Louis voters approved all of the propositions by a six-to-one margin, including a hefty $10 million for slum clearance. The entire bond issue package amounted to over $110 million, putting St. Louisans on the path to the largest public improvement program in the city's history.[18]

As the focus of slum clearance shifted to publicly underwritten commercial development, inner-city renewal was increasingly geared toward the infusion of private capital. At the same time, the potential for luring outside investors existed only to the extent that St. Louis's civic boosters could present a more "attractive" downtown. Although racially innocuous on its face, "massive redevelopment" concealed anxieties about black working-class slums overrunning the Central Corridor. Mill Creek Valley, located at the periphery of the central business district, would simply have to go. Indigenous white corporate, civic, and political leadership simultaneously contemplated an overhaul of St. Louis's governance structure, eliminating bases of resistance to their progrowth agenda—as well as bringing more centralization to a historically decentralized municipal government. As had long been the case, the mayor's role in budgetary affairs was constrained by the existence of a Board of Estimate and Apportionment, composed of the mayor, comptroller, and president of the Board of Aldermen. The Mayor's Office, moreover, lacked authority even over the city's police department, which was overseen by the governor-appointed Board of Police Commissioners. Ward bosses, who derived their power from the city's weak-mayor system, and who were typically more concerned with jobs, services, and neighborhood zoning laws than with larger issues of fiscal and development policy, were a chief source of opposition to urban renewal schemes. The black vote, gaining in potency, was regarded as another. Civic Progress, and the racial-class interests it embodied, resolved to deal with them both. The existing charter, groundbreaking perhaps for 1914, had become a fetter on efficient municipal government, prominent residents insisted. Thus, a campaign to draft a new city charter was born. Leading the civic and media support for revising document was the St. Louis Citizens Charter Committee, chaired by Boatmen's Bank executive (and Civic Progress member) Tom K. Smith.[19]

Many black St. Louisans generally favored urban redevelopment, with few disputing the need for more playgrounds, hospital care, and other social infrastructure that an expanding, and segregated, black working-class citizenry needed. Yet black discourses of civic improvement largely rejected demolition schemes, which severed communal ties and institutions, displaced marginally employed African Americans, and cast them to the mercies of a segregated housing market. In rejecting previous slum clearance and renewal bond proposals, they had demonstrated their preference for neighborhood revitalization, and their emphases on fair employment and open housing in reconstruction projects. Black voters had, moreover, rejected a previous charter revision in 1950 that had lacked broad civil rights measures. Chambers, representative of other black ward-level insiders, therefore regarded the renewed impetus toward a new charter as a stealthy move to "cut the Negro's throat," as he confided to David Grant. At Chambers's prodding, Grant filed for candidacy in a special May 1956 election for a City Charter Board of Freeholders, the body of local property owners constituted to draft the new charter. With Chambers's organization strongly behind him, Grant joined a slate of twelve other candidates, including another black man, school principal and Urban League official Colbert B. Broussard. Endorsed by the Citizens Charter Committee and Mayor Tucker, the entire slate won, with Chambers's precinct workers delivering impressive votes for Grant.[20]

Racial and class fissures emerged as soon as the freeholders began their public deliberations. Speaking for many black St. Louisans, the *Argus* editorialized that at a moment when black citizenship had become a matter of national prominence, any new charter should embrace civil rights. Other outspoken African Americans insisted on tougher enforcement of the antidiscrimination clause in the city's existing civil service code, as black workers had complained for decades about the faulty "merit system" that prevented them from getting high-ranking municipal jobs. In the meantime, a resolution to retain the existing mayor-council arrangement passed, and a freeholder majority adopted proposals to expand mayoral authority in budgetary and fiscal matters, as well as bring several city departments under the mayor's direct purview. The new formula for electing city legislators, however, became the freeholders' most explosive issue. Heretofore, St. Louisans had elected twenty-eight aldermen on a ward basis, and the mayor and aldermanic president citywide. At a series of public freeholder meetings, representatives speaking for prominent civic groups called for reducing the Board of Aldermen. Hostility to the idea came mainly from aldermen and ward organizations, the St. Louis Industrial Union Council, the Central Trades and Labor Union—and most vociferously, black leaders acutely aware that with the numbers of African Americans growing in various wards, black St. Louisans were poised to elect a larger share of representatives.[21]

During a February 1957 meeting, several prominent freeholders made a surprise motion to adopt a "7-7-1" plan cutting the number of wards by over half, and creating seven at-large aldermanic seats. The aldermanic president would continue to be elected citywide. The proposal carried against dissenting votes from Grant, Broussard, and white labor leaders William Webb and John McNally, each of whom represented constituencies with vested interests in a more robust aldermanic structure. Proponents framed the newly revived "7-7-1" measure as a protection against the evils of corrupt, ward-based politics, though Calloway publicly countered that the proposal was nothing more than "a studied attempt to amputate present and potential Negro representation." "The whole face of the city is going to be changed within the next five to ten years," he emphasized. "This is going to involve millions of dollars in investment, jobs and profits. The local and absentee bankers see this Negro political and legislative potential as a 'problem' of major significance in their future investment plans." Lacking protections against racial discrimination, and sundering black people from the strength of their numbers, the charter inscribed their disenfranchisement in the face of urban "progress." With fewer wards to represent, and at-large elections pitting them against larger white constituencies, grassroots black candidates would find themselves at a disadvantage to those with elite financial and political backing.[22]

Consistently outnumbered and outmaneuvered among the freeholders, Grant could attest to how supposedly representative civic bodies ensured white racial-class hegemony. When, in early May, the Board of Freeholders held its final meeting, he alone refused to sign the proposed new city charter. The final eighty-nine-page document adopted by the board was completely mute on civil rights, the major constitutional issue of the day. The formula to reduce the Board of Aldermen was deemed the charter's most dangerous feature by far, where black interests were concerned. The proposed charter had also given the Mayor's Office additional executive power, which many feared would fortify this shroud. Eight aldermen and a mayor, all elected citywide, would make total the political authority of local banking and business leaders.[23]

The War within the War: Division within the NAACP
and St. Louis's Black Leadership

Yet the charter proposal had to pass a public vote, scheduled for August 6. While many accepted its passage as fait accompli, the NAACP's grassroots contingent began to galvanize mass response. During a tense meeting in late June, the NAACP's executive council voted overwhelmingly to oppose the charter, and brought the matter before the general membership. Heated debate ensued when more than 150 NAACP members gathered at the Pine Street YMCA for the special meeting. Days before the summit, anonymous sources in the NAACP had given the media pledge cards printed by the association on behalf of a "Citizens Assembly" against the charter. Representatives from the NAACP Youth Council strongly criticized Calloway and his cabinet for the preemptory act of printing anticharter pledge cards in advance of a membership vote. Yet Grant drew a standing ovation when he denounced several unnamed "pandering Negroes" who "stooped to steal information from the NAACP office and take it downtown to the white people." Nor did Grant spare Broussard, an erstwhile ally on the freeholder board who had emerged as a staunch charter supporter. Targeting Broussard in his blistering remarks, he denounced him as "a school principal charged with our young, who would duck the issues and stick his head in the sand." An effort to table the vote, led by executive board member Joseph W. B. Clark, failed by a wide margin, and the NAACP membership voted 142–11 against the new charter.[24]

Nonetheless, several board members, including NAACP vice-president Frankie Muse Freeman, remained outspoken charter advocates. The black press, which had pledged to fight the very type of city charter now before the public, made an about-face and issued support. Howard B. Woods and Nannie Mitchell-Turner, the *Argus*'s executive director and publisher, respectively, were especially vocal in their defense. Echoing a common argument, they based their support on the fact that the existing Board of Aldermen, with four black members, had failed for years to pass a public accommodations bill. For them, this proved that "mere numbers from so called 'Negro wards' do not necessarily assure good legislation, but rather how many of the total aldermen will Negro voters select." Staffers at the *American*, the city's other black newspaper, reached similar conclusions in a lengthy editorial supporting the charter.[25]

Meanwhile, the public feud between Grant and Broussard precipitated a flurry of attacks. A scathing open letter, signed by Grant and widely distributed in the black public sphere, accused procharter black St. Louisans of "selling out the race for 30 pieces of silver." Implicit in this rhetoric was a connection between black corporate racial interests and an imagined working-class identity. This was juxtaposed to a black bourgeois elitism rooted in treacherous individualism, a slavish identification with whites, and personal advancement at the expense of the wage-laboring black majority. The polemic closely paralleled sociologist E. Franklin Frazier's blistering 1957 study, *Black Bourgeoisie,* which castigated black middle-class professionals for their alienation from the working-class majority, their unrequited desire for white recognition and acceptance, and their world of "make-believe" that masked self-loathing. Not to be outdone, black charter supporters retaliated by casting Grant, Calloway, Weathers, and Chambers as symbols of a decadent system of ward politics. They pointedly skewered Calloway for his Teamsters membership, taking advantage of the fact that organized labor, and particularly the Teamsters, were under intense federal scrutiny for racketeering and rumored links to organized crime. More than any individual, Detroit Teamsters leader Jimmy Hoffa—a close associate of Gibbons, and a rising star in the union hierarchy—had become the embodiment of the unscrupulous, mob-connected labor boss. Gibbons himself had been a target of a sweeping federal grand jury investigation more preoccupied with the union's collective bargaining strength than with uncovering illegal activity. Allegations of wrongdoing had all been dismissed, but a lingering pall of corruption contributed to a perception that Calloway—"a paid employee of the Teamsters Union," as the *Globe-Democrat* dutifully reminded readers—was turning the NAACP into a stalking horse for crooked ward politicians and depraved labor thugs seeking to preserve an outmoded city government.[26]

The dispute around the charter also signified a changing trajectory of black life at midcentury. Relationships among St. Louis's African American population had always been deep and multiple, particularly among its political leadership. But with class stratification growing—evident in the greater opportunity for political appointments, professional advancement, new blue-collar jobs, and inroads into organized labor—the community had become more complex. The escalating charter struggle revealed how sharply articulated these internal dynamics had become. At root, some segments of St. Louis's black civic leadership were more than comfortable with the idea of limiting grassroots participation in local politics. Reacting to circumstances in which whites judged African Americans according to the "lowest common black denominator," many black middle-class professionals historically had sought to both distance themselves from, and regulate the behavior of, black laboring classes. Many black political leaders clung to the belief that they and their white counterparts could build a class-based unity, and preserve racial peace, by jointly managing their respective "lower classes." Such a racial "peace," however, had usually mandated an unspoken black racial subordination. Nevertheless, to the extent they viewed white workers as Jim Crow's core constituency, this wing of black leadership perceived a collective racial interest in undercutting the power of the South St. Louis "Dixiecrats" who pandered to white working-class bigotry. In their place, black procharter advocates envisioned a Board of Aldermen peopled by mild-mannered, dispassionate white Democratic technocrats like Mayor Tucker, or civic-minded white Republican businessmen.[27]

Their faith in the goodwill of white patricians was consistent with the related presumption that they, as the "better class of Negroes," shouldered the responsibility for "uplifting" the rowdy black masses prone to vice and improvidence. As the ideological pillar of black middle-class consciousness, "racial uplift" in fact exhibited deep ambivalence toward the black majority. From this standpoint, a reduced Board of Aldermen cleared the way for a small number of "sober-minded" and well-connected black professionals to bargain for token seats. They could do so, further, without competition from baser elements within the African American community. Consequently, many black professionals, like their white counterparts, agreed with the principle that working-class people had no place in formal politics, except as it related to following the stewardship of the educated and "respectable."[28]

Yet it was a telling statement of class politics in the African American community that most registered black St. Louis voters stood firmly in opposition to the charter. Through community meetings—a strategy that historian Lance Hill describes as "a rudimentary form of working-class control over the black middle class"—anticharter organizers built mass support for its defeat, and checked the activities of their opponents. On August 6, the proposal failed in twenty-two of the city's twenty-eight wards, losing by a count of 106,855 to 71,146. The heaviest votes for the charter came from the Twenty-fifth and Twenty-eighth wards, both bastions of white wealth. In contrast, the Board of Aldermen, ward organizations, the Teamsters, the St. Louis Industrial Union Council, and the Central Trades and Labor Council, who all favored the existing twenty-eight-ward structure, were instrumental in its defeat. A decisive factor in the upset was the black electorate. In contrast to the 20 percent who normally came to the polls, some 60 percent of all registered African Americans turned out to oppose the charter by disproportionate margins. In the Eighteenth and Nineteenth wards, strongholds of Weathers and Chambers, the ratios of defeat were four to one and five to one, respectively.[29]

"Negroes Must Eat Too!": The NAACP Job
Opportunities Council

On the heels of this victory, the St. Louis NAACP began fashioning a comprehensive black employment strategy, which Calloway had forecast upon first assuming the presidency. Margaret Bush Wilson, who had been prominent among the anticharter forces as chair of the NAACP's legislative committee, envisioned an organization semiautonomous from the association that would spearhead an aggressive mass jobs campaign. In August 1957, she was named secretary of the newly formed Job Opportunities Council (JOC), with McNeal selected as chairman. For the council's steering committee, the NAACP drafted, among others, Reverend John J. Hicks, pastor of the Union Memorial Methodist Church; NAACP Youth Council leader William Clay; and St. Louis CORE president Charles Oldham. Other civic and church groups were invited to send representatives to the council and have a voice in shaping its program.[30]

With urban redevelopment plans in the works, the JOC's goals were targeted, foremost, to documenting violations of presidential decrees and municipal laws associated with fair employment on public contracts. In 1953, the Eisenhower White House had ordered nondiscriminatory hiring provisions by private businesses receiving government contracts, and established a Committee on Contract Compliance to oversee the mandate. Echoing the defunct NNLC, JOC leaders announced they would lobby the committee to make inquiry into violations committed by local firms with federal contracts. They promised to do the same regarding breaches of the city's Fair Employment Practice law governing businesses with municipal contracts. Addressing the predictable absence of black labor in the skilled construction trades, JOC members also pledged themselves to "investigate the extent of exclusion of Negroes within the Apprenticeship Training Program sponsored by the U.S. Dept. of Labor in co-operation with the Board of Education, industry and unions." The fourth plank in the JOC's platform spoke to the employment discrimination still practiced by local utilities with publicly granted monopolies. Points 5 and 6 recognized the acute need for more and better jobs for black residents. At 15 percent, the local black unemployment rate had been nearly three times that for whites in 1954. The JOC called for "greater employment of the Negro in the sales, administrative and clerical fields," as well as the removal of "all discriminatory bars against Negroes practiced by many unions in the St. Louis area." These, by far, were the council's most pressing tasks. "The tremendous income gap between Negro and white workers in the St. Louis area constitute the foremost social and economic problem of our community," Calloway insisted at an early JOC meeting held at the Pine Street YMCA. "When figures indicate an income gap of more than $1,000 a year and Negro income represents 56 percent of white income the total community certainly faces a social and economic problem of major proportions."[31]

Activists began with expanding black employment opportunities in retail and mass consumer industries. Beginning with this approach could, in accordance with the local NAACP's overall mass-action strategy, put the most numbers of community residents into motion. To do this, the JOC spoke to a broad black worker identity, encompassing clerks and cashiers equally with butchers, bakers, and construction tradesmen, for the reality was that many such "white-collar" jobs, especially those occupied by women, were working-class in their nonsupervisory, routinized character. Calloway was also keenly aware that the JOC's broad-based, semi-independent character, and its direct action orientation, placed it at odds with the more centralized, legalistic activity favored at the NAACP's New York headquarters. "[P]erhaps some of our methods and techniques will be frowned upon by our national leaders," he stated forthrightly at the JOC's inaugural meeting, "but we must move in a direction that makes sense to us in a mass community approach to a most difficult problem. If we are going to carry the community with us in this effort we must provide the vehicles for mass participation."[32]

Council leaders chose three major supermarket chains—A&P, Kroger, and National Tea—as their first action project. Food constituted the largest single expense in black household budgets, and the three firms together operated some eighteen grocery stores in and around black St. Louis neighborhoods. Their black workers, however, were primarily porters and stock clerks. Of the three stores, the A&P was widely regarded as the worst offender; aside from janitors, the store employed only four full-time black workers, and less than ten part-timers. The chain had no black typists, file clerks, butchers, or administrative personnel. In late November 1957, JOC organizers began a "customer concern" educational campaign. Circulating among shoppers, volunteers distributed cards reading, "We want more than token employment of Negroes in your business—A Regular Customer," which they encouraged shoppers to deliver in silent protest to store managers. While executives at Kroger and National Tea soon expressed interest in coming to terms with the JOC, three weeks of wrangling failed to bring local A&P managers to the negotiating table. Reminiscent of the Colored Clerks Circle during the early 1930s, JOC leaders announced plans of a boycott. Wilson published a short pamphlet titled "Negroes Must Eat Too! (and Not Just Stew)," that bore directly to the heart of the conflict. "[T]he 'consumer dollars' of Negroes flowing into A & P cash registers are far from 'token dollars,'" the document argued. "WHY THEN ARE NEGROES GIVEN ONLY TOKEN EMPLOYMENT???" Wilson concluded:

"We must walk in protest, and every Negro who wants a 'fair share' of jobs—not 'token employment' must protest too by refusing to cross our 'freedom lines.'"[33]

Focusing on an A&P store on Easton Avenue in the Ville, Wilson, Clay, and other JOC activists, many of them belonging to the NAACP Youth Council, walked an around-the-clock picket at the site. Black shoppers, urged by the young protesters to give their business to other competing chain grocers, responded in droves. Within days, "this A&P supermarket was completely free of customers," Calloway later reminisced. Ten days into the boycott, a vice president from the supermarket chain's Chicago office arranged a series of meetings with JOC officials, resulting in a multifaceted agreement to employ more black clerks in the stores serving their communities, hire black workers above custodial positions at the company warehouse and bakery, and integrate clerical jobs. In coordination with the butchers union, the supermarket chain also agreed to open its meat-cutters apprenticeship program to black residents. The JOC additionally negotiated a review program to monitor progress toward these goals.[34]

The JOC-CORE–NAACP Youth Council Alliance

The A&P campaign provided the basis for similar equal job opportunity "treaties" with National Tea, Kroger, and the Laclede Gas Company the following year. While Oldham sat on the JOC steering committee, his organization, St. Louis CORE, struggled for direction. By 1955, he and his new spouse, Marian O'Fallon, were barely keeping the chapter afloat; notwithstanding the fact he became CORE's national chairman in 1956, the local branch barely registered a pulse by the spring of 1957. Key members, such as Bernice Fisher and Joseph Ames, had left, and even at its most active the organization had not commanded a mass base. Beyond a handful of African American members, and despite founder Irv Dagen's regular column in the *Argus*, the group had few black community ties.[35]

Among other border-city and northern-based chapters, fair employment was emerging as a critical CORE battlefront. Oldham's involvement in the JOC therefore presented an opportunity to refocus the St. Louis branch programmatically. In the summer of 1958, Marian Oldham (née O'Fallon) led CORE in negotiations for black sales and clerical workers at the Famous-Barr department store, which had taken a step toward integration by opening a basement lunch counter to African Americans. Like the Stix department store, Famous-Barr was considered a "softer" target than other establishments holding fast to Jim Crow. Activists were surprised, then, when Famous-Barr management curtly ended the talks. The capriciousness of the act confronted the activists with their own frailty, which sharply contrasted with the NAACP's newfound vigor. (From twenty-seven hundred members in 1955, St. Louis's NAACP membership had grown to eighty-six hundred in 1958, the highest ever in the branch's history, while life memberships increased from four to nearly two hundred.) CORE representatives approached the JOC about a formal collaboration, and the NAACP, eager for community-wide participation in its jobs opportunity program, agreed. The two organizations were soon announcing preparations for a mass demonstration against Famous-Barr.[36]

Concerned with the possibility of an embarrassing protest campaign that might tarnish its image and cripple sales, department store officials attempted to foster another black political split. While black leadership generally favored the end of Jim Crow employment, certain sectors—black school administrators, and some prominent ministers—tended to be more strategically and tactically conservative than those whose status and welfare did not depend directly on white decisions. Even many top black businesspeople, given their transactions with white capitalists, eschewed the strategies and tactics of protest. To be sure, a number of African Americans had made comfortable lives for themselves managing segregated institutions and currying the favor of powerful white patrons. The St. Louis NAACP's self-consciously grassroots strategy had only heightened their sense of alarm, convincing them that the locus of black leadership needed to return to "more responsible" representatives.[37]

Encouraged by downtown merchants, or at their own initiative, vocal black critics condemned the NAACP branch as irresponsible for planning the Famous-Barr picket line, since no team of negotiators had first sought a conference with company executives. Others questioned whether the JOC had even received the proper authorization from the NAACP membership to mount the protest. The Associated Retailers' Association, representing decision-makers from the leading department stores, held a series of meetings with black leaders of their choosing, then shrewdly announced a new policy to integrate the stores' tea rooms. Many well-heeled black professionals may have been placated by the move. Months earlier, CORE also might have considered this a victory. With the triumph over the city charter, however, and with a string of modest victories against job discrimination, the context of struggle had changed. As JOC and CORE organizers reminded their adversaries, job upgrades were now the central issue. A motorcade by the NAACP Youth Council, JOC, and CORE demonstrated the coalition's determination not to let downtown retailers pacify them with last-minute symbolism. The mobilization also sent Famous-Barr officers a clear message about the volunteers' capacity to carry out a campaign of mass picketing, for the NAACP Youth Council alone numbered between three hundred and four hundred people. But with St. Louis's black political and civic activists divided on whether to take to the streets, JOC leaders privately questioned whether they could sustain a prolonged boycott. With the wounds still raw from the charter fight, few wanted to risk the demoralization that another major schism might cause.[38]

NAACP and CORE activists were handed an unexpected chance to retreat when Famous-Barr envoys sent word that management was willing to enter talks. The would-be protesters weighed the offer. At a mass meeting at the Lane Tabernacle Christian Methodist Episcopal Church, one day before the scheduled August 18 demonstration, they announced an immediate suspension of the picket line to accept Famous-Barr's invitation to the bargaining table. In a statement prepared for the church meeting, Calloway dismissed the notion that the pro-picket forces had been outflanked by opponents in the black community, though he did admit that the NAACP-CORE allies had not consolidated the level of communal support needed for an offensive against the department stores. However, he stopped short of conceding that the threat of demonstrations against Famous-Barr was ill conceived. "It has been my experience that when you talk to business men in terms that they can understand and quickly grasp, you make an immediate impression and you are able to get through and communicate with them," the NAACP president maintained. "This means that there is very poor communication when you approach business men and firms from the vantage point of sociology, anthropology, political science or Christian morality and ethics. On the other hand if you approach them in terms of economics—wage rates, hours of work, markets, purchasing power, consumer expenditures and the price of pork chops they become all ears and the interest heightens."[39]

The talks became stalemated when Famous-Barr representatives asserted that white personnel would not accept black employees in sales and clerical positions—an old line of argument that obscured white employers' own diffidence. JOC negotiators discovered an unexpected way out of the impasse. It was, ironically, on the basis of the effects of automation on black employment. "At the time," Calloway later described, "Famous-Barr was installing mechanical elevators and eliminating elevator operators," who mainly had been black women. Activists suggested training the women for sales jobs, since they were already in the company's employ, and in many cases had had prior interaction with white employees and patrons. Typical of a liberal integrationist approach, this solution sought to mollify white managers and workers by legitimating their angst—in this case, an aversion to "strange" black workers joining them on the sales floor. The strategy worked, however, and Famous-Barr accepted the proposal for hiring its first black salespersons.[40]

The JOC-CORE–NAACP Youth Council alliance forged another breakthrough when, following a yearlong campaign of agitation, executives at the Taystee Bread Company agreed to hire black delivery truck drivers and other workers in more better-paying classifications. Just as its leaders had hoped, St. Louis CORE experienced dramatic recovery through this joint work. One outcome was the close relationship that blossomed between CORE and the much larger NAACP Youth Council. During the Famous-Barr controversy, CORE had halted the march to the picket line far more reluctantly than the NAACP, for its earlier demonstrations against segregated accommodations had never depended on mass support. This mode of protest appealed to NAACP Youth Council leaders like Clay, who tended toward a greater militancy than their elders. The affiliate had asserted its independence from the NAACP branch in 1957, when Youth Council leaders openly criticized Calloway's administration for printing anticharter pledge cards without a membership vote. This underscored their general opposition to the NAACP's top-down organizational structure, which contrasted sharply with CORE's comparatively more democratic style.[41]

Independent of the senior NAACP branch, Youth Council members began, in August 1960, a picket of the Scruggs department store, whose management had become resistant to hiring black clerical and sales workers. NAACP youth had also joined CORE in another series of loosely coordinated protest actions against segregated public accommodations. That same month, police arrested Clay and Raymond Howard, a law student at St. Louis University, during a sit-in demonstration at a Howard Johnson restaurant. Mobilized by schoolteacher and CORE leader Norman Seay, students from Vashon and Sumner high schools picketed the diner, precipitating more than fifty other arrests. The protests widened the gulf between the Youth Council and the parent NAACP, whose leadership chastised the young activists for moving too spontaneously and tried vainly to bring them under tighter rein. It was perhaps ironic that Calloway, a man criticized for being too aggressive himself, had little patience for demonstrators who acted, in his view, on a "purely agitational, piece-meal, highly emotional and isolated basis." The real concern was that the parent NAACP body exercised no direct control over its unpredictable youth wing.[42]

As the conflict mounted, Clay and other members left the NAACP's youth wing, sparking a mass defection to CORE that further energized the latter's rank and file. For the first time in its relatively brief history, the organization had the makings of a significant black base. In their classic study of CORE, historians August Meier and Elliott Rudwick argue that the St. Louis committee reemerged as the nation's most important chapter, and certainly its most vital branch among the border state cities. Few other branches were having as much of an impact on CORE's national leadership. Oldham remained in the position of national chairman, while Henry Hodge, a black St. Louis social worker, had become national vice chairman in 1959. Marvin Rich, another founding member of St. Louis CORE, had also been hired to the post of community relations director that same year. Few other chapters, too, worked as diligently around the issue of black employment opportunity.[43]

The "Negro Proclamation"

Although hit hard by the exodus of much of its youth wing, the St. Louis NAACP continued its growth, in 1959 becoming the nation's sixth largest branch—larger than Philadelphia, Washington, D.C., Los Angeles, and Pittsburgh. The branch's profile had received a boost in 1958 when two of its prominent members, Grant and Freeman, were appointed charter members of Missouri's new Advisory Committee of the U.S. Civil Rights Commission. Consistent with the federal commission's aims, the exercise of the franchise loomed largest among civil rights priorities. To be sure, the local NAACP's voter registration campaign, its opposition to the city charter, and its subsequent demands for fair employment, was fastened to the goal of expanding formal black political representation locally and statewide. Although a small stratum of the black middle class stood to gain directly, the promise of black elected officialdom also carried with it the prospects for better public sector work and services for black laborers. Notwithstanding the dispersed nature of power among the city's Democratic ward fiefdoms, a coterie of Irish political bosses continued to wield power over the fifteen-ward area of North St. Louis. Foremost among them were John J. Dwyer, city treasurer and Democratic committeeman of the Fourth Ward, who controlled hundreds of patronage jobs. A strong supporter of Mayor Tucker, Dwyer had been chairman of the St. Louis Democratic Central Committee since the early 1940s. Equally entrenched was Michael Kinney, a state senator since 1913. Closely connected to the city's downtown business patriarchs, he also held the post of Sixth Ward Democratic committeeman. A third major center of power belonged to state senator Edward "Jelly Roll" Hogan, who had been in office since 1944.[44]

The advance of urban renewal increasingly impinged on black voting strength in the Sixth Ward, but with the black population shifting steadily north from Delmar to Natural Bridge, a new racial voting bloc was developing. Alongside the black citizens' campaign to end overcrowded schools in the early 1950s, African Americans had made repeated attempts to win seats on the board of education. Two black men—Edward Grant and Walter Younge—had been appointed to fill unexpired vacancies on the school board, but no black candidate had as yet won a citywide election to a full six-year term. With black youth forming 45 percent of the total public school enrollment, many parents and teachers were adamant that African Americans had a right to more than token appointments to fill white vacancies. After Younge's second attempt to win a slot failed in 1957, McNeal and Weathers began searching for another promising black candidate to support, which snowballed into talks with other civic activists.[45]

In early 1959, organizers approached John J. Hicks, pastor of the Union Memorial Methodist Church, chairman of the NAACP's Education Committee, and a JOC steering committee member. He agreed to run, and the committee backing him drafted Calloway as campaign director. Having served, as of December 1958, three consecutive terms as NAACP president, he had decided not to seek a fourth, and had supported as his successor Margaret Bush Wilson, who became the first woman to assume the branch's leadership. Under Calloway's direction, meanwhile, activists revived the Committee For a Representative School Board, which had sponsored Younge in 1955. Ward-level citizens assemblies, vital to defeating the 1957 charter proposal, were also reactivated and given the "spade work" of building black grassroots support for Hicks. Weathers and Chambers, further, used their influence to broker behind-the-scenes support from several white Democratic leaders. Twelve ward organizations, as well as the Urban League Federated Block Units, the AFL-CIO's public education committee, and the liberal *Post-Dispatch*, lent endorsements. Hicks captured thirteen of the twenty-eight wards, winning a school board seat (James Hurt Jr., another popularly supported black candidate, won a seat on the board in 1961).[46]

The popular mobilization of black working-class votes propelled two other African Americans into elected office that day—Lawrence Woodson, who won the aldermanic race in the Twentieth Ward, and William Clay, who became alderman of the Twenty-sixth. Aldermen Mayberry, Blaine, Smith, and Lawson all retained their seats, raising the total number of black aldermen to six. Suddenly, St. Louis led the nation in the percentage of African American representatives elected to ward-based municipal government—more than Chicago, Cleveland, and Philadelphia. Community efforts to unseat white North St. Louis politicians reached a new peak in 1960, a national election year. From fifty-six thousand black registered voters in 1955, the number had leapt to approximately one hundred thousand. This was over 70 percent of the community's voting age populace, and its highest ever. Multiple factors had converged in favor of this electoral upsurge. The municipal charter fight, the subsequent school board and aldermanic races, and a larger, stronger NAACP had stimulated, and simultaneously reflected, the high level of political consciousness among black St. Louisans. Further, next to Detroit, St. Louis had experienced the largest black population increase (40 percent) of any major city since the 1950 U.S. census. Years earlier, the Missouri Supreme Court had ordered the St. Louis Election Board to redistrict the city's state senatorial districts, making them more compact and uniform in size. The new Seventh Senatorial District, encompassing the Fourth, Eighteenth, Twentieth and Twenty-second wards, contained a black majority. A new Fifth Senatorial District, also, enveloped the Third, Fifth, Sixth and Nineteenth wards, another concentration of black residence. The remapping had created, for the first time, the possibility of electing black officials to the thirty-four-member Missouri Senate.[47]

"Jelly Roll" Hogan, nonetheless, had won the Seventh Senatorial race in 1956. Aside from the support he enjoyed from the Steamfitters union, six black candidates—including *American* publisher Nathaniel Sweets—had split the black vote in the Democratic primary, raising speculation that some had been paid to run. Now, four years later, the state senator's reelection loomed, and activists were prepared to put up a more determined fight. In a virtual replay of the Hicks school board campaign, Weathers, Grant, Alderman Smith, and Calloway convinced McNeal to challenge Hogan, with Calloway again serving as campaign director. Leaders of the Dining Car Employees, and representatives from other trade unions and civic institutions, immediately joined the campaign. Weathers's political patron, Democratic Party chief John Dwyer, also lent McNeal's candidacy his considerable support. McNeal, further, proved uniquely suited to rallying a black working-class base. The campaign played on the strength of his labor and civil rights activism, and his ongoing leadership in the BSCP. Popular among the rank-and-file porters he directed, McNeal also commanded respect through his close friendship with Randolph, who even appeared at a community fund-raiser. A largely female Volunteer Telephone Corps, whose members had worked around the clock for Hicks, mobilized again, this time to oust Hogan.[48]

The August Democratic primary served notice that the era of Irish political control in St. Louis was at an end. McNeal took 90 percent of the vote, defeating Hogan by a count of 12,660 to 2,110. The middle-aged MOWM veteran also swept the November general election by a five-to-one landslide, besting his Republican opponent by a vote of 33,571 to 6,550. In another upset victory, former Tuskegee airman Hugh White beat John Lavin in a contest for the Sixteenth State Legislative District. Similarly, Leroy Tyus, a black state representative, and Seay, of CORE, both won seats as ward committeemen of the Twentieth and Twenty-sixth wards, respectively—replacing white "absentee" politicians Pat Lavin and Martin Tozer. Paradoxically, as they ushered Irish politicos out of local and state offices, black St. Louisans voted overwhelmingly for an Irish Catholic Democrat, John F. Kennedy, in the presidential race. In fact, it was only because he received 83 percent of the city's black votes that Kennedy carried Missouri by nine thousand ballots.[49]

Like the fight around the city charter and Famous-Barr, the expansion of black electoral politics had also brought new intraracial challenges. Since Clay's election as Twenty-sixth Ward alderman in 1959, the goodwill and support he had enjoyed from established black political patrons had evaporated amid complaints about his ego and personal opportunism. Clay had begun building his Twenty-Sixth Ward Democratic Voters Organization as an alternative black political base to Ida Harris' Twenty-Sixth Ward Independent Democratic Organization. Key former campaign workers, including DeVerne Calloway, had left Clay's operation, complaining of his "immaturity," "lying and double-dealing." It seemed apparent to others, too, that he had manipulated his connections to CORE to further his own ambitions. Exuding youth and charisma, the alderman had also begun a campaign to supplant Chambers, as well as Weathers, Grant, and Calloway. Taking up familiar recriminations made during the charter fight, Clay portrayed his political elders as emblems of a dying mode of patronage politics, more concerned with spoils than with representing black communal interests. Neither Chambers nor Weathers, he chastised, had ever publicly supported or even expressed a position on the civil rights legislation that the Board of Aldermen had continually refused to pass. He likewise scored Calloway for the racial discrimination the Teamsters maintained in the chain grocery stores, particularly in the milk, bread, beer, and soda delivery jobs the union controlled. Reiterating the accusation that Calloway was using the St. Louis NAACP to build a Teamsters monopoly on the black community's growing electoral power, Clay exploited the union's growing disrepute in national politics. Following Hoffa's election as the Teamsters international's general president in September 1957, Gibbons had become his executive assistant, an international vice-president, and president of Teamsters Joint Council 13. Widely considered Hoffa's heir-apparent, Gibbons had been the subject of a U.S. Senate probe focusing on Hoffa and former general president Dave Beck. The Teamsters' subsequent expulsion from the AFL-CIO in December 1957 had further tarnished the union's image.[50]

To the extent that his denunciation of Calloway's Teamsters affiliation played to perceptions of organized labor as crime-ridden, Clay implicated himself as well. Indeed, he had become politically allied with Larry Callanan and John Lawler of the Steamfitters Union Local 562, who also had reputed ties to the underworld. For Clay, the Steamfitters' massive cash reserves to finance electoral campaigns, coupled with the city's growing black population, was a heady combination well worth any guilt by association. The fact that the Steamfitters had a formidable presence among organized labor also made them attractive to an aspiring young politician seeking an alternative to the Teamsters as a union base. But when, in the spring of 1960, Clay had joined the crowded primary race for St. Louis sheriff against incumbent Martin Tozer, the white Democratic committeeman of the Twenty-sixth Ward, his rivals had treated it as evidence that he had been seduced by a coalition of white South St. Louis "Dixiecrats" and racist union leaders seeking control of key citywide law enforcement posts and patronage jobs. Clay had abandoned the campaign, though he blamed the Teamsters, and the Chambers and Weathers factions, for pressuring his supporters to withdraw.[51]

Clay had faced equal opprobrium when he advanced Seay and Evelyn Davis as the Twenty-sixth Ward Democratic committeeman and committeewoman against Austin Wright, a liquor salesman, and Ida Harris, both supported by Chambers. Raymond Howard, a Clay ally, had also challenged Chambers for the Nineteenth Ward committeeman's seat. Clay had scoffed at the suggestion he was trying to build a political dynasty. "This is just a manner of covering up the program that Austin, Weathers, Calloway and Pop Chambers are engaged in," he had countered. Coming from those with close connections to Chambers, an entrenched kingmaker known for political ruthlessness, criticisms of Clay for his political ambitions were, at a fundamental level, disingenuous. It was a telling statement of St. Louis's sharpening black class politics, however, that Seay's supporters were mainly young schoolteachers, attorneys, and other professionals like Marian and Charles Oldham, many of them affiliated with CORE. Clay's support for Seay, moreover, had also hinged on the latter's greater "educational qualifications"—for which critics had rebuked him for "establish[ing] class consciousness in the Negro community by insisting that Seay is an educated 'high-type' individual," and that his opponents were "low-type."[52]

Clearly, a new stratum of college-educated black professional politicians was emerging to challenge the older generation of grassroots ward bosses for ownership in the new field of public offices—at the city, "county," and state levels—achieved by black freedom struggle. With the black public engaged in a broad social movement, both factions tied their fortunes to championing the interests of an African American working-class majority for jobs, political rights, and increased social wages. Following the 1960 elections, campaigners in both factions had to have taken stock of what African Americans had achieved over a brief span of years. Black people were almost 30 percent of the St. Louis citizenry, yet accounted for 40 percent of the Democratic vote. From Calloway's perspective, formal political power had become a realistic means of addressing the deep racial inequities in employment, housing, and education. This outlook was compatible with the basic tenets of U.S. liberalism influential among civil rights activists, but it was also consistent with Calloway's own radical social democratic vision, which posited that an egalitarian society could be achieved through far-reaching electoral and bureaucratic means. To position themselves in office, he suggested, African Americans would need more than just their numbers; rather, they would have to marshal critical mass behind a pragmatic, unifying set of minimum goals. Both the white media and black press had heavily endorsed the 1957 charter, proving their subservience to the boardrooms of Civic Progress. Savvy to the uses of the press in crafting agendas and building constituencies, Calloway began assembling staff and materials for a newspaper.[53]

In December 1960, the Calloways launched the activist-oriented *Citizen-Crusader* (reorganized the following year as the *New Citizen*), and recruited Wilson, McNeal, and Oldham, among others, as editorial consultants. The newspaper covered not only issues pertaining to black politics and labor, but also sports and entertainment—that is, it spoke to the whole of the experiences and interests of a black working-class reading public. Early in its publication, the editorial staff also put forth a "St. Louis Negro Proclamation," envisaged as a modest ten-point guide to action in electoral politics. The manifesto called on black grassroots freedom workers to organize toward achieving, among other objectives, the appointment of African Americans to municipal commissions and at least one top cabinet-level post in the Mayor's Office. Other planks prioritized the election of another black school board member, passage of a tougher Fair Employment Practice ordinance by the Board of Aldermen, and preparations for the eventual election of a black U.S. congressional representative from St. Louis.[54]

The Breakthrough in Public Accommodations

Passage of a strong civil rights law also ranked high on the proclamation's list of priorities. Beginning in 1953, St. Louis's public accommodations bill had come before the Board of Aldermen every year, only to be thwarted. A bill drafted by members of the Council on Human Relations had made it to a floor vote in 1956, but opponents had defeated it by a count of sixteen to ten. Yet the fact that the measure had been discharged from the legislative committee, where it had so often died, indicated mounting civic pressure. Civil rights measures failed by even slimmer margins between 1957 and 1959, again suggesting heightened support, particularly following other NAACP-CORE successes. By 1960, moreover, a new configuration of power had taken shape on the Board of Aldermen. Clay and Woodson had both campaigned on strong civil rights platforms. Aside from the presence of six black members, several white aldermen new to the board had also run in support of a public accommodations ordinance. Despite the prospects these developments raised, antagonists had killed the civil rights bill yet again, this time by a seventeen-to-eleven vote.[55]

As always, the main thrust of racial reform emanated neither from the Mayor's Office nor city legislators, but rather from black freedom workers. A promising new front in the "heroic" civil rights struggle had opened in February 1960, when four students from North Carolina A&T College staged a sit-in at a Woolworth's lunch counter in Greensboro. This was hardly novel as a form of protest. The Citizens Civil Rights Committee and CORE had helped pioneer the tactic in St. Louis during the 1940s. In February 1959, moreover, four members of Washington University's student NAACP chapter, legally represented by Charles Oldham, had been arrested during a sit-in at a segregated restaurant near the campus. The 1960 Greensboro sit-in, however, sparked a cluster of student-led protests that quickly enveloped cities throughout the South. Southern CORE affiliates helped plan local sit-ins, while St. Louis members picketed two Woolworth's stores in solidarity. Heretofore, Tucker's record as a black civil rights advocate had been mixed, but in their renewed assault on St. Louis's Jim Crow eating accommodations, demonstrators began to receive the tacit support of the Mayor's Office. Perhaps weighing the prospects for a coming reelection bid, Tucker privately ordered police to cease their arrests of protesters. By August 1960, thus, the Missouri Restaurant Owners Association was stuck between relentless picketing and inaction by authorities. Once determined foes of desegregation, representatives from the association quietly began working on a voluntary program of integration.[56]

In the hotly contested mayoral election of spring 1961, Tucker barely won a second term, though the black electorate voted for him at a higher percent than previously. Addressing a lingering complaint from black St. Louis leaders, Tucker called for strengthening the city's FEPC ordinance to include private employers. In the same statement, he joined the list of civic representatives urging passage of a public accommodations ordinance. The mayor's attitudes toward black civil rights, swayed by the initiatives of movement activists, may have evolved since the early 1950s. Or perhaps the growth of a local movement, rooted in tactics of mass direct action, had left him little choice but to accede to certain core demands. In either event, St. Louis's black freedom community had gained an important new ally. Given the earlier CORE campaigns, and the recent pact with the Missouri Restaurant Owners Association, many downtown and midtown restaurants already had desegregated. Consequently, when the Mayor's Council on Human Relations sponsored another public accommodations bill that year, CORE and the NAACP Youth Council already had laid the groundwork for its success. As the African American populace had grown, many white politicians, particularly those with citywide aspirations, were also beginning to understand that continued antagonism to basic black civil rights had become a liability. With fewer political costs to pay, St. Louis aldermen finally passed a civil rights ordinance on May 19, 1961 by a vote of twenty to four. The new law prohibited racial and religious discrimination in all places offering food, shelter, recreation, amusement, and other services to the general public. It also established an Anti-Discrimination Division on the Council of Human Relations, empowered to investigate complaints, issue cease and desist orders, and refer cases to the City Counselor's Office for legal action.[57]

Mayor Tucker again won praise when, in September, he named as director of welfare Chester Stovall, executive secretary of the Council on Human Relations. Stovall, who had helped move the Council of Human Relations beyond a standpat policy of simply "encouraging" better race relations, was the first black St. Louisan appointed to a high-level city cabinet position. Six months since the *New Citizen* had issued the "Negro Proclamation," then, black activists and white liberals had brought several of its planks into being. Taking into account the whole of recent events, Calloway mused optimistically that Stovall's appointment, recent additions to the Board of Aldermen and board of education, passage of a local civil rights act, and the election of McNeal to the Missouri Senate, constituted the beginning of a genuine civic partnership between black St. Louisans and the liberal Tucker administration rooted in mutual respect, rather than racial paternalism and empty "civility." With his gaze fixed on automation and industrial stagnancy, which threatened to aggravate black unemployment, Calloway argued that such racial rapprochement would be necessary to face a range of municipal issues looming before the urban body politic.[58]

In the final analysis, the St. Louis charter fight embodied the resurgence of a black workers' political bloc, one that initiated a "heroic" civil rights struggle for full employment, black electoral power, public accommodations, respect, and self-determination. Its preeminently working-class nature was evident in activists' overall agenda (jobs, representation, and justice), targeted constituency (the black laboring majority), and strategy (mass-directed community mobilization). The class character of this postwar Black Freedom Movement was also apparent in its leadership, whose central actors included Ernest Calloway, Theodore McNeal, and other labor and grassroots organizers. Black Democratic ward leaders like Jordan

Chambers could also be described in this vein, for their power ultimately rested on catering to an overwhelmingly working-class electorate. If anything, St. Louis's early "heroic" civil rights battles were rooted in the concerns and activity of "everyday" working people. Despite the fact that it objectively expanded the black political elite, even the campaign to increase the number of black officeholders emanated from popular, mass-based impulses. Appropriately, many of the black officials elected during the 1956–61 period, like McNeal, had earlier proved themselves in arenas of working-class activism.[59]

This initial period of "heroic" civil rights activism also illustrated deepening postwar class stratification within urban black communities. Internal class conflict surfaced around the charter, and reemerged when black activists and civic leaders chose differing sides in the Famous-Barr dispute. Further, the bitter warfare between the black Democratic bloc led by Chambers and Weathers, and the upstart faction by Clay, may not have been a clear instance of conflict between the black working and middle classes, but it did attest to a developing rivalry within the evolving electoral wing of the black professional minority. In St. Louis, the struggle would reach its zenith in a prolonged battle for jobs and justice in schools, housing, and industry. In the process of carrying out these campaigns, activists would again wrestle with each other over sharply differing strategies and tactics. Such intramovement schisms would heighten racial-class tensions. A host of external political and economic developments—automation, mass communal displacement, and emerging forms of de facto racism—also brought St. Louis's black freedom workers to a new crossroads.

FIG. 1. Mill Creek Valley, circa 1950s. Until its demolition at the end of the decade, the district was the heart of St. Louis's black working-class community, and a point of entry for waves of black southern migrants. Photo: Missouri History Museum Library and Research Center.

Fig. 2. *(top) From left:* John J. Hicks, Margaret Bush Wilson, NAACP executive secretary Roy Wilkins, and Ernest Calloway, circa 1959. Calloway, an official of Teamsters Local 688, brought a black labor and working-class politics to his tenure as St. Louis NAACP president. With Wilson and others, he was part of an action-oriented local leadership that emerged from a municipal charter fight to defend black electoral power. Photo: Western Historical Manuscript Collection, St. Louis.

Fig. 3. *(bottom)* Sit-in protest by parents at the St. Louis Board of Education, early 1960s; acting school superintendent William Kottmeyer is seated in the background. The continuing segregation of public education joined black St. Louisans across class lines, though the effects of automation made the issue especially vital to working-class African Americans. Photo: Missouri History Museum Library and Research Center.

FIG. 4. *(top)* CORE demonstrators at St. Louis police headquarters following the arrest of marchers at Forest Park, February 14, 1964. Standing in the center of the throng are Richard Daly (wearing eyeglasses), Percy Green (in the Astrakhan-style hat), and Eugene Tournor (in the overcoat and scarf), who were all subsequently involved in forming the Action Council to Improve Opportunities for Negroes (ACTION). Photo: Missouri History Museum Library and Research Center.

FIG. 5. *(bottom)* Mayor Alfonso J. Cervantes meeting with select black leaders at City Hall around the issue of equal employment, August 1965. Sitting in the front row (in suit and bow tie) is James E. Hurt Jr., one of the city's first black school board members and later a proponent of "Black Capitalism." Standing in the background against the wall is Arthur J. Kennedy, one of the "Young Turks" allied with the Twenty-sixth Ward leader William L. Clay. Photo: Missouri History Museum Library and Research Center.

Fig. 6. *(top)* Jefferson Bank boycott defendants (from left): Danny Pollock, Norman Seay, Michaela Grand, Lucian Richards, Bill Clay, Charles Perkins, and Robert Curtis, circa 1967. The drama of the boycott both heightened racial and class fissures among movement activists and paved the way for Clay's election as Missouri's first black U.S. representative in 1968. Photo: Missouri History Museum Library and Research Center.

Fig. 7. *(bottom)* Charles Koen (center, in dark turtleneck shirt and glasses) leading a Black Liberators press conference at the "Wall of Respect" mural, September 1968. To the far right (in suit and tie) is Robert Curtis, a veteran of St. Louis CORE and the Liberators' attorney. The Liberators, while clearly the most audacious, were only one of the many local organizations that proliferated during the heady Black Power period, when the movement's internal class politics became increasingly fractious. Photo: From the St. Louis Globe-Democrat Archives of the St. Louis Mercantile Library at the University of Missouri–St. Louis.

FIG. 8. *(top)* St. Louis public housing rent strike leaders (from left) Irene Thomas and Jean King, February 1969. The first of its kind in the nation, the strike was both a manifestation and rebuke of local Black Power politics, and ushered in major reforms at the local and federal levels. Photo: Missouri History Museum Library and Research Center.

FIG. 9. *(bottom)* The Black Liberators' damaged patrol car in front of the group's ransacked headquarters, September 1968. The Liberators brief, yet intense, war with St. Louis police was symptomatic of the widespread repression of radical black freedom organizers, and the ascension of a cross-class "New Right." Photo: Missouri History Museum Library and Research Center.

FIG. 10. *(top) From left:* William Douthit, Rodman Rockefeller, William R. Hudgins, and Darwin W. Bolden at a conference to organize a local chapter of the Interracial Council for Business Opportunity, October 1968. Support for black business development by corporate leaders and the Nixon administration answered a legitimate grassroots movement demand, but it also promoted the growth of a "new" black middle class as a shield against grassroots working-class insurgency. Photo: Missouri History Museum Library and Research Center.

FIG. 11. *(bottom)* Protest march up the steps of City Hall to see the mayor about complaints of police brutality, September 1965. Photo: Missouri History Museum Library and Research Center.

CHAPTER FIVE

Black Freedom at the Crossroads of Automation and De Facto Racism, 1962–64

WHEN JORDAN CHAMBERS DIED in August 1962, he had recently won the primary race for reelection as constable. Having held the Nineteenth Ward committeeman's seat since 1938, he was the oldest member of the city's Democratic Central Committee, and the key broker of black electoral cohesion. The black vote, constituting 40 percent of the local Democratic Party's support, certainly had become a force with which to be reckoned. Of the 750,000 people living in St. Louis in the early 1960s, more than 250,000 were African American. They occupied a "political corridor" engulfing nine of the city's wards and forming a substantial presence in seven others. Black St. Louisans still claimed the largest percentage of black representatives on any municipal legislative body in the United States. With two black members out of twelve, they also had the largest percentage of African Americans on the board of education. One of them, John Hicks, had become vice president by 1962, and was soon to become president. When illness forced the aged Henry Winfield Wheeler to retire during his second term in the Missouri House of Representatives, *New Citizen* publisher DeVerne Calloway ran a spirited race to fill his seat, and became the first black woman to hold a statewide elected office in Missouri.[1]

News editors pondered who would succeed the deceased "Negro Mayor of St. Louis." With the diversification of black electoral leadership, and the class conflict and political schisms widening within St. Louis's African American community, two groups of black officials vied for the mantle. The first consisted of established insiders like Eighteenth Ward Democratic committeeman Fred Weathers, Grant, Ernest Calloway, and Missouri state senator Theodore McNeal. Tied to the St. Louis Democratic Party's dominant wing, they had developed close relations with the administration of Mayor Tucker, who, in the period following the charter fight, had become sympathetic to the city's civil rights alliance. The second faction, known as the "Young Turks," consisted of the brash ward alderman William Clay and his allies.[2]

Both groups, nevertheless, were part of a collective leadership that had been built in the 1930s and 1940s, and renewed in the heat of the charter fight. Rooted in working-class grievances and mobilization, this bloc had brought to fruition many racial reforms, including the passage of St. Louis's public accommodations ordinance in the spring of 1961. Since then, the Missouri General Assembly had passed a fair employment practice law, while the St. Louis Board of Aldermen had amended the city's FEPC law to cover private businesses as well as municipal projects. Responding to the momentum generated by the local NAACP Job Opportunities Council, and following the example set by the President Kennedy's Committee on Equal Employment Opportunity, Mayor Tucker had formed his own twenty-member Commission on Equal Employment Opportunity in 1963. In late May, white liberal Protestant, Catholic, and Jewish leaders formed the St. Louis Conference on Religion and Race, lending St. Louis's escalating civil rights struggle greater legitimacy among the white citizenry. The conference's founding members had been awakened both by local events and Martin Luther King's "Letter from Birmingham City Jail," a widely circulated broadside that indicted white southern clergy for their inactivity around the cause of black citizenship.[3]

Border states like Missouri, which had been the first former slave territories to impose racial segregation as Reconstruction faltered, ironically were the first to formally end Jim Crow. St. Louis's public accommodations ordinance, for instance, was passed in a climate of growing brutality against peaceful demonstrators in the South. And though black freedom workers in the Lower South endured arrests, bombings, and death for attempting to register African Americans to vote, black Missourians not only exercised the franchise but also occupied influential public offices. But while St. Louisans essentially had resolved, by 1961, many issues around which black freedom activists in southern communities would fight for several more years, they now began to confront an emerging postsegregation pattern of black racial control.[4]

With the legal demise of Jim Crow in St. Louis, the city's black freedom struggle reached a critical turning point. More and better jobs, equitable education, and open housing became even more vital to the substance of local movement activities. While these campaigns were by no means limited to black workers, the issues involved spoke most directly to their concerns at a moment when employment practices, urban redevelopment and black residential displacement, and new forms of segregation, were consigning a younger generation of African Americans to economic and social isolation. Evident since the 1950s, automation had become an additional threat to black working-class gains in semiskilled industrial employment. By the early 1960s, it had contributed to a new phase of black working-class formation, principally in the form of "structural unemployment." Fair employment remained an important goal among activists, but conditions now forced them to take up the additional demand for *full* employment. "Manpower development"—retraining for black workers displaced by mechanization, and job training for young African Americans—emerged as another popular working-class-oriented movement strategy. As the trajectory of the movement shifted in response to a new corporate capitalism, Black Nationalist ideology would gain broader currency among younger civil rights workers, and stimulate a reinterpretation of working-class black identity.

The Gateway City on the Northern Civil Rights Front
⌀

Given the long-term effects of the red scare, the Black Freedom Movement had become the main antisystemic social movement in the United States. Adding to its significance was the fact that the technological revolution had weighed heaviest on black workers, who suffered disproportionately from the labor speedups, depressed working conditions, and permanent joblessness. Shunted to the front lines of economic disposability and postindustrial social anomie, African Americans had become the nation's key revolutionary force. An unrestrained civil rights revolution could, for instance, overturn the long-standing wage differentials between the North and South, from which northern investors, as well as white southern landowning elites, had benefited. Further, in reclaiming the black vote, Calloway remarked, a "total and unconditional struggle for civil rights" would uproot Dixiecrat control of the "Solid South," fundamentally realigning national politics. However much they trumpeted the virtues of a free market economy, many northern business magnates were not prepared, he mused, to "gamble in an open political market" on the outcome of such social transformations. Calloway likely had in mind St. Louis's "massive redevelopment" alliance, led by City Hall, that had worked to isolate the St. Louis NAACP and split the black activist community. Despite the defeat of the 1957 city charter, this governing circle of commercial, manufacturing, financial, real estate, and public utility interests had maintained, and even surreptitiously tightened, their overall control over the city's economic and physical development. Through local banking institutions, in which many business leaders were active as board directors and shareholders, they held many of the bonds being used to fund the urban redevelopment plans they themselves directed.[5]

Interstate highway construction had begun directly west of St. Louis City in 1956, promising an unprecedented level of traffic through the central city. Civic Progress leaders had been active in the formation of Downtown St. Louis, Incorporated, a group of businessmen formed in 1958 specifically to promote greater planning in the development and use of the central business district. With the shift to U.S. corporate capitalism, greater demand for downtown office, rather than retail, space had also grown. Officers at the First National Bank made plans for a new six-story downtown headquarters during the early 1960s, while Famous-Barr, the Ralston-Purina Company, Anheuser-Busch, and the public utility companies also felt the spasms of corporate expansion. The growth of university and medical centers, and high-tech research and development industries, also figured in corporate growth schemes. With a $1 million donation, St. Louis University was able to purchase more than twenty acres of land being redeveloped by the city. This complemented the work of executives involved in the recently established St. Louis Regional Industrial Development Corporation, and the St. Louis Research Council—many of them Civic Progress members—who envisioned a metropolitan "research corridor" with St. Louis City's Central Corridor as its epicenter.[6]

Corporate capitalism likewise placed a premium on conventions and tourism. President Kennedy, who authorized $10 million for the Jefferson National Expansion Memorial, joined the list of the U.S. presidents since Roosevelt who had supported the project's completion. In collaboration with the LCRA, the Civic Center Redevelopment Corporation, a private group of investors, had gained ownership of a thirty-block area immediately south of the memorial grounds. The consortium focused its energies on building a new $80 million downtown sports stadium to replace Sportsman's Park. First National Bank, the May Company, and Anheuser-Busch (the owner of the St. Louis Cardinals baseball franchise) were all contributors to the fund-raising drive for the project. East Coast investment groups, drawn to the city by the promise of downtown revitalization, had shepherded the acquisition of several locally owned firms, including the Scruggs-Vandervoort-Barney department store, and Stix, Baer & Fuller. By the 1960s, moreover, McDonnell Aircraft, the metropolitan area's largest single employer, was at the cutting edge of the nation's burgeoning aerospace industry. Its prosperity was a potent symbol of a federal budget skewed toward military spending by the Cold War, as the company was a major recipient of lucrative contracts from the National Aeronautics and Space Administration and the Department of Defense.[7]

Focused on creating a unified regional economy, Civic Progress patriarchs tried to concentrate the levers of public administrative power, this time through attempts at a St. Louis City-County merger. The "Borough

Plan," proposed as an amendment to the Missouri constitution in 1962, sought to consolidate a unified "Municipal County of St. Louis" with twenty-two boroughs and a legislative council. From the standpoint of rescuing the city from the doldrums of economic isolation and decline, the plan made good sense, as it created a framework for regional cooperation with its thriving neighbors. Supported by Civic Progress, the *Globe-Democrat*, the AFL-CIO St. Louis Labor Council, and Teamsters Joint Council No. 13, the plan was opposed by the Mayor's Office, elected officials, St. Louis County business leaders, and a broad swath of black St. Louis leaders. Notwithstanding their support for limited projects like the creation of a metropolitan-wide sewer district and junior college system, African Americans vehemently believed that regional government would substantially dilute black legislative power. With local ordinances subject to amendment or repeal under the new system, they argued that legislative gains in public accommodations and fair employment would fall to the mercy of the racially conservative politics of the county. Objections also came from the white suburban citizenry who, while supporting metropolitan-wide cooperation to build highways, were hostile to sharing the costs of St. Louis City schools, public housing, and welfare assistance. The plan failed miserably. Metropolitan development, like voting rights and public accommodations, remained a Civil rights battleground where the policy interests of downtown developers and black working-class leadership competed and collided.[8]

Black Workers in the Automated Age

The inequalities embedded in corporate-led urban redevelopment were painfully visible in the evolving patterns of black economic underdevelopment. At the beginning of the 1960s, black St. Louis families earned an annual income of three thousand dollars, half of that earned by whites. In 1960, only 22 percent of the African Americans employed in the entire St. Louis metropolitan area worked in professional, managerial, clerical, sales, and skilled jobs, as opposed to over 50 percent of white area residents. In city government, further, Homer G. Phillips Hospital was the only entity employing black professionals in significant numbers. One in every three black people was either in unskilled work or household service. One of the ironies of the 1950–54 period of job expansion in St. Louis was that even when black employment had grown, so too had the Gateway City's black unemployment—the consequence of African American workers remaining the proverbial "first fired." "You gotta realize," remarked the comedian Dick Gregory, "my people have never known what job security is. For in-

stance, comes another recession and the economy has to tighten its belt—
who do you think's gonna be the first notch?" Younger African Americans
were the most vulnerable to the trend of structural joblessness, with one of
every six black youth absent from the nation's official workforce. While the
proportion of black workers in durable goods industries may have been increasing, the increase was disproportionately in menial labor and service
tasks. "And many of them," Calloway soberly commented in 1963, "will
never work again at gainful employment during their lives."[9]

St. Louis's industrial base historically had been light and highly diversified, which had limited the range of mass-production work typically
available to black workers in other midwestern cities. As the pace of industrial expansion slowed, even this foundation was in jeopardy. Although positions were slowly opening for highly skilled black stenographers, electrical technicians, and computer operators, "modernized" industrial
production was permanently destroying many of the semiskilled and unskilled jobs black workers had gained after World War II. This coincided
with the coming of age of many of St. Louis's "war babies," who were doubling the ranks of those seeking paid work. At a 1963 *Argus* awards dinner,
Arthur Chapin, special assistant to the U.S. secretary of labor, assured black
St. Louisans that the federal government was "ready and will be increasingly ready" to hire African Americans in managerial jobs, though he has-
tened to add that technological changes were demanding greater skills
from job seekers. True as this may have been, Chapin sidestepped the fact
that many employers and unions opted to use new technology to buttress
racism in the workplace. Automated machinery did not simply eliminate
black occupations, as in the case of department store elevator "girls" and
similar categories; it also enabled the transferral of many "Negro jobs" to
white workers, which employers blithely justified as the natural consequence of higher skill requirements. When, in the early 1960s, the Missouri
Pacific Railroad installed an electronic conveyor system at one of its warehouses and created a new job classification, many black St. Louis laborers
lost their livelihoods to members of an all-white local of the Railway
Freight Handlers and Clerks union.[10]

Union racism, then, was another entrenched obstacle to meaningful
black employment in the Gateway City. St. Louis's skilled trades, especially
in construction, continued to hold black workers at arm's length. The national NAACP, selecting St. Louis as a test case in 1962, gave renewed attention to widespread complaints that AFL-CIO unions and building contractors systematically excluded black people from apprenticeship
programs. As the St. Louis NAACP's Job Opportunities Council had highlighted in its seven-point program, the Board of Education was wholly
complicit in these arrangements. At the previously all-white Hadley Tech-

nical High School, students could not enroll in building trades courses without the sponsorship of a construction contractor or union, both of which gave preference to the children of craft unionists, and thus to whites. Moreover, Hadley had become, in the estimation of black school board leaders John Hicks and James Hurt, a "second-class" institution. Its classes in shoe repair and dry cleaning, they pointed out, paled in comparison to the aeromechanics, pre-engineering, and other state-of-the-art courses offered at the newer, predominantly white O'Fallon Technical High School in South St. Louis. True, the AFL-CIO Carpenters Joint Apprenticeship Committee approved its first black trainee at O'Fallon Technical High School in April 1962. Still, of 797 skilled trade apprentices, fewer than 10 were black, and they had been accepted over the stiff opposition of joint union-management committees. When one high school apprenticeship program was desegregated, Local 562 of the Steamfitters left altogether. National NAACP labor secretary Herbert Hill coldly assessed the vicious cycle this perpetuated: Denied apprenticeship training and other quality educational opportunities, black St. Louis youth were subsequently held back from good jobs through a lack of "qualification."[11]

Mechanization, a shallow industrial foundation, and racism in the building trades consequently buttressed black St. Louisans' reliance on employment in commercial and financial enterprises. In the dairy, soft drink, and brewing industries, which employed over 10,000 employees, black workers constituted a meager 3.6 percent, or 367 people. Not only were they absent in the better-paying driver-salesman, office, and plant production jobs, but they were also denied work as janitors and porters at some companies. Most public utilities, like Southwestern Bell and Laclede Gas, maintained "Negro tokenism" in their hiring and placement. Of the thirty-five thousand estimated public utility workers in the area, fewer than seven hundred were black, and most of them were marginally employed. The major retail department stores downtown were hardly better. Famous-Barr, which had narrowly averted a NAACP-CORE boycott in the late 1950s, had hired twenty-three sales workers by 1963. This was more than the combined black sales force at Stix, Baer & Fuller, and Scruggs-Vandervoort-Barney—though with 1,129 sales employees, Famous-Barr's concession to black workers was hardly evidence of fair employment. In the insurance industry, African Americans were barely 1 percent of the workforce, and none were salaried. In the entire financial industry, two black workers held supervisory positions, one of them supervising a janitorial crew.[12]

As had been the case historically, the low wages and unemployment of black men exerted pressure on spouses to take paid employment, most often in domestic or service work. Job-wise, St. Louis had long been, in many

African Americans' estimation, a "woman's town," with black women finding employment easier than black men—in 1959, 46 percent of the total local black workforce was female. But the fact that African American women were more easily employed did not necessarily mean they were better employed. In 1960, 62 percent of black women in paid labor earned under two thousand dollars annually. "[T]he Negro community of St. Louis cannot survive under the traditional trickle down results in the matter of job opportunities," Calloway had warned in the late 1950s. Now, less than ten years later, Alderman Clay similarly cautioned: "[T]he absence of a normal and healthy circulation of income through the Negro community deadens not only opportunities for Negro self-support, but stifles the advances possible for the Greater St. Louis community as a whole." Both men connected, in compelling ways, issues of economic justice, racial equality, and postwar urban and economic development.[13]

The Negro American Labor Council and a "Fair Share of Jobs"

Few could have been shocked when St. Louis's NAACP Youth Council found in a 1960 street survey of four hundred pedestrians that most people regarded jobs as the city's most pressing issue. The NAACP and CORE had made inroads in this area since the 1950s, and newer initiatives emerged on the outskirts of organized labor. The sleeping car porters, members of the old black laboring elite, again played a transformative role—though with the steep drop in railroad passenger travel, the BSCP was in the throes of decline. For many, the elderly BSCP president A. Philip Randolph had become a political anachronism, even as he remained the nation's foremost black labor statesman. While publicly asserting the need for black workers to form groups free from white participation, he had become contented as a "loyal opposition" within the House of Labor, criticizing the AFL-CIO from within its own executive council. At critical moments in his career, he actually had shied away from mass mobilization. Nevertheless, a dispute between Randolph and AFL-CIO president George Meany had come to a head in 1959, setting the seventy-one-year-old on a well-worn path of black worker self-organization. The result had been the creation of the Negro American Labor Council (NALC), which promoted an independent, dual strategy of attacking the racism of white-dominated unions, and underscoring the "economic revolution" at the core of the civil rights struggle.[14]

Calloway, who shared Randolph's anticommunist socialist pedigree, as well as his commitment to a black labor agenda, had joined the fledgling organization to harness and redirect the remnants of the black union caucus movement. He succeeded McNeal as president of the NALC's St. Louis Metropolitan Division, with McNeal assuming the vice presidency. The branch drew its officers and most of its seven hundred members from the Teamsters and BSCP, though others came from the ranks of longshoremen, as well as packinghouse, communication, steel, bakery, and brick and clay workers. Consistent with the leadership he had provided the St. Louis NAACP and its Job Opportunities Council, Calloway helped craft and supervise "Operation Now," an aggressive mobilization project against job discrimination. The project was part of an expansive "Fair Share of Jobs" campaign that included the forming of community block groups, and recruitment for the eagerly anticipated "Emancipation March on Washington for Jobs" that the NALC was sponsoring jointly with the NAACP, CORE, SNCC, and the Southern Christian Leadership Conference (SCLC).[15]

Local NALC organizers proposed drafting unemployed African Americans into a program of "militant, non-violent mass pressure" to force "Fair Share Employment Covenants" from employers and trade unions, agreements that would guarantee nondiscriminatory hiring and on-the-job training. The branch also pursued retraining programs for black workers displaced by mechanization, and "crash" job training programs for black youth and high-school dropouts. One job training conference, cosponsored with State Representative DeVerne Calloway and tenant council leaders at the Pruitt projects, concerned the opportunities available under the new Manpower Development and Training Act, passed in 1962. Harold Crumpton, a Howard University student and local NALC organizer, also headed a special research group that examined black consumption patterns in the city. The team estimated that black St. Louisans spent approximately $400 million a year on consumer items. As the JOC had done previously, the NALC division hoped to mine black St. Louisans' racialized identities as workers, patrons, and citizens in the fight for employment in the consumer industries.[16]

Through the Teamsters, Calloway had also conducted an exhaustive study of the main centers of decision-making power in the city and their personnel practices. The existence of a standing NALC "Workshop on Public Utility Employment," in particular, stemmed from the adroit observation that the public utilities exercised the greatest authority among St. Louis's "omnipotent decision makers." The $3 billion empire run by Southwestern Bell president Edwin M. Clark made him—alongside David R. Calhoun of the St. Louis Union Trust Company, and J. Wesley McAfee of the Union Electric Company—one of the three most powerful men in the metropolitan area. Hiring policies at the telephone company, likewise, had been a guidepost for those at the other utilities. Southwestern Bell employed some 7,000 persons in the St. Louis metropolitan area. A three-month study of the firm revealed that only about 123 were African American, and 84 of them were custodians and matrons. A meager number of black employees held accounting, clerical, stockroom, truck driving, and mechanic jobs. In a press release, Calloway seethed that despite Southwestern Bell's formal commitment to equal employment, "the mainstream of telephone company employment has been completely closed to Negro applicants and workers," even to military veterans who had gained experience through the Signal Corps. NALC communiqués also charged the Communications Workers of America as a culprit aiding and abetting the company's tokenism and discriminatory practices, principally by maintaining a Jim Crow local.[17]

In the past, activists' attention had focused on getting black women into telephone operator jobs. While lobbying continued in this regard, Calloway asserted that the contemporary period demanded more than ever that movement workers fight for male wage-earner jobs in the higher-paid commercial and plant crafts. In a report at a special St. Louis NALC meeting, Calloway called for full-scale "community education, picketing, mass demonstrations and organized customer resistance" at the company's long-distance and toll offices. Members voted unanimously in favor of the plan, and publicized Monday, July 15 as the launch date. Following a three-hour parlay between Calloway, McNeal, and three of the company's vice presidents, however, local NALC leaders canceled the picket. At a standing-room-only meeting, Calloway announced to the rank and file that Southwestern Bell brass had made assurances to pursue an open hiring and upgrading policy. "We are informed enough in the ways and habits of industrial management to know the long, tedious distance between high sounding policy at the top of the heap, and how it operates with lower level management at the bottom of the heap," he assured the membership. Yet one of the main goals of planning and announcing the demonstrations was to open lines of communication and negotiation, which activists hoped to use to "thaw out at the top management level many of the ice blocks in the Company's stated personnel policy." In achieving this end, he contended, the branch had been successful. Yet as the momentum moved from the streets, where the "masses" could participate, to the rarified spaces of the corporate boardroom, the NALC arguably fell into the phone company's designs, not vice versa.[18]

Eleven African Americans had applied for high-paying plant crafts jobs, and Southwestern Bell managers advanced two of them. Mayor Tucker also promised to facilitate new lines of communication between employers, labor unions, and the black community. The *Argus* characterized the settlement as a "real breakthrough" in fair employment, but other black observers were less sanguine. For many "Young Turks," the canceling of demonstrations in exchange for two placements, especially after NALC leaders had beat the drums against "Negro tokenism," reeked of a crass sellout. "There is an old adage that says: 'You don't get a hungry dog to watch the smoke-house,'" concluded a July 17 editorial in the *St. Louis Defender*, a black newspaper. As if the implications of the statement were not clear enough, a cartoon accompanying the commentary depicted Calloway and McNeal as dogs salivating at the doorway of a "Bell Telephone Smoke-house" stocked with meats labeled "Jobs," and a trough brimming over with "Bell Payola." The compact fed critics' misgivings about Calloway's ties to the crime-linked Teamsters, and led to renewed charges from Clay that he was the union's "espionage agent" in the black community. At the national level, Randolph was also facing challenges from a militant young rank-and-file who criticized the NALC's goals as too narrow, and clamored for the organization to break squarely from the AFL-CIO. Thus, the Southwestern Bell controversy contributed to younger black freedom workers' perception of the mainline labor movement as hopelessly reactionary, and of aging black trade unionists as politically bankrupt. Predicting that the debacle had "ended the reign of gladiator Ernest Calloway as king-maker and string-puller in the Sepia community," the *Defender* announced that the incident "has caused this newspaper to say 'Amen' to the growing segment in the Negro community who are demanding an agonizing re-appraisal of the aims and methods of the Negro leadership structure in St. Louis."[19]

Conflict with local soft drink bottling yielded similarly dissatisfying results. Claiming that black residents spent nearly $2 million a year on soda, an NALC negotiating committee led by Calloway, McNeal, Crumpton, and Beatrice Allen, initiated a series of meetings with the St. Louis Bottlers Association. In early October 1963, the NALC, Teamsters Local 688, and major beverage firms reached a three-year voluntary covenant, creating an industry-wide fair employment practices commission and a joint arbitration panel with binding authority. Within weeks, however, many of the soft drink company heads began backpedaling on the agreement. Highlighting the fact that no other civil rights organizations, or the Bottlers union, had endorsed the initial covenant, local presidents of Coca-Cola, Canada Dry, and Vess refused to formally sign, effectively undermining the covenant.[20]

In the meantime, civil rights leaders reacted creatively to the pressure to consolidate their forces. NAACP branches in St. Louis City, St. Louis County, East St. Louis, and neighboring Edwardsville, Illinois, formed the St. Louis Metropolitan Council of NAACP Branches. In December 1963, its leaders entered talks with management at a local Lever Brothers plant. A subsidiary of one of the world's largest producers of soaps, detergents, margarine, and cooking oils, the company employed 375 people at its St. Louis County plant, only about 7 of whom were black. In February 1964, after months of unanswered correspondence and unreturned phone calls, the Metro NAACP Council created a new, expanded Job Opportunities Committee under Calloway's leadership. At his suggestion, the metropolitan-wide JOC recommended plans for a community boycott, which the local NAACP branches adopted in April. News of the imminent "selective buying" campaign leaked to the daily press, and representatives from Lever Brothers' local management and New York City headquarters requested a private meeting. Similar to the NALC's earlier proposal to the soft drink companies, Metro JOC representatives put forth the idea of a "Fair Share" jobs covenant involving Lever Brothers, the Metro NAACP, and the Chemical Workers union. Unlike before, however, black activists now raised the issue of crafting a covenant national in scope, covering plants in Baltimore, Chicago, Los Angeles, and Hammond, Indiana.[21]

Unable to reach an accord with Lever Brothers executives, Metro NAACP activists resumed preparations for "a long consumer siege." Several of St. Louis's prominent black churches read special announcements at Sunday services announcing the boycott, while other civic and neighborhood groups joined the mobilization. A Mass Education Committee, headed by St. Louis NAACP president Evelyn Roberts, printed and distributed an initial one hundred thousand leaflets urging customers to "SUPPORT EQUAL JOB OPPORTUNITY FOR NEGROES IN THE METROPOLITAN ST. LOUIS AREA" by not purchasing any item from a detailed list of Lever Brothers products. A hastily scheduled meeting between the NAACP and Lever Brothers again ran aground when JOC envoys continued to insist on a nationwide fair employment agreement. Ten days into the boycott, organizers were making preparations to extend it across the state, as well as into Kansas, Nebraska, and as far away as Colorado.[22]

The results of these skirmishes were mixed, at best. Black employment patterns had not remained static, in part because of costly boycotts by the NALC and NAACP. Representatives from McDonnell Aircraft, Southwestern Bell, Union Electric, and other major employers also had become active participants in Urban League–sponsored youth career guidance conferences at the city's predominantly black high schools. Notwithstanding these gestures, and the formal removal of hiring barriers by the city, African Americans still comprised a staggering two-thirds of the area's jobless. The mantra "Fair Share of Jobs" encapsulated a popular postwar black demand, but this "fair employment" rhetoric had grown antiquated. Mainly, it presumed the existence of an expanding, full-employment economy. The reality had become quite different, with both productivity and permanent unemployment rising in tandem. What was needed was a greater social-democratic thrust aimed at crafting new federal tax policies, raising the minimum wage, creating government-sponsored job training and public works, and expanding federal aid to education. M. Leo Bohanon, executive director of the St. Louis Urban League, pithily summarized the new dilemma. "What you need in addition to more democratic practices in employment," he maintained, "is more jobs for everybody, period."[23]

Mill Creek Valley Destroyed: Dilemmas of
Race, Class, and Housing

Changes in the city's black working-class formation, wrought by automation and corporate capitalism, had spatial dimensions, chiefly in the mass displacement of black families from Mill Creek Valley. In the early 1950s, the LCRA had selected the 460-acre black ghetto as its main renewal site. Even black voters, whose experience with urban renewal had been bitter, favored slum clearance. Virtually all of the structures in the district were in need of major repair, while 80 percent of its homes lacked private baths and toilets—67 percent were still without running water. Many Mill Creek Valley families, eking by on Missouri's meager relief payments, saw urban renewal as a chance at better low-income housing, not to mention construction work. But black freedom workers, recalling the controversial Plaza Square bond issue in 1953, were skeptical about African American families finding new housing on a nondiscriminatory basis. They were mindful, also, of the black craftsmen who had been left out of building the city's public housing. In March 1958, the St. Louis NAACP had supported the Mill Creek redevelopment, though the association had urged open housing for relocated households, and the use of black labor at all stages of clearing and rebuilding.[24]

With $7 million from the 1955 bond issue and $21 million from the federal government, the LCRA had begun razing Mill Creek Valley in February 1959. Despite Urban League and NAACP vigilance, construction jobs did not materialize for black workers. Because the city performed the demolition phase of the project, African Americans were hired in sufficient numbers, albeit in the labor-intensive and unskilled work they would have performed anyway, with or without an FEP ordinance. But once the LCRA sold the cleared land to private investors, the agency effectively absolved itself of responsibility for the practices of developers, building contractors, subcontractors, and trade unions. In what had become a distressingly familiar pattern, black workers received only a token number of the skilled construction jobs generated by downtown reconstruction. The Mill Creek Valley project itself displaced an initial 1,772 families. Pockets of white working-class residents in the downtown business area felt the effects of the wrecking ball, but none so directly as black St. Louisans. An estimated twenty thousand black residents, or 10 percent of the city's African American population, were forced to move.[25]

Many of the displaced bee-lined to the Carr Square, Pruitt-Igoe, Darst-Webbe, and George L. Vaughn housing projects that had been funded through federal housing acts in 1949 and 1954. Circa 1957, St. Louis had over seven thousand public housing units, all of them concentrated on the near north and south sides. Although greeted with fanfare when they opened, public housing projects had not fundamentally altered relations of race, poverty, and place. If anything, the new settlements had reinscribed them. The earliest public housing tenants may have been stably working-class, but the projects had become a "second" ghetto for the poorest African American workers, employed and otherwise. This was particularly the case when, in 1959, a massive tornado had devastated the central city, requiring the emergency resettlement of many Mill Creek Valley residents by the St. Louis Housing Authority. Low-income public housing had once been the primary commitment in urban revitalization plans, but its importance had declined as private enterprise emerged as the main purveyor of redevelopment. Some developments, like Carr Square Village, consisted of cozy single-family homes with porches and communal yards. But most federal projects, notably Pruitt-Igoe, were hulking mazes of concrete that were poorly designed and isolated from public transportation and other social amenities. Routine janitorial and maintenance services declined, while public housing administrators gradually phased out regular apartment inspections. Robberies became more common as security guards were removed from duty. Such neglect had much to do with the public's retreat from a commitment to federal low-rent housing as a concept and a legitimate social good. The fact that public housing had become associated with the supposed poverty and moral dissolution of black workers only sharpened popular hostility to the idea.[26]

Other black refugees from St. Louis urban renewal settled in the mid-town area. In the previously swank West End area between Kingshighway and the city's western limits, the black population had exploded from 1,150 in 1950 to 57,300 in 1960. The white population there had simultaneously dropped from 81,500 to 24,400. South St. Louis remained predominantly white, but neighborhoods north of Delmar Boulevard and south of Natural Bridge Avenue became solidly black as white St. Louisans quit their homes for residences in Berkeley, Ferguson, Creve Coeur, Clayton, and other growing St. Louis County settlements. White residency, while declining in the city, had expanded in the county from 406,349 to 703,532. Much of the new spatial mobility African Americans experienced was due to these very patterns of white panic and flight. Executive Order 11063, signed by President Kennedy in November 1962, prohibited discrimination in federally owned housing and properties receiving federal funds, but like St. Louis's public accommodations ordinance, it did not apply to the racially contested terrain of apartments, rooming houses, and other places governed by private landlord-tenant relations. As with the 1948 *Shelley* ruling, this was a loophole that preserved housing segregation by other means. The paradox was that even as the areas of the city available to black residents had expanded since 1950, African Americans became more densely concentrated, not less, with continuing migration from the South intensifying the overcrowding.[27]

The Mill Creek Valley dispersal, the western movement of the displaced, the pressures of additional black migration, and the demand for housing all encroached on the Ville. The community's changing social composition also upset the existing class relations among black St. Louisans, narrowing the relative social and spatial distance that the "better Negroes" historically had maintained from the black laboring majority. With the new influx of poorer, more transient families, the old geographical markers of black class stratification were crumbling, which black middle-class observers like Sidney Redmond noted. School desegregation in 1955 suddenly meant that attendance at Vashon and Sumner high schools was no longer determined by whether one lived east or west of Grand Avenue. "No one bothers to stop and wonder whether they come from 'downtown,' 'uptown' or 'across town,'" Redmond commented. More Ville residents began to move west into white-vacated homes and neighborhoods, though ironically all of the 150 square blocks newly opened to black settlement had been designated as blighted by the City Plan Commission. In 1960, the Urban League reported, 70 percent of the city's 214,337 African Americans lived in or near deteriorating housing stock, much of it built prior to 1939. Denied home improvement loans, even many "respectable" black St. Louisans suffered substandard housing.[28]

While homeownership historically had been a marker of black "elite" status, the aspiration to own a house was by no means a middle-class quality. Denied the full fruit of their labor, African Americans in St. Louis City and nearby Kinloch viewed the possession of a home not only as a measure of independence and "self-respect," but also as a protection against old age, infirmity, and economic disaster. African Americans who had the means left the city for municipalities in St. Louis County, many of them becoming the first black residents in previously all-white areas. Most of these relocations occurred without major incident, though violence could rear its head with sudden ferocity. When, in late 1963, a black crane operator, his wife, and their four daughters moved into Jennings, a white neighborhood, they were singled out for several nights of anonymous harassment. The abuse included threatening phone calls and vandalism. Most black families, however, were not so "fortunate" as to break the color line in housing. Despite the *Shelley* decision, the Real Estate Board (formerly the Real Estate Exchange) still condoned racially exclusive sales in St. Louis's choice markets. In St. Louis County, the board required a minimum of three black families in residence before showing properties to African Americans; those who violated the directive were subject to expulsion. "Blockbusting" realtors nurtured and exploited fears of declining property values to scare white homeowners into selling their houses at below-market prices, which they then sold to black families at artificially high costs. Black real estate brokers were able to acquire properties for sale in white residential areas mainly through white "straw parties" who bought homes on their behalf. Yet the Federal Housing Administration maintained the practice of denying loan supports to black families seeking homes in all-white communities. Nor did loan agencies extend credit to whites looking to buy houses in older central-city neighborhoods.[29]

There was, at the same time, a counterhegemonic white politics buoyed by racial liberalism and the city's heritage of religious ecumenicalism. The West End Community Conference, a consortium of homeowners, reflected the sentiments of white St. Louisans who resisted being frightened into selling their homes by warnings of black invasion and lowered property values. In March 1962, members had been involved in forming the Greater St. Louis Committee for Freedom of Residence, an interracial coalition committed to "work[ing] for an open, democratic and competitive housing market" in the area, and "develop[ing] a climate of acceptance whereby good neighbors of any race or creed may be welcomed to full participation in the responsibilities and benefits of Greater St. Louis neighborhoods." Most participants were professionals and prominent civic activists who resided in fashionable communities in the city or surrounding county. Its officers included individuals like chairman William G. Lorenz, the white pastor of the Grace Presbyterian Church; T. H. Mayberry; Joseph W. B. Clark; Paul Hanlon, a sociology professor at St. Louis University; and Ruth Porter, director of the Kinloch YWCA. Consistent with the paradigm of liberal interracialist boards and commissions developed in the 1940s, the committee was not conceived as a mass membership organization, but rather as a small executive body of black educated professionals and "sophisticated" white elites who, in Lorenz's own earnest description, "occasionally invite Negroes to their homes for visits or cocktails."[30]

Similar also to previous liberal interracial coalitions, Freedom of Residence organizers adopted a path to integration eschewing policy-oriented agitation in favor of voluntarism, and imagined they could stimulate the dismantling of Jim Crow by patiently cultivating racial goodwill on a person-to-person basis. Interracial elites would, through their example, demonstrate fair and just race relations for the rest of civil society. Characteristically, "education" figured heavily into the group's goal of providing "opportunity for neighbors of various backgrounds to know, understand and respect each other." The committee established a speaker's bureau to address the widespread perception that black families depreciated property values in white neighborhoods. "Open house" gatherings at members' homes provided another model of ideal race relations. In its regular newsletter, the organization listed homes and apartments available on an integrated basis. Nevertheless, Freedom of Residence leaders seemed less interested in fair housing for African Americans per se than in introducing black pioneer families into upscale white areas like University City. The class bias in this approach was especially telling in the fact that leaders forthrightly dismissed helping potential homebuyers in working-class "fringe areas," where "an expanding Negro community is likely to come anyway." It was in large part due to the committee's efforts, nonetheless, that the St. Louis Board of Aldermen subsequently passed, in early 1964, an ordinance prohibiting discrimination in private housing markets.[31]

The Campaign against "School Resegregation"

Although black displacement and resettlement were fraught with class politics of difference, African American workers and professionals found greater commonality on the matter of public education. Youth marches on Washington, D.C., in 1958 and 1959 had decried the violent opposition to school integration in the South, but black parents north of the Mason-Dixon had struggled just as heroically, if less auspiciously, against unequal education. Indeed, racial barriers to open housing in St. Louis were intertwined with persistent forms of segregated public schooling. As the discriminatory nature of high school trade apprenticeships demonstrated, the St. Louis Board of Education was deeply involved in the racial oppression and economic exploitation that plagued African Americans in the automated age. After a promising start in the 1954–55 academic year, the city's progress toward school desegregation had rapidly deteriorated. In 1959, Missouri's Advisory Committee of the Federal Commission on Civil Rights could claim that 95 percent of the state's black children attended desegregated schools, and overall the greatest leaps in integrated education had occurred in Missouri and the other border states. Still, by the committee's own allowance, this bore no direct relation to the numbers of African Americans actually attending schools with whites. "Even where desegregation has been sincerely attempted on all grade levels, the vast majority of Negro pupils are still attending segregated schools," the report had concluded. It was no coincidence that school integration slowed in St. Louis at the same time that the numbers of school-age African Americans swelled. Between 1953 and 1963, total public school enrollment increased from 90,327 to 112,361, with black students doubling from 31,000 to 64,000. White pupils, on the other hand, decreased from 59,000 to 47,000. In 1964, 838 more white St. Louisans exited the system as 3,200 new African Americans entered.[32]

Many white families still residing in the city routinely transported their children long distances when the nearest public school was predominantly black. Of the city's 134 elementary schools, 71 were completely black in 1963–64. Fifty were thoroughly white. Among the public high schools, Cleveland, Roosevelt, and Southwest were predominantly white, while Beaumont, Soldan-Bluett, Sumner, and Vashon were almost all black. McKinley, Central, and the recently built Northwest high schools approached modest levels of integration, but the fact was that 90 percent of all black high schoolers attended racially homogenous institutions. Thus, while legally sanctioned school segregation had been abolished, black St. Louisans now confronted a "de facto" segregation deliberately maintained by the gerrymandering of school district boundaries, arguments for "neighborhood schooling" in areas where the residential majority was white, and the selective transfer of white pupils from neighborhood schools when the numbers were predominantly black. This practice of "open enrollment," involving cross-neighborhood mixing, formally allowed students to attend any public school with vacancies. In practice, political scientist Jeanne F. Theoharis writes, it "served largely as an administrative shield against charges of racial privilege within the system—and in many ways functioned like 'freedom of choice' plans did in the South." Nor were black St. Louisans deceived by innocuous sounding rationales for neighborhood school preservation. Summarized one irate woman responding to an Urban League survey: "The closer Negroes get to any school, the more of a sanctuary it becomes." The fact that "open enrollment" and "neighborhood schooling" were contradictory concepts, yet resonated with the same constituents, undermined the race-neutral assertions of white parents who promoted these programs. By 1965, 40 percent of white elementary school attendance in St. Louis was outside the public system altogether. The common, though unspoken, premise was that white students not go to school with black students.[33]

Throughout the spring and summer of 1963, a coalition challenged the board of education's bus transportation program and other "open enrollment" policies maintaining a dual, Jim Crow system of schooling. Even when black youth were transferred by bus to white receiving schools, administrators frequently isolated them from white pupils. Parents, clergy, and members of CORE had physically blocked school buses to demonstrate opposition to such policies. A new vehicle emerging from this battle was the Parents of Transported Children (later renamed Parents for Integrated Education), an ad hoc body chaired by Jerome Williams, a mild-mannered black physician. Supporters were a veritable who's who of the local movement, including the West End Community Conference, Urban League, NAACP, CORE, *Argus* editor Howard Woods, the *New Citizen* collective, Weathers, Clay, and Margaret Bush Wilson, who had recently become state NAACP president.[34]

The coalition presented the school board with 136 allegations of preserving segregation, singling out school superintendent Philip Hickey and assistant superintendent William Kottmeyer. Protest leaders highlighted the fact that the racial makeup of schools in the Central West End was 90 percent black, though African Americans were only 60 percent of the area's population. Attaining an even ratio of black and white pupils per classroom was not the goal in itself, but rather the prime strategy for uprooting disparities in education whereby white students had a surfeit of underused resources and black students went without. Specifically, civil rights advocates urged that black students transported by bus go to white receiving schools in South St. Louis, and that teaching assignments be issued without regard to race. They petitioned, also, for a remapping of St. Louis school district boundaries so as to achieve integration. Siding somewhat with the community dissidents, the Council on Human Relations urged the school board and its allied Citizens Advisory Committee to honestly examine the coalition's charges of "school resegregation," and seriously consider reforms. But promises to study the matter and make a report came much too late to placate critics, who scoffed at the need for "further study of obvious inequalities." Several, including Clay, vowed to mobilize black St. Louisans' considerable electoral power against future bond issue and tax proposals until the matter of school integration was resolved. Others contemplated withholding their children from classes in the fall.[35]

Rejecting appeals to wait for an investigative report by the Citizens Advisory Committee, Clay, Williams, and national CORE chairman Charles Oldham emerged as prime movers in plans for a June march against the school board. Aside from secular organizations like the NAACP, their efforts enjoyed strong support among black clergy, most notably the Ministers and Laymen's Association for Equal Opportunity. Like the Conference on Religion and Race, the association had been organized in April, mainly as a result of dissatisfaction with the Board of education. The group had over one hundred active members, and its steering committee consisted of pastors from some of the city's oldest and largest black churches—I. C. Peay of the Galilee Baptist Church, John E. Nance of the Washington Tabernacle Baptist Church, Frank Reid of St. James AME Church, Joseph Nicholson of All Saints Episcopal Church, and Amos Ryce of Lane Tabernacle Church. Six white ministers, including Reverend Lorenz of the Freedom of Residence Committee, also held membership in the association.[36]

A week of tense negotiations between community activists and school board officials failed to avert the publicized rally. On the afternoon of Thursday, June 20, an estimated 125 demonstrators amassed downtown. Gathering in front of the board of education headquarters, black and white protesters carried NAACP printed placards with such admonitions as "Don't Treat Our Children Like Prisoners," "Don't Teach Segregation," and simpler yet, "We Protest School Segregation." Others unfurled twelve-foot-long banners emblazoned with "Freedom Now" in bold black and red letters, which they used to barricade the intersections at Ninth, Tenth, and Locust streets. On Hickey's orders, the building's 150 office employees had left work early to avoid the angry throng, which grew as hundreds more spectators turned out. They watched and listened as Williams and several pastors led the crowd in prayer. "We are tired of proclamations without practice, tired of tokenism, tired of committee reports, tired of hearings where the truth is not heard," proclaimed Reverend Reid. In the midst of prayer, he iterated, "We desire more action, not study and talk. We want implementation of action to assure us the dignity due unto us." Swelling first to three hundred, then five hundred, the demonstrators began moving in an oval line that blocked traffic. Flanked by Clay, Calloway, and numerous other white-helmeted parade marshals, the marchers sang "God Bless America," "The Battle Hymn of the Republic," and similar preselected songs. These musical choices, juxtaposed with banners bearing the militant declaration of the southern black revolt, strategically adapted the trappings of American patriotism to criticisms of white supremacy and its denial of full citizenship to African Americans. Like the St. Louis MOWM's flag-waving parade marches in the 1940s, the pageantry was simultaneously an embrace and a rebuke.[37]

It is evident that, when properly contextualized, the mass demonstration was a direct consequence of automation. That is, the black parents who mobilized against the school board were aware of the conclusion, announced by labor experts and federal bureaucrats, that postwar mechanization had produced a greater demand for technical skills among workers. For many, this realization would have placed an even higher premium on fighting for quality education. If little else, it had to have made them even more keenly aware and resentful of black students' isolation from skilled apprenticeships sponsored through the board of education. "Our people have said they will not have children transported to segregated units in the fall," Williams informed the press, promising more protests. "We will stand behind this decision with continuing demonstrations." The

Parents for Integrated Education faced the prospect of following through on this vow, particularly when, the following month, the school board adopted a report by Hickey that only modified the city's open enrollment and integration policies. Responding in late August, NAACP attorneys Wilson and Robert Witherspoon, and lawyers from the New York headquarters, filed a legal suit against the board of education. Accusing the twelve school board members of maintaining a Jim Crow school system, the complaint requested a temporary injunction to halt the current desegregation program.[38]

Under branch president Evelyn Roberts, the St. Louis NAACP was also assembling a "Pupils Stay at Home" campaign, set for September 5. Black parents in Boston, and other cities where school boycotts were staged, had formed temporary "freedom schools" that operated in private homes, churches, and other black communal spaces. St. Louis organizers elaborated no such intentions, which may have undercut potential support. Thus, an *Argus* spot survey of black citizens in the midtown area revealed mixed attitudes toward the idea. One young man interviewed on the street considered that the tactic might actually yield results. "If it helps our cause, and I think it will, they ought to keep the children out," he responded. "People don't ever give you something for nothing." Most grassroots respondents, however, seemed to fear that the children would suffer from missed days in the classroom. "Keep those kids in school," one elderly man stated, speaking for many black St. Louisans. "Children can't do nothing without an education. We should keep our children in school, above all, even more so than anybody else." Hurt and Hicks, the two African Americans on the school board, also opposed the idea, as did State Senator McNeal. Another crippling blow came when the Ministers and Laymen's Association withdrew support from the proposed strike. An orderly retreat was the only option. At a public gathering following a September 1 rally, Roberts announced that the branch was shelving the campaign, but only to give the school board another opportunity to ameliorate its segregated classroom conditions.[39]

But by January 1964, little had changed. If anything, school board actions after the summer of 1963 had continued to exacerbate black grievances. Board members had recently approved the construction of transportable classroom units to relieve congestion in predominantly black West End schools, though as community activists bristled, buses were available to transport students to less crowded accommodations across town. The Parents for Integrated Education, now chaired by Timothy Person, demanded that the city either build permanent structures to house students in black neighborhoods, or transport them to available classrooms on an integrated basis. Kottmeyer, then acting school superintendent, also remained a lightning rod of discontent. In early February, the St. Louis NAACP demanded his ouster, as well as the recall of all school board members who had voted for the "portables." Person led five women and a small boy in a sit-in demonstration at Kottmeyer's office in the board of education building. One of the uninvited visitors held a hand-printed sign questioning, "Kottmeyer, Do Your Children Attend Portables?"[40]

The Parents for Integrated Education, meanwhile, revisited the possibility of mustering black community sentiment against school-related tax levies and municipal bond issues. James Hurt and John Hicks, who had since become board president, forcefully condemned the idea as defeatist. The split in black popular opinion likely killed the proposal before it could ever gain serious momentum. Hurt and Hicks had coasted into office on a tailwind of black grassroots activism, but their victory had been contradictory, as it had meant their incorporation into an entity—the board of education—with an entrenched culture of segregation. As citywide officeholders, moreover, they had become answerable to constituencies beyond black voters. This implied a degree of accommodation to interests at odds with their core supporters. While the two men had spoken against racial inequalities in the school system, their willingness to fight alongside movement insurgents apparently had its limits. And as the tone of opposition sharpened, with activists like Person threatening to disrupt the normal functioning of the school board, Hurt and Hicks—by virtue of their social location—opted to protect the institution. Although black working-class people formed the spearhead of racial reform, the postwar diversification of black occupational life, itself a result of the movement, contributed to divergent agendas within the African American public. Like the charter fight, and the JOC campaign for black department store sales workers, the anti-school tax controversy attested to the splintering of black political agendas along class lines.[41]

The Linchpin of Police Abuse

Intensifying the problems of unemployment, residential displacement, and renewed housing and school segregation were the adversarial encounters between working-class African Americans and the St. Louis Police Department. The black community's relationship with the department historically had been strained, and police stations were notorious for the mistreatment of black citizens. In the context of corporate redevelopment, police surveillance and control had become even more systematic. In the early 1960s, the department instituted a mobile reserve unit to conduct nighttime searches of automobiles and pedestrians under the guise of "routine" traffic stops.

As Clay complained, 70 percent of those arrested were released after a few hours. More than twenty thousand searches in June 1961 had netted only 122 weapons, which for many critics had raised troubling questions about the unit's effectiveness, necessity, and very legality. Not even "respectable" black St. Louisans were exempt from wanton searches—including David Grant, whom police arrested that summer when he refused to let them search his car.[42]

Later that same year, a citizens group led by M. Leo Bohanon of the Urban League had complained to the St. Louis Board of Police Commissioners about police dragnets that indiscriminately rounded up black residents. The group, which included Calloway, Wilson, James Hurt and John Hicks of the school board, and journalist Bennie Rodgers from the *American*, charged that police were especially heavy-handed in their methods when searching for African Americans suspected of robbing or attacking whites. In one scandalous episode in September 1960, a nineteen-year-old white woman had alleged that a group of black men abducted and repeatedly raped her. Amid the general panic that had ensued, authorities had arrested over three hundred suspects, more than one hundred of them booked on suspicion of rape. Most were black workers detained on their way to their jobs. The discovery that the entire story was false had done little to salvage the detainees' reputations. Saddled with public police records listing their arrests "on suspicion of" numerous crimes, many black civilians were similarly shut out of quality job opportunities, Bohanon argued in a letter to the police commissioners. This, of course, exacerbated the unemployment African Americans already encountered under the "normal" circumstances of rampant job discrimination.[43]

These new patterns of police abuse stemmed, on the one hand, from a public sense of white peril accompanying black population growth and dispersal, and the need to discipline an expanding group of jobless black workers. But as Wilson also argued, racism by police also reflected a long history of employment discrimination by the department. NAACP researchers reported that from 1930 to 1961, the force had only hired 138 black officers. Between 1950 and 1960, the percentage of black police had risen only from 5 to 7 percent. The police department had two black captains and a lieutenant, but few black civilian workers. As in the past, African American officers were confined to black areas, and in all but one district patrolmen were assigned partners according to race. Twelve of the city's police sergeants were black, though this was out of a total of 203. While 7 out of 1,800 white officers had college degrees, 45 of the department's 135 black officers were similarly educated. Norman Seay, a CORE veteran, Twenty-sixth Ward committeeman, and chairman of a special NAACP committee on police affairs, viewed the disparity as proof that black applicants had to pass higher educational standards than their white peers. Calloway, another member of the NAACP police committee, chronicled that from May 1960 to May 1961, only 5 of 481 black applications to the police force were accepted. "However," he noted wryly, "we can take heart in the increase from 45.9 to 52.8 per cent in custodial (non-commissioned) personnel in these five years."[44]

In April 1961, St. Louis's new police chief, Curtis Bronstron, had delivered a speech vowing to eliminate hiring discrimination and segregation in the department, in accordance with the city's new equal employment policy. Yet he had passively avoided meeting with NAACP representatives to outline how the police department would implement the dictum. Police commissioners had similarly eluded the NAACP, citing as the source of their refusal an unsavory attempt by Seay to use his committeeman office to "force" the promotion of two black policemen. Wilson angrily dismissed the objection as a "cheap public relations gimmick" to avoid a conference, where Bronstron and H. Sam Priest, the police board president, would have to offer concrete details and time lines for integrating the department. A full year later, the requested meeting still had not materialized, and by the spring of 1962 a small coterie of NAACP activists had begun picketing police headquarters downtown.[45]

Police abuse was both the linchpin of black racial oppression and the spark that ignited a series of postwar black urban working-class rebellions in cities like Birmingham, Alabama, Cambridge, Maryland, New York City, and Philadelphia. In early July 1964, St. Louis police responding to a fight between two siblings touched off an hourlong clash in North St. Louis. Police dispersed a crowd of rock- and bottle-throwing black youth with tear gas, and arrested three people. Thirty minutes after the clash ended, about forty-five demonstrators marched to the nearby Lucas Avenue police district station, where bricks were hurled through two windows. Officers drove the protesters away with police dogs. The gender, generational, and class character of these racial disturbances becomes clear when one considers the profile of the typical rioter later described by the National Advisory Commission on Civil Disorders. He was commonly unmarried, between the ages of fifteen and twenty-four years, and an unskilled or menial laborer who suffered frequent bouts of joblessness. Although usually a high-school dropout, he was nonetheless well informed about current events, and had Black Nationalist leanings. A lifelong resident of the city, he often did not have a prior arrest record or criminal convictions. Rather than looting and burning randomly, the rioter targeted symbols of white property and authority, most often white-owned retail businesses and police patrols, as well as fire crews that for decades had also excluded black workers from employment.[46]

Authorities in black-run municipalities were not spared the frustrations of unemployed and restless black workers, either. In late September 1962, some three hundred residents of Kinloch, Missouri, had picketed City Hall after a seventy-four-year-old member of the city's small, beleaguered police force shot and killed a twenty-year-old during a traffic stop. As the evening progressed, assailants fired gunshots on the Kinloch police station, while roving groups of young arsonists set fire to the police chief's home, several vacant buildings, and an elementary school portable—which, as the school protests in St. Louis City revealed, was a hated symbol of inferior black education. At the request of Mayor Clarence Lee, fifty white law enforcers from St. Louis County and seven nearby municipalities, many of them outfitted with machine guns, tear gas, and canines, arrived to restore order. Three county officers and a bystander were hit by shotgun blasts as sporadic gunfire and arson continued for the next three days. The burgeoning national phenomenon of black working-class rioting spoke to a new level of alienation, particularly among the adolescents and young adults, whom black middle-class leaders alternately pitied as victims of economic change, and despised as "thugs," "hoodlums," "riffraff," and "wineheads."[47]

Early Signs of Black Nationalist Rebirth

❧

Beyond the condescension of many black professionals, working-class youth held fast to the goals of stable, remunerative employment, decent shelter, substantive social amenities, respect, and self-determination. When spoken to, and not spoken for, they were poignantly cogent in articulating this agenda. As Urban League staffers discovered when they polled poor and unemployed black workers, respondents expressed the desire to "free" themselves from welfare aid offered in the absence of meaningful work, the residential segregation that hampered their ability to choose quality housing, and the police harassment that deprived them of their dignity. Black working-class male heads of households, in particular, looked forward to, as one St. Louis man described it, "the right to earn our money at any trade or profession open to everybody else." Elaborated another interviewee: "We want a chance to do, or learn to do, skilled labor in plants and factories alongside any workman of any race, especially in the plants turning out billion of dollars' worth of goods with our Government money."[48]

Millenarian Black Nationalism had resonated among the Midwest's black working class since the 1930s, and the trend now harvested a new bounty of frustration caused by automation and its social aftershocks. The most notable beneficiary was the NOI. In St. Louis, Muhammad's Mosque

No. 28 had been active since the early 1950s, with members "fishing" for converts in prisons, poolrooms, taverns, and the sidewalks outside black churches. Muslim women, covered head to toe in flowing white, exemplified moral virtue. The men, with their suits, bow ties, and close haircuts, embodied the racial pride, manhood, and discipline found in the teachings of Elijah Muhammad. Young war veterans were particularly drawn to the military-like precision of the NOI's Fruit of Islam. Even still, Muhammad's Mosque No. 28 had struggled to attract members. Minister Clyde X, a former Detroit autoworker and Korean War veteran, had been dispatched to St. Louis in 1958 to oversee a concerted recruitment campaign. Boosted by Malcolm X, the organization's energetic national organizer, membership had begun to climb.[49]

By the early 1960s, the "Black Muslims" had over two hundred temples around the country. Mosque No. 28 moved into a two-story building on North Grand Boulevard, and operated an ice cream parlor and several other small businesses. Its membership, however, was a matter of dispute, with NOI officials claiming 1,100 and local media placing the number somewhere between 150 and 200. The St. Louis press emphasized the Black Muslims' failure to attract a following, but by any estimate Mosque No. 28 had become dramatically visible. Its leadership had made news in October 1960, when police arrested William X, the mosque's captain of security, and three other members who were posting advertisements for a planned appearance by Muhammad. Between forty and one hundred members gathered outside the Deer Street Police Station while Clyde X successfully negotiated their release.[50]

Among St. Louis's civil rights leaders, opinion about Muhammad's Mosque No. 28 ranged from dismissive to concerned, especially when they considered the influence the NOI might exert over younger African Americans who had come of age in the midst of the black revolt following *Brown*. With their clean-shaven appearance, star-and-crescent flags, and martial bearing, the Black Muslims certainly had a psychic impact among younger African Americans similar to the Garvey movement of the 1920s. An August 1962 appearance by Muhammad at the Kiel Auditorium attracted thirty-five hundred people, who heard his apocalyptic prediction that the "rule of the white man over the black man" was nearing its end. In the spring of 1963, Malcolm X also drew a sizable audience to Finney Avenue's Crystal Roller Rink, where he delivered a speech defining "America's No. 1 Problem" as "the Presence of 20,000,000 Unwanted Negroes." The NOI's most visible and eloquent figure, Malcolm had been the single individual most responsible for expanding the organization's membership. An effective organizer equally at home among diplomats and the unemployed, he had popularized, among a broad African American public, a number of

Black Nationalist conventions that simultaneously made whiteness explicit and turned it into a slur. Most egregiously, at least to black middle-class activists and professionals who valued light skin and straight hair as symbols of elite identity, he had rejected the designation of "Negro" in favor of "Black."[51]

Hailing from a working-class background, and a former hustler and convict, Malcolm was able to communicate with the black working masses and articulate their grievances in a manner elusive to most of his contemporaries. At the Northern Negro Grass Roots Leadership Conference in Detroit, where he gave his seminal "Message to the Grassroots" speech to dissident civil rights workers in early November 1963, Malcolm related the parable of the pampered "house Negro" who identified with the master, and the overworked "field Negro" committed to torching the plantation. Emblematic of his skill as an orator, the allegory drew a contemporary line of demarcation between African Americans who enjoyed comfort and respectability accommodating to white dominance, and the black majority who created white wealth through their toil. From the standpoint of historical accuracy, the house Negro–field Negro metaphor may have been faulty—house servants suffered close surveillance and habitual violence in the slave owners' household, and often plotted insurrection in concert with field slaves. But as an elementary rendering of black class relations, and as a critique of black elites who bargained away workers' interests for their own gain, it was an effective formulation.[52]

Despite Malcolm's critical interventions into the discourse of civil rights, the thrust of political action in the early 1960s belonged to the liberal integrationists, and they were adamant that African Americans not concede citizenship in the nation they had helped create. "I doubt seriously that discrimination will ever be eliminated 100 per cent," Bohanon confessed to the *Globe-Democrat* in late 1963. "But the more injurious forms of segregation with respect to the Negro community—housing, employment, education and overt acts—will be eliminated in St. Louis in five years, I predict." Horrified, yet inspired, by events unfolding in the South, many had no trouble believing the Urban League director's forecast. SCLC president Martin Luther King Jr., fresh from a high-profile campaign of civil disobedience in Birmingham, had visited St. Louis in late May 1963 to promote the upcoming D.C. march. Amid great fanfare, over three thousand people attended a "Freedom Rally" at the Washington Tabernacle Baptist Church, where he was the featured speaker. While praising the progress local civil rights activists had made toward desegregation, King identified housing and employment as areas deserving greater attention from the movement.[53]

The southern minister merely told the audience what many already recognized, for common black people had been demanding equal employment, housing, and educational opportunities. Notwithstanding their success in the areas of employment, electoral politics, and public accommodations since the late 1950s, however, black freedom workers were unable to exert the same influence in urban renewal and housing policies. In the long run, the local "massive redevelopment" alliance proved helpless to reverse the city's economic decline. Because indigenous suburban political and economic elites, and their citizenry, had no intentions of supporting a city-county merger, St. Louis's corporate capitalists were politically weakened by the continued proliferation of suburban municipalities. And while downtown businessmen envisioned highway construction as a means of preserving central-city health, they merely accelerated the ongoing exodus of citizens, industry, and retail to St. Louis County. By the early 1960s, the neighboring suburb of Clayton rivaled downtown St. Louis as a central business district. The opening of the Northland Shopping Center, in St. Louis County, was also emblematic of the movement of population and commerce outside the central city.[54]

Through several organizational outlets, black St. Louisans confronted these effects of automation, structural unemployment, corporate-led urban renewal, and the growing central-city concentration of black poverty. Motivated by the southern black revolt and other crosswinds of activism, the tempo of protest in the Gateway City was increasingly driven by a new militancy oriented toward civil disobedience. As the following chapter discusses, the result was a mass "strike" to topple Jim Crow employment practices at the Jefferson Bank and Trust Company, and end the job discrimination of St. Louis's "white power structure" more generally. Although this struggle gained broad-based support, its most dynamic contingent was black working-class youth, who had the most at stake in the changing economic environment, and who were most receptive to an emergent black proto-nationalist politics. While emancipatory in its effects, the black freedom "strike" campaign nevertheless highlighted, and intensified, the contradictions of class within the black community.

CHAPTER SIX

The Jefferson Bank Boycott and the "General Strike" against Racism, 1963–64

Departing by bus from the NAACP and NALC headquarters, three hundred St. Louisans began a twenty-hour journey on August 27, 1963, to attend the D.C. March for Jobs and Freedom. Margaret Bush Wilson and Ernest Calloway sat among the four busloads of travelers, as did leading members of the city's white religious, human rights, and ecumenical communities. Robert B. Curtis, the energetic new chairman of St. Louis CORE, also joined the upbeat delegation. However, David Grant, who two decades ago had publicly challenged the national leadership of the March on Washington Movement to stage its threatened mass rally, was forced to cancel his trip when he fell ill. For him and many other veterans of the 1940s, the expedition may have fulfilled plans long deferred; yet the nationwide mobilization, closely coordinated with a cautious Kennedy administration, lacked the insurgent thrust of the original March on Washington Movement. Pressured from above, organizers had de-emphasized the march's focus on jobs in favor of supporting the passage of a federal bill. But if the White House had managed to co-opt the event to its purposes, as critics like Malcolm X alleged, it was precisely because federal officials recognized the militant black grassroots possibilities contained in a platform of full and fair employment, massive federal works programs, decent housing, and meaningful civil rights laws.[1]

Many local delegates, with imaginations fixated on Washington, D.C., could not have guessed they were leaving St. Louis on the eve of a local insurgency that caught city leaders, and some movement activists, by surprise. Within days, St. Louis civil rights militants would launch a boycott against the Jefferson Bank and Trust Company, which escalated into a "general strike" against the corporate employment practices of the Civic Progress patriarchy. At the same time that the NALC, NAACP, and the Parents for Integrated Education were waging local protest campaigns against the effects of automation and de facto racial oppression, St. Louis CORE was involved in the continuing issue of black job opportunity. Inspired by the militancy of the southern revolt, and renewed by an influx of young black workers sensitive to the appeal of Black Nationalism, CORE brought a new cultural verve to the unfolding struggles for fair—and full—black employment. With the bank boycott, the organization ignited a level of mass civil disobedience that had been absent from black St. Louis protest at least since the 1930s. That most of St. Louis CORE's leading members opposed the civil disobedience campaign attested to the group's changing internal configurations of race and class. Like the 1957 charter fight marking the origins of St. Louis's postwar civil rights struggle, the Jefferson Bank protest was a moment of political fissure among the black citizenry, magnifying intraracial class divisions. In their successes and shortcomings, CORE and the Jefferson Bank boycott foreshadowed the proliferation of postwar black political interests and agendas.

No More Tea and Donuts: CORE in Transition

Three events had catapulted CORE to national prominence as a major civil rights organization. The first had been the sympathy boycotts of local Woolworth's stores that members in St. Louis and other cities had organized in solidarity with the 1960 southern sit-ins. The second event had been James Farmer's appointment as CORE's national director in February 1961, which had helped revive many chapters and stimulated the formation of new chapters, including an active East St. Louis affiliate. Farmer had since become a black movement spokesman of a stature second, perhaps, only to King. The creation of new field secretary positions had also augmented CORE's developing new image as a black grassroots organization. Third, and most important to CORE's new image, had been the Freedom Rides of May 1961. The project had sought to test federal enforcement of the 1960 *Boynton v. Virginia* Supreme Court ruling banning Jim Crow at interstate terminals. In June, three members of St. Louis CORE had embarked on their own "Freedom Ride" by plane to test observance of integration in airport terminals. Departing from Lambert Field, the trio was arrested in Jackson, Mississippi, attempting to enter "whites only" restrooms and receive service at the airport restaurant. The following month, four other CORE Freedom Riders, leaving St. Louis by bus, had spent several days in a Little Rock, Arkansas, jail after refusing to leave a "whites only" section of the bus terminal.[2]

Following the wide publicity the Freedom Rides generated, CORE had accelerated the pace of registering black voters in the South, and challenged discrimination in housing and schooling. Redressing unequal job opportunities in the North and border regions also remained important to its national agenda, though the principal targets had shifted from retail stores to financial institutions, the construction trades, and major manufacturers. Charles Oldham and Marvin Rich, both white St. Louisans heavily involved in CORE's national affairs, had been instrumental players in this shift. Not coincidentally, the St. Louis chapter had been the first to develop a full-fledged employment campaign—a likely result of members' interaction with skilled labor strategists like Calloway, and their association with the St. Louis NAACP Youth Council. Since January 1960, local leaders had been involved in protracted discussions with banks and retail stores, and by the end of the year they had helped obtain jobs for more than twenty white-collar black workers at downtown businesses.[3]

The passage of the city's public accommodations ordinance in the spring of 1961 had also emboldened their efforts. With the integration of lunch counters and other public commercial spaces formally accomplished, employment had become even more of a priority. In June 1962, St. Louis CORE had begun picketing the Kroger supermarket on Easton Avenue, previously a target of NAACP JOC protests. Demonstrations had forced the hiring of four black butchers, but the treaty had fallen apart when Kroger officials reneged on hiring African Americans in more skilled jobs. Picketing had resumed that September, this time with the additional support of alderman William Clay's potent Twenty-sixth Ward Democratic Organization. Protesters now demanded a timetable for hiring black workers across all classifications. This new offensive had dissipated, too, when in December Kroger had negotiated a separate agreement with the senior NAACP branch and other leaders. This latest subterfuge had further fanned hostilities between younger and older movement activists.[4]

As Rich pondered in an article written for the radical journal *New Politics*, the mass-oriented nature of CORE's recent campaigns had broadened the organization's horizons, allowing people to make practical contributions to the movement—walking a picket line or distributing literature—whatever their occupation or level of education. This development had enabled many local affiliates, for the first time, to enlist substantial numbers of working-class African Americans. In terms of its structure, CORE remained a small, highly motivated cadre governed by strict membership requirements. But by 1962, it had metamorphosed from a national organization with a predominantly white, northern, middle-class membership to one more evenly balanced between white and black activists, workers and professionals, and northerners and southerners. Ivory Perry, a Korean War veteran, was among the black workers who joined St. Louis CORE during this turning point. A recent migrant from Pine Bluff, Arkansas, he had been court-martialed, sentenced to hard labor in the stockade, and dishonorably discharged from the Army on faulty narcotics and insubordination charges. Since relocating to the Gateway City, he had drifted among itinerant jobs as a machine operative, warehouse worker, taxicab driver, and bakery employee. Profoundly embittered by racism in the military and by marginal work in St. Louis, Perry had come to a stark conclusion: "I shouldn't have been in Korea in the first place because those Korean people they haven't ever did anything to Ivory Perry. I'm over there trying to kill them for something that I don't know what I'm shooting for. I said my fight is here in America."[5]

Another working-class black St. Louisan, Percy Green, was similarly drawn to CORE. The son of a packinghouse worker and a homemaker, he had grown up on the near south side in the Compton Hill district, and like many of the "boppers" in his neighborhood had been a member of the Compton Hill Angels. A Vashon High School graduate, Green had been hired at McDonnell Aircraft, becoming one of the firm's few black skilled workers. Returning to the city in 1960 after a two-year stint in the army, he had resumed his well-paying job as a radio and electrical mechanic. At $1.57 an hour, the twenty-seven-year-old earned ten cents more than his father had made in thirty-eight years of employment. At the suggestion of a white assembly line coworker, Green had accompanied him to a CORE meeting in 1962. The chapter was, at the time, engaged in protests against Kroger for better black employment. Green was radicalized by what he witnessed. "They were talking about the white power structure," he recalled, remembering how black soldiers had been given the dirtiest details in the army, and how his own father had always come home "tired and sweaty" after a day at the packinghouse. "They described it as this invisible wall that black men came up against. It was the first time I heard a rationale that explained all the things I'd seen. There was a wall out there keeping us on the outside. There was a wall that we had to break through."[6]

He continued attending meetings, though from the start he was ill at ease. Foremost, he was startled by the leadership's naive approach to negotiating with employers:

After a couple of Sundays . . . I got the understanding that they were negotiating with Krogers for some jobs. And the report back from a committee, I guess, it was considered an employment committee—they were stating that the personnel manager appeared to have been much different in attitude at this most recent meeting as opposed to a meeting in the past. Because this time at the meeting, he was pleasant, he did some smiling and he served all of the participants some tea and donuts and what have you. And before, they said, that this was a big contrast with the first meeting because he was hostile and everything. For some reason they thought this was meaningful.[7]

Green, who had honed keen instincts as a streetfighter, was unconvinced by the symbolism of interpersonal niceties. "My thinking was 'why would they be placing so much significance on a person who was rude to them one moment, and the next time he was serving them tea and donuts?'" he recounted. "'Can't they understand that that's 'game'? I mean this is all part of a confidence game. What is more significant is whether or not there were any jobs.' I'm saying this to myself, but still a little bit reluctant to say anything outwardly."[8]

His reluctance to speak up was more than a matter of feeling insecure in a new social environment. Although CORE had been propelled toward a greater focus on working-class African Americans, its internal culture had not become more readily inviting of their actual presence.[9] Green found many of the better-educated members, both black and white, politely dismissive in their relations with their working-class peers. He remembered:

> If you were a new face, "How are you, we're glad that you've come to the meeting" and everything, and then eventually we'd get to the point of "where did you go to school" and if you happen not to be one of those that went to St. Louis University, Washington U., or some school of higher learning—then the conversation seemed like it was a little bit short and abrupt. "Maybe you'll come back to the meeting sometime." That kind of thing. . . . And not only I felt it at the time, but there were other persons who were pretty much in the same category as myself. You know, not having this college thing.[10]

Still, he joined the organization and became a regular participant in the boycott picket line. The pickets eventually forced Kroger to hire black clerks and butchers at its three stores in the city's black community. Yet CORE's organizational practices continued to rankle him. He observed, for instance, that while many of the "important" movement people made occasional appearances, those walking the picket line were mainly, like him, working class in background. He remained, in the meantime, a skeptic of the liberal interracialist "tea and donuts" approach to integration, noting: "I had gone through a phase of gang fighting in the community where real people lived and was not so prone to accepting everything that people would say, except how close their actions followed up what they said, you see."[11]

Such objections derived from Green's organic experiences, and longstanding modes of working-class "self-respect" and conduct. But they also mirrored CORE's changing tactical outlook. After 1961, the organization had begun emphasizing coercive pressure over interracial civility and other passive methods adhering to the law. This strategic shift was contested, of course, as an older cohort of white liberals, including Oldham, remained adamant about avoiding rowdy public disturbances, and urged restraint. Yet this group was losing ground to a younger bloc of "direct actionists" who saw only injustices that demanded immediate remedy, by whatever means.[12]

St. Louis CORE's new chairman, Robert Curtis, was an avatar of this trend. The twenty-seven-year-old black attorney had led the affiliate in several actions over the objections of the influential Oldham faction, which heretofore had dominated the chapter. Curtis's staunch defense of militant protest tactics emanated from a deep well of personal commitment, and reflected his upbringing. His mother, Mabel B. Curtis, had been director of the People's Art Center, a creation of the New Deal and Popular Front, and an important base of support for integration since the 1940s. As a child, he had been one of several black youths who had desegregated the Fairgrounds Park swimming pool. While president of the student NAACP at Washington University, further, Curtis had been one of the four collegians arrested at an off-campus restaurant during the 1959 sit-in demonstration. After graduating from law school, he had joined the army, and organized similar sit-ins at segregated commercial accommodations near Fort Hood, Texas. By the time he was discharged in 1962, military and civilian police had arrested him on at least three separate occasions.[13]

As embodied in Curtis's chairmanship, a new civil rights front was emerging in St. Louis, and CORE was at its cutting edge. "Street oriented" members like Perry and Green were discovering an affinity with the trained intellectuals and professionals belonging to the "actionist" wing of leadership. Curtis, a fellow military veteran, was one. Others, like Eugene and Roberta Tournour, were young white radicals who had attended Washington University and had been inspired to join CORE during Oldham's fight to reverse the convictions of Curtis and his fellow University City sit-in protesters. Amid the socializing, drinking, and music at Green's apartment gatherings, tough black activists from the grass roots, black professionals with civil disobedience backgrounds, and white political bohemians seriously reassessed CORE's direction. In the process, they consolidated a subculture of young dissidents ready to redefine the local Black Freedom Movement.[14]

The CORE Ultimatum

The changes in CORE's base, strategic thrust, and political program were apparent in the confidence with which the St. Louis branch approached the local banking industry in August 1963. Despite hiring advances at St. Louis's Federal Reserve Bank, this sector had remained largely closed to African Americans. Not only was banking a vital source of employment in the local economy, but financial institutions also had a symbolic importance that escaped few seasoned organizers. "The bank is a powerful institution," DeVerne Calloway summarized, contrasting it to the other employers the NAACP-CORE alliance had targeted in the late 1950s. "We had been picketing grocery stores because they didn't have enough checkers or no blacks working in the stores, but gosh when you hear a bank, then you're treading on some very powerful feet." To be a janitor in a bank— "where white people's money was sleeping"—conferred status, but at $1.25 an hour, it hardly offered a comfortable living. Yet many whites feared that even this menial labor might result in black people moving behind the tellers' cages.[15]

The NAACP and CORE had been in hiring negotiations with bankers since at least 1958. Now members of CORE were willing to press harder their demands. This fearlessness emanated from the growing militancy of the rank and file, though the SCLC's Birmingham campaign, and the popular demand for "Freedom Now" that fed it, had also "cognitively liberated" civil rights militants to believe they could challenge the city's financial elite and win. Closer to home, Missouri NAACP leader Margaret Bush Wilson, and Norman Seay, had mobilized NAACP members from around the state, who on August 10 marched on the Capitol building in Jefferson City. Over one thousand people, representing all of the state's fifteen branches, reacted to the Missouri Senate's failure to pass a state public accommodations law or support civil rights legislation in the U.S. Congress. Lieutenant Governor Hilary Bush, a Democratic gubernatorial candidate, had received a delegation composed of Wilson and every NAACP branch president in the state.[16]

Mass protest against the St. Louis Board of Education and an NAACP lawsuit filed against the school board were also part of the backdrop encouraging CORE's "direct actionists." Curtis and Tournour, who had traveled among other cities with active CORE affiliates, were further influenced by similar campaigns in locales like Brooklyn, New York. From their comrades, and through their own experiences, they had come to the realization that employment campaigns in the retail and finance sectors, relative to the building trades, had great potential for success. On the east side of the Mississippi River, meanwhile, militant East St. Louis activists had set a more direct example. In early August, the city's NAACP Youth Council had begun a series of job discrimination protests at three banks and two savings-and-loans associations in the downtown area. Led by white activist James Peake, black freedom workers had halted financial transactions by forming human chains in front of the tellers' windows.[17]

Against this national and local background, St. Louis CORE called on five banks to hire thirty-one African Americans in sales, clerk, and teller jobs within two weeks. "In 1963, we look over the situation and find there is just one Negro bank teller in the whole City of St. Louis," Oldham complained. Although a moderate by the standards of other members in his organization, the veteran white civil rights attorney was adamant as the showdown neared: "CORE is tired of empty statements of high purpose. We plan to break the pattern of discrimination and quota system that has been imposed by the banking industry in assigning white collar jobs to whites only for the last 130 years." Of particular interest was the Jefferson Bank and Trust Company, where activists claimed many black St. Louisans deposited their money. In the early 1950s, Jefferson Bank had employed about ten African Americans in nonservice positions, but by 1958 this number had fallen to only one. Currently, the company employed one African American in an administrative position and two in petty labor. CORE's leadership demanded the immediate placement of four white-collar workers at the bank within fourteen days, or activists would begin demonstrations. "I regret that we have to ask for a certain number of jobs," Curtis explained to the press. "I wish we could depend on the various institutions to hire on the basis of equality, that they would hire Negroes on their qualifications without coercion, but through long experience we've found that this does not often work. They need to be forced into doing the right thing." Previous negotiations had produced unfulfilled promises, as Oldham and other activists had discovered. "We're concerned with jobs, not with promises," Curtis avowed.[18]

Bank spokesmen rebuffed the ultimatum. Several pointed out they had frequently requested applicants from the Urban League, and spotlighted their support for Mayor Tucker's new Commission on Equal Employment Opportunity. Answering the popular claim that large numbers of black people deposited at his institution, Joseph McConnell, executive vice president of Jefferson Bank, retorted that only 4 percent of business came from African Americans. In an equally resolute tone, bank attorney Wayne Millsap lectured Curtis that demands for a quota of jobs, or a demonstration by CORE, would "impede the progress which is being made toward obtaining equal job opportunities for Negroes in the St. Louis area."[19]

The First Arrests

Nevertheless, city leaders took the threats seriously enough to try half-heartedly to mollify the dissidents. Members of the Council on Human Relations called a meeting of representatives from seven of the city's major banks, including Jefferson, First National, Boatmen's, and the Mercantile Trust Company. On August 29, they adopted a ten-point program by the city's Commission on Equal Employment Opportunity for hiring African Americans in the industry. W. J. Duford, commissioner of the Council on Human Relations, announced the provisions, which included publicizing the banks' written antidiscrimination policies, reviewing employment records, and contacting the Urban League for "qualified" black job candidates. For militant civil rights workers, especially those who had vainly lobbied the banks before, the pronouncement came as little more than a public relations ploy. Vague and noncommittal in language, it lacked any real mechanisms for implementing fair employment.[20]

Millsap, in the meantime, approached St. Louis City Circuit Court judge Michael J. Scott for a restraining order barring CORE from interfering with transactions at Jefferson Bank. By then, CORE members had voted to picket the bank, and over the objections of Oldham and other leaders, they had resolved to disobey any court injunction. Judge Scott issued the restraining order on Friday, August 30, naming in it CORE and nine of its prominent members. Around four o'clock that afternoon, more than one hundred demonstrators began picketing the sidewalk in front of the bank. Under the watchful eye of law officers, they marched with placards announcing, in bold lettering, the protest's most immediate demand—"JOBS NOW." Other placards, reading "Full Employment Plus Civil Rights Mean Freedom," forcefully linked the issue of black employment with ongoing crises in housing, education, and political citizenship. Some participants—particularly many high schoolers and other youth who casually joined the demonstration en route from school or work—departed from the picket line to escalate the protest. Ignoring entreaties by CORE leader Raymond Howard to observe the court order, twenty people locked arms and sat on the front steps of the bank. Another group moved to the building's rear exit, creating a logjam. As sheriff's deputies reacted to the congestion, a handful of protesters entered the bank's front door. The entire group poured in behind them, chanting, clapping, and choking all business activity inside. Borrowing a tactic from the East St. Louis bank boycotts, several men, women, and youth sat three-persons deep in front of the tellers' cage.[21]

On Saturday, August 31, a round of meetings occurred involving McConnell, Millsap, Tucker, St. Louis chief of police Curtis Bronstron, Board of Police Commissioners chairman H. Sam Priest, and Governor John Dalton. Hours later, Dalton delivered a tough statement against the protests. "I trust that our laws will be enforced," the governor said. "The alternative is anarchy." Mayor Tucker, who days earlier had praised the March on Washington gathering, now called for law and order, maintaining that St. Louis

City was making greater strides toward equal employment. Charging contempt of court, Judge Scott ordered the arrest of the nine leaders named in the restraining order, most of who had vigorously opposed violating the injunction. The following day, police arrested two of them—Marian Oldham and Herman Thompson, both former chairpersons of St. Louis CORE. On Sunday, the seven others—Curtis, Clay, Seay, Charles Oldham, Lucian Richards, Ray Howard, and minister Charles Perkins—surrendered at the City Jail. They met an enthused throng of supporters, many of them having just adjourned from the NAACP's earlier mass rally against the board of education. "Mr. Millsap tells us we've set the Negro movement back 10 years," Clay said to the audience before turning himself in. "But 10 years ago the median income of the Negro was $1,000 a year less than the white man. Today it's $1,800 less." The Reverend I. C. Peay, president of the Ministers and Laymen's Association for Equal Opportunity, led a forty-minute prayer vigil.[22]

Prominent attorneys David Grant, Robert Witherspoon, and Alphonse J. Lynch and Missouri NAACP president Wilson joined the legal defense for the nine CORE leaders, who faced charges of criminal contempt. Questioning the legality of the arrests and the harshness of the charges, they argued that none of the defendants had participated in the civil disobedience except Curtis, who they insisted had entered the bank at Howard's instructions to get the demonstrators to leave. Clay, Thompson, Howard, and Marian Oldham were released, though on excessively high bail. The others remained voluntarily in jail in symbolic protest. At the CORE rally that followed at Grace Presbyterian Church, Clay and Thompson appeared before an overflow crowd, which passed a motion unanimously in favor of continuing bank demonstrations.[23]

In a blatant conflict of interest that outraged movement activists and other fair-minded citizens, Millsap was appointed special prosecutor in the case against the nine defendants. Not only was Millsap a Jefferson Bank attorney, but he was also the son-in-law of bank president Dillon J. Ross. Millsap and Judge Scott, further, were both members of the exclusive, lily-white Missouri Athletic Club. Given the dense relationships between the bank and the men prosecuting and presiding over the case—and the broader Civic Progress interests to which they adhered—it was hardly a shock when the court convicted the nine activists. On October 4, the following day, police arrested seven other leaders on contempt charges in connection with another episode of disruptive bank protests. The group included Roberta Tournour, Benjamin Goins, Louis Ford, and Taylor Jones, one of the leaders in the East St. Louis bank demonstrations. On the eve of their court appearance, members and supporters of CORE held a mass meeting where they adopted a plan to stall bank operations with petty transactions. This type of disruption, activists agreed, was less likely to lead to arrests, unlike the sit-ins that had occurred so far. The idea had come largely from field secretary Eugene Tournour, who, since the arrests of several of the organization's leading members, had become a main coordinator. Among the one hundred people in attendance at the meeting were members of an undercover police decoy squad, who alerted authorities about the plan. Consequently, when the militants attempted to implement their new tactic on October 7, four protesters, including East St. Louis NAACP Youth Council organizer James Peake, were arrested on contempt charges and for blocking police vehicles at the bank.[24]

A Circle Expands

Despite the three waves of arrests, the bank boycott had become a magnet drawing a broad cross-section of black and white St. Louisans. The black press unanimously supported the picketers. Supporters held fund-raisers to raise money for demonstrators' bail and fines. Teachers, laborers, and housewives walked the picket line, some with children in tow. Hershel Walker, the former chairman of the St. Louis Negro Labor Council, participated in the protests; so did William Massingale, a sixty-three-year-old former state representative and leader of St. Louis's Civil Rights Congress. Missouri state representatives Hugh White and DeVerne Calloway, both of them vocal civil rights proponents, were also on hand. Other locally elected black officials joined them, if for no other reason than to demonstrate a connectedness to black grassroots interests. As the arrests of Taylor and Peake indicated, activists even came across the river from East St. Louis to lend their encouragement and numbers. As the scale of the demonstrations escalated, members of CORE quickly found themselves outnumbered by unaffiliated sympathizers. The most critical component among the newcomers were the youth who attended the local high schools—Soldan, Beaumont, O'Fallon, Hadley, and East St. Louis's Lincoln High—as well as Washington and St. Louis universities.[25]

Although responsive to CORE organizers, black youth nonetheless were prone to act unpredictably. On October 11, demonstrators marched in the street from Jefferson Bank to the St. Louis Police Department headquarters, frustrating detectives who had to shut down traffic. The following day, authorities arrested thirty-two more people at the bank when, according to the *Post-Dispatch*, "leaders lost control of the crowd" during a demonstration. One hundred fifty people were picketing when a few, ignoring a large "No Trespassing" sign, marched onto the bank parking lot, and began circling the drive-in windows. Informed they were under arrest, they fell limply to the ground, prompting police to carry them by stretcher to waiting police vehicles. Other protesters followed suit by sitting and lying in groups at several other spots. Twenty youth lay together in a knot, blocking the bank drive-in, and even defying the cars that inched toward them. Tournour, Gretchen Carter, and Loretta Hall, a veteran from the St. Louis NAACP Youth Council protests of the late 1950s, were among the experienced activists arrested in the fray. To prevent police from loading the protesters, Clay, Hugh White, and Twentieth Ward alderman Lawrence Woodson sat on the bumper of a police truck. When they refused orders to move, police arrested them, as well. What had developed spontaneously into mass civil disobedience threatened to escalate further when a group of black youth surrounded the police truck to prevent it from leaving. Father Joseph Nicholson, a leader of the Ministers and Laymen's Association, tried to disperse the crowd, but he was ignored. The crowd was enticed to leave only when Louis Ford, standing atop a truck fender, instructed them to march to police headquarters. Seventy-five people followed.[26]

Fearing the worst, the Mayor's Office managed to convince protesters to consent to a two-week "cooling-off" period, beginning October 14. In the interim, Tucker hoped the two sides could negotiate a settlement, and an end to the boycott. For their part, CORE militants expected Jefferson Bank officials to use the truce to show "tangible evidence" of hiring more African Americans. The sentencing of the nineteen defendants associated with CORE's protests, therefore, could not have been more ill timed. On October 24 and 25, Judge Scott sentenced all of them to jail terms spanning sixty days to a year, and imposed hefty fines ranging from five hundred to a thousand dollars. In a final rebuke of the protests, he refused to release them on bond while they awaited appeal. "These defendants have aroused juveniles and young persons in the formative stages of their lives to act in contempt of the law," he railed, "and for this they should be severely denounced."[27]

The *Globe-Democrat,* a local bastion of white racial conservatism, congratulated Scott, while the more liberal *Post-Dispatch* ruminated that the sentences may have been too severe. Defense attorneys, in the meantime, filed applications for writs of habeas corpus. Foremost, they argued, the boycott was essentially a labor dispute, and as such belonged under the jurisdiction of a federal agency or court. Thus, Scott had had no power to issue a restraining order in the first place. Second, they maintained that the three groups of defendants had been deprived of due process, most egregiously through Millsap's appointment as special prosecutor. Moreover, the prosecution had not demonstrated the defendants' guilt beyond a reasonable doubt. That is, Judge Scott's restraining order had been issued against CORE as a group, and select members who were specifically named. Yet five of the defendants convicted for the disruption on August 30, and all ten individuals convicted in connection with the civil disobedience on October 4 and 7, were neither official members of CORE, nor individuals named by Scott. Thus, they were not bound by the injunction.[28]

While this appeal took shape, and the "Jefferson Bank 19" languished in jail, another bombshell exploded. The Council on Human Relations published a report disclosing that since late August, when Jefferson Bank officials signed the ten-point program against job discrimination, the bank had hired five new white employees. Bank representatives insisted that four of the five hires had been made prior to the August agreement, and the fifth was a temporary replacement. Whether this was true or not, the disclosure damaged prospects for a speedy end to the conflict. Inflammatory also was a high-handed statement by Jefferson Bank executive vice president Joseph McConnell, who likened the demonstrators to animals. "We were at first disgusted with the demonstrations," he declared. "Now we are angered. When aldermen and ministers and physicians picket your bank and block police vehicles, we wonder what our society is coming to." Mayor Tucker rather futilely called for full implementation of the ten-point employment agreement, and appealed to protesters not to resume any further "disorderly, illegal or violent demonstrations at the bank."[29]

The "General Strike" against Racism

As soon as the "cooling-off" period ended, demonstrators resumed the bank protests with missionary verve. As a means of mediating social conflict, cooling-off periods typically favored the powerful, who used the time to strengthen their opposition, often through co-optation or the law. Insurgents, on the other hand, usually faced the task of maintaining their momentum, typically amid economic and personal hardship. In this instance, however, the two-week armistice between the bank and the demonstrators had worked to the advantage of the latter. The civil rights grass roots had not only maintained mass support, but had also consolidated enough forces to actually broaden the scope of protest. What had begun as a bank boycott quickly matured into a general strike against the racism of the entire Civic Progress economic edifice.

Not only had Jefferson Bank executives refused to take any affirmative action toward hiring black clerical workers, but the City of St. Louis and its agencies had also tacitly supported this discrimination by continuing to deposit millions of dollars at the bank. On October 28, CORE helped stage a mass rally at City Hall that involved some one thousand people. A follow-up rally occurred that evening on the St. Louis University campus. The following afternoon, demonstrators picketed the offices of the St. Louis Land Clearance and Housing Authority. They appealed to the bureau to withdraw Mill Creek Valley redevelopment funds and other monies from the bank. Eighty people, mostly black, including two women carrying infants, then paraded to City Hall. Many carried signs demanding, "Remove City Money from Jim Crow Banks." Black freedom workers marched around the second-floor rotunda singing freedom songs and clapping their hands. They gathered at the office of city treasurer John J. Dwyer, the powerful chairman of the St. Louis Democratic Party and committeeman of the Fourth Ward. Sitting outside his door, they demanded the divestment of public monies from the bank.[30]

When, at the end of the day, Mayor Tucker emerged from his office with a plainclothes police escort, sit-in demonstrators began singing the freedom song, "Which Side Are You On?" As he boarded the elevator, several protesters raced downstairs and gathered around his waiting limousine, but did nothing to stop it from leaving. Later, 225 people gathered outside the City Jail to sing to the nineteen jailed activists. Fifty demonstrators returned to City Hall the next day, led by Reverend Frank Reid, a member of the Ministers and Laymen's Association and an organizer in ongoing protests against the board of education. Sit-ins at Dwyer's doorstep also continued. On November 6, Percy Green and twenty-four other protesters crowded outside the City Treasurer's Office. After the other demonstrators left that evening, Green stayed behind to conduct a silent hunger strike and vigil. Clutching a copy of Louis Lomax's *The Negro Revolt,* he passively refused to leave, forcing police to hoist him out of the building on a stretcher. In another episode, Winston Lockett, a national field secretary for CORE, led seven men and a sixteen-year-old girl in an overnight "sleep-in" in front of the city treasurer's office.[31]

By this time, a special squad from the Lucas Avenue police station had been assigned to monitor and control the "racial demonstrations." Rather than suppressing the protests with German shepherds, water hoses, or other forms of state brutality, the detail chose the less auspicious path of surveillance. This was consistent with St. Louis's civic culture as it regarded race, though this restraint was also likely at the behest of Mayor Tucker, who had demonstrated similar judiciousness during the 1961 protests against Jim Crow restaurants. Few city leaders, particularly those north of Dixie, wanted images of bloodied demonstrators splashed on front pages and television screens across the world. If nothing else, this might thwart Civic Progress efforts to attract commercial capital for downtown and riverfront redevelopment. An organized black contingent within the mayor's party, an expanding African American voting populace, and growing interracial and ecumenical support for the bank-related demonstrations, also accounted for the absence of rampant police violence against the movement under Tucker. Since the sentencing of the nineteen CORE workers, nightly vigils outside the City Jail, attended by hundreds of people, had become the norm. On October 29, 350 Catholic laity, priests, and nuns, mostly white, had held a silent march and candlelight prayer service on the steps of the Civil Courts Building. Another procession, organized by the predominantly white Conference on Religion and Race, brought thirty-five thousand people to the riverfront. Occurring on November 24, it also served as a memorial for the recently slain President Kennedy.[32]

The Ministers and Laymen's Association had also begun a petition for the defendants' release, and a reconsideration of their sentences. "This fight is no longer CORE's fight," the group had announced. "It is now the fight of every Negro and every person in this community who stands for human rights. Let us not confuse the issue. The issue is jobs." Expanding the parameters of protest even further, the black clergymen's group argued that if the city government was guilty of endorsing Jefferson Bank policies through their deposits, so too was the downtown business community. Not only did commercial elites transact regular business with discriminatory banks, but they also upheld a general pattern of job discrimination through their own activities. Citing the racial inequalities in employment, education and housing, Reverend Peay convinced the congregants at Galilee Baptist Church and seventy-five other churches to support a general consumer strike. In late October, the ministerial association urged St. Louisans to observe a boycott of the downtown stores on November 14 and 15.[33]

Following the announcement of the two-day "economic retreat," Downtown St. Louis and the Associated Retailers of St. Louis made their own announcement—a "Downtown Sale Days," plus free bus transportation for shoppers returning home. Coinciding with the planned consumer boycott, the commercial campaign appeared specifically designed to deflect the possible blow to retail revenues. When November 14 came, substantially fewer black shoppers were downtown, and their numbers diminished steadily throughout the day. Peay and other supporters passed out handbills at department store entrances, while an automobile, festooned with the sign "No Jobs—No Money Today" cruised the downtown streets. Short in duration, the boycott did not require a sustained community mobilization to succeed. Coordinated in the midst of heightened militancy, it gave nonmilitant civil rights supporters a passive way of contributing to the bank campaign, one that did not expose them to arrest.[34]

"Ne'er-Do-Wells" versus "Uncle Toms"

✐

At the same time, other dynamics were splintering the continuity among civil rights activists. On November 1, a week after Judge Scott had handed down his sentences, CORE attorneys won the temporary release of all nineteen defendants pending a hearing on the writs of habeas corpus. Nevertheless, the legal battle had disrupted the coordination of protest activities, while the activists' time behind bars had stymied experienced leadership. In Curtis's absence, Lucian Richards, and then Richard Daly, held CORE's local chairmanship, with Eugene Tournour as an anchor. Percy Green, still new to the movement himself, assumed responsibility for coordinating the picket line at the bank, and shortly thereafter became chairman of CORE's employment committee.[35]

Since the beginning of demonstrations on August 30, active membership had leapt from a close-knit group of 25 to 175. By late November, nearly three hundred people attended CORE's organizing meetings. Many were young black working-class participants who were unschooled in—or like Green, disdainful of—polite noncooperation. The central principle of this approach—putting white citizens at ease—not only overlooked the structural foundations of racism, but also implied that black people should be willing to stoically "earn" respect as human beings. Comfortable members of liberal interracial social networks may have been able to afford the luxury of a "tea and donuts" path to better black employment opportunities. But as the black laboring majority was making plain through its activity, the black grass roots was not willing to submit to this tactic. In the rush of events that had sped working-class people to the front lines, few had received training in CORE's philosophy and tactics of nonviolence. As the near-riot on October 11 suggested, the bank demonstrations had the latent potential to become outright rebellion.[36]

Black working-class youth's growing presence on the picket line had prompted black physician Jerome Williams, a leader in the school board protests, to mobilize his peers in the medical community to play a bigger role in the boycott. From this standpoint, it was important to project middle-class respectability in order to legitimize black popular demands for an end to Jim Crow. With picket signs declaring "Responsible People Want Justice" and "We Cannot Condone Recklessness or Stubbornness," Williams and other black medical professionals strove to offset the visibility of the black working-class "ne'er-do-wells," who he believed were discrediting the movement with their unruly conduct. The recent disturbances by black laboring-class youth in nearby Kinloch, which had similarly grown out of picketing, also would have impressed Williams with the urgent need for "responsible Negroes" to maintain order over the crowd. The

Reverend Amos Ryce, pastor of Lane Tabernacle Church and a member of the Mayor's Commission on Equal Employment Opportunity, echoed these sentiments, and those of the mayor and Governor Dalton, when he publicly rebuked the civil rights militants for their "immaturity and irresponsibility." Politically more conservative than his peers, Ryce had been perhaps the only member of the Ministers and Laymen's Association to oppose the June 20 street demonstration at the board of education building, not to mention the association's two-day moratorium on downtown shopping.[37]

The desire to show the more "respectable" face of civil rights activism to white authorities was symptomatic of the larger class, intergenerational, and ideological schisms that had developed around the protest strategies of the Jefferson Bank campaign. "Antagonisms among Negroes themselves have grown as debate and disagreement have sharpened over methods of struggle," commented the influential Detroit radical James Boggs, taking a national view of the movement. "Negroes have begun to realize that they will also have to fight Negroes before they win their freedom." Thus, the St. Louis Urban League and the NAACP, both initially supportive of the boycotters, had turned against the protests when militants continued to defy the court injunction. This staid opposition to CORE's tactics, voiced by NAACP branch president Evelyn Roberts, could have just been a cynical act of one-upmanship in the two organizations' ongoing competition since the late 1950s. But even old militants like State Senator McNeal upbraided the protesters for violating the restraining order. He contrasted the boycotters unfavorably with the MOWM activities of his own youth. "We were marching on the biggest plants in St. Louis for equal employment rights 22 years ago, but no one was ever arrested," he remarked during a Sunday evening address at the Union Memorial Methodist Church. "The political climate was not nearly as favorable then—the mayor didn't like us—but we were careful to obey the law and no one went to jail." Like Williams and Ryce, McNeal feared that the boycott was threatened by a lack of "respectable" leadership. From the pulpit, he urged the churchgoing audience to participate in the civil rights struggle so as to protect the movement's integrity from the "hate and violence" of disorderly insurgents.[38]

Ernest Calloway, at the time president of the St. Louis NALC and vice president of the NAACP, offered a more nuanced appraisal. He forcefully denounced Jefferson Bank officials, who "went into court with dirty hands, pious statements and a built-in contempt for the well-being of the community," and the St. Louis NALC publicly supported the call to remove all municipal funds from the bank until its executives complied with the spirit of the city's FEP ordinance. An ally of CORE, Calloway also advised his peers to close ranks behind the group because its destruction, he warned, would establish a dangerous precedent for isolating other black freedom organizations. Yet the local NALC chief, too, had politely disparaged the CORE protesters, whose undisciplined methods he contrasted with the "symphonic composition" of coordinated planning. The assessment was consistent with Calloway's earlier discord with the NAACP Youth Council. The Jefferson Bank militants were trying to re-create the Birmingham struggle in St. Louis, he observed, but the spontaneity of their actions paid no heed to objective differences in local conditions. Despite the city's quasi-southern culture, black St. Louisans had political tools at their disposal that their counterparts in Alabama lacked, including a supportive Mayor's Office, and the vote.[39]

Animated by "pre-conceived notions of the 'Negro Revolution,'" the bank boycotters hurtled forward with emotional zeal, but no well-defined goals. "The new young school of thought evidently seeks to create a crisis situation for massive community educational purposes," Calloway proffered. "This is supported by the theory that if the Negro community develops a deep sense of concern on the need for profound social change, the objective has been achieved." To Calloway, the weakness of this approach was evident in the fact that, rather than capitalizing on the ten-point program they had wrested from the banking industry in August, CORE's leaders had sought "total and unconditional surrender from one minor banking institution," Jefferson Bank. Better to have boycotted the larger, and more powerful, Mercantile Trust Company, if any example had to be made. A more effective strategy, he insisted, would have been organizing black public sentiment and votes against the passage of future bond issues, since investment in municipal and school bonds was a major local bank activity. By arbitrarily violating a court-ordered injunction, CORE had sacrificed its most articulate leaders to court trials and appeals, and allowed opponents to shift the conflict from black employment to "law and order."[40]

Civil rights militants responded to established black leaders like Ryce, McNeal, and Calloway by dismissing them as "Uncle Toms." The NALC president rejoined that the crude insult evaded principled differences, and sympathetic criticisms, about protest strategies and tactics. Making oblique references to Clay, Calloway also averred that personal claims to "militancy" provided a front for empty posturing and political ineptitude. He cautioned that at a moment of heightened struggle, when clarity among activists was of the essence, these could be costly errors. For one thing, unfocused emotional zeal and spontaneity made the movement vulnerable to opportunists who might exploit civil rights demands for personal gain. In all fairness, Calloway may have overestimated the control CORE's leadership exerted over the path of civic disobedience. The first bank demonstrations had exploded from the rank and file, and since then St. Louis CORE had fought to keep pace with, much less lead, its growing constituency. In the "spirit of urgency" that prevailed after Birmingham, grassroots movement workers were ready to storm the gates of racial apartheid for "Freedom Now." Unlike during the 1957 charter struggle, appeals to institutional politics in the current climate would have been tantamount to demobilizing the masses.[41]

The slurs traded between "ne'er-do-wells" and "Uncle Toms" formed the rough coating of a political dispute shaded with class tensions. It reflected, on the one hand, the anxieties of black professionals like Williams and Ryce, who viewed the rowdiness and illegal behavior of working-class people as a threat to their own personal and group respectability. Accordingly, not only did the "better sort" of black people stand to be publicly embarrassed, but black people as a whole also stood to lose legitimate claims to citizenship with their indecency. The dispute revealed, on the other hand, the straightforwardness of a grassroots rank-and-file that, facing structural unemployment, had no commitment to the rituals of deference and decorum governing relations among interracial elites. They were, moreover, ideologically antagonistic to the coercive "civility" of local race relations. Intergenerational differences were also enmeshed in these hostilities, for many of the boycotters' detractors had come of political age during the 1940s, or earlier. Clay suggested as much when he asserted that younger African Americans were "destined to become the real leadership for the extremely simple reason that they are in tune with the attitudes of the overwhelming majority of newly awakened Negroes."[42]

While containing great truth, Clay's statement nevertheless oversimplified the actual relationship between older and younger activists. The involvement in the protests of aging Communists like Walker demonstrated the intergenerational character of black working-class militancy. Yet old radicals, marginalized in the 1940s and 1950s, did not have the same visibility as their anticommunist contemporaries. The so-called old guard was also internally differentiated. Unlike individuals like Ryce and Williams, Calloway and McNeal were working-class leaders, albeit of a bureaucratic stripe. It is likely that the two labor chiefs had grown politically moderate, even more conservative, over time. But neither Calloway the Teamster, nor McNeal the former Pullman porter, had ever been willing to accommodate white supremacy, and this stance had not changed. Their criticisms of CORE were wholly consistent with black militancy, but the distinction was that they had been schooled in earlier paradigms of black insurgency. Calloway, a veteran of the mass movements of the Depression, had not graduated from the rowdy street battles between Communists and police that had nurtured left-wing organizers like Walker. On the contrary, his politics derived from a socialist outlook that regarded social change as fully attainable within a more democratic capitalism. MOWM demonstrations led in the 1940s by McNeal and Grant had openly confronted Jim Crow, but it had done so within the strict boundaries of the law. The bank boycotters, in contrast, applied the methods of civil disobedience—breaking laws, incurring arrests—that MOWM leaders had only vaguely considered. Black St. Louis activists traditionally had sought clearance from police in planning marches and demonstrations. The bank demonstrators, in contrast, frustrated authorities with their volatility. St. Louis MOWM leaders like Grant had studiously quashed spontaneous working-class agency when the rank and file had threatened to overwhelm the union officials, attorneys, and other black laboring elites forming the MOWM's executive leadership. But the Jefferson Bank protests, increasingly, were led by the rank and file.

As trade unionists with decades of experience in contract negotiations, Calloway and McNeal had considered protest from a largely instrumental perspective, viewing mass agitation as simply a means of bringing authorities to the boardroom table. This was evident in Calloway's leadership of the NAACP's aborted boycott of Famous-Barr in the late 1950s, and the St. Louis NALC's more recent backtracking on the planned protests against Southwestern Bell. The Jefferson Bank militants, on the other hand, viewed themselves as crusaders charging full tilt at the local "white power structure." They were willing, literally, to put their bodies "on the line" in front of bank entrances, tellers' cages, City Hall offices, and even the tires of police vehicles and cars. On many levels, then, the Jefferson Bank boycotters, who engaged in civil disobedience and practiced a more decentered form of organization, presented a model of protest that someone from Calloway and McNeal's generation could neither comprehend nor appreciate. At the same time, the strategies and tactics they deemed common sense appeared, to many younger black freedom workers, characteristic of the "house Negro" leadership reviled by Black Nationalist spokesmen like Malcolm X.[43]

It bears reminding, too, that Calloway and Clay also represented competing factions of a maturing black elected officialdom. Thus, the dispute between the "old guard" and "Young Turks" around the boycott's conduct manifested, in a different form, the continuing rivalry between two blocs of black electoral politicians and strategists jousting for power in the North St. Louis wards. Clay's Twenty-sixth Ward organization, for example, was a powerful base of CORE's black grassroots influence, leading Calloway to speculate that CORE unwittingly had become, through the young alderman, an appendage to a rump faction of Democrats led by former Board of Aldermen president Alfonso J. Cervantes, who hoped to embarrass and weaken Mayor Tucker's administration. Clay, from his own position in St. Louis Democratic politics, regarded McNeal and Calloway's cautiousness about civil disobedience as symptomatic of their debts to party chairman and city treasurer Dwyer, who had been a benefactor in McNeal's and DeVerne Calloway's electoral campaigns, and reputedly issued marching orders to Weathers. These relationships, Clay implied, tied them too closely to the sitting mayor, and compromised their integrity at a critical moment.[44]

Countermovement in the Media and Courts

However opportunistic or naively sincere they may have been, the "Young Turks" had nonetheless rallied many among the young black working-class public to their side. Thus, the objections to civil disobedience voiced by the "old guard" fell largely on deaf ears. Ignoring an exasperated NAACP leadership who asked them to call off the protests, St. Louis CORE proposed a Christmas shopping strike as a follow-up to the November 14–15 downtown boycott. That same day, Winston Lockett had led fifty demonstrators in a march through the central business district, where they tied up traffic for a half hour. Many were arrested as they lay in front of police cruisers. A few groups, including Beauticians United, a black barbers organization, the Delta Sigma Theta sorority, and the new Midtown Neighborhood Citizens Council, endorsed a renewed boycott, but most, even the Ministers and Laymen's Association, ignored the idea. Plans proceeded, nonetheless, and on November 21 thirty demonstrators marched in front of the department stores handing out leaflets. Before day's end, police arrested many of them on charges of disturbing the peace. On December 4, another contingent paraded through the stores, stuffing leaflets into merchandise. Twenty-five people, including Perry and Lockett, were arrested at Scruggs.[45]

The lack of broad support that St. Louis CORE received for its Christmas campaign stemmed from two likely sources. First, few other civil rights organizations were confident they could maintain a boycott during the Christmas shopping season, when social pressure and custom led families to purchase gifts. Second, consistent with the tensions among local civil rights moderates and militants, segments of the "old guard" hoped to minimize CORE's influence by undercutting any new initiatives its leaders developed. The daily media, which criticized the protesters, also took advantage of the breach among movement leadership to try to discredit the militants. One avenue was comparing Clay, Curtis, and other militants unfavorably to more responsible and "quiet" leaders like St. Louis Urban

League director M. Leo Bohanon. The other means involved loaded accusations of "subversion" against CORE. As had been the case since the 1940s, southern segregationists continued to use the rhetoric of racial paternalism and anticommunism to deride black freedom workers. The *Globe-Democrat*, whose leading editorial writer, Patrick J. Buchanan, embodied the newspaper's enmity toward civil rights struggle, borrowed this strategy as part of a countercampaign to strip the bank protest of its legitimacy. In late December, the newspaper began publishing a ten-part "exposé" series on the "pro-Communist" affiliations of several national members, regional organizers, and local members and supporters of CORE. Reporter Denny Walsh highlighted, as an example, the presence of old Communists at the bank and City Hall picket lines. Reporters also implied that Tournour and Lockett, both full-time organizers for the national CORE, were essentially "outside agitators" who had imported a foreign black militancy to St. Louis.[46]

As "outside agitators" and "communist instigators" had become synonymous in meaning, such revelations were meant to insinuate that the protests were part of lurid, insurrectionary plots. More pointedly, the taunts were designed to deflect public support from black grievances by shifting the focus to the disrepute of those making demands for greater employment opportunity. The *Globe-Democrat* report did acknowledge, in a backhanded manner, that the boycott had gained greater mass appeal since beginning; yet Walsh interpreted this growth as evidence that St. Louis CORE, like its parent organization, was losing the ability to screen and "control" members. This, of course, made the group susceptible to Communist infiltration. To reinforce this claim, the series spotlighted Sam Riley, the former chairman of Chicago CORE who had resigned in July 1963 out of disgust with the "ultramilitant tactics of the kids." The newspaper subtly linked these political and generational fissures to the specter of domestic subversion. Walsh also quoted Ryce, who freely expressed his misgivings about the growing trend of mass civil disobedience. America had to resolve the problem of black civil rights, he advised, "lest the Communists do try."[47]

Significantly, the FBI provided the *Globe-Democrat* with classified documents and other information used to compile the series of articles. Acting under the guise of containing domestic threats to U.S. security, FBI director J. Edgar Hoover had long sought to immobilize black freedom struggles through interwoven tactics of red- and race-baiting. Thus, much of the bureau's intelligence, shared with the White House and Congress, was filtered through the prism of the bureau's own virulently racist and anticommunist culture. If anything, the *Globe-Democrat* series merely gave the boycott's opponents further justification for their resistance. For their part, leaders and participants in the bank demonstration were hardly dissuaded from their goals by the negative coverage. State Representative White, for one, already had prompted the Missouri Commission on Human rights to begin a full-scale investigation of employment discrimination at Jefferson Bank. The year 1963 ended with police arresting Hall, Carter, and twenty other members of CORE outside Dwyer's office when they refused to leave City Hall on New Year's eve. On bail pending his appeal, Clay strongly advocated continuing the general strike. The nightly harassment of the working-class black family in an all-white neighborhood in Jennings had made the local news, and for many the episode reinforced the need for a total war on the triad of segregated housing, education, and employment. Speaking at a January 1964 conference on civil rights at St. Louis University, Clay averred, "[T]he white man's promises of 'tomorrow' falls on deaf ears. The Negro wants his freedom now." Acknowledging that it was possible, even likely, that he would return to jail, he intimated that he and his codefendants could "endure cold winters in jail if the white man can endure the long hot summers in the streets."[48]

Such comments are noteworthy for what they reveal about the changing mentalities among St. Louis's civil rights workers. Like the "white power structure," another newly popular term, "the white man" had not been commonplace in mainstream public discourses of postwar black politics until Malcolm X's standardization of postwar Black Nationalism. The "white man" certainly had not been a trope in Clay's pronouncements before his surrender at the City Jail in early September 1963. The change in speech may have been a result of being personally radicalized by legal repression: He and Robert Curtis had, in fact, received the stiffest penalties in Judge Scott's courtroom—270 days and one thousand dollars each. Yet Clay was, among other things, a savvy and ambitious young politician. However ambivalent he may have been at the outset of the bank protests, he recognized the emergence of a new politics, and sought to respond to it, as well as galvanize it. Thus, he spoke to a rising constituency among the black working class, particularly young jobless adults, who had long since become agitated by the pace of change. Shaped by declining opportunities for full employment, this segment was caught between militant liberalism and Black Nationalism. Drawing from this base of discontent, the alderman's militant, proto-nationalist rhetoric mirrored among younger "Negroes" a growing self-designation as "Black." His insinuations of "long hot summers in the streets," which was becoming shorthand for discussing black urban working-class insurrections, also played to this growing element among the grass roots. It conjured, as well, public fears about the potential for rebellion among unemployed black youth.[49]

"Gateway to What?"

A few days later, Clay and fifteen of his codefendants were remanded back to jail after their appeals failed, while the convictions against Howard, Thompson, and the Oldhams were overturned. Charles Oldham, Hugh White, and the precinct captains from Clay's ward organization led sixty people in a raucous motorcade outside the City Jail. While nightly vigils in front of the lockup resumed, and pickets in front of City Hall and Jefferson Bank continued, attorneys appealed to the Missouri Supreme Court. The high court denied the appeals on February 1, 1964, leaving CORE's legal defenders to consider action in federal court. (The following month, lawyers again secured the defendants' release pending an application for a writ of habeas corpus.) Meanwhile, civic leaders had begun celebrating St. Louis's bicentennial. Amid the inconveniences of the Jefferson Bank boycott and its offshoots, they looked forward to a calendar of events—including a touted visit by President Lyndon B. Johnson—that would advance the city's downtown redevelopment plans, particularly the Jefferson National Expansion Memorial. While guests celebrated an evening "pre-bicentennial" affair at the swank Chase-Park Plaza Hotel, forty CORE demonstrators picketed outside. Challenging the pomp of Civic Progress boosterism, they carried signs admonishing, "Desegregate—Then Celebrate," and "200 Years, Yes—Progress, No." "Gateway to What?" another protester's sign asked. The question was somewhat enigmatic, raising doubts about the historical meanings of U.S. expansion west of the Mississippi. Viewed in its more contemporary, immediate context, the sign highlighted the discrepancies between the optimism of urban redevelopment, embodied in the Gateway Arch project, and the unequal benefits the black laboring majority had derived in housing and work.[50]

Perhaps unwisely, civil rights workers publicized their intentions to demonstrate at other glitzy bicentennial engagements, including the February 14 ceremony, also at the Chase, where President Johnson was scheduled to appear. Like the Civic Progress elite, CORE strategists saw the president's visit as an important opportunity; in the activists' case, it presented a chance to draw the nation's attention to racial discrimination in St. Louis, and the jail sentences of civil rights leaders. On the night of the affair, eighty-six members and supporters of CORE gathered on the edge of Forest Park, four blocks from the hotel. Just as they began a single-file march, two police trucks and five cruisers interceded, and officers arrested the entire procession. Claiming they posed a threat to the president's safety, authorities whisked them away to the downtown police headquarters for questioning. As capriciously as they had detained them, police released them, without any charges or fines, immediately after Johnson and his entourage left the city. Furious over the detentions, White, acting as the group's attorney, undoubtedly spoke for many others, declaring, "I'm getting sick and tired of this non-violent business. The next time we're going to give the police a good excuse for arresting us. If they're going to treat us like mules, I'm going to act like a mule." Although speaking in an obvious fit of anger, the state representative nonetheless underscored the frayed consensus around the validity of nonviolent movement tactics.[51]

Indicative of the other class, ideological, and generational differences that had splintered black leadership, the St. Louis NAACP refused to support any demonstrations during Johnson's visit. Many of the branch's prominent members, including president Evelyn Roberts, attended the gala at the Chase while demonstrators were spirited to jail. Another attendee, NAACP member Frankie Freeman, had been part of the 1957 charter controversy that had similarly heralded the growing differentiation of St. Louis's postwar black community. As associate counsel for St. Louis's Land Clearance and Housing Authority, she was, in the likely view of young civil rights militants, implicated in the "white power structure" protecting inequitable employment practices and downtown "negro removal." Immediately before the bicentennial program, Freeman—a member of the Missouri Advisory Committee of the U.S. Civil Rights Commission—had also had a private audience with President Johnson, who informed her of his intentions to name her the first woman to the federal commission. The two had also discussed the importance of defeating communism. Given the *Globe-Democrat*'s red-baiting of CORE, discussing the need to combat subversion was hardly casual conversation, and allowed Freeman to assure the president of her stance against the city's ongoing protests.[52]

This latest mass arrest proved to be among the final attempts at repressing the boycott's energy. On March 31, 1964, Jefferson Bank relented in the hiring of six black bank tellers. Over the following months, between thirty-five and forty-five (and later, eighty-four) African American employees were hired at the bank and fourteen other financial institutions. Several other companies, fearful that protests "would come to them next," according to Seay, endorsed the St. Louis Commission on Equal Employment Opportunity's ten-point program. Eight months earlier, perhaps, activists might have considered this an unqualified victory. Given the tremendous sacrifices involved, however, the concessions seemed tokenistic. For most, the arrests had been both financially and politically costly, while legal repression had frightened a number of activists from the movement. The boycott's uneasy denouement had also widened the split between St. Louis CORE's "liberals" and "direct actionists," and the gulf between an older, "whiter" leadership and younger, "blacker" rank-and-file. Many of

CORE's veterans from the 1940s and 1950s, ill at ease with the attention-grabbing civil disobedience characterizing the "general strike," disavowed any future such disruptions. Another faction, headed by St. Louis chairman Lucian Richards and Percy Green, called for heightened nonviolent confrontations with other major employers. When the moderates won a critical vote for leadership of the chapter, Green and his allies began quietly forming a separate organization.[53]

A fragmentation of political agendas also remained evident in the feud among black factions within the St. Louis Democratic Party. The time he spent incarcerated had nearly destroyed Clay's ward organization, but it had also strengthened his movement bona fides and political stature, and fed his long-range ambitions. Urban renewal may have attenuated the city's black electoral bloc in the Central Corridor, but this strength had been reconstituted in other areas of concentration. With the August 1964 primary looming, the "Young Turk" alliance of William Clay, Hugh White, T. H. Mayberry, Lawrence Woodson, and Leroy Tyus, the Democratic committeeman of the Twentieth Ward, made public their intentions to defeat Mayor Tucker, who would soon stand for reelection. In the process, they hoped to establish control in the black Fourth, Eighteenth, Nineteenth, Twenty-first, and Twenty-second wards, and sweep aside older "Uncle Tom" leaders like Weathers and the Calloways. Supported by White and Clay, Arthur J. Kennedy, a sheet metal shop operator who had led a struggle to enroll black students at the all-white Rankin trade school, put up a spirited fight for the Fourth Ward committeeman seat. Dwyer fended off his opponents to keep the post. (In 1963, he already had used his influence to unseat Mayberry as Fourth Ward alderman and install Joseph W. B. Clark.) White also ran unsuccessfully against Weathers for committeeman in the Eighteenth Ward, and lost his seat in the Missouri General Assembly to Ray Howard. Meanwhile, Benjamin Goins, another bank protester, won the office of Twenty-first Ward committeeman. Clay, who since his election had quickly discerned the greater power a Democratic committeeman could wield in the Twenty-sixth Ward and the party, had also vacated his aldermanic seat to challenge Norman Seay, a former ally with whom he had severed political ties. With Ida Harris campaigning at his side as committeewoman, and with her Democratic organization in firm support, Clay ousted his protégé in a bitter contest.[54]

The Clay-White coalition's next putsch occurred in the race for the 1964 Democratic gubernatorial candidate. Most black leaders in St. Louis and Kansas City endorsed Lieutenant Governor Hilary Bush. For others, Bush was not able to escape his association with Governor Dalton, who had come out forcefully against the Jefferson Bank protests. Working to forge a new statewide political bloc, the Clay-White faction backed Bush's opponent, Missouri secretary of state Warren E. Hearnes. "It was obvious that I would not be able to penetrate the inner circle of the established Democratic Party," Clay later wrote. "Therefore I was compelled to seek alliances with other aspiring politicians. Hearnes fell into that category." Yet Hearnes, as a state legislator, had publicly defended racial segregation and opposed the *Brown* ruling. The sharp animosity between Calloway and Clay became even more lacerating as the Teamsters leader railed against the "Young Turks" for approving a candidate whose support included cotton planters, White Citizens Council members, and other blocs of white racist reaction in Missouri's Bootheel and Ozark regions—not to mention the "arch racists and segregationists" among St. Louis's Steamfitters and south side politicians. As with his reputed ties to racially retrograde South St. Louis politicians, Clay was again derided for choosing expediency over principle. Undaunted, the "Young Turks" stood with Hearnes as he won an upset victory over Bush, and bested his Republican opponent. Notwithstanding the fact that the governor-elect had lost in every one of St. Louis's black wards, Clay continued his political ascent.[55]

The group of black elected officials surrounding Clay and White had been especially skillful in capitalizing on the campaign of civil disobedience to challenge older white political bosses, and older black representatives, within the St. Louis Democratic Party. In many respects, Clay's rise resembled that of Jordan Chambers or David Grant during the tumultuous depression years. But in the changed climate of the mid-1960s, as white political elites anticipated that black St. Louisans would soon elect one of their own to higher offices, the temptations for political co-optation had become far greater. Calloway bitterly joked that if Clay "could keep his mouth shut long enough, his ears close enough to the heart-beats of the Negro community, and his naked ambition properly dressed, he could easily achieve the dizzy heights of Negro leadership to which he aspires." The aging Teamster worried, however, that this "local young man of destiny" would put his newfound power to self-serving and dangerous uses. In the meantime, the dream of a unified and collective black leadership, as contained in St. Louis's "Negro Proclamation," was horribly dashed.[56]

The overlapping conflicts in St. Louis's black electoral and social movement politics had also spilled over into the local NAACP. Charging that the current leadership had grown ineffective and "sterile," a slate headed by NAACP secretary Pearlie Evans and attorney Clyde Cahill challenged the incumbency of president Evelyn Roberts and vice president Ernest Calloway. The opposition slate also included Ruth Porter, executive director of the Freedom of Residence Committee, and state NAACP president Margaret Bush Wilson. Using the weight of her office and reputation, Wilson argued that under Roberts's tenure, the St. Louis branch had drifted aimlessly, contributing virtually nothing to the movement. She was especially incensed by the branch's decision to drop a suit against the board of education for perpetuating school segregation, which had alienated local constituents and squandered the base that she and others had built in the 1950s. As proof of the NAACP's decline in St. Louis, she pointed to membership rolls that had dwindled from eight thousand in 1961 to less than five thousand.[57]

Once an ally of Calloway's, Wilson had by now defected to the "Young Turks." Evans, a social worker, and Cahill were also both tied to Clay and White, and were rumored by their opponents, as well as by the *Argus,* to be planning to use the organization to support the former South St. Louis alderman Alphonso Cervantes in a mayoral bid against Tucker. The fight to control the NAACP became so acrimonious that when the branch held elections for officers and board members in early December 1964, two national officials were on hand. An unofficial vote declared Evans the winner by nine votes, and Cahill and Calloway tied. Yet more than one hundred NAACP members signed a petition requesting another election when it became evident that hundreds of certified voters had been locked out or otherwise thwarted in obtaining ballots. With the results in dispute, the national NAACP headquarters authorized a recount in early January, which resulted in Roberts and Calloway winning by extremely small margins. Not to be outdone, the Evans group filed a complaint with the national NAACP, which ordered another recount. Following six hours of balloting, Roberts and Calloway were reelected, accompanied by all of the top officers on their slate. In a gesture of unity, Roberts appointed Evans to the NAACP's housing committee and Cahill to the board, but the assignments could not mask the deep divisions that remained within the association.[58]

As the Jefferson Bank struggle was coming to these multiple and fretful conclusions, Henry Winfield Wheeler died. Battling age and illness for years, the seventy-six-year-old had been living in the care of his daughter, Ruth Mattie Wheeler. One of St. Louis's last remaining "race men" from the period prior to the Depression, he had become known locally as "Mr. Civil Rights." Crediting him as a movement architect, the *Argus* eulogized that Wheeler had "fathered direct action in the St. Louis area," preceding the "social revolution of the sixties" by four decades. "The irony of it is," editors noted, chastising the Jefferson Bank protesters, "that so many of the youngsters engaged in direct action programs have scoffed at any activity of by-gone years. Yet, had it not been for the Henry Wheelers, or more specifically—Henry Wheeler, conditions would not have progressed enough for the antics of the modern-day militants."[59]

To be sure, the bank demonstrations and "general strike" had not dramatically altered black workers' overall circumstances, but neither had black employment conditions remained the same. In July 1964, the Mayor's Commission on Equal Employment Opportunity boasted that the number of African Americans employed at twenty-one retail and department stores had increased from 1,231 to 1,631 since the previous summer—a growth of 32 percent. New employees included 170 sales workers, 154 semiskilled and service employees, and twenty-six skilled craftsmen. Yet commission members also made public their disappointment with the small number of black St. Louisans in skilled apprenticeship training. This was painfully true of the St. Louis Building and Construction Trades Council, which—aside from the Teamsters Joint Council No. 13, and the International Association of Machinists District Council No. 9—represented the largest number of unionized workers in the entire metropolitan area. Despite a housing boom in the early to middle 1960s, a shortage of skilled labor, and formal nondiscrimination pledges, few building contractors and building trades unions admitted black apprentices. The exclusion was most acute among the city's electricians, as well as the membership of Ironworkers Local 396, Steamfitters Local 562, and Plumbers Local 35. Even with authorities in Washington, D.C., closely watching their apprenticeship programs, none of the organizations in the St. Louis area had had their government certification revoked or suspended for failing to meet federal guidelines. Laying blame on a shortage of black applicants, construction tradesmen continued to rebuff the claim that their history of racism obligated them to go beyond "passive nondiscrimination," and ignored angry entreaties by national NAACP labor secretary Herbert Hill to actively recruit in black high schools and communities.[60]

In August 1964, one year after the bank boycott had begun, Marian Oldham spoke before an audience at the city's private Fontbonne College. Only a month earlier, President Johnson had signed into law the nation's most comprehensive civil rights act, which prohibited discrimination in all public accommodations, outlawed school segregation, and reinforced black voting rights. Title VII of the act banned job discrimination, and created the Equal Employment Opportunity Commission (EEOC) to oversee private employers. The Office of Federal Contract Compliance, another provision created under the Department of Labor, monitored the employment practices of firms receiving government contracts and subsidies. With a mixture of hope and despair, Oldham portrayed employment discrimination as the most stubborn form of racism in the metropolitan area. "Of the 53,000 Negro males working in Greater St. Louis, only 354 are earning $10,000 or more," she stated:

> Only 15 per cent earn $5,000 or more annually and about 70 per cent of the Negro youths who tried to find summer jobs were un-

successful. The backbone of the Negro home is the woman who makes up 46 per cent of the Negro work force. And much of this is in the field of domestic help where she meets little competition from the white work force.[61]

In a few deft verbal strokes, she encapsulated black adults' marginal work lives, and the rampant joblessness among African American adolescents. The consequences, as civil rights organizations from CORE to the NALC understood, were far-reaching. Continuing employment discrimination stunted black St. Louis's overall economic development, affecting both workers and middle-class professionals in the areas of housing, education, and other living standards. Dreams of a just and prosperous interracial civic partnership, articulated in the "Negro Proclamation" by local civil rights workers, seemed further from realization than they had been in 1961.

These dismal economic conditions, paradoxically, had energized the burgeoning group of black freedom dissidents led by Percy Green. A wave of black-led insurgencies, begun by Philadelphia CORE in 1962, had been sweeping construction sites in New York City, Newark, and Cleveland. In the aftermath of the Jefferson Bank employment campaign, these struggles provided St. Louis activists with fresh inspiration. As construction proceeded on the Gateway Arch in the summer of 1964, the direct-action militants dramatically announced both their split from CORE and the arrival of a creative new nonviolent resistance. On July 14, while the Arch work crew lunched, Green and Richard Daly, a white activist, climbed 125 feet up the north leg of the unfinished monument. Another group of protesters, gathering for a press conference nearby, explained the action as a dramatization of black workers' exclusion from well-paying skilled employment opportunities on the publicly supported project, and demanded that African Americans receive at least 10 percent of the jobs at the site. Refusing orders by workers, National Park Service officers, and the project's assistant superintendent to disembark from their perch on a steel surface ladder, Green and Daly shut down work for the entire afternoon. When they did descend, four hours later, police arrested them on charges of trespassing, peace disturbance, and resisting arrest. Daly spent the night in police holdover, while Green bonded out in time to make his midnight work shift. The demonstration marked the debut of the Action Council (later Committee) to Improve Opportunities for Negroes (ACTION).[62]

Civic decision-makers, hoping to save the city from decline, continued to seek an economic future at the banks of the Mississippi, where the St. Louis metropolis had been born. They hoped the sprawling Jefferson National Expansion Memorial, exemplifying the past glory of frontier exploration and "Manifest Destiny," would serve as the harbinger of a present-day downtown revival. The memorial's centerpiece, the Gateway Arch, would embody St. Louis as the doorway to the western hinterlands, and serve as a portal to renewed prosperity in the Central Corridor. But as the Arch demonstration powerfully asserted, many black St. Louisans facing the brunt of the postwar urban crisis were determined to resolve the question: "Gateway to What?"[63]

In the Jefferson Bank conflict, two diverse cross-class groupings of black activists had clashed. The first grouping encompassed middle-aged leaders representing the stably unionized segment of the working class, Jordan Chambers-era black electoral politics, and spokespersons from older black middle-class professions such as medicine. The second grouping included younger, more economically tenuous segments of black workers, ambitious upstarts in the electoral arena, and a budding stratum of black professionals versed in an emerging new political language.

As early as 1963, and certainly after 1964, liberal integrationism had steadily ceded ideological ground to a Black Nationalist renaissance. By 1966 "Freedom Now" had become "Black Power," a new phase of movement activism more directly oriented toward the cohort of urban black youth who had gained political consciousness through the Jefferson Bank boycott, and similar struggles around the nation. Like civil rights, Black Power also had a grassroots foundation, evident in both its rhetoric and stylizations. Unlike civil rights, however, Black Power projects were more multidimensional in scope. As they proliferated, they created new strains on the movement's working-class bases.

CHAPTER SEVEN

"What Do We Want?": Black Power and the Growing Contradictions of Class, 1965–71

THE PASSAGE OF THE 1964 Civil Rights and 1965 Voting Rights acts were vividly symbolic of the movement's many triumphs, but they also unraveled the tenuous consensus that had fastened together the national civil rights coalition of the SCLC, NAACP, SNCC, CORE, and the Urban League. The already strained relations between SNCC and CORE on the one hand, and the NAACP and the Urban League on the other, frayed as black freedom militants and moderates divided on whether movement workers should intensify their insurgency, or pursue group interests in the arena of electoral politics. Escalating U.S. militarism in Southeast Asia further widened the chasm as black moderates and white liberals rallied behind the Johnson administration, while many of the younger activists spoke against American empire. Battle-fatigued militants had also begun to divide around such issues as the place of white activists in movement organizations, the importance of black leadership, and the need to adopt programs of sustained inner-city "community organizing."

These broad transformations, coupled with the growing racialized poverty of the nation's declining industrial centers, seeded the soil for an array of political and cultural developments that collectively became known as "Black Power." Black Power emerged in the late 1960s not only as a new stage of the Black Freedom Movement, but also as another juncture of black working-class formation. This new stage consisted chiefly of automation and the erosion of black advances in semiskilled labor. It also involved urban renewal and central-city redevelopment that resulted in "negro removal," the working-class riots in Watts and most other major cities, and the advent of federal antipoverty programs to stabilize an expanding black "hardcore jobless." Further, this phase of working-class formation was defined by U.S. social movements waged by other racially oppressed peoples and white antiwar radicals, as well as prolonged anticolonial and anti-imperialist struggles in Asia, Africa, and Latin America.

Black Power took numerous organizational forms in the St. Louis metropolitan area, most notably the Black Artists Group, Black Liberators, the
Zulu 1200s, CORE, and ACTION. The most significant of these local
groups, ACTION, served as a bridge between civil rights and Black Power
and demonstrated the wide-ranging nature of black working-class politics.
Eventually coalescing into a loose "Black Liberation Front," these organizations all participated in highly publicized disruptions of Sunday worship
services, which targeted religious institutions for the deepening impover-
ishment of the city's black working-class enclaves. The demonstrations
were informally tied to a national reparations campaign centering on a
treatise known as the "Black Manifesto." Another formative moment in St.
Louis's Black Power ferment occurred in 1969, when female public housing
tenants waged the nation's first, and largest, citywide rent strike. At a time
when both white liberal and Black Nationalist discourses associated matriarchy with the black community's poverty, these women claimed the right
to respect, fair rents, and the ability to maintain autonomous households.
Black Power was programmatically amorphous, amenable to both Democratic functionaries and radical democrats. Thus, it became the language of
competing class politics as a developing new post-civil-rights stratum of
African American entrepreneurs, professionals, and elected officials vied
against working-class leadership to define, or rather redefine, the corporate
black interest.

The Cervantes Administration and Black St. Louis

Because of the interrelated character of St. Louis's social movements and
institutional politics, some of the most immediate effects of the Jefferson
bank protests were in elected officialdom. Having worked for Hearnes's
victory in the 1964 gubernatorial race, the Clay-White camp redoubled its
efforts to fashion a new political bloc at City Hall. Raymond Tucker's
twelve-year tenure as St. Louis mayor thus came to an end in the spring of
1965, when he lost the Democratic primary to Alfonso J. Cervantes, the former Board of Aldermen president backed by the "Young Turks." In contrast
to Tucker's standoffish posture toward many grassroots leaders, Cervantes
had mobilized small merchants, white workers, and other ward-based loy-
alists dissatisfied with the downtown capitalists influential in Tucker's administration. Despite the cordial relations he had developed with older
black political insiders, Tucker also had never been popular among most
black St. Louisans. A succession of controversies—the Mill Creek Valley
clearance, his noncommittal stance regarding the possible closure of
Homer G. Phillips Hospital, and his favoritism toward the banks during

the Jefferson Bank drama—had further damaged his image. With five of the city's eight black wards offering endorsement, Cervantes received nearly 60 percent of the black vote.[1]

Lamenting Tucker's removal as the end of a long period of racial reform in St. Louis, Calloway pointed out that the incoming mayor had no strong record on behalf of African Americans. As a South St. Louis alderman, Cervantes had undermined public accommodations bills several times by voting not to release them to the Aldermanic floor. While campaigning for mayor in early February 1965, he had also caused a furor when, during a speech to a white audience, he related how the decline in municipal services had generated "shabby and rundown neighborhoods, urbanized jungles peopled with mechanized savages." The description called to mind tropes of barbarism that had grown widespread in commentaries about urban areas that were becoming heavily black. The *Argus* had raised other questions about the Democratic hopeful when editors ran a story accusing the Laclede Cab Company, which Cervantes owned, of racist hiring practices. His campaign had protested the newspaper's numbers, claiming that five of the company's taxicab drivers were black, and not three, as the *Argus* had alleged. "How does this change the employment record of this vast operation, which it is charged, hires upwards of 300 drivers?" asked an *Argus* editorial, fully conceding the error. "Does the candidate really feel that this is fair employment and something to headline?" Fourth Ward alderman Joseph W. B. Clark, a staunch Tucker supporter, was equally irate. "If all employers in St. Louis hired Negroes on the same percentage basis as Mr. Cervantes," he snapped, "the unemployed Negroes could reach all the way to Jefferson City where they could pass their welfare checks back to St. Louis by hand." Almost from the moment Cervantes took office, moreover, Tucker's Commission on Equal Employment Opportunity languished.[2]

The mayor muted growing opposition through a new rapprochement with selected black leaders. In August 1965, he convened a summit on black unemployment, assembling a citizens committee to craft an agenda on black economic opportunity. He appointed M. Leo Bohanon, who had been promoted to regional director of the National Urban League; William Douthit, the St. Louis Urban League's new executive director; Ruth Porter, who led the Greater St. Louis Freedom of Residence Committee; and Pearlie Evans, who had lost the bitter 1964 race for NAACP branch president. Clay, who had delivered a margin of nearly three thousand votes for Cervantes in the Twenty-sixth Ward, was elected committee chairman. Percy Green, whose group ACTION had been gaining notoriety for its flamboyant street protests against job discrimination, was notably not invited to the summit. His absence made clear the meeting's key purpose, to incorporate tractable black activists and supporters and solder them to a revised politics of liberal interracial gradualism. "Little will be gained by demonstrations and nuisance marches, which bear little relation to problem-solving," Mayor Cervantes scolded. "The time is now at hand for problem-solving and they will be much easier to solve if we direct our energies to the harder work of negotiation, persuasion and motivation."[3]

That some prominent members of St. Louis's black public sphere were amenable to this reasoning was indicative of the growing class cleavages that had widened in African American postwar politics. Popular agitation may have made such political diversity possible in the first place, but even erstwhile militants like Clay argued that the time had come to leave behind mass demonstrations and focus on "politics"—implied as electoral participation and private negotiation. Many spoke as if the grassroots dynamism that had fed the 1963–64 "general strike" was exhausted. "Some of the nineteen that got arrested at the Jefferson Bank, never got arrested again," Ivory Perry sourly recalled of the high-profile leaders of CORE. "Never picketed again." Many of the defendants had not even been in favor of protests. Several of them had paid a steep personal price for their association with CORE, nonetheless. When the U.S. Supreme Court, in February 1967, refused to review continuing legal appeals, eight defendants returned to jail. Embarrassed by the lingering reminders of the bank protests, St. Louis business leaders quietly convinced Judge Michael Scott to offer parole. He agreed, albeit on the condition that the activists publicly apologize for their antics. Most of them flatly rejected the circuit court judge's compromise, and chose to serve the remainder of their sentences. Notwithstanding private attempts to soothe racial discord, many black working-class activists rejected the idea that such rapprochement with Civic Progress patriarchs made protest unnecessary. "The whole problem of street demonstrations is that there are too many people who are pretending that they are supporting civil rights activity behind closed doors," Green complained. "The majority of people who say demonstrations are no longer appropriate are either tired or contented or they have given up the fight."[4]

If Cervantes convinced some black activist-politicians to forgo future protests, he could not so easily dismiss black workers' stagnating conditions, which made insurgent politics a continuing possibility among the masses outside the mayor's inner circle. "With machines now replacing human labor," sociologist Sidney M. Willhelm wrote in the late 1960s, "who needs the Negro?" On the basis of employment patterns in the U.S. corporate capitalist economy, the answer was grim. A 1966 report sponsored by the federal EEOC found that African Americans in the St. Louis metropolitan area remained underrepresented in high-salaried fields, with 69 percent of surveyed firms employing no black males in white-collar and crafts-men positions, and 80 percent reporting no black women in skilled occu-pations. In St. Louis alone, an estimated 60,000 black workers were "sub-employed," a category encompassing those either working below their skills or at wages that kept them mired in poverty. By 1968, the Department of Labor reported that some 19,000 (or 12.7 percent) of the 150,000 African Americans in the workforce on both sides of the Mississippi River were job-less. This was higher than in Detroit, which at the time had 10.7 percent. That spring, Urban League director Douthit hailed as a "major break-through" the hiring of three black steamfitters at Anheuser-Busch; two years earlier, Clay had brokered the entry of ten black journeymen and five black apprentices into the union. Yet these inroads hardly addressed the fact that the area had developed the worst case of black unemployment among the nation's fifteen largest metropolitan areas. This corresponded to the stark reality that between the early 1950s and 1967, St. Louis City had lost 50,000 jobs in manufacturing, and 35,000 in wholesale and retail, while St. Louis County had gained over 75,000 and 47,000, respectively. With St. Louis's boundaries long since locked, and competing municipal govern-ments mushrooming beyond its borders, political power and economic de-velopment had shifted from the central city, intensifying black joblessness.[5]

A cruel paradox of the city's unusually high number of unemployed black adult males was that it existed alongside a major downtown con-struction boom. Between 1945 and 1964, nearly $1 billion in urban renewal work had occurred in the city. The Mill Creek Valley redevelopment ven-ture, and the $17 million Memorial Plaza Apartment project, had both evinced a downtown renovation at full tilt. Civic Progress boosters dedi-cated the new Busch Memorial Stadium in 1966. After numerous delays and controversies, the gleaming, 630-foot Gateway Arch opened to na-tional fanfare in 1967. Completed during this period, three expressway routes connected the central business district with St. Louis County and, it was believed, renewed commerce. In observance of the city's colonial Spanish past, Cervantes had also purchased the Spanish Pavilion from the 1964 New York World's Fair. The structure, a popular tourist attraction, was located between the Arch and Busch Stadium sites. Other corporate construction projects came to fruition, including the Stouffer Riverfront Inn, the Pet Incorporated Building, and the Ralston Purina Building and Checkerboard Square. Yet the urban renewal coalition's continuing inat-tention to racial discrimination at construction work sites had given union tradesmen carte blanche to bar African Americans from skilled work. By 1966, Green and Daly's protest at the Gateway Arch site had become part of a chain of events leading the U.S. Justice Department to file its first "pattern or practice of discrimination" suit against the St. Louis AFL-CIO Building and Construction Trades Council and four of its member unions under Title VII of the 1964 Civil Rights Act. The suit marked the federal government's first attempt to put teeth in the enforcement of nondiscrimination policies in government construction contracts. Nonetheless, the wage work associated with downtown reconstruction persisted as a boon primarily to white workers and contractors.[6]

In other facets of their lives, most working-class African Americans during the late 1960s continued to scramble, in Calloway's words, "for mere survival." Food prices in the St. Louis area were the nation's second highest, with inner-city residents known to pay 6 percent more for their groceries than suburbanites at the same chain supermarkets. Meanwhile, policy changes in the federal Aid to Families with Dependent Children (AFDC) program had coincided with an increase in black working-class mothers receiving assistance. In 1963–64, about 31 percent of all live births to black St. Louis women had been out of wedlock, and by 1966 African Americans received some 80 percent of AFDC payments. As a "culture of poverty" thesis took root in scholarly and public policymaking circles, such statistics served to stigmatize black female recipients in their poverty. Despite their depiction as indolent, most "welfare mothers" were painfully aware that means-tested social wages substituted poorly for meaningful employment, especially in St. Louis, where public assistance benefits were among the nation's lowest.[7]

Black working-class people continued, also, to live in substandard homes. This was not only the result of absentee slumlords, but also city officials who, intent on clearing blighted properties for redevelopment projects, were lax in enforcing building codes. One consequence was that thousands of black children were exposed to lead poisoning from the chipped paint and peeling plaster of deteriorating rental properties. Despite the Mill Creek dispersal, and the passage of a fair housing ordinance in the mid-1960s, residential overcrowding in older areas of the city was still a prevailing fact of life for black workers. Although 40 percent of the population, St. Louis's "Black Archipelago" was largely confined to about 19 percent of the gross acreage of the city. Overall, the Gateway City possessed the fourth highest percentage concentration (38 percent) of African Americans among the major northern and border urban centers, exceeded only by Washington, D.C., Newark, and Baltimore.[8]

Even the Greater St. Louis Freedom of Residence Committee, which mainly represented African Americans with the means to move outside the city, continued to flail against the walls of housing discrimination. Filed in the U.S. district court by a Freedom of Residence staff attorney, *Jones v. Mayer* became a national cause célèbre when it reached the U.S. Supreme Court in early 1968. In a coda to the 1948 *Shelley* ruling, the nation's High

Court decided that the federal government could regulate the sale or rental of private property in order to prevent racial discrimination. Coming two months after the passage of the federal Fair Housing Act, the decision broke the remaining legal barriers to fair housing. Nonetheless, a growing number of black St. Louisans literally could not afford to avail themselves of these new opportunities. Thus, when the Freedom of Residence Committee received a sixteen-thousand-dollar grant in 1967 specifically to help black working-class families locate housing in St. Louis County, project organizers were quickly frustrated with the obstacles they met. "Low income families and decent housing just don't match," lamented a member of the group.[9]

In the county, as well as the city, racism was squarely to blame. With plans to create alternative housing for St. Louis's black working-class poor, the Inter Religious Center for Urban Affairs received federal funding in 1970 to build a low- and moderate-income apartment complex in an unincorporated area of St. Louis County. Residents of the all-white area began a petition drive that resulted in the incorporation of the City of Black Jack. One of the new city council's first acts was to pass a zoning ordinance prohibiting the construction of new multiple-family dwellings. In *United States v. City of Black Jack, Missouri* (1974), an appellate court would rule the measure a violation of the Fair Housing Act. In the meantime, however, many black workers remained wedged between the predations of private landlords and the unfulfilled promises of the St. Louis Housing Authority.[10]

While the massive Pruitt-Igoe homes became the chief national symbol of failed public housing, nearly one hundred county municipalities surrounded St. Louis City. This at once manifested the metropolitan fragmentation wrought by home rule in Missouri and reflected the hardening racial-class dichotomies of privilege and deprivation that, according to the Kerner Commission report, underlay the black working-class riots of 1967. Rebellion came to East St. Louis that year on September 10 following a visit by SNCC chairman H. Rap Brown. Evening disturbances erupted in the city's downtown, with at least two hundred people involved in the destruction of white-owned property, looting, and firebombing. Several residents were arrested, and a nineteen-year-old was shot to death as he fled police in a stockyard parking lot just outside the city limits. The following day, forty people marched to police headquarters to protest the shooting and demand the release of those under arrest. Scattered looting continued into the following evening, requiring the intervention of over one hundred state and city police officers.[11]

On purely statistical grounds, St. Louis was also poised to become a hotbed of black working-class rebellion. By early 1968, however, no major disturbances had occurred. "There is a lot of cause [to riot]," pondered one twenty-four-year-old North St. Louis resident in an interview with the *Post-Dispatch.* "People living eight in a room, eating beans and fatback and molasses. Only place they want to let you move is the places they have torn up. Landlords patch up the front and let the plumbing go to hell. And rats." Despite the ascendance of black working-class rebellion evoked in such comments, St. Louis's long history of biracial civility, liberal-integrationist negotiation, and electoral paternalism proved durable enough to avert major disturbances. "We had a core of black and white people, in which there was communication," Frankie Freeman later pondered. "There was dialogue." Thus, when mass uprisings shook Kansas City, Chicago, Detroit, and most other major U.S. cities following Martin Luther King Jr.'s assassination in April 1968, local media, City Hall, Civic Progress, police, and a cross-section of black civic leadership acted quickly to quell developing signs of unrest. Mayor Cervantes crafted an interracial, ecumenical coalition that sponsored a thirty-thousand-person eulogy procession and prayer service. Such gestures may not have satisfied black grievances, but they may have secured enough of an abeyance. More concretely, Democratic committeemen in black wards, who exercised a level of power and autonomy uncommon in more centralized machine systems, were sources of welfare, security, and support that tied many black working-class clients to the routinized processes of institutional politics.[12]

The "War on Poverty" and Its Discontents

Another widely acknowledged factor undercutting widespread rebellion was the Johnson administration's developing "War on Poverty." The mid-1960s became a period of domestic social welfare reform rivaling the New Deal, though this time the legislation was aimed primarily at the conditions of the black poor. The 1964 Economic Opportunity Act, then, was as much a product of black grassroots struggle as the recent Civil Rights and Voting Rights acts—and like the 1962 Manpower Development and Training Act, it more explicitly acknowledged the movement's working-class demands for social wages. Coordinated under the newly formed Office of Economic Opportunity, the omnibus law created Head Start for preschool youngsters from working-class poor households, and Upward Bound for those of college age. The act also established the Job Corps for youth, and expanded the Manpower Act to include work training for the unemployed. Legal services for the poor, Food Stamps, and Volunteers in Service to America, a domestic iteration of Kennedy's Peace Corps, were the bill's other key provisions.[13]

Title II, the Community Action Program, authorized $300 million for local antipoverty initiatives premised on the "maximum feasible participation" of community residents in their development and administration. In St. Louis, the Human Development Corporation (HDC) became the city's chief antipoverty agency, focusing on skills training, social services, and job placement for "unemployables." By the end of 1967, the HDC had over seven hundred employees, and a budget of more than $13 million. The Model Cities Act, passed in 1966, was similarly geared toward the black urban working-class poor. Approved by the Board of Aldermen in November 1967, the program funded proposals to rebuild slum areas, with emphases on community beautification, health, and public recreation. Congress also passed the Housing and Urban Development Act, creating the Department of Housing and Urban Development (HUD), and the Elementary and Secondary Education Act that made Head Start a permanent program. Amendments to the 1935 Social Security Act, further, produced Medicare, a health insurance program for the elderly, and Medicaid, which covered the health care expenses of working poor families.

In the flurry of initiatives that produced President Johnson's vaunted "Great Society," many local black freedom activists were swept into new antipoverty bureaucracies. Freeman, Teamsters leader Harold Gibbons, and Irvin Dagen, a founding member of St. Louis CORE who had since become acting executive director of the LCRA, all served on the Model Cities steering committee in 1966. Margaret Bush Wilson, a veteran of the 1957 charter battle and the Jefferson Bank boycott who had led the state NAACP, became the agency's deputy director in April 1968, and later its acting director. The St. Louis NAACP, meanwhile, became an administrator in federal work-training programs for the city's growing population of black high-school dropouts, while the Urban League received HDC funds for programming. Norman Seay and Ivory Perry, both veterans of CORE, became involved in the HDC, and even Percy Green worked for the agency for a time. Involved initially in federal antipoverty work himself, Ernest Calloway had since become a vocal critic. While this may have reflected his personal frustration with the major roles his younger rivals played in such agencies targeted at youth, he genuinely also viewed the programs as little more than "ghetto pacification" that constricted grassroots mobilization. National antipoverty initiatives also pivoted on assumptions of black cultural deprivation, as the focus on work training presumed that "hardcore" joblessness stemmed mainly from black workers' lack of competitive skills, rather than from racial hierarchies of economic opportunity and deindustrialization.[14]

Yet the emergence of antipoverty agencies did not altogether foreclose mass movement self-assertion. Indeed, the "War on Poverty" evolved in tense interaction with an ongoing transformation in black freedom strategies, tactics, symbols, rhetoric, and ideas. It thus provided vehicles for black working-class mobilization. "Citizen participation" in antipoverty programs held the potential, at least, of militant disruption as constituents pressed for provisions that administrators were unwilling to meet. With the expansion of the HDC bureaucracy, moreover, the grassroots participants who made up the agency's Community Advisory Council began calling for increased board representation, and the hiring of more black staff. The neighborhood corporations and community activists connected to St. Louis's Model Cities similarly became embroiled in a fight with the Cervantes administration to maintain, and expand, authority in the program's administration.[15]

Dissatisfaction also mounted as low rates of job placement dashed hopes for a comprehensive remedy to the problem of black "hardcore" joblessness. Pickets of HDC staff became commonplace. In August 1967, nine black women and their children staged a ten-day sit-in occupation of HDC offices. Having recently completed a training program in electronics assembly, they were frustrated by the inability to find employment—the result, they claimed, of racial discrimination practiced by McDonnell Aircraft and fourteen other firms, as well as the HDC's hollow promises of placement. Several top white HDC officials, including the general manager, resigned, and Clyde Cahill, who replaced him in October 1967, subsequently expanded black representation at all levels of the HDC. Antipoverty programs also provided bases from which black freedom organizers jumpstarted independent neighborhood initiatives. From his HDC post, Perry confronted the lethargy of city officials and medical professionals in the face of exorbitant rates of lead poisoning in North St. Louis, and led popular mobilizations for screening, the detoxification of homes, and a lead-control ordinance. Likewise, the League for Adequate Welfare (LAW), part of the city's nascent welfare rights activism, formed in June 1966 to protest meager public assistance, long waiting periods for receiving benefits, and capricious social workers who terminated social wages without proper investigation. In September 1966, thirty-five LAW members had demonstrated at the city welfare office, demanding an audience with the director. Continuing demonstrations in St. Louis and Jefferson City forced him to meet with 250 activists in November—the first time in two decades that he had met with welfare recipients. East St. Louis's Project IMPACT, geared toward cultural and recreational outlets for black youth, was similarly a beneficiary of federal funds. Another was St. Louis's Jeff-Vander-Lou (JVL) Community Action Group, which formed in 1966 in the heart of the black neighborhood from which it took its name. The JVL focused mainly on housing rehabilitation, and the corollary opportunities of black employment and homeownership. Established that same year, the Mid-City Congress (MCC) also promoted militant black community development and control from within the federal antipoverty bureaucracy.[16]

Other challenges to the "War on Poverty" establishment came through the creation of movement vessels wholly apart from the HDC and Model Cities. Teamsters Joint Council 13 became one such source. While claiming forty-five thousand members in the late 1960s, the union's radical democratic leadership had stagnated in a crisis of purpose. Denigrated as an "Uncle Tom," fifty-seven-year-old Calloway had become alienated from the emerging generation of black freedom workers. The electoral victories of Hearnes and Cervantes, in solidifying Clay's status as the city's black political boss, had isolated him even further. Like A. Philip Randolph and other older African American trade unionists involved in the NALC, he had quit the council in 1966 amid complaints that it had fallen under the sway of young "separatists and Communists" in the rank and file. Similarly, Joint Council 13 president Gibbons had fallen out of favor with his mentor, Hoffa, and had since resigned as his top aide. By 1967, his national influence in the union had faded. Like Calloway, he was also at odds with younger rank-and-file Teamsters in St. Louis who called for a more democratic union. Searching for a way to remake themselves politically, both men began to imagine a St. Louis business-labor-government civic partnership that would creatively address declining capital investment, suburban flight, faltering municipal services, and most importantly, the racialized poverty within the city's working class.[17]

Nearly five hundred black Local 688 members, including Calloway, lived in the Ville, giving the Teamsters a solid base of black trade unionists for an active community project. Using these resources as a point of departure, the Teamsters formed the Tandy Area Council (TAC) in 1966, and began what Calloway christened a "trade union oriented war on the slums" of North St. Louis, which the union eventually expanded to the white working-class neighborhood of Carondolet. TAC-led pickets at local grocery stores wrested price reductions in food, and gave the group solid moorings among welfare recipients and underemployed workers. Through the involvement of Teamsters Frank Boykin and Leroy Graham, TAC also became LAW's designated representative in negotiations with Missouri's welfare system. Establishing ties with the community's black working-class youth, Boykin and Graham also helped the council mobilize campaigns against police brutality. TAC's support for the hiring of black firefighters, and its advocacy of black history courses in the public schools, were other initiatives that helped broaden the horizons of the "War on Poverty" beyond the mere provision of social services to working-class clients.[18]

From "Freedom Now" to "Black Power"

❧

From a very different corner of the ideological spectrum, Malcolm X had a powerful influence on the changing contours of black working-class politics, and in death had become a model to younger activists of a revivified, radical Black Nationalism. This transition from "Freedom Now" to "Black Power" had been a gradual one, first evident within the militant civil rights wing and its thrust toward inner-city community organizing. By 1966, both CORE and SNCC were endorsing interpretations of the slogan "Black Power." When CORE held a demonstration at the St. Louis Police Department's downtown headquarters in September 1966, a group of black teenagers, recruited from the vicinity of Carr Square Village, began chants of "Black Power." As the protest concluded, some pitched garbage cans in the streets, broke car windshields and antennae, and ripped bunting from streetlamps. One group shattered the windows of a laundry on Washington Boulevard, and injured two motorists with a metal disk thrown at their windshield. Firefighters responding to false alarms were pelted with flying glass and bricks, as were uniformed police. Thirty-four patrolmen converged on the area and ended the confrontation with two arrests.[19]

A year earlier, St. Louis CORE had mobilized after the Bi-State Transit System absorbed the city's ailing Public Service Company. As part of the purchase agreement, the Consolidated Service Car Company, in which Cervantes held ownership, was discontinued. Despite public promises of employment with the Bi-State system, the arrangement put nearly one hundred black service car operators out of work. The new consolidation, moreover, threatened the livelihoods of the many more black working-class commuters who had relied on the jitneys for transportation, and who now faced fare increases. On November 30, a delegation of sixty drivers visited the Mayor's Office, bringing with them a petition with fifteen thousand signatures demanding the preservation of the service car system. Nearly twenty drivers picketed City Hall as officials met to approve the sale. CORE spearheaded a boycott of the new bus system, and in its place organized a network of "freedom cars" piloted by the displaced drivers. The boycott drew the support of many black elected officials, the *Argus*, and most importantly black community residents, who responded enthusiastically to the independent jitneys. An irate Cervantes administration retaliated by ordering police to cite the "freedom drivers" for license violations. The boycotters also ran afoul of black taxicab drivers, who complained to City Hall that the cars were unfair competition. The combined opposition broke the boycott in March 1966, forcing the drivers to accede to earlier concessions offered by the city. As part of a deal between CORE and the Bi-State agency, charges against one hundred freedom car drivers were dropped. Despite this setback, or maybe because of it, the Gateway City became a test site in 1967 for CORE's national program, "Black Power, a Blueprint to Success and Survival," which focused on strategies of black control of community institutions. By then, much of St. Louis CORE's white founding membership had long since resigned. When, at CORE's 1968 national convention in St. Louis, attendees voted to officially bar white members, they merely acknowledged a fait accompli.[20]

The best example of this uneven transition from "civil rights" to "Black Power" in the Gateway City was ACTION, which had evolved as a motley group of veteran black working-class activists affiliated with CORE, middle-class professionals who had been part of the NAACP Youth Council, educated white radicals steeped in traditions of pacifism and ecumenical religion, and militant black youth. Notwithstanding the organization's diverse racial and class base, black workers formed its core, indicative of the broad, expansive character of the city's black working-class bloc. Like SNCC's Mississippi Freedom Labor Union, formed in 1965, and CORE's Maryland Freedom Union, formed a year later in Baltimore, ACTION signified more generally the working-class agenda that had grounded the civil rights struggle. Further, at a time when CORE and SNCC were nationally adopting the policy that white members should organize separate antiracist campaigns in their own communities, ACTION remained interracial. Yet its black members self-consciously reserved the uppermost leadership positions for themselves, guided by the idea that African Americans had the right to play the central role in their own struggles for self-determination—and that white activists, who often had been privileged in organizations like CORE, benefited from the "therapy" of black leadership.[21]

With the passage of the Civil Rights Act, and its equal employment provisions under Title VII, black freedom workers had a vital new incentive in their fight for jobs and justice. Thus, continuing the jobs campaign that had reached its apex in the Jefferson Bank boycott, ACTION expanded the focus to the area's major corporations: Southwestern Bell, Laclede Gas, Union Electric, and the formidable McDonnell Aircraft (which became the McDonnell-Douglas Corporation following a 1967 merger). Refuting the widespread claim that black workers did not possess the necessary experience or skills for better jobs, activists asserted that in well-paying, working-class occupations like gas meter reading, and telephone installation and repair, skills were learned on the job, and workers needed only basic formal education. This was both a response to employers and a trenchant critique of ideas about black skills deficiency underlying the "War on Poverty."[22]

Given the organization's preoccupation with black working-class men, demands for greater job opportunities for black women were largely superficial, as they were deemed the extension of male wage earners. The leadership's attention centered on the ideal of the black "family chief breadwinner," which would "rescue" black working-class women from out-of-wedlock births and welfare dependency. This logic paralleled a contradictory folk assumption that corporate managers were more favorable to hiring black women in order to preempt the meaningful employment of black men. Granted, many local phone companies had begun employing a select number of educated black women as clerks, telephone operators, and stenographers, which conferred middle-class respectability and "ladyhood." It was also true that black male unemployment was especially acute in St. Louis, relative to most other major industrial cities. Yet most black St. Louis women, though more regularly employed than their male counterparts, were in classifications subject to low wages and irregular hours. ACTION's male-centered jobs platform, thus, overlooked the particular ways in which racism restricted black women's opportunities, preventing them from forming autonomous households with or without male wages. Rallying around the slogan "More and Better Paying Jobs for Black Men," ACTION followed in the ideological footsteps of earlier organizations equating black freedom with a male-oriented vision of social citizenship, and the redemption of black manhood premised on the patriarchal household. Although grounded in earlier conceptualizations of struggle, this thought was also part of an emergent thesis of cultural pathology attributing black poverty to the dominance of matriarchy in working-class communities.[23]

During the spring and summer of 1965, when ACTION first began exerting its presence, members grabbed news headlines through unorthodox demonstrations that exploited corporate leaders' latent fears of negative publicity. Black members, outfitted in military berets and dark T-shirts emblazoned with the words "A.C.T.I.O.N. GUERRILLA FORCE," transformed civil disobedience into guerrilla theater. Marching in front of Southwestern Bell's downtown headquarters, activists carried placards with such admonitions as "Negroes Can Dial Telephones! Why Can't Negroes Install Telephones?" and "Dial O-J-T—N.M: On-The-Job Training for Negro Men." Reassembling a short time later, they walked into the middle of the street in front of the building and blocked evening rush-hour traffic. Green and another ACTION worker, Hamid Khalil, lay down in the street, while other demonstrators ignored police orders to end the disruption. Homeward-bound motorists were stalled for nearly thirty minutes before authorities arrested Green and Khalil for peace disturbance and obstructing traffic. In the aftermath of the protest, the young protest organization found itself at odds with the St. Louis NAACP, whose leadership issued a press statement praising the phone company's hiring program for opening opportunities to African Americans. The *Argus* noted the timing of the statement and the phone company's purchase of a table at the NAACP's annual dinner. Public suggestions of collusion compelled branch president Evelyn Roberts into a subtle retreat as she denied that the NAACP would be used to attack another civil rights organization. Publicly, at least, the imbroglio between the two groups subsided, and downtown protests at the Southwestern Bell headquarters continued.[24]

In a concurrent thread of activity, ACTION militants pursued the McDonnell Aircraft Corporation over its alleged noncompliance with the 1964 Civil Rights Act. Green's own troubles with the company extended back to August 28, 1964, when the corporation had fired him as a radio and electrical mechanic. Dismissed a month and a half after his televised exploits on the beams of the Arch, he believed the firing was a response to his political activities. Protesting his dismissal and McDonnell's hiring and upgrading practices, Green had picketed the home of James McDonnell, chairman of the corporate board of directors. In October 1964, he and a group of activists had also staged an automobile "stall-in" near the plant, tying up traffic during a shift change. In July 1965, ACTION workers staged a "lock-in" at the company's downtown offices, chaining shut the building's entry and exit doors. The group had, that same day, filed employment discrimination charges with the new EEOC, alleging that of the five hundred African Americans employed among more than thirty-five thousand McDonnell workers, 90 percent did janitorial and other menial labor. The complaint also claimed that personnel administrators routinely discouraged black workers from participating in on-the-job training programs and other venues for promotion. ACTION's demands rested on the immediate hiring of seventeen hundred black men and women at the corporation, the upgrading of all black employees across job categories, and Green's reinstatement to his former position with back pay.[25]

Parallel ACTION initiatives also displayed the small organization's energy and breadth. Among other activities, the group lent its growing reputation to protests against police brutality. Since February 1965, the NAACP's Police Affairs Committee had fielded a growing number of citizen complaints, which the association routinely turned over to the police department. Relations between the department and black community residents became especially tense in June, when a police officer shot and killed seventeen-year-old Melvin Cravens, a burglary suspect, in the driveway of the Lucas Avenue station. Unarmed with his hands cuffed behind him, the youth had died from a gunshot to the back of the head. As angry crowds of black St. Louisans confronted police during scattered neighborhood disturbances, ACTION joined the NAACP, CORE, the Urban League, and black aldermen in demanding a full police investigation. Public outrage led Mayor Cervantes to hold a meeting with representatives of the city's civil rights organizations, including ACTION, to air grievances. Yet the matter remained in the hands of the Board of Police Commissioners, whose members answered to the governor. When the board ruled the shooting a justifiable homicide and cleared the patrolman involved, it came on the heels of disclosure that the former head of the police department's Community Relations bureau was a member of the right-wing John Birch Society. In August, Green and representatives from sixty-four other community organizations urged city officials to adopt a "crash program" to alleviate the dire economic conditions in areas of the city believed to be susceptible to rioting. By early September, when police shot another black youth during an alleged school break-in, many like Urban League director Douthit voiced fears of civil violence on the magnitude of Watts barely a month earlier.[26]

The tissue connecting these multiple campaigns was ACTION's attack on the yearly Veiled Prophet parade and ball. Many working-class African Americans, like other St. Louisans attracted to its visual splendor, frequented the annual fall procession downtown. But to black freedom militants, the Mystic Order of the Veiled Prophet of the Enchanted Realm embodied the hegemony of governmental, business and civic interests denying black workers a humane quality of life, either by active discrimination, indifference, or empty "lip-service liberalism." Many Civic Progress patriarchs belonged to the secret society, and each year during a televised gala at the Kiel Auditorium, the veiled oracle crowned a young "Queen of Love and Beauty" selected from among the daughters of the local elite. ACTION workers declared their intentions to unmask the Veiled Prophet and drive the exclusive, all-white affair from the tax-supported city auditorium. On October 2, 1965, as the Veiled Prophet Parade passed Twelfth and Olive streets downtown, Green pitched himself on the pavement in front of the oracle's float, and two other ACTION members, Loretta Hall and Dallas Jackson, chained themselves to the Veiled Prophet Queen's float. The cavalcade was forced to halt for twenty minutes while police disentangled and arrested the protesters. This was only the first in a string of confrontations with the Veiled Prophet organization that continued over the next several years. Responding to the constant disruptions of militant black activists, the parade route steadfastly avoided downtown after 1967. Concerned that ACTION demonstrations posed a danger to the daughters of the local white bourgeoisie, the selected Veiled Prophet Queen and her maids quit their participation in the yearly float parade, as did the Veiled Prophet himself. By 1969, continuing harassment, and related fears of urban black unrest, had prompted parade organizers to move the outdoor spectacle from the evening to the daytime.[27]

"What Do We Want?"

*

ACTION's accent on civil disobedience and black leadership interfaced with the groundswell of "Black Power" that emerged in 1966 and became dominant after King's assassination. At a diffuse level, "Negroes" embraced a new "Black" identity as "brothers," "sisters," and "youngbloods." The "white power structure," "crackers," "honkies," and "pigs" emerged, at the same time, as negative condensation signifiers that sought to delegitimate institutions and practices of white racial control. Reaching into the chasm of the past, many black people across class lines adopted the "afro," goatees, beards, and similarly African-derived grooming styles and clothing. Some assumed new names and social practices, such as the study of Kiswahili. Others founded Black Nationalist–oriented boutiques, bookstores, publishing houses, and periodicals like St. Louis's *Pride* magazine. The clench-fisted "Black Power" salute became emblematic of these new framing symbols.[28]

In 1966, ACTION had begun sponsoring its own "Black Veiled Prophet" Afro Festival to crown a "Queen of Peace and Justice." Aside from lampooning the regular Veiled Prophet gala, the ball promoted an increasingly popular "Black is Beautiful" ethos. ACTION's history committee, chaired by Luther Mitchell, became another vehicle in the advocacy of black culture. A veteran of Chicago's South Side Community Art Center, Mitchell conceived the idea of creating the "Wall of Respect," a community-driven mural modeled after Chicago's "wall of respect" project, and duplicated in other cities. Initiated in the summer of 1968, St. Louis's mural featured a color collage of faces that included Jomo Kenyatta, W. E. B. DuBois, Malcolm X, Martin Luther King Jr., and Muhammad Ali. Located on a three-story brick building at Easton and Franklin avenues, near the Pruitt-Igoe projects, the wall became a popular gathering space for political speakers, organizers, and cultural workers in the midtown area.[29]

The popular working-class sentiments generating the "Wall of Respect" remained ever present in the threat of insurrection, hovering even at the margins of peaceful demonstrations. "A significant group of trained and intelligent black people are saying 'Freedom yesterday or destruction of the country,'" explained the black East St. Louis poet, Eugene B. Redmond. "And since it is today, not yesterday, we are already too late." Some younger black freedom workers returned to the popular demand for African Americans' right to self-determination in the "Black Belt Nation." Others, more immediately influenced by Third World upsurge, and intellectuals like Frantz Fanon, had discovered the domestic colonial thesis. Reflecting the momentous black population shift that had occurred since the 1920s, majority-black U.S. cities—not the cotton-growing states of the

Lower South—were reimagined, in the words of James Boggs, as "the Black Man's Land." The "Black Belt" South, nonetheless, remained a potent symbol of land-based independence in the Black Nationalist imaginary. Positing that African Americans constituted an internal colony of the United States, movement theorists like Robert Allen argued that black workers' long-term interests lay not in reform, but rather in a substantive break with the U.S. nation-state. North St. Louis thus became indivisible from southern Africa, the Caribbean, and Southeast Asia. Along the lines preached by Malcolm, black communities were radically reconceptualized as constituents in a broad anticolonial and anti-imperialist movement among the world's people of color. As a consequence, the black working-class political bloc was connected discursively to the interests of the laboring peasantry and proletariat of the global South.[30]

Emblematic of this changing worldview was widespread black grassroots antipathy to military service. Perceived by generations of African Americans as a route to claiming a substantive U.S. citizenship, enlistment had become contradictory to black self-determination. In 1966, the Johnson administration sought to resolve problems of black unemployment and military manpower through Project 100,000, a recruitment program for low-income black working-class men into the armed forces. Theoda Lester Jr., a young black shipping clerk and former student activist at St. Louis's Forest Park Community College, was typical of his peers who judged U.S. conflict in Vietnam as an unjust "white man's war." After receiving his draft notice, the twenty-one-year-old attempted to get himself declared unfit for service. When the ruse failed, Lester sought another escape.[31] He recounted:

> So the time came for them to break me on down like all the other recruits, and I said, "You can't cut my hair"—had this big 'fro. "It's against my religion. And that's Black Nationalism." I didn't realize what I was saying when I said that, nobody else had ever said that. If all brothers who came through there said that, and they let that slide, then there was a lot of us not going.[32]

Lester was court-martialed for refusing to shave or be fingerprinted. The case received national scrutiny, gaining him legal representation from the ACLU. Initially facing ten years, he received a three-year sentence of hard labor, and a dishonorable discharge. Upon further review, authorities reduced the sentence to two years; a final review shortened it to the nine months he had served. During his imprisonment, Lester had befriended other black soldiers, a number of whom were serving time for assaulting or killing white officers in Vietnam. "We all pulled together, you know," he said, "and exchanged experiences about how we ended up in prison, and our ideas about what we needed to be trying to do once we got out." Certainly, Black Power politics appealed to the raw sensibilities of young working-class black veterans, many of whom returned from the war "confused and bitter," as the *New York Times* described them. Clarence Guthrie, a twenty-three-year-old black veteran from St. Louis, attested to the feelings of thousands of other returning "bloods": "We fought for the honkie and now we're going to fight for ourselves."[33]

This was, however, easier proclaimed than done. During the 1966 "March Against Fear," when SNCC organizer Willie Ricks and chairman Stokely Carmichael had confronted a carefully prepared Greenwood, Mississippi, crowd with the question, "What do we want?" the masses had responded, "Black Power!" But neither side had elaborated much beyond that. A series of national Black Power conferences announced the arrival of a "Modern Black Convention Movement." Yet Black Power represented no unified thought or program, aside from a few key Black Nationalist precepts: black peoplehood and self-determination in the United States and Africa; the institutional character of white supremacy; self-consciously autonomic institution building; cultural awareness and pride; and the explicit advocacy of the right of self-defense. Notwithstanding its grounding in black grassroots sentiments, it also possessed no singular class content. Rather, the new Black Nationalist spirit emanated both from a college-educated middle class rejected by modern bureaucratic society and the black working-class "masses" cast aside by automation and urban renewal. Thus, Detroit's League of Revolutionary Black Workers emphasized organization at the point of production, Oakland, California's Black Panther Party for Self-Defense romanticized the "lumpen," and the US Organization, formed in Los Angeles by Maulana Karenga, stressed the need for black cultural transformation.[34]

St. Louis's Committee for Africa, which raised funds for African liberation movements and sponsored public forums to connect black residents with the larger African Diaspora, mainly attracted students and faculty from area colleges and universities. Many black students were also involved in the Association of Black Collegians (ABC), which in 1968 staged a series of building takeovers at St. Louis and Washington universities, and Forest Park Community College, leading to the creation of Black Studies curricula and programs and the recruitment of black faculty. By the end of that year, ABC had chapters on seven campuses in the metropolitan area. The group was part of a wave of militant black student unions that emerged at historically white institutions of higher learning following the urban riots after King's death, when black working-class youth were first admitted as full-time students in substantive numbers. As a result, campus-based black insurgency often merged with grassroots community organizing. Allied with the TAC, ABC joined the fight against inner-city slumlords, and lobbied city officials for the enforcement of housing codes. Another cohort of youth, meanwhile, adopted the ideology of Black Christian Nationalism espoused by Detroit minister Albert Cleage Jr., and sought to transform the "Negro" church into a tool of black nation building. Black clerics formed caucus movements in the major Christian denominations to demand greater white church accountability around issues of black poverty. One result was the National Committee of Negro (Black) Churchmen, which held its major 1968 gathering in St. Louis.[35]

Like younger activists, older black organizations were equally divided in their responses to the new Black Nationalism. Roy Wilkins of the NAACP, for example, was openly hostile to the call for "Black Power," but the Urban League, despite denunciations by spokesman Whitney Young, was willing to fight over its definition. St. Louis Urban League leader Douthit played a key role in forming a local branch of the Interracial Council for Business Opportunity (ICBO), a national organization promoting black capitalist enterprise. The opening of the black-owned Gateway National Bank, three years earlier, had simultaneously refuted the endemic racism in St. Louis's banking industry, provided a source of credit and loans for working-class African Americans, and announced the arrival of a burgeoning new black entrepreneurial middle class. It was a far cry from Redmond's assertion that the new activists were not trying to square their goals with the status quo. "What [young black militants] are really asking for is to be cut into the system," insisted Douthit. "What could be more middle-class than that?"[36]

Others equated Black Power simply with the extension of electoral pluralism. In 1964, the U.S. Supreme Court had mandated redrawing legislative districts at all levels of government, and a federal court ruling ordered the Missouri General Assembly to reapportion the state's U.S. congressional districts. In a powerful show of unity, Jefferson City's twelve black legislators agreed to collaborate in electing an African American from St. Louis to the U.S. House of Representatives. Led by Missouri state representatives James P. Troupe and DeVerne Calloway, they successfully fought a redistricting bill to gerrymander St. Louis's eight black wards into three separate districts. Federally ordered remapping, sustained by the U.S. Supreme Court in 1967, resulted in the creation of the new First Congressional District, enveloping the majority of the city's three hundred thousand African Americans.[37]

Troupe, a ward committeeman, state representative, and Steelworkers union official, pursued the Democratic candidacy for the seat in 1968. Clay, endorsed by the Steamfitters, also joined the race, as did Calloway and Alderman Joseph W. B. Clark. With the candidates potentially splitting black Democratic votes, the press speculated upon a Republican victory. Concerned activists approached McNeal to run as a consensus candidate, but the ailing sixty-five-year-old, who had recently announced his retirement from the Missouri Senate, declined. A three-hour meeting of black newspaper publishers, black Democratic committeemen, and black congressional hopefuls failed to reach an agreement on the need to back a single candidate. By the second such summit, however, Clay had emerged as the frontrunner, having secured endorsements from four of St. Louis's seven black ward organizations, and the *Argus*. With the five Democratic candidates remaining in the contest for the August primary, he beat his opponents with nearly 24,000 votes. Calloway, placing third, received 6,405. For those who had witnessed Clay's rapid political rise, it came as little surprise when, in the November 1968 general election, he defeated black Republican candidate Curtis Crawford to become Missouri's first black congressman, joining eight other African Americans in the U.S. House of Representatives. Calloway's embarrassing loss was the "final blow" ending his long-standing battle with the "Young Turk" who had fulfilled the major plank of Calloway's own "Negro Proclamation." Both politically and personally, the aging Teamster leader never fully recovered from the setback.[38]

That same year, Raymond Howard, another CORE veteran who had participated in the Jefferson Bank insurgency, ousted ninety-three-old Michael Kinney in the midtown-area Fifth District to become Missouri's second black state senator. Like McNeal, who had won his seat in 1960, Howard's victory further nullified Irish political dominance of St. Louis's black "plantation wards"—Kinney had held his seat since 1913. In all, St. Louis City sent nine black representatives to the Missouri General Assembly, including the incumbent DeVerne Calloway. Black electoral influence had been a theme of St. Louis's black working-class bloc, and the seizure of formal political control in areas where African Americans constituted a majority was consistent with demands made by Black Power organizers. The founding of the Congressional Black Caucus, led in 1969–71 by Clay, Shirley Chisholm of New York, Louis Stokes of Ohio, and California's Ronald Dellums, further manifested the pursuit of black self-determination through electoral means. From the standpoint of grassroots working-class activism, however, black electoral politics looked entirely different in the late 1960s than ten years earlier. At a moment when black freedom radicals were attacking the very legitimacy of the U.S. state, the continued rise of black elected officialdom appeared conservative indeed. "Things aren't better," Redmond said, castigating the emerging black political elites as stand-ins for the "white establishment." "They are worse."[39]

A Grassroots Black Nationalist Front
✍

Thus, despite the symbolic and substantive importance of Clay's election, a range of activists remained rooted to the heterogeneous politics of black community organizing. In November 1967, Clarence Guthrie and other black Vietnam veterans formed the Zulu 1200s, a youth "action arm" of the MCC. Operating out of the MCC's Delmar Boulevard office, the Zulus helped generate the Wall of Respect project. They also gained public notice in May 1968 when they provided security for the eight hundred working-class African Americans, whites, Native Americans, and Chicanos arriving from the West Coast en route to the SCLC's Poor People's gathering in Washington, D.C. "We don't agree with the Poor People's Campaign, always asking and asking the man for what they need," Guthrie averred. "But they're brothers and sisters trying to do something for black people so we support them." The Zulus, serving as an honor guard, led the visitors in a symbolic trek across the Eads Bridge before the marchers departed by bus.[40]

In the meantime, Redmond was involved in organizing Southern Illinois University's new Experiment in Higher Education (EHE) in East St. Louis. The program became another hub of Black Studies activity, attracting many black working-class youth affiliated with the Imperial Warlords and Black Egyptians, two East St. Louis gangs. The EHE also contained the Performing Arts Training Center, helmed by Katherine Dunham, the internationally renowned choreographer and anthropologist of the African Diaspora who had adopted East St. Louis as her home. The Black River Writers Press, founded by Redmond and fellow poet Sherman Fowler, further popularized the new Black Arts aesthetic on both sides of the Mississippi through chapbooks, published fiction, spoken-word recordings, and community poetry readings at the Wall of Respect. If East St. Louis and St. Louis "served as a meeting point between the Black Arts movement in the South and in the Midwest," the Black Artists Group (BAG), founded in St. Louis around 1968, was a prime illustration. Heavily influenced by Chicago's Association for the Advancement of Creative Musicians, the collective sought to raise a black social consciousness through multimedia works of poetry, dance, theater, visual arts, and free-jazz music. Unusual for combining so many different genres of art within its ranks, BAG contained over fifty members at its peak, including saxophonist Julius Hemphill, poet Quincy Troupe, and playwright Ntozake Shange. Headquartered in a renovated industrial building in the city's declining midtown area, the group staged performances in the churches, storefronts, public housing centers, auditoriums, public schools, and sidewalks of black working-class communities. Reminiscent of the People's Art Center, the group also ran a free youth arts academy.[41]

Formed in the summer of 1968, the Black Liberators were perhaps the city's most audacious manifestation of Black Power. Charles Koen, the Liberators' founder and "prime minister," had, at sixteen, been chairman of the Cairo Nonviolent Freedom Committee, a SNCC affiliate in southern Illinois. A former ministerial student, the twenty-two-year-old had moved to East St. Louis and become the spokesman and main coordinator for the Black Economic Union, a regional umbrella organization of antipoverty, youth, and cultural organizations from the metropolitan area and Peoria, Illinois. A dynamic organizer, Koen had recruited heavily from both the Warlords and Egyptians to build the Liberators, and envisioned the new group as the nucleus of a militant black working-class youth alliance. Although their actual membership ranged between 150 and 300 people, the Liberators soon developed statewide influence in Illinois. Koen had recently become a national deputy chairman of SNCC, and through this connection the Liberators were joined to SNCC's efforts to create local black political formations modeled after Alabama's Lowndes County Freedom Organization. He was, additionally, drawn to St. Louis, whose cultural environment closely resembled his native Cairo, a small, aging commercial city at the confluence of the Mississippi and Ohio rivers. The Liberators established their base of operations in the Franklin Avenue area of North St. Louis, taking up residence in an office around the corner from the Wall of Respect.[42]

Fitting the group's self-image as a band of male warriors, the paramilitary Liberators patterned themselves after Oakland's Black Panther Party. Members sported black berets and leather jackets, held weekly military drills, published a short-lived newspaper, ran a free children's breakfast program, supplied draft counseling to black youth fighting military conscription, and worked closely with the ABC and white antiwar student activists. Koen's vocal interest in working with white youth suggested, like the Panthers, praxis explicitly attuned to Black Power's multiracial, universalist tendencies. "What we need to begin to relate ourselves to right now is human rights, the philosophy that no person should infringe upon anybody else's rights," he insisted. "If you try to speak in terms of ghetto problems and not make them relevant to the total problems of the nation then we're not doing a damn thing." Developing at a critical moment when SNCC and the Oakland-based Panthers were attempting an alliance, the Liberators' platform was similarly a manifesto of radical Black Nationalism

that demanded community self-determination, and an end to police violence and capitalist exploitation.[43]

Like the Panthers, too, the organization drew immediate media attention through brash, well-publicized activities. In August 1968, the Liberators approached the mainly white Franklin Avenue Businessmen's Association about making donations to the group and hiring its members as night
watchmen. The protection plan, which the merchants rejected, was both an
obvious fund-raising strategy, and a step toward the group's overarching
goal of achieving community control of the schools, social services, businesses, and police in the predominantly black Franklin Avenue area. "The
cops out in St. Charles are from St. Charles, and the cops from Ladue are
from Ladue," Koen complained. "But in this city [St. Louis] you have cops
who are not from this city. . . . Now, by no means can they deal with the
problems in the ghetto. Therefore, they need to change the whole concept—
if you live in the area, you work in the area, if you don't live in the area, you
don't work in the area in terms of being a cop." That same August, the Liberators had provided an armed escort to black New York congressman
Adam Clayton Powell Jr., whom they had invited to town for a speaking
engagement. A standoff between police and Liberators occurred as Powell
attended a rally at the Wall of Respect. His aides spirited him away, and the
small Liberator delegation dispersed. Police arrested two members on
weapons violations charges.[44]

In the relatively small activist community of a midsized metropolis like
St. Louis, it was common for young black freedom workers to hold multiple and simultaneous affiliations to ACTION, the Zulu 1200s, CORE, BAG,
and the Liberators. Several black freedom workers, including Green, Ivory
Perry of CORE, and BAG's Julius Hemphill and Oliver Lake, resided in Laclede Town, a stable, integrated community in the midtown area known for
the bohemian lifestyles and radical politics of its residents. The Liberators
also had a connection to ACTION through the Reverend William Matheus,
a white ACTION member who allowed Koen the use of St. Stephen's Episcopal Church as the Liberators' second headquarters. Although ideologically dissimilar, the Zulus and the Liberators had overlapping members
and activities, beginning with their shared involvement in the Wall of Respect project. In June 1968, Koen and Guthrie met with representatives
from local radio station KATZ, which catered to a mainly black audience.
Threatening boycotts, they voiced a common interest in more on-air opportunities for Black Nationalist viewpoints. In late August, when the Liberators sponsored a mass rally featuring former SNCC chairman Stokely
Carmichael, a joint contingent of Liberators and Zulus guarded him. Accordingly, both groups were part of a larger bloc of local organizations
known as the Black United Front (later renamed the Black Liberation

Front), whose other members included CORE, ACTION, MCC, the Jeff-Vander-Lou action group, and the Black Nationalist Party formed in 1969. In the spring of 1968, the alliance presented Mayor Cervantes with a fifteen-point mandate calling for upgrades of black municipal workers, city contracts for black businessmen, greater efforts to recruit black police officers, and a massive restructuring of the Model Cities program. That fall, students at the predominantly black Vashon High School rioted after administrators banned a prom queen candidate because of her afro. Students and members of ACTION, the Liberators, and the Zulus met with school officials to negotiate a series of student demands, including the adoption of Black Studies curricula and the creation of a student advisory committee.[45]

The Black Liberation Front also became a local purveyor of the "Black Manifesto" published by Detroit's Black Economic Development Conference (BEDC), an affiliate of the League of Revolutionary Black Workers. The document had garnered national publicity in May 1969 when James Forman, SNCC's former executive secretary, interrupted services at New York City's Riverside Church to read it. It called on white religious institutions to render $500 million in reparations for black institution building. The BEDC steering committee exhorted grassroots activists to engage in similar acts of civil disobedience, and that summer St. Louis's Black Power front inaugurated "Black Sunday" disruptions at the city's major churches. Directly implicating the Missouri Episcopal Diocese and the St. Louis Catholic Archdiocese in the ownership of slum properties, ACTION's leadership demanded, among other concessions, that both institutions publicly list all of their property holdings and end any investments in Laclede Gas, Union Electric, Southwestern Bell, and McDonnell-Douglas until the corporations ceased their racist employment policies. Initially, several pastors willingly granted the young insurgents time to address their congregations, while church representatives of the Mayor's Council on Human Relations attempted to negotiate an end to the protests. ACTION workers, with characteristic aplomb, publicized their intention to spit in the communion chalice at the revered Old Cathedral.[46]

As the protests continued, Cardinal John Carberry, head of the St. Louis Archdiocese, directed Catholic churches not to indulge the militants' requests for speaking time, and many clergy made arrangements for police intervention. The Board of Aldermen, meanwhile, passed a resolution enabling officers to arrest those disturbing the sanctity of church, even in the absence of congregants' complaints. A temporary restraining order also barred the Black Liberation Front from the Old Cathedral. Members of the Pilgrim Congregational Church, however, allowed Yusuf Shabazz, a Black Liberation Front spokesman, to speak during services. Luther Mitchell, who led several of ACTION's "Black Sunday" demonstrations, was also granted time to address St. Stephen's and several other Episcopal churches. Members of the Episcopal Society for Cultural and Racial Unity, and the Lutheran Human Relations Association, even formally endorsed the "Black Manifesto," while not commenting on the ongoing demonstrations.[47]

The National Baptist Convention openly condemned Forman and other "Black Manifesto" proponents for their sacrilege, as did local black ministers. "They [the protests] are the work of splinter groups and don't represent the thinking of the Negro community," complained the Reverend Victor Wells of St. Louis's West Side Missionary Baptist Church. "White leaders should not submit to them, shouldn't even give it a thought." The local Baptist Ministers Union, an organization of black pastors that included among its officers the conservative Reverend I. C. Peay, deplored the protests with equal vehemence. "[T]he so-called Negro church cannot afford to sit idly by and not say anything while these unholy acts are being committed," the group announced in a public statement. Evoking white political benevolence to distance themselves from the insurgents, they added: "These methods tend only to alienate the friends of the Negroes and create more hate and animosity between the races." Characteristic of the seething class politics among African American St. Louisans, grassroots organizers responded by expanding their Sunday disruptions to black houses of worship. Carrying protest signs, two members of the ACTION's youth Guerrilla Force were arrested when they "invaded" services at Reverend Peay's Galilee Baptist Church. During a separate ACTION protest at the New Bethlehem Baptist Church, an eighteen-person phalanx stood in the sanctuary's center aisle while Guerrilla Force leader Ahmed Naseem strode behind the altar and painted a white Jesus statue with black paint.[48]

ACTION's participation in the Black Liberation Front's protests occurred at the same time that the group's obstinate efforts against McDonnell-Douglas had taken a pivotal turn. In July 1969, the organization had issued a report describing job discrimination at the corporation. Based on a clandestine, eight-month survey, the brief stated that 98 percent of the company's black workers were in the most menial, dispensable categories, and of the two thousand people who had been laid off that year an estimated 60 percent were black. In the following months, black workers' caucuses publicly alleged that African Americans were also more readily disciplined than their white coworkers. Drawing on his own federal statistics, the freshman U.S. congressman William Clay wrote McDonnell urging him to address the company's noncompliance with equal employment laws. Senator Edward Kennedy of Massachusetts exerted his own pressure when he called for a review of a $7.7 billion F-15 fighter plane contract the U.S. Department of Defense had recently awarded the corporation. In January 1970, the U.S. Civil Rights Commission held public hearings in St. Louis to review the employment policies not only of McDonnell-Douglas, but also the Chrysler Corporation and Mallinckrodt Chemical Works. Testifying before Frankie Muse Freeman and other commissioners, Green used the occasion not only to air many black workers' standing grievances against McDonnell-Douglas, but also to blast the Defense Department for effectively underwriting the company's racism by awarding it a major contract. The following month, the St. Louis Housing Authority fired Freeman as general legal counsel—a reprisal, NAACP leaders claimed, orchestrated by the *Globe-Democrat* and McDonnell-Douglas because of her vocal role in the commission hearings.[49]

ACTION's chairman, meanwhile, had been waging his own legal struggle against the corporation for terminating him in August 1964, and refusing to rehire him in July 1965 for an advertised position he had held. Green had filed suit in 1968, demanding reinstatement, back pay, and attorney fees. He had enjoyed the backing of the EEOC, which had submitted a brief on his behalf with the district court. The start of the trial had coincided with the Civil Rights Commission's hearings in St. Louis, and began eventfully with McDonnell-Douglas vice president Richard Crone testifying that he would not rehire Green "unless I was ordered by the Supreme Court." In September 1970, U.S. district court judge James H. Meredith ruled the company was not guilty of racial discrimination, given Green's illegal disruptions of company business. Meredith dismissed Green's complaint with prejudice, prohibiting him from bringing suit again on the matter, and ordered him to pay over two thousand dollars in court costs. The case went to St. Louis's Federal Court of Appeals, which reversed the decision and remanded the case for trial. The lawsuit continued to move in fits and starts as the corporation, making good on Crone's vow, petitioned the case to the nation's highest court.[50]

The "Small October Revolution"
❧

Notwithstanding the significance of ACTION's battle with McDonnell-Douglas, the struggle was a telling statement of the group's odd mixture of liberal and Black Nationalist ideology, and the limitations of its jobs-oriented platform. While objecting to the corporation's employment practices, ACTION's leadership was largely silent on the ethics involved in producing aircraft to be used against a "people's war" in Southeast Asia. Given the "domestic colonialism" framing black freedom struggles in the late 1960s, the antiwar sentiments prevalent among black grassroots activists, and ACTION's involvement in the Black Liberation Front, this tacit acquiescence to U.S. militarism, for the sake of gaining black employment, was contradictory—not least of all to ACTION members' growing conscious-ness of their group as a "human rights protest organization."[51]

Then, too, ACTION's strategic focus remained fastened on securing jobs for black men. Consistent with the gendered class politics of Black Power, the Liberators and the Zulus also made black women invisible, or cast them as mute symbols of male heroism and redemption. At the same time, individuals like Green, Koen, and Guthrie became supporting actors in the increasing militancy among St. Louis's working-class black women and mothers receiving public assistance and housing. Signs of their grow-ing dissatisfaction had been evident since 1967, when groups of black women led protests at the HDC offices. That same year, sixty demonstra-tors, the majority of them black women, had picketed the offices of the St. Louis Housing Authority, calling for rent reduction, better janitor services and pest control, and greater tenant representation. These rumblings of dis-content had turned thunderous as the women, drawing on their identities as parents, public housing tenants, and AFDC recipients, more assertively voiced their right to social citizenship, autonomous households, and lives with dignity. In laying claim to entitlements independent of any male breadwinner, they implicitly rejected masculinist discourses assigning them a passive place in the Black Freedom Movement, and had begun pro-jecting a new one rooted in "welfare rights."[52]

In May 1968, two hundred public housing residents marched to City Hall to dramatize the need for jobs at a minimum wage of two dollars, a re-duction in public rents, reforms in Missouri's means-tested welfare system, and the investigation of seventy-six caseworkers accused of unethical prac-tices. Organized by LAW, the marchers walked twelve abreast with the Zulu 1200s and ACTION's Guerrilla Force serving as parade marshals. Holding signs with such pronouncements as "Idle Hands, Empty Stom-achs, Hot Weather = Riots," demonstrators played on the white public's anxieties about urban rebellion to further goad city officials into action. The breaking point came in February 1969, when housing authorities an-nounced their second rent increase in two years. "They just did not concern themselves with whether or not people could pay," said Loretta Hall, an ACTION member and Jefferson Bank boycott veteran. Because the public housing and land clearance authorities functioned as one entity, a glaring conflict of interest was also at work, she argued. "I think at that time they were putting money in urban renewal and that's where they wanted most of their money to go so they could do the redevelopment in the city."[53]

Over one thousand tenants living in the city's six public housing devel-opments organized a general rent strike. Its leadership, including Jean King, Ruby Russell, Hall, and the Reverend Buck Jones, a community or-ganizer, demanded that rents should not exceed a quarter of a given family's income. "We're suffering down here," King explained during an interview, recounting how twelve- and thirteen-year-old children in her community often sold sex to augment their families' income. "There are times I've had to stop little children from eating garbage off the ground." Initially, however, participants in the strike did not constitute even half of the Gateway City's seventy-eight hundred public housing residents, many of whom had been threatened with fines and eviction. They also received little support from elected black officials, though other members of St. Louis's black public took careful notice. ACTION, the Liberators, the Zulus, and St. Louis's Legal Aid Society, all lent support, and St. Stephen's Episcopal Church—a hub for both ACTION and the Liberators—became the strikers' headquarters.[54]

Calloway enthused that the rent strike was "by far the most meaningful engagement in social action the St. Louis black ghetto has witnessed in recent years," and "a classic example of grassroots self-determination" that had produced its own leadership. Through TAC organizers Frank Boykin and Leroy Graham, both of whom had worked with welfare rights activists, Teamsters Local 688 became a critical source of financial and logistical support. Like Calloway, Gibbons could not help but compare the dispute to the labor upheavals of the 1930s. "As trade unionists," he wrote in a widely circulated editorial in the *Missouri Teamster*, "we have a stake in their struggle—not just because the main purpose of our movement is to fight for the rights of the poor, but also because the health of our community affects the gains we have already made for ourselves. Thus, we have two main interests in the rent strike—to see that the poor win justice, dignity, security and hope through the power of organization; and to see that the community where we live is a decent, humane city in which to live, raise our children, and share human concerns."[55]

Not since the 1930s, when African American women disrupted St. Louis's food-processing industry, had black working-class women so boldly demonstrated their autonomy from the male-centered leadership that had characterized most periods of local activism. The rent stoppage became the largest of its kind in the nation. By September, twenty-four hundred of the city's tenants had withheld more than $600,000 in rent, bringing the Housing Authority to the brink of bankruptcy. The strike's goals, moreover, had expanded to encompass a fundamental restructuring of the entire housing authority system, with a central emphasis on tenants' control. Further, while the strikers picketed City Hall, the protest threatened to spill over into the private housing markets occupied by other segments of the city's black working-class poor. As the crisis commanded the attention of Housing Authority staff and the Mayor's Office, all of whom were concerned about the direction the conflict might take, HDC and Civic Progress officials traveled to D.C. to confer with anxious federal officials. HUD dispatched the Reverend Kirk Walsh, a young Jesuit priest, to work with both sides to bring the strike to an end.[56]

Gibbons, meanwhile, had become the strikers' chief negotiator, and the key broker in any potential agreement. A settlement plan, developed by Gibbons and the strike leaders after arduous meetings, proposed disbanding the five-member Housing Authority and placing the developments under the trusteeship of a citizens committee of tenants, trade unionists, clergy, and corporate and civic leaders. The plan also called for the creation of tenant units, and a Tenant Affairs Board made of one member from each of the city's housing projects. It also established a tenants' "bill of rights" that included the right of appeal; protection against arbitrary charges for apartment damage, unless tenant culpability could be established; a maximum 25 percent rent-income ratio; the right to a fixed rent between lease expiration dates; and the right to transfer from one development to another.[57]

On October 29, 1969, at a press conference attended by Mayor Cervantes and business, religious, civic and labor leaders, tenant organizers announced the strike's end and the formation of the St. Louis Civic Alliance for Housing. King, Hall, and Earline Jackson were among the six public housing tenants named to the new seventy-person body. Boykin became the chair of the alliance's board of directors, which ran the projects for the next two years. Acceding to the strikers' other main demands, the settlement included rent reductions, the establishment of tenant management boards, better upkeep and policing of housing sites, and the separation of the land clearance and housing authorities. The compact, Calloway bragged, amounted to a "small October Revolution" that had radically altered the landscape of public housing in St. Louis, and provided a model for other tenants around the nation. Addressing a black middle-class and white public skeptical of working-class self-management, he admonished: "The public housing tenants with their new sense of self-determination and responsibility are entitled to at least one failure. Everyone else involved professionally in public housing for 35 years has been failing, and far too often these social failures have been compounded without public reckoning." Nationally, the strike had a direct impact on the drafting and passage of the Brooke Amendment to the 1969 Housing Act, which placed a ceiling on public housing rents and provided subsidies for rent reductions.[58]

In its participant base, strategies and objectives, the rent stoppage was further illustration of the working-class character of local Black Power campaigns. Consistent with Rhonda Y. Williams's work on black female public housing activists in Baltimore, St. Louis's housing struggle and the involvement of ACTION, the Liberators, and the Zulus challenge characterizations of Black Power as singularly masculinist and antiwoman. Granted, the strike paralleled the work of St. Louis's Black Liberation Front more than it overlapped, and the fact that male organizers aided the largely female rent strikers did not mean they jettisoned their ideal of the patriarchal, male-centered household. At the same time, many single-parenting mothers on AFDC may have harbored the same ideal, even as they fought to maintain independent households of their own. Beyond the public pronouncements of both putatively antifeminist Black Power activists and ostensibly proto-feminist black welfare rights workers, their actual mobilizations were nuanced affairs.[59]

Responding to the crisis of social meaning that attended automation, and the antipoverty programs that sought to render them politically listless, black working-class youth, men, and women had continued to assert themselves as a transformative force, projecting their interests through an historic bloc of forces. "As the Negro perceives the nation's unwillingness to undertake the task of compensating the dispossessed black laborer," Willhelm observed, "he embarks upon a more radical program: increasingly, he advocates 'economic justice' to restore all America. The Negro now develops into a creative minority endeavoring to found a radically different society for both black and white." This was manifested in the urban rebellions, and the reemergent Black Nationalist strategies, tactics, institutions, and theoretical frameworks that became known as "Black Power." While this political and cultural shift mirrored, at a fundamental level, a new period of black working-class formation produced by automation and postindustrial decline, Black Power was nonetheless a concept whose meanings were internally contested by practitioners with varied class standings and interests. Increasingly, an expanding post-civil-rights black middle class began to rival black workers in articulating the platforms and priorities of the larger African American community. External factors would converge to support one wing of the movement, while moderating, even silencing, the other.[60]

CHAPTER EIGHT

Broken Bloc: "Law and Order," the New Right, and Racial Uplift Redux, 1968–75

Despite black power's contradictory class character, its popular association with communal insurrections was indicative of "the issue of black poverty and unemployment" that had become the central domestic crisis of the 1960s. Since 1950 a large swath of the black working class had become a "semiproletariat" barely suspended above permanent unemployment. Meanwhile, as a result of Title VII of the 1964 Civil Rights Act, the size of the black middle class doubled between 1960 and 1970, and the diversity of its occupations expanded. Continuing desegregation of graduate and training schools, and new sources of federal aid for higher education, expanded its professional wing, while the implementation of the 1965 Voting Rights Act fortified the black electorate, feeding the development of new political officeholders. However, the "old" class of African American middle-class entrepreneurs had experienced decline as corporate expansion, and corporate-led urban renewal, disrupted segregation-era black business institutions. To the extent that Black Power represented a fusion of the dual Black Nationalist politics of professionals and workers, government actors and corporate capitalists responded to black urban working-class uprising, and the "skidding" of the old black middle class, by cultivating a new entrepreneurial elite. Consequently, "Black Power" received an unlikely endorsement from Richard Nixon, the Republican nominee in the 1968 presidential election, who articulated it specifically as "Black Capitalism." During his presidency, the federal state for the first time directly supported black business, albeit on the White House's own narrow terms. That is, the fundamental goal of set-asides, loans, and logistical support for "Black Capitalism" was to project models of individual achievement and responsibility—and provide a social barrier to black working-class militancy. The maturation of post-1965 black elected officials, though not directly tied to this project, ultimately served a similar function.[1]

One result of these processes was increased class polarization among

African Americans. At the same historical moment that these new dynamics of class formation were magnifying the fragmentation of black political agendas, the postwar U.S. police state expanded through popular appeals to "law and order," and a cross-class white coalition consolidated under the banner of the "New Right." It was through a combination of government repression and co-optation, and antiurban social welfare policies that the black working-class political bloc prevailing since the Great Depression was finally eroded. The "New Right," paradoxically, produced conditions for a new black historic bloc along dramatically altered lines.[2]

Interracial Incivility

The public housing rent strike settlement, and the creation of the Civic Alliance for Housing, had been possible in large measure because of St. Louis's culture of "civility." For many prominent white citizens, the pride they took in the city's "good" race relations was vindicated by the pact, and more generally by the absence of major rioting. Yet local authorities responded to Black Power activists largely through coercion. The Liberators, arguably St. Louis's most radical Black Power organization, weathered the brunt of police harassment, though their own tendencies toward "adventurism" may have further inflamed the conflict. On September 4, 1968, Koen and four other members were arrested on peace disturbance charges following a dispute with police, who stopped them on a minor traffic violation. That evening, a group of Liberators arrived at the Lucas Avenue police station, where the five had been taken. Indicative of the growing class stratification among African Americans in St. Louis, they confronted the black station watch commander, Lieutenant Fred Grimes, who rebuffed their demands to release their comrades. In separate incidents that same evening, unidentified snipers fired shots through the front window of the station, and at Grimes's home. Arsonists also attempted the firebombing of the real estate office of Clifton W. Gates, a black member of the Board of Police Commissioners.[3]

The following day, vandals ransacked the Liberators' headquarters and set their patrol car ablaze. (A witness later claimed to have seen Lieutenant Grimes fire a shotgun blast through the Liberators' office window.) That night, police rounded up twenty-one members of the Liberators and the Zulus for questioning. Claiming that the spate of shootings and firebombings was the result of a Liberator-Zulu feud, the president of the Board of Police Commissioners, Mayor Cervantes, and Missouri governor Warren Hearnes, endorsed a police crackdown on both groups. Similarly enraged was the staff of the *Globe-Democrat*, whose main news columnist, Patrick

Buchanan, had since become a Nixon aide. "This community cannot permit a small band of men to operate as a guerrilla unit within its boundaries," proclaimed one editorial. Mindful of the Liberators' ties to national Black Power spokesmen widely suspected of fomenting ghetto riots, and evoking the Cold War rhetoric of "subversion," the missive continued: "And it cannot allow outside agitators such as [Stokely] Carmichael to preach the overthrow of the government and civil war."[4]

On September 7, Koen and several other Black Power activists, including national SNCC chairman Phil Hutchings and Chicago SNCC organizer John Wilson, were arrested following an antiwar rally on charges of inciting violence. Wilson and Hutchins were charged with unlawful assembly, and fined the maximum five hundred dollars each. While the *Globe-Democrat* continued to insist on a policy of zero tolerance against Black Power dissent, editors at the more liberal *Post-Dispatch* reviewed the latest arrests with alarm. "[T]here was no unlawful act, and no force or violence, at the meeting or after it," a *Post-Dispatch* editorial declared. "Three of those arrested did not even speak on the program. Reporters described the tenor of the meeting as subdued." Not to be mistaken for favoring Black Power organizers, however, the editorial asserted: "Few St. Louisans of whatever race have much sympathy with the Black Liberators who sponsored the rally and other extremist groups. The public expects the police to apprehend anyone or any group committing overt acts of violence." At the same time, the news staff reasoned, "It is another matter to treat a peaceable assemblage as an unlawful one." Typical of local white liberal discourse, the editorial ended by applauding the city for its history of civic cooperation, and cautioning against further police excesses. "For a large city, St. Louis has so far enjoyed an unusual record of secure community relations, and to a considerable degree that record is a credit to past police restraint, which prevented trouble swiftly but provoked none," came the boast. "We hope the Police Board and the Police Department will consider the unnecessary risks of changing that successful policy now."[5]

But the chain of events crescendoed on September 13 when Koen and Leon Dent, another leading Liberator, were seriously injured while again in custody at the Lucas Avenue station on traffic charges. While Dent suffered facial lacerations, Koen's hands and skull were fractured. Disputing charges that they had assaulted officers, the two claimed that police had beaten them with brass knuckles and clubs in the station house basement. The incident unified black freedom activists, and white liberals and radicals, across generations and political tendencies. A coalition of black ministers, who were by no means ideological friends of the Liberators, demanded answers from the police commissioners and Chief Curtis Bronstron. Others were not as convinced that the board was an appropriate vehicle for an investigation. Highlighting the threat that police harassment of the Liberators posed to other dissenting community groups, a broad "Save Our City Coalition" formed around ACTION, CORE, the Zulus, the MCC, the NAACP, Teamsters Local 688, the St. Louis Archdiocese, the Washington University chapter of the Students for a Democratic Society (SDS), and the ACLU. About 150 people demonstrated outside the mayor's home on September 14, while a subsequent mass rally drew 1,000 people, including Norman Seay, Percy Green, Fourth Ward alderman Joseph Clark, Margaret Bush Wilson, State Representative Raymond Howard, Harold Gibbons, and William Clay, then a congressional candidate. Following the rally, 200 people marched in a drizzling rain from the Wall of Respect to the Lucas Avenue station to demand the suspension of the officers involved in the altercation. The group dispersed after seven delegates presented their demands to a police representative. Clay subsequently telegrammed U.S. attorney general Ramsey Clark requesting an investigation by the Department of Justice. In October, Koen, Green, and Joel Allen of SDS became plaintiffs in a lawsuit seeking an injunction against police mistreatment of local black and antiwar activists.[6]

Massive Retaliation: FBI Counterinsurgency

Forced, like so many St. Louis mayors before him, to symbolically protect the city's image, Cervantes announced that he favored outside participation in the police board's inquiry on the Lucas Avenue incident. The Board of Police Commissioners suspended two officers involved and reprimanded four others. The following year, Koen, Hutchings, and the others arrested on the unlawful assembly charges were acquitted, again vindicating the city's reputation for political moderation. Still, while public scrutiny made the police department more circumspect in its dealings with local Black Power organizers, it did not qualitatively change the relationship between law enforcement and black activists. Violence had flared again in November 1968, when St. Louis police arrested a nineteen-year-old Liberator "lieutenant" on suspicion of stealing. An anonymous caller phoned the Lucas Avenue station and, upon confirming the youth's arrest, informed the desk sergeant, "We're tired of you locking up the Black Liberators; we are coming over and blow up your station." In the early hours of the morning, occupants of a passing automobile fired seven shots into the station, injuring a detective. In Atlanta working on SNCC project at the time of the shooting, Koen denied his group's involvement in the attack, retorting that the police themselves may have staged the incident to frame the Liberators.[7]

Ongoing conflict and recriminations between police and urban "militants" at the local level were also contributing to a thickening atmosphere of repression against black freedom activists nationally. In the aftermath of urban revolts following King's murder, HUAC recommended a strategy against black guerrilla warriors that included sealing off the nation's black working-class ghettoes, imposing strict curfews, and suspending civil liberties. Although never formally adopted by President Johnson, the recommendations conditioned the further growth of a de facto police state. Accusing the federal government of "coddling" black rioters and revolutionaries through Great Society programs, U.S. senator John McClellan's Permanent Subcommittee on Investigations called for the reassertion of "law and order" through the passage of an omnibus crime bill. Passed in 1968, the act toughened antirioting measures, increased expenditures for police training and equipment, and expanded discretionary authority in the use of electronic surveillance. The Nixon administration later extended such measures through "no-knock" searches and seizures, and provisions for preventive detainment.[8]

Rampant fear of genocide spread across class and political lines in Black America, driven by rumors that Nixon was preparing concentration camps for political dissidents. Clay and other members of the burgeoning Congressional Black Caucus vocally supported repealing Title II of the anticommunist McCarran Act, which sanctioned mass arrests and detention. Employing a two-tiered strategy, police contained the street rebellions to their ghetto epicenters, and waged war on SNCC, the Black Panthers, the Revolutionary Action Movement (RAM), the Republic of New Africa (RNA), and other Black Power radicals. State violence extended to upwardly mobile black students, as well. When students at Missouri's Lincoln University staged a sit-in protest against administrators in the spring of 1969, armed guards beat and arrested them, sparking arson and sniper fire on campus. Deadlier encounters involving student demonstrators, National Guardsmen, and police would occur the following year at Kent State University and Jackson State College.[9]

Unbeknownst to most citizens, further, the FBI had begun its own separate campaign against black freedom organizations and their allies. Updating the anticommunist crusade of the late 1940s and 1950s, FBI director J. Edgar Hoover launched the bureau's Counterintelligence Program (COINTELPRO) to undermine civil rights, Black Power, and white antiwar organizations. Expanded in March 1968, COINTEL operations instigated police raids, arrests, and assassinations, bankrolled informants, maintained surveillance of individuals and groups, and fed negative stories about activists to cooperative newspapers. The *Globe-Democrat*, a consistent opponent of black freedom activism, had in fact been one of five initial newspapers selected by the FBI to aid its counterintelligence agenda, with Buchanan serving as the bureau's chief contact. When, in March 1968, a march led by King had turned into a melee between police and black working-class youth in Memphis, the FBI had urged media contacts to emphasize King's inability to control the rowdy throngs he was seeking to mobilize for the SCLC's upcoming Poor People's March on Washington, D.C. Claiming to have unmasked the "real" Martin Luther King, the *Globe-Democrat* editorialized that he was in fact more "dangerous" than Black Power firebrands like Carmichael. "[King] continues to talk non-violence even as it erupts all about him," the editorial accused. "He purports to be genuinely distressed when it breaks out after his incendiary speeches or during marches he leads. . . . Memphis could only be the prelude to a massive bloodbath in the nation's capital in several weeks." Accompanying the editorial was a cartoon depicting King with a jerrybuilt halo over his head, heedlessly firing a pistol whose report echoed in "Looting," "Violence," and "Trouble." "I'm Not Firing It," the caption explained. "I'm Only Pulling the Trigger." Published at the end of March, the inflammatory editorial and cartoon had clearly aimed to discredit the SCLC leader. But it may also have bolstered the plot that had taken his life a few days later. In one scenario later investigated by the U.S. House Select Committee on Assassinations, a group of white Missouri businessmen had offered fifty thousand dollars for King's life, news of which had circulated in the state penitentiary, where James Earl Ray—King's convicted assassin—had been an inmate before escaping in 1967.[10]

As part of its psychological warfare against black freedom workers, the bureau also circulated phony correspondence and anonymous cartoons to spread distrust and paranoia, and exploit the latent friction among organizations. *The Blackboard,* ostensibly an underground black student newspaper based at the nearby Edwardsville campus of Southern Illinois University, was a product entirely of the FBI's making, and it specialized in rumors and misinformation about activists in the St. Louis–East St. Louis metropolitan area. Agents mailed copies to virtually every black organization in the bi-state region. The Liberators and Zulus were specific targets of such efforts. In October 1968, the FBI distributed an unsigned flyer praising the Zulus and denigrating the Liberators for, among other transgressions, "work[ing] with white college honkies" and dressing like "honkie truck drivers and motersycle [*sic*] cats." The circular, according to an internal bureau memorandum, was "purposely slanted to give the impression that the Zulus may have had a key role in its preparation although this is not stated." The widely disseminated polemic fed news media speculation about a rift between the Liberators and Zulus, and built on the claim by St. Louis police that the two groups were engaged in a war. FBI agents simi-

larly weighed the possibility of promoting animosity between the Liberators and ACTION. Observing that the two organizations were drawing
closer, an FBI memorandum, dated January 8, 1969, declared that the bureau was looking into plans that would "frustrate any strong degree of cooperation" between them. Authorities likely also fanned the intense rivalry
that developed between the Liberators and the Black Nationalist Party, a
feud that police used in early 1970 to justify a raid on the Black Nationalists' headquarters to seize a cache of weapons.[11]

The convergence of local and federal anxieties about the Liberators' activities were evident, too, when Lieutenant Earl Halveland, chief of St.
Louis police intelligence, appeared in Washington, D.C., before the McClellan Committee in June 1969. "Koen, in the name of SNCC, is trying to organize East St. Louis militant groups such as the War Lords, Black Egyptians and local Black Liberators into an alliance, with himself as a SNCC
representative being the directing force," he testified. Connecting this to
the Liberators' previous efforts to extort money from local business owners, and their sponsoring of "outside agitators" like Brown and
Carmichael, he undoubtedly fed the McClellan Committee's claim, shared
by the FBI, White House, and Department of Justice, that black urban upheaval and campus unrest were the work of a network of domestic and foreign conspirators.[12]

Yet a succession of costly arrests in 1968, the indictment of Koen and
Dent on charges of assaulting police, and the presence of at least one confirmed police agent within their ranks, had hampered the Liberators' ability to function by the end of 1969, despite a publicized merger with SNCC.
The group faded steadily from the St. Louis movement—as did the Zulu
1200s, who had become largely defunct by the spring of 1969. By then,
Koen had returned to his native Cairo, where he had formed a local black
united front. Demanding equal employment and the appointment of high-
ranking African Americans in the police and fire departments, the coalition
had sustained an economic boycott of the city's downtown merchants
amid pitched battles with white police and vigilantes. The struggle became
a movement flashpoint, drawing wide attention from other black activists,
white supremacists, the state capitol, and the federal government. Convicted of attacking St. Louis police, Koen was sentenced in 1971 to six
months in jail. Beginning his sentence in July, he began a highly publicized
fast that not only defied his own incarceration, but also demonstrated his
solidarity with black Communist Party leader Angela Davis, Black Panthers Huey P. Newton and David Hilliard, and other black freedom workers then behind bars. Transferred to Phillips Hospital the following month
as his body atrophied, he was paroled when U.S. representative Bill Clay
intervened. Dangerously weakened by the forty-eight-day fast, he had nev-

ertheless elevated his status further among black freedom activists and sympathizers around the nation.[13]

With Koen's energies concentrated in Cairo, St. Louis field agents had focused their attention on ACTION, which according to a September 1969 memorandum was "the only Black group of any significance other than the NOI [Nation of Islam]." Percy Green had made the FBI's "Rabble Rouser Index" in 1967, and by 1970 his name was among fifteen thousand activists who were to be arrested on sight in the event the federal government declared martial law. Between 1970 and 1971, police often harassed community residents around ACTION's Newstead Avenue address, and in a later complaint filed with the Department of Justice, members detailed what amounted to an armed police raid of the group's headquarters. By early 1970, the FBI was also developing a plan against an unnamed white female active in the organization. Through apparent surveillance, agents learned that her husband, who was uninvolved in the group, felt threatened by the woman's close interactions with black men. The bureau mailed him a phony letter, signed by "A Soul Sister," intimating that his wife had had assignations with ACTION members:

> Look man I guess your old lady doesn't get enough at home or she wouldn't be shucking and jiving with our Black Men in ACTION, you dig? Like all she wants to integrate is the bed room and us Black Sisters ain't gonna take no second best from our men. So lay it on her, man—or get her the hell off Newstead.[14]

The couple soon separated and later divorced, and subsequent FBI correspondence noted approvingly that the woman's political involvement waned. It was not until November 1975 that the U.S. Senate Select Committee on Intelligence disclosed the full extent of these tactics against the era's progressive social movements, both locally and nationally. By then, radical Black Power organizations like SNCC, the Panthers, the RNA, and RAM were either defunct as national entities or entirely destroyed. Another wave of Black Nationalist organizations had since emerged, including the Congress of African People, the Student (Youth) Organization for Black Unity, and the African Liberation Support Committee. Influenced by revolutionary Pan-Africanism, their leadership had turned increasing to "scientific socialism," which, while recalling the "Third Period" of the 1930s, drew inspiration from such Third World figures as Mao Zedong, Amilcar Cabral, and Fidel Castro. Splintering under the weight of their own ideological factionalism, they also succumbed to the state harassment that had plagued other black freedom workers.[15]

Vocally "Silent": New Right Populism

ø

COINTEL terrorism was not just the result of Hoover's vicious intolerance of any form of black militancy. It was also the product of a major electoral realignment in response to black working-class rebellion, antiwar activism, the counterculture, and a perceived disregard for "law and order." Responding to the rising tide of black protest signaled by the Jefferson Bank struggle, organizers had formed a St. Louis affiliate of the White Citizens' Council in 1964–65. Although small and short-lived, it portended a full-scale campaign of white reaction whose seeds had been planted by the anticommunism of the 1950s. This had generated "a new populist class politics" that was both anti-establishment and fundamentally conservative, calling for a smaller federal state, lower taxes, the dismantling of New Deal and Great Society welfare liberalism, an end to government regulation of racial affairs, and the restoration of religious traditionalism. Such politics had borne early fruit in the 1964 presidential campaign of Republican Barry Goldwater, who lost to Johnson but nonetheless had helped codify the main precepts of a white countermovement. On the one hand, its proponents stigmatized the Democratic Party—the party of the "Great Society"—by associating it with the black urban poor and an attitude of permissiveness that rewarded inner-city rioters with tax-funded welfare programs. On the other, they popularly recast the Democrats as the emissaries of an effete "Eastern Establishment" elite. These combined discourses legitimized a broad white racial-class politics of resentment. Beginning in the midterm elections of 1966, the Republican Party surged to victory by affiliating with a working-class populism borrowed from the "southern strategy" of George C. Wallace, Alabama's outspoken segregationist governor. The "Solid South" crumbled as Dixiecrat legislators and voters defected to the Republicans, completing the revolt begun in 1948.[16]

Yet the "New Right" more specifically emanated from white-collar, suburban voters in the emerging Sunbelt South, enabling their ascendance as "the driving force behind the steady postwar growth of the southern wing of the Republican party" and their convergence with a national politics of white middle-class entitlement. As in other metropolitan centers, a rejuvenated GOP had followed white St. Louisans to their new, racially homogeneous communities outside the city. Eschewing overtly white supremacist appeals, this "New Right" took great pains to cast its efforts in nonracist terms. As sites where whites had had a long history of enforcing Jim Crow while endeavoring to shun association with the racial politics of the Deep South, the border states were a key incubator of this national conservative consensus. St. Louis native Phyllis Schlafly, for instance, had helped deliver the 1964 Republican nomination to Goldwater through the publication of *A Choice Not an Echo*, establishing herself as a leading voice of grassroots conservatism. Wallace had used another border state, Maryland, as a proving ground in refining a public persona for the North. Maryland governor Spiro T. Agnew, selected as Nixon's 1968 running mate, shared Wallace's penchant for blunt denunciations of militant black leaders, but was free of any baggage as a defender of segregation. As Nixon's "hatchet man," he became perhaps the most popular icon of the "New Right." Agnew had been heavily touted for the vice presidency by Buchanan, who as a speechwriter likewise shaped the style and rhetoric of the Nixon campaign and White House. Among other things, the St. Louisan coined the term *silent majority*, used to describe an expansive new conservatism spanning the North and South.[17]

Thus, even as Nixon nominated southern conservatives to the Supreme Court in tribute to former Dixiecrats like South Carolina's Strom Thurmond, who had rallied southern support for his campaign, his administration also typified a sea change uprooting the Democrats' historic base among northern white ethnics. The transformation even swept the ranks of Teamsters Local 688, exposing rifts between the union's radical-democratic leadership and its general membership. The Tandy Area Council may have embodied social unionism at its most idealistic, but many white rank-and-file Teamsters had opposed the union's actions in the black working-class neighborhoods of North St. Louis. Even for more progressive rank-and-filers, Gibbons's "war on the slums" was largely a public relations fraud that covered his inattention to shop floor issues of job security, safety, speedups, and grievance procedures, and reflected his distance from the membership. Many members, moreover, lacked an immediate stake in addressing the problem of urban decline: By 1967, only 44 percent of the local's members lived in St. Louis. These antiurban sentiments thinly masked white unionists' more general hostility toward the rhetoric of racial justice, and in particular Gibbons's support for the Black Liberators. A majority of Local 688's membership, in fact, supported Wallace's independent presidential campaign in 1968. Similar to the formation, thirty years earlier, of a black grassroots political bloc oriented toward the Democrats, many white workers in the late 1960s migrated to the Republicans in an emerging new historic bloc of working- and middle-class whites that carried Nixon into office.[18]

The "silent majority" may have fundamentally reflected a "powerful politics of middle-class warfare," but the new president identified white male blue-collar workers as his key constituency and mounted a campaign to strengthen the administration's support among this base. Tellingly, these overtures were absent of any concrete concessions to organized labor; Nixon's "blue-collar strategy," in fact, was a largely symbolic politics that mined white working-class masculinity, racism, cultural conservatism, and patriotism. Not coincidentally, the construction worker had reemerged as the "archetypical proletarian," and the hard hat became the chief emblem of U.S. labor and "Middle America." Skilled construction tradesmen in the Midwest had been a bastion of conservative working-class politics of race and gender for generations. Now, however, they fought to maintain the exclusivity of their unions—and their white masculine identities—against the demands of the women's movement and black working-class campaigns for desegregation of the construction industry. The Justice Department had dropped several charges against St. Louis's Building and Construction Trades Council in 1967, and a judge had dismissed the remaining charges a year later.[19]

Nevertheless, the black popular furor embodied in ACTION's 1964 protest at the construction site of the Gateway Arch had forced public officials to implement affirmative action mandates to improve black access to the skilled trades. In September 1969, the Nixon administration announced the "Philadelphia Plan" requiring goals and timetables for minority hires in the construction trades. Although the measure failed to satisfy black worker advocates, who criticized the absence of strict monitoring and enforcement, many whites reacted angrily to what they perceived as preferential treatment for African Americans. Four thousand white Pittsburgh workers rallied against a mayoral decision to suspend construction work until the city completed negotiations with black protesters. In Chicago, some two thousand white building craftsmen fought police and harassed witnesses outside a federal courtroom where a hearing on union discrimination was occurring. Nixon, who had proposed the "Philadelphia Plan" in part to undercut construction union power as a source of inflation, soon backpedaled on the plan as he moved to consolidate craft unionists behind the war. In line with the administration's new emphasis on voluntary "hometown plans" (and to avoid the strife that had occurred in Pittsburgh and Chicago), the Gateway City's Associated General Contractors and five building trade unions adopted as part of all city contracts the "St. Louis Plan," an agreement with the Council on Human Relations to increase the training and employment of black construction workers.[20]

With the White House's tacit endorsement, racially conservative "hard hats" turned their grievances against other segments of political and cultural dissidents, as well, becoming instigators of the first major street clashes between civilians over the war. On May 8, 1970, white construction workers in New York City violently attacked antiwar demonstrators protesting the killing of several students at Kent State University. St. Louis's Building and Construction Trades Council was the main organizer of a similar parade on June 7, in which nearly forty-five thousand people marched four miles along Lindell Boulevard. As in New York, several physical confrontations occurred as scattered groups of marchers singled out long-haired, bell-bottomed male passersby for verbal abuse and beatings. The most serious incident occurred as the procession went by the home of William and Mary Anne Hodel, where twenty-two-year-old Timothy Kirby, a recently discharged solider, was sitting outside with a sign announcing "Veterans Against the War." Fifty marchers charged onto the lawn, attacked Kirby, and beat and kicked Mary Ann Hodel before turning their wrath on William Hodel and his son-in-law. A *Post-Dispatch* photographer shooting the incident was hit over the head with a bottle.[21]

Just as Nixon borrowed tropes from George Wallace, the cultural politics of the "silent majority" echoed in explicitly fascist projects that recalled Gerald L. K. Smith's earlier Christian Nationalist Party. In December 1969, the National Socialist White People's Party attracted local media attention as it waged a recruitment campaign in South St. Louis. Organizers circulated a swastika-adorned leaflet warning, "Communist revolutionaries, using the militant Black masses, are at this moment preparing for a terror-campaign in the city of St. Louis." Juxtaposing the specter of "Black Terror" with a hope for "White Unity," the party voiced sentiments that would have been familiar to the "hard hats" joining the Republican fold. "The honest White workers will suffer the arrogance of Black rabble-rousers who demand high positions on the job line without earning those positions," the circular read. "This criminal intrusion by a stupid, savage minority will slow construction in St. Louis and result in the loss of employment for thousands of White working men."[22]

Reactivated in late 1968, St. Louis's Citizens' Council addressed its own appeals to white South St. Louisans. "We believe it is time everyone became concerned," declared one invitation to a neighborhood meeting. "Our government has become the captive of minority groups and no longer represents the majority community." The accusation reflected the anxieties many white working-class residents felt as the city's racial composition changed, and as the metropolis became a battleground between Black Power radicals and police. The silence of the majority, according to the flyer, "makes it easy for the hoodlums and thugs to wreck our schools, peddle dope, murder, rape, steal, turn our neighborhoods into slums and pave the way for Communist takeover in America." It would be difficult to indict the white working class en masse for the activities of small groups of white supremacists, or equally inaccurate to suggest that white workers were, on the whole, characteristically retrograde. Many younger working-class whites, like others of their generation, adhered to antiracist and progressive—and even revolutionary socialist—politics. And while it is difficult to discern how reading audiences reacted to the literature distributed by groups like the National Socialist White People's Party, the views of the latter may have been more representative of popular opinion than some white St. Louisans wanted to admit. Nixon's "class struggle" was deadly precisely because it drove deeper the wedge between left-oriented white labor leaders and the membership they ostensibly represented. Harold Gibbons was one tragic case in point. Bypassed as Hoffa's successor when the Teamsters general president went to prison on criminal charges, Gibbons had steadily lost clout in the union. Marginalized by the right in his union, he was also despised by rank-and-file workers oriented toward the New Left, who regarded him as a staunch business unionist hiding behind the facade of progressive politics. One of the most nationally visible, and outspoken, labor leaders against the war in Vietnam, he cast the only dissenting vote on the Teamsters executive board against endorsing Nixon's 1972 reelection. Summarily dismissed as director of the Central Conference of Teamsters, he was forced in 1973 to resign his posts in both Joint Council 13 and Local 688. Ernest Calloway followed him into retirement shortly thereafter, taking a teaching position at St. Louis University.[23]

Johnson's "War on Poverty," predictably, was an attendant target of white reaction as U.S. social and urban policy veered to the right. During a series of planning sessions for a White House Conference on Civil Rights, which took place in June 1966, A. Philip Randolph had proposed a $180 billion "Freedom Budget for All Americans." Tightly controlled by a Johnson administration distracted by war and obsessed with suppressing criticism, the conference was largely a failure, and Randolph's proposal never received genuine consideration. Indeed, the Revenue and Expenditure Control Act, signed in June 1968, required the federal executive branch to cut domestic spending by $6 billion. Congress eviscerated the budget of the Office of Economic Opportunity, and among other revanchist measures voted down a $40 million rat control plan for working-class communities. In Missouri, Governor Hearnes proved intensely hostile to Legal Aid, Job Corps, the HDC, and the Great Society more generally. Many St. Louisans shared his sentiments. In December 1969, the Legal Aid Society lost financial support from the city's United Fund, whose board castigated the agency for defending black revolutionary militants like the Liberators rather than the more abstract "needy." Late the following year, when the *Globe-Democrat* reported that two black HDC federal job trainees had been involved in promoting a St. Louis CORE boycott against Anheuser-Busch, HDC general manager Clyde Cahill was also forced into contrition. According to the newspaper, grocery, tavern, and liquor store owners in the declining West End area claimed to have received threats from CORE representatives to stop stocking products by the brewery. Cahill subsequently ordered drastic cuts in the number of trainees assigned to CORE, and through written agreement restricted them from participating in any partisan activities, whether on or off duty. The damage to the city's antipoverty agency, however, had been done. A U.S. attorney called for an FBI investigation, while the *Globe-Democrat* stoked readers' antipathies toward liberal waste and black criminality. "In view of the loose administration shown in this case and the brazenness of the abuse, there would be grounds to review the whole program here," asserted a *Globe-Democrat* editorial. "When two men with long police records, one of them a convicted felon, can go about the city promoting a boycott when they are supposed to be learning a job skill, it's time to clean house."[24]

With waning support for public housing among federal officials and civic leaders, moreover, the St. Louis Civic Alliance for Housing disbanded in May 1972. The demolition of the massive Pruitt-Igoe complex, beginning during this period, rid the city of a development that had become thoroughly unlivable. The nation's first high-rise public housing project to face the wrecking ball, Pruitt-Igoe also signaled the beginning of the federal state's abandonment of affordable housing. Through a strategy of decentralization, meanwhile, the Nixon administration siphoned power from federal antipoverty programs, bolstering the authority of local officials against organized community participants. The passage of the 1973 Comprehensive Employment and Training Act, and the Housing and Community Development Act of 1974, also diminished programming resources, according state governments the right to determine funding priorities through federal block grants. Given the racial politics dividing predominantly black urban centers from their white suburbs, let alone the white constituencies dominating state capitols in Missouri and elsewhere, this "new federalism" assured the instability of social welfare programs targeted to marginal black workers. A continuing cyclical downturn in the U.S. economy, stemming from the Vietnam debacle, gave additional impetus to the hostility toward black social wage demands. African American working-class activists appealed for economic justice at the same time that the nation's economy contracted, rendering domestic social spending a lowered priority.[25]

Nixon may have elevated the "benign neglect" of the cities to official policy, but the "War on Poverty" had been far from perfect even during the heyday of the Johnson years. Foremost, it rested on assumptions of black cultural pathology, and as a consequence of the war in Vietnam, antipoverty measures never received the funding appropriate to their ambitious goals. Vital matters of urban redevelopment also fell outside the purview of federal antipoverty agencies, which made it impossible for them meaningfully to affect the structure of local power relations. Indeed, the existence of the HDC and Model Cities often insulated Civic Progress decision-makers from popular protests by redirecting them to beleaguered antipoverty administrators. With few exceptions, too, grassroots interests remained subordinated within these bureaucracies and subject to reprisals from city officeholders resentful of working-class activists receiving federal programming money. Supported by HUD, Mayor Cervantes wrested authority from St. Louis's Model Cities agency; neighborhood corporations subsequently lost their planning and operating autonomy, and their input into policy. Margaret Bush Wilson, an outspoken proponent of maximum community participation, was forced out of the Model Cities directorship in July 1969 when the mayor appointed, in her place, Arthur Kennedy. Demoted to Kennedy's deputy, she was dismissed the very next month. Notwithstanding Alderman Joseph Clark's spirited resistance, Cervantes also succeeded in revising the Model Cities ordinance, which shifted control over the program to his administration.[26]

"A Piece of the Action": A New Black Entrepreneurial-Political Bloc

The repression of Black Power radicals, the crafting of a "New Right" populism, and the evisceration of the Great Society were but part of a multilayered countermovement strategy. The federal state had also adopted policies to pacify the black "semiproletarian" masses. Johnson's "War on Poverty," despite his administration's rhetoric, had never endeavored to be an unconditional war, and in fact had sought merely to stabilize the poor in their poverty. The same applied to Nixon's ill-fated proposal for a Family Assistance Plan, whose miserly guaranteed annual income of $1,600 was opposed by welfare rights activists and liberal politicians. Another facet of this co-optation was more extensive in its consequences. Unlike President Johnson, whose major black policy thrust had been employment and job training, his successor found it more cost-effective to increase the number of African American business owners, who constituted less than 2 percent of the total black population. Many of the black hotels and other segregation-era businesses that had survived the Great Depression, or had formed during or shortly after World War II, had since suffered as urban renewal demolished black communities, and as African Americans had taken advantage of public accommodations legislation to patronize white businesses. Therefore, while Nixon courted blue-collar "hard hats" among the white electorate as a counter to eastern "limousine liberals," he cultivated a new black middle-class stratum to forestall working-class black insurgency. Under Nixon, the Small Business Administration (SBA) for the first time began targeting black entrepreneurs for government assistance. SBA

7(a) guaranteed loans made to minority businesses, while SBA 8(a) provided set-asides for government contracts. The Office of Minority Business
Enterprise (OMBE), established in the U.S. Department of Commerce
through executive order in 1969, coordinated other federal agencies' involvement in black business development.[27]

Thus, the same president who ratcheted up state terror against organizations like the Panthers on behalf of the "silent majority," actively endorsed "Black Power," though he framed it distinctly as "Black Capitalism." The SBA and OMBE, through its partnerships with "consensus-
seeking organizations" tied to the white elite, formed a web of "corporate
liberalism." Foremost among these vehicles of civic cohesion and corporate
hegemony was the Ford Foundation, which in late 1968 had given St. Louis
University a thirty-thousand-dollar grant to fund full tuition scholarships
for working-class black St. Louisans. The foundation had also underwritten summer internships for black youth involving nearly sixty local firms.
Both the Ford and Rockefeller foundations, as well as major corporations
like PepsiCo, had similarly financed the ICBO, a national entity created to
aid the development and expansion of black-owned enterprises. Home-
grown "corporate liberal" patrons were also prominent in defining this
strategy. Since the early 1960s, Civic Progress had sponsored "dialogue
groups" to bring together select black and white leaders, and promote
"community reconciliation." "The term 'dialogue' was a misnomer because it implied discussion between two or more people; the only people
talking were the blacks," Clay observed. "The leaders of Civic Progress did
all of the listening and received enough information to effectively develop
strategies to offset any serious challenge to the welfare of the downtown
business interests." Designed as a preemptive measure against black urban
rebellion, the meetings were wholly consistent with the city's tradition of
interracial negotiation, and for all intents and purposes functioned as "an
effective mechanism for establishing a safety zone between the victims of
injustice and the victimizers." In the aftermath of Watts, Civic Progress had
declared civil rights the city's most pressing issue, and since then had become the leading private entity in generating business-oriented alternatives to Black Power radicalism, with its affiliates providing millions of dollars in grants for business management training.[28]

With the full support of St. Louis's white civic institutions, the SBA and
the ICBO had opened local offices in September 1968—the same period,
significantly, when organizations like the Liberators were gaining notoriety. Not coincidentally, the ICBO made its debut at a well-publicized lun-
cheon hosted by *Globe-Democrat* publisher G. Duncan Bauman, and attended by the city's leading white business executives. In his remarks at the
gathering, Urban League executive William Douthit, who was the ICBO's

acting local chairman, carefully reconciled Black Power with the goal of economic and social inclusion, as he had so many times before. "When you hear people yelling black power, " he insisted, "what they mean is green power." Douthit could point to the purchase of a white-owned car wash by an African American, who had received a $25,000 SBA-guaranteed bank loan. He could boast, with equal optimism, about the two black lathe operators at McDonnell-Douglas who, in early 1969, opened their own drive-in restaurant. The largest beneficiary of St. Louis's black capitalist initiative was the Central City Foods Company, which with fifty-eight employees became the city's first major black supermarket. Financed by the General American Life Insurance Company and the SBA, the shopping center's investors included the black-owned Vanguard Redevelopment Corporation, chaired by board of education member James Hurt.[29]

On the heels of a $47,000 grant from the Department of Commerce, the Danforth Foundation provided $25,000 in seed money to establish the ICBO's full-time office in 1969 and hire an executive director. Satisfied with the results, the foundation contributed an additional $130,000 to the ICBO in early 1970. Consistent with the ICBO's goal of expanding businesses outside the service industry, Hurt was involved in forming an all-black construction association, which attracted architects, subcontractors, and U.S. Civil Rights Commission member Frankie Muse Freeman as legal counsel. "Let's face it," Hurt remarked, singing what must have been music to the ears of City Hall and the local corporate elite, "the United States is a country that operates on economic power—the dollar. If we are going to live in this society, we are going to have to do what has been successful in this society. . . . We must convince Negroes that they can be successful within the system." The *Globe-Democrat,* a chief purveyor of this outlook, led the local media in the late 1960s and early 1970s in lavishing favorable publicity on black private business ventures, readily contrasting the black capitalist slogan "Build, Baby, Build!" with caricatured militants urging followers to "Burn, Baby, Burn!" Racial inclusion in white corporate America was also part of the black corporate expansion, and many firms hired their own minority "intrapreneurs"—as did McDonnell-Douglas, which in April 1970 named Luther Bellinger director of equal opportunity. Others were tied to white corporate capital through joint business ventures and franchise deals, which enabled one black St. Louisan to start an All Pro Chicken eatery, and another—former Cardinals baseball player Johnny Lewis—to open a Jack-in-the-Box restaurant.[30]

To be sure, corporate liberalism easily meshed with the outlook of many Black Nationalists, for whom the desire for business development was as legitimate an expression of Black Power politics as community control of police and schools. Although comprising about 40 percent of the city's population in 1968, African Americans were only a little over 7 percent of St. Louis's business proprietors and managers. Historically denied personal and collective wealth, many black activists and their constituents rightfully demanded, in Nixon's words, "a piece of the action" as a form of self-determination. Green viewed ACTION's jobs campaign as a way of securing the type of wages that would sustain black business development, and the fact that McDonnell-Douglas workers were prominent among the aspiring black entrepreneurs who received SBA approval was a testament to his logic. MCC spokesman Ocie Pastard openly pursued joint-venture partnerships with white financiers to generate black-owned businesses, and in July 1968 he announced the beginning of a "Buy Black" campaign urging suburbanites to spend ten dollars a week in the North St. Louis ghettoes. Like the Jeff-Vander-Lou Community Action Group, the MCC was among the black grassroots recipients of Danforth Foundation grants. CORE's approach to Black Power also had been oriented toward capitalist enterprise, in large part because of the influence of individuals like Floyd McKissick and Roy Innis. The national organization formed its own CORE Enterprise Corporation in search of joint ventures in industry and commerce. In St. Louis, CORE worked just as vigorously to bind white capital to the project of black economic development. In the summer of 1969, members held a two-day seminar on business management that brought to the table both activists and representatives from Southwestern Bell, the Ralston Purina Company, and other corporations. Even the Black Nationalist Party, once the target of police raids and surveillance, had by 1971 formed Black Nationalism for You, Inc., a construction consortium funded by Gateway National Bank, the Urban League, and the FHA. The group had begun construction on four homes in the West End area, with plans to build another twenty-six in North St. Louis.[31]

The launching of *Black Enterprise* magazine in 1970, and Chicago's star-studded Black Expo affairs during the same period, announced the arrival of this new entrepreneurial class on the historical stage. Between 1969 and 1975, SBA-sponsored procurement from minority-owned firms grew from $9 million to $250 million. Between 1970 and 1974, the number of minority-owned banks nearly doubled from twenty-eight to fifty, with public and private deposits springing from $400 million to more than $1 billion. Ultimately, however, the president's commitment to nascent black capitalists was as shallow as his support for white blue-collar workers. This was evident in the general criticism, made by many would-be black entrepreneurs themselves, that Nixon's "Black Capitalism" was a hoax. It was, first of all, underfunded by the federal state and corporate leadership, and the resources never came close to approximating the public subsidies extended to white businesses; as late as 1973, OMBE's budget was only $60 million.

With some exceptions, the SBA and ICBO offered mainly technical training and advice, and little of the capitalization necessary for genuine racial parity. When, in late 1970, members of an SBA-appointed task force visited St. Louis and other cities to build interest in $100 million worth of promised government contracts, they encountered skepticism and indifference. "The SBA is putting blacks out of business," complained one disillusioned black St. Louis businessman in early 1971. "It practically guarantees failure by not giving businesses adequate capital. A black man accepts whatever he can get, not knowing enough to realize that he is cutting his throat by taking whatever he can get."[32]

Even these meager funds were subject to competition from white businessmen who used African Americans as "fronts" to apply for government funding. One 1969 HDC report, overseen by ACTION member Luther Mitchell, also concluded that 80 percent of the city's black-owned businesses were in marginal areas of the economy, such as beauty salons, barbershops, taverns, and similar "mom-and-pop" ventures. Despite the good intentions of the ICBO, self-sustaining black-owned corporations remained lacking: Eight of St. Louis's 2,000 manufacturing firms had black proprietors, while 10 of its 2,230 wholesale businesses were similarly owned. Gateway National Bank was a key source of black venture capital. Still, as a young financial institution serving an undercapitalized, overwhelmingly working-class community and facing an inordinately high level of risk, the bank was too predictably conservative in its lending habits to function on the scale that a genuine black capitalist program required.[33]

Mitchell's study had promoted, as a solution to this dilemma, creating buying pools to lower the cost of purchases from wholesalers, and lower costs to customers. Yet "Black Capitalism," particularly under the aegis of the SBA, had been narrowly constructed on the model of small, owner-operated ventures that employed few individuals, presumed economic prosperity, and ignored the reality of an increasingly global economy defined by multinational corporations. This model also effectively preempted other workable paradigms of black economic development, including the demands raised in the "Black Manifesto" for meaningful reparations. Consistent with the racial paternalism embedded in SBA and ICBO skills-building programs, further, "Black Capitalist" entrepreneurs, even under the best circumstances, could not escape the role of junior partners. The same was true of salaried black corporate "intrapreneurs" at white firms, who often served in highly visible, yet relatively powerless, positions in human resources, community relations, and public affairs.[34]

Rather than wielding any real agenda-setting authority, or exercising the economic self-determination many had envisioned, the new black entrepreneurial class was largely subservient to white capital. What made them "new" in the first place was precisely that they were tethered to corporate capitalists and dependent on their prerogatives. Indicative of such relationships were the funding difficulties that had beset the Performing Arts Training Center and BAG, which had been recipients of Rockefeller and Danforth largesse in 1968. Black Arts activists rejected condescending white assumptions of black cultural deprivation, leading both foundations to withdraw support the following year amid concerns about the artists' racial stridency. Likewise, the act of identifying which African Americans possessed "the potential to succeed as entrepreneurs," making them eligible for corporate liberal support, privileged the judgment of white economic-political elites. "The hard part of this program," ICBO executive director John G. Seay freely admitted, speaking for his corporate backers, "is going to be explaining to some who want a business of their own that they may not be qualified by experience or temperament to assume the responsibilities of running a company." In some cases, applicants for grants and federal contracts were required to affirm their support for the president as a measure of this fitness.[35]

With the violent suppression of more insurgent movement tendencies, "Black Capitalism" became the dominant expression of Black Power by the early 1970s. The failures of this strategy, even from the standpoint of its proponents, were beside the point. As with Johnson's antipoverty initiatives, the endgame of "Black Capitalism" was only secondarily black capital formation; the primary objective was the reinscription of racial-class hegemony. In fostering networks of indebtedness and loyalty, government and private institutions like Ford, Rockefeller, Danforth, and Civic Progress hoped to harvest a generation of middle-class black political moderates who, exactly like Douthit and Hurt, would confidently articulate corporate capitalist hegemony and defend it against disruptions from below. A few veteran activists, like McKissick, demonstrated their appreciation by endorsing Nixon's 1972 reelection.[36]

Not surprisingly, "Black Capitalism" paralleled the continued rise of black elected officialdom. The relationship, in fact, was symbiotic, as black politicians put the new black business class on firmer footing by securing equity in municipal contracts and federal set-asides, and advocating legislation on their behalf. Between 1965 and 1975, the ranks of black elected officials sprang from 280 to 3,503. Although theoretically part of the same class as their entrepreneurial siblings, the post-1965 black public officials were not so much the result of Republican initiative as they were the progeny of Democrat-backed voter registration drives. Corporate liberals were active even on this front, as in Cleveland, where the Ford Foundation gave CORE a $175,000 grant to register black voters, aiding the 1967 election of Carl Stokes as the first black mayor of a large industrial metropolis. Ford also aided the development of the Joint Center for Political Studies, a black think tank that promoted supplanting black working-class militancy with a more adaptable elected leadership. By 1970, Gary and Newark had joined Cleveland in electing black mayors, and East St. Louis followed in 1971. The Mayor's Office eluded black St. Louisans, though they gained other major elected citywide offices. Benjamin Goins, a political opponent of Clay who Governor Hearnes had appointed to the "county" post of city license collector in the late 1960s, was elected to the office in 1970. In 1972, former school administrator John Bass became St. Louis's first black comptroller, making him the city's second most important municipal officeholder. Between 1968, when Clay was first elected to the U.S. House of Representatives, and 1973, when he began his second term, the number of African Americans in Congress had risen from six to sixteen.[37]

Unlike the black "corporate liberals" favored by Nixon, however, black liberal Democrats did not enjoy the goodwill of the White House. Nixon refused requests to meet with the CBC for a full year, prompting the caucus' boycott of his 1971 State of the Union address. The administration also studiously ignored black legislators' recommendations for public works jobs, a guaranteed annual minimum income of $6,400 for families of four, a federal development bank for black business, and withdrawal from Southeast Asia. Openly attacked by Vice President Agnew, CBC members were subjected to government harassment, as well. But while not politically congruent with Nixon's "silent majority," the rapid ascendance of African American officeholders undercut the agenda of the black working-class bloc in other ways. The emergence of the CBC, National Conference of Black Mayors, and the National Black Caucus of State Legislators, while reflecting the explosion of black politicians at all levels of U.S. government, functioned as vehicles of middle-class consciousness similar to their "Black Capitalist" cognates. They provided, in political scientist Robert C. Smith's words, "a way for middle-class blacks to embrace the principles of black power while simultaneously pursuing their narrow professional or political interests."[38]

Consistent with the Joint Center strategy, as well as his own political proclivities, Clay became prominent among the CBC leaders consciously seeking a shift from black grassroots mobilization to "politics." As even he recognized, however, this project contained the danger of new forms of political opportunism. "On the local level, too many Black elected officials are engaged in divisive, guerilla-type activities which can only impede the progress of Blacks," Clay wrote in a 1972 essay appearing in the periodical *Black World.* It is clear that Goins, though unnamed, was one of his intended targets. "It is inconceivable that in this day and age some Black ward leaders, councilmen and representatives would become the 'pawns' of outside forces which are determined to divide Blacks." There had emerged, he later recounted, "an assortment of black nihilists, hustlers, and obstructionists" without even a passing involvement in black freedom activism—individuals who sought to exploit St. Louis electoral politics for purely personal gain. In the mid-1970s, Clay, who had often been accused of political cynicism himself, was investigated for everything from padding his office payroll and income tax evasion to illegal campaign contributions and drug trafficking. Most of the probes stemmed from sensational stories printed in the *Globe-Democrat*. Although exonerated in each case, Clay became arguably the most publicly maligned black elected official since Adam Clayton Powell Jr.[39]

The 1972 National Black Political Convention, held in Gary to craft a collective racial agenda for that year's presidential election, also signaled the "zenith and decline" of a working-class black freedom politics. Organized by a coalition of elected officials and grassroots Black Nationalists, and attracting nearly three thousand formal participants, the gathering starkly revealed the extent of black class differentiation in the post-1965 period. Influential black professional politicians had steadfastly opposed the idea of a convention when it was initially proposed, instead preferring "small and exclusive meetings of the black elite to establish themselves as the patronage referees for the emerging national black political community." To be sure, a convention had been suggested in part because of popular concerns that the CBC was too parochial to adequately represent the spectrum of black interests. In a lengthy, fiery summary published in *Black World*, Imamu Amiri Baraka—a pivotal Gary convener, and a chairman of the Congress of African People—took polemical aim at Clay and Ohio representative Louis Stokes, who, he identified as "the main movers" in the CBC and who, Baraka insisted, covertly tried to sabotage the mass effort. Reluctantly acceding to pressure to support the convention call, the CBC subsequently withdrew its sponsorship in frustration with rules privileging the selection of community-based delegates. Many of the officeholders who attended, and stayed to the convention's adjournment, were ambivalent about the "Black Agenda" delegates adopted, and they abandoned the newly formed National Black Political Assembly (NBPA). In a final repudiation, the CBC issued its own "Black Declaration of Independence and Bill of Rights." "The hands of Clay and Stokes in this are obvious," Baraka declared, lambasting the document as "a Negro Bill of Sale" to the Democratic Party for individual positions of black brokerage.[40]

The schism growing out of the Gary Convention at root reflected an antagonism among the budding new class of politicians toward the idea that national black agenda-building should come from the working-class grassroots—the same grassroots that had made their very offices possible. This was a hostility premised on the idea that only those with the connections and resources to win high office had the right to represent and pursue collective black interests. In essence, CBC leaders rejected the direct democracy of mass assemblies, which had both anchored black working-class politics and prevented middle-class leaders from negotiating secret agreements with white elites. Their flight not only fed the gradual decline of grassroots Black Nationalists in the burgeoning national black political community, but it also ensured that expanding black electoral power would be negotiated within an increasingly diffident Democratic Party seeking to separate itself from black popular interests. While black St. Louisans increased their numbers by nearly 20 percent between 1960 and 1968, their voter registration declined by 23.1 percent, and their participation in city elections dropped 27 percent. By 1971, less than four in ten were registered voters. As Calloway would later comment, the "dry-rot" of black St. Louis politics during the 1970s was particularly evident in the sharp decline in school board elections, once a rallying point of community mobilization. Estranged from an active black working-class constituency, black politicians reached their own accord with corporate capitalists to retain office. In doing so, they helped further institutionalize an elite brokerage paradigm.[41]

Epilogue
◢

If the appearance of the new black entrepreneurial-political stratum marked the emergence of one historic bloc, Randolph's retirement in some respects embodied the decline of another. In 1968, the seventy-nine-year-old doyen of black labor withdrew from the presidency of the BSCP and the AFL-CIO Executive Council. The BSCP, like the man who had led it since 1925, was by then a faded shadow of its former self. With the growth of air travel, the Brotherhood, which had never been a major force within the AFL-CIO, had declined to a membership of two thousand, and within a decade merged into a larger union. Yet its legacy of independent black worker activism persisted. With black St. Louisans still lagging behind whites in well-paying work, African American workers remained far from quiescent as the 1970s proceeded. In May 1969, St. Louis's United Black Alliance had begun a boycott of the Krey Packing Company, charging the company with racial discrimination against black employees and accusing the United Packinghouse Workers of failing to protect them. The coalition sent letters to grocers in the city's black neighborhoods warning them not to handle Krey products. Two Kroger stores were bombed, with signs left on the windows declaring, "Krey Meats Must Go." Ongoing protests brought into being the local Brotherhood of Black Packinghouse Workers, whose members lifted the boycott in August 1970 when the plant appointed a black foreman and restored employee benefits. The caucus was consistent with continuing black militancy inside the U.S. labor movement, which in 1972–73 produced the Coalition of Black Trade Unionists (CBTU). One of its founding members, Cleveland Robinson, had been a leader of the NNLC in the 1950s, as well as Randolph's successor as president of the NALC. Like its predecessors, the CBTU became a vehicle for increasing black union organization, participation and leadership, and "providing active support for civil rights, civic and related groups to improve living and working conditions in the Black community."[42]

The CBTU model inspired black women to join other female unionists in the fight for new gender relations within organized labor. In April 1973, eight top women union officials—including Addie Wyatt, a black representative of the Amalgamated Meat Cutters and Butcher Workmen—met to discuss a strategy for expanding women's involvement in the AFL-CIO and other labor organizations. This modest beginning led to their convening over two hundred people in Chicago. In preparation for the founding of a new organization, the delegates agreed to hold a series of regional conferences. Through the coordinating efforts of black garment worker Ora Lee Malone, tradeswomen in St. Louis were the first to hold such a gathering. Hosted by Teamsters Local 688, the meeting attracted 350 attendees, and featured Wyatt as keynote speaker. In March 1974, over three thousand people, representing more than fifty unions, took part in the founding of the Coalition of Labor Union Women. In its statement of purpose, the organization called for the unionization of unorganized women, a federal livable minimum wage, full employment and job opportunities across gender and race, universal childcare, and mass mobilization to ratify the Equal Rights Amendment.[43]

In the realm of black working-class struggle outside the labor movement, ACTION continued plaguing the local utility companies with its baroque protests well into the 1970s. Entering Southwestern Bell's headquarters disguised as janitors, two members staged a "stick-in" at Southwestern Bell's employment office, pouring thick molasses over furniture and carpeting to inform the corporation that, in Green's words, "number one, we're going to stick right with them until they do the things that we want done." At the Union Electric Company's downtown building, activists posing as laborers sprayed a strong, ammonia-based substance over desks and typewriters, symbolizing their determination to "clean up" the company's service and employment practices. ACTION leaders also adopted a strategy of forcibly halting white Laclede Gas repair crews at several North St. Louis sites, demanding that 50 percent of the jobs go to black workers, proportionate to their numbers in the city. At the gas company's offices, Green and another ACTION member shocked employees by decorating walls, floors, glass mirrors and elevators with dog manure, graphically expressing their opinion about explanations for the low numbers of black employees. The protest left arresting officers to debate who would bodily carry the men to the waiting police vehicle.[44]

In the midst of these struggles, ACTION culminated its long campaign against the Veiled Prophet Organization. During the 1972 ball, Gena Scott, a white ACTION member "disguised" in full evening dress, slid from the ballroom balcony on a spotlight cable, landing near the oracle's throne. Despite injuring herself, she was able to snatch his crown and gossamer veil before authorities apprehended her. The unmasking sparked outrage among the city's civic leaders, and most media maintained their deference to the corporate elite by withholding the exposed official's name. Breaking ranks, the *St. Louis Journalism Review* disclosed his identity as Tom K. Smith, a Monsanto Corporation executive vice president and Civic Progress alumnus. Although entirely symbolic, the caper stripped a seemingly omnipotent icon of white capitalist hegemony of its mystique, and subverted the public rituals of power the gala had embodied since the nineteenth century. A subsequent class-action lawsuit, also instigated by ACTION, forced the Veiled Prophet Organization to relocate its annual affair to a private venue.[45]

ACTION had continued to afflict McDonnell-Douglas, as well, despite the hiring of Luther Bellinger as corporate director of equal opportunity. In March 1970, as the corporation had continued to evade details of a hiring plan, four ACTION members had gained entry to an aircraft building, where they had staged a brief sit-in before police arrested them for trespassing. This had been only the first of several "maneuver-ins" that occurred over the next few years. With Clay's involvement, the U.S. House of Representatives, through its special Subcommittee on the Armed Forces, had called McDonnell-Douglas's vice president to testify about the firm's hiring timetables in August 1970. That same month, the U.S. Civil Rights Commission had reviewed the corporation's affirmative action hiring plan, and deemed it deficient in employment goals and outlines for training programs. Scrutinized by federal legislators from above, and hounded by grassroots organizers from below, the corporation eventually made reforms. Deputies for U.S. Secretary of Defense Melvin Laird sent Green a letter "thanking ACTION for information it had provided about job discrimination allegedly practiced by local defense contractors." In an unmistakably arch gesture, Green mailed the Defense Department a billing statement for "consulting services."[46]

Through a series of appeals, further, Green's suit arrived on the docket of the U.S. Supreme Court. In *Green v. McDonnell-Douglas Corporation* (1973), the court ruled that plaintiffs in a racial discrimination suit needed only to establish "minimum proof" that they were denied employment or discharged due to racism. The decision gave plaintiffs in private discrimination suits a powerful new weapon, and like the outcome of the Gateway Arch controversy set a standard for subsequent cases. It became the most recognized case ever decided under Title VII of the 1964 Civil Rights Act. Green himself never regained employment at McDonnell-Douglas, though as his case had proceeded through the courts, he had earned a B.A. in Urban Affairs from St. Louis University, and a Master of Social Work from Washington University.[47]

With the success of the "New Right" against the Black Freedom Movement, his case was largely an epilogue to several decades of black working-class struggle in St. Louis and other cities. Police and FBI-supported violence marginalized the movement's most insurrectionary and grassroots segments in the late 1960s, and Black Power was channeled toward the creation of new entrepreneurial and administrative strata of the black bourgeoisie. "Black Power" essentially became "Black Capitalism," a version of middle-class racial uplift sanctioned by the federal state and corporate largesse.[48]

Granted, "Black Capitalism," as promoted by the Nixon administration, was largely a myth—as late as 1977, the top one hundred black businesses combined employed only 8,389 individuals. Among other weaknesses, it served to undermine the working-class project of full employment that would have made small business-development schemes possible in the first place. But as historians Robert E. Weems Jr., and Lewis A. Randolph maintain, "[A]lthough Nixon did not achieve his institutional goals (campaign promises) related to Black capitalism, he did, indeed, achieve his larger ideological goal of subverting African American radicalism." The rise of black elected officials, though emerging from civil rights and Black Power struggles, was equally a factor in this demise, largely because of the new officeholders' changing set of priorities. In the conflict that split the 1972 Gary Convention and crippled the NBPA at birth, historian Komozi Woodard contends that "a line emerged between, on the one hand, rising black leaders, accountable to the group politics of the black community, and on the other hand, black public figures and professional politicians, retreating to the habitual politics of individualism, brokerage, and clientage." By the mid-1970s, according to political scientist Robert C. Smith, the latter had triumphed, "render[ing] post-civil rights era black politics largely an elite, hierarchical phenomenon that is largely irrelevant to the internal problems of the black community."[49]

Still, as the grumblings against the Nixon administration by struggling black middle-class entrepreneurs attested, schemes of black political co-optation were not seamless, and individuals did not numbly play their as-signed roles. That is, black entrepreneurs and "intrapreneurs" were not white corporate dupes. Rather, they fought the white racism of lending in-stitutions, sought to smash the glass ceilings of their corporations, con-tested white colleagues who resented their competition, and, increasingly, confronted hostile federal officials who began an attack on affirmative ac-tion policies. Nor were black elected representatives necessarily less racially conscious or militant than their working-class constituents, as Clay's solidly progressive voting record, and the formation and activities of the CBC, all suggest. By the late 1970s, moreover, a series of economic downturns had slowed black middle-class growth; by the early 1980s, black professionals were losing ground altogether. But while their class lo-cation proved too tenuous to narrowly prescribe their politics, the ideas of the black racial interest held by members of the new black economic-polit-ical elite were not always compatible with those of the working-class ma-jority. Indeed, they diverged as state-sponsored black middle-class forma-tion, like state-supported violence against black radicals, demobilized grassroots black freedom struggle. At a historical moment of heightening joblessness among working-class African Americans, this divergence both reconstituted black racial domination and set the stage for intensified black class schisms.[50]

It would be a mistake, nonetheless, to conclude that "the black bour-geoisie was the primary beneficiary of the movement," as some black lib-erals and radicals alike have contended. In St. Louis, the combined pres-sure of work stoppages, EEOC suits initiated by ACTION, and the embarrassment and federal scrutiny caused by insurgent protests, com-pelled firms like Laclede Gas to implement minority hiring plans by the late 1970s. This was a narrative repeated in many other cities as on-the-job training and hiring programs paved the way for black gas meter readers, telephone operators and linemen, bank clerks, and skilled workers in con-struction, steel, and other basic industries—to say nothing of the much greater numbers of African Americans who joined fire and police depart-ments, or successfully pursued other working-class occupations in munic-ipal, state, and federal employment as mail carriers and postal clerks. These reforms, particularly in the realm of public employment, were, in one sense, concessions to the movement akin to "Black Capitalism." Yet such affirmative action training and hiring programs affected a much larger cross-section of African Americans, freeing them from the common labor and domestic servitude that had constrained generations of black workers. The fact that these reforms were mightily resisted, moreover, speaks to the unlikely success of working-class black freedom struggle, notwithstanding the spreading misery of black workers' conditions at work and at home. This was a legacy of struggle for more and better employment, meaningful political representation, union protection, social wages, and respect—a legacy from which even many liberals, freed from the demands of a vibrant black working-class bloc, actively began to retreat by the end of the 1970s.[51]

Conclusion

At the end of the 1970s, "St. Louis was clearly the patron saint of the nation's urban crisis" that for many residents in the surrounding county epitomized the danger and dysfunction of urban life. In 1980, two sociologists ranked it one of the nation's most depressed cities, as measured by housing stock, per capita income, and degree of population decline. By then, 453,000 people lived within St. Louis City's borders, 46 percent of them black. Between 1970 and 1977, nearly 100,000 people had left the riverfront metropolis. An estimated 69,000 African Americans quit the city, doubling their numbers in St. Louis County by 1979. Their absence, among other things, exacerbated municipal government's retreat from providing "social wages" to the city's black working class. During this period, City Hall closed Homer G. Phillips Hospital, once a source of pride and identity among black St. Louisans. With national fiscal crises in the mid-1970s, capitalist disinvestment in older cities, and an aggressive campaign by business to radically restructure the U.S. economy, the working class that had once steeled local black freedom struggles was consigned to the margins of a new postindustrial landscape oriented toward tourism, recreation, corporate capital, privatization, and low wages.[1]

The movement also lost much of its black working-class leaders from the preceding decades. Theodore McNeal, the former MOWM chairman, BSCP leader, and state senator, died in 1982. David Grant lost a long fight with lung cancer in 1985. Ernest Calloway died in December 1989, one day shy of his eighty-first birthday. At the time, DeVerne Calloway, who had retired from public service after ten terms in the Missouri House of Representatives, was in a hospital recovering from a stroke. She died of a heart attack three years later. Although he never fully recovered politically from the anticommunist offensive of the early Cold War, Hershel Walker had also remained a committed activist. During the 1970s, he had coordinated local defense work for Angela Davis, and helped form the National Al-

liance Against Racist and Political Repression. By the 1980s, he was involved in the South Africa divestment movement, and organized family
visits to inmates at the Missouri State Penitentiary. His life came to a tragic
end in May 1990, when a pickup truck crashed head-on into his car.[2]

Margaret Bush Wilson, who had served as assistant attorney general of
Missouri, spent nine terms in office as chairperson of the NAACP National
Board of Directors. Symbolic of many activists adjusting to the postindustrial retreat from "social wages," she had "served on several corporate
boards as she pushed for less reliance on government and more on the private sector." Like Frankie Muse Freeman, who served on the U.S. Commission on Civil Rights until 1979, Wilson had returned to private legal practice since leaving her post as NAACP board chair. Her fellow former
"Young Turk," William Clay, retired in 2000 after several terms in the U.S
House of Representatives. As a measure of the extraordinary influence he
had amassed during his incumbency, voters elected his son, William Lacy
Clay Jr., to fill his seat. The younger Clay was part of a new generation of
black politicians that had matured after the civil rights–Black Power period, taking advantage of the city's changing racial demographics to win
higher government positions. In 1982, attorney Freeman Bosley Jr., the son
of a well-known ward alderman, had won the powerful "county" office of
circuit clerk. By the late 1980s, he had outmaneuvered the entrenched white
leadership of the St. Louis Democratic Party to become its first black chairman. Buttressed by his control of the city's largest patronage office, the activist networks he had developed as a student at St. Louis University, lib-
eral-progressive support, and divided white opponents, paved the way for
his election as the city's first black mayor in 1993.[3]

Among the grassroots black freedom workers hired into the new administration was Percy Green, who, despite enduring frequent periods of
unemployment, had continued his wide-ranging activism. ACTION, however, had disbanded in the early 1980s. Accepting an appointment as director of the city's minority-participation program, he became responsible for
investigating and certifying minority- and women-owned businesses for
involvement in municipal contracts. The task was consistent with Green's
general commitment to achieving racial parity in the distribution of economic opportunity, though the office corresponded more directly to the interests of the new black entrepreneurial elite that had grown since the
1970s. Indeed, the Bosley administration was typical of other post-civil
rights "black urban regimes" favorable toward the progrowth strategies of
corporate capital, provided that black executives and business interests
had an expanded role in these arrangements. Yet the young mayor's insis-
tence that black professionals and entrepreneurs share meaningfully in city
appointments and business set-asides intensified hostility among white

South St. Louisans. Exploiting a series of missteps and scandals involving mayoral staffers, a contingent of politicians, residents, and corporate leaders supported a challenge to Bosley's reelection by Clarence Harmon, who had been the city's first black police chief and a known adversary of the mayor. In the 1997 Democratic primaries, 94 percent of white voters chose Harmon, giving him his margin of victory. The contest betrayed not only the city's complex racial dynamics, but also the stark class politics among African Americans, the overwhelming majority of whom favored Bosley and derided Harmon as an "Uncle Tom." That the black electorate turned out in underwhelming numbers, however, suggested a grassroots disconnect from the entire process—most black working-class people remained mired in deteriorating conditions impervious to the swearing-in of another black elected official. By 2001, St. Louis ranked as the nation's ninth most segregated city, plagued by high black unemployment and low household income.[4]

Lost in the Flood

Black workers could still be moved to action, as the 1999 Highway 70 construction protest demonstrated, but their energies were channeled toward the interests of a middle-class historic bloc. The construction trades remained almost solidly closed to black workers. In 2002, only 5.5 percent of construction workers in the city were African American, leading Theodore D. McNeal Jr., to publicly raise the age-old question, "Where Are the Construction Jobs for African-Americans?" The nadir of a visible black working-class politics became painfully visible in the late summer and fall of 2005, when Hurricane Katrina overwhelmed the Gulf Coast. In New Orleans, working-class African Americans comprised the largest and most noticeable segment of those who, unable to flee rising floodwaters, crowded rooftops and sports arenas for days without adequate food, fresh water, medical attention, or a timely federal response. Media coverage became increasingly fixated on "looters" and lawlessness, and when evacuation efforts on their behalf finally began, they often assumed the character of search-and-destroy military operations. Several federal, state, and local officials spoke as if their task was one of quelling a dangerous mob, not rescuing citizens.[5]

Early references to the black urban hurricane victims as "refugees," likely meant to evoke public compassion, only served to further separate them from the U.S. polity. During his belated tour of the devastation, President George W. Bush studiously avoided the streets of New Orleans, and its stricken residents. New Orleans mayor Clarence Ray Nagin, beleaguered, shocked, and angered at federal negligence, may have reflected black sentiments across class. But it bears reminding that Nagin, a former cable company executive, had personified a style of post-1960s black urban politics steeped in "progrowth" initiatives favoring corporate tax give-aways, and antilabor policies directed at largely black municipal work-forces, privatization, and the urban renewal-driven displacement of the black poor. The desertion, distancing, and vilification of the black "under-class" were emblematic of a broader social abandonment of black working-class people in the period after civil rights and Black Power.[6]

In contemporary times, black working-class people have been "lost in the storm of controversy" surrounding discussions about a triumphant black middle class and a scrambling African American "bottom class." Yet the fact is that black workers have not disappeared as subjects in popular discourse; rather, they have simply been discursively reconstructed, politi-cally suppressed, and publicly maligned. In the 1970s, the "underclass" emerged as a main signifier of cultural pathology and social deviance in the United States. In the conventional wisdom, this group is distinguished not simply by its members' poverty, but more importantly by their defective values and dysfunctional behavior. While this social category may not be explicitly racialized, it is casually associated with people of color, who com-prise a disproportionate share of the working-class poor. Generally defined as the marginally employed, high school dropouts, female-headed and sin-gle-parenting households, petty criminals and hustlers, and dependents of means-tested social welfare programs, the term *underclass* is heavily freighted with moral assumptions about race, gender, class, and poverty.[7]

Even Ernest Calloway, who committed his adult life to championing working-class activism, had capitulated ideologically to such sentiments. With the flight of middle-class African Americans, he argued in 1978, black communities had become economically and socially isolated ghettoes. The result, Calloway wrote, was cultural underdevelopment and moral insta-bility. "Consequently," he counseled, "one would conclude that what the ghetto 'underclass' is in need of today, above everything else, is a continu-ing revolution in aggressive self-hood. In the absence of this new self-view in the bowels of the urban ghetto, federal and local welfare programs have only limited value." While promoting "self-awareness" as a prelude to re-newed struggle, the wizened labor intellectual nonetheless reified the de-veloping consensus about black working-class cultural pathology. Al-though employed by others committed to social justice, the image of the "underclass" was used increasingly to roll back social welfare programs as-sociated with black working-class recipients. By discrediting social entitle-ments and means-tested subsidies as handouts to a primarily black unde-serving poor, movement opponents succeeded in realigning U.S. politics.

Although conspicuous as the archetype of urban decline and poverty, the black working class has become largely voiceless in debates about public policy. As illustrated by the Katrina crisis, "underclass" rhetoric hides the growing inequities of wealth in U.S. society, the retreat of federal government from "social wages," and continuing patterns of urban renewal and their marginalizing effects on working-class communities.[8]

Class Politics, Place, and Black Freedom Struggle

This project responds to the fact that scholars have lost sight of the intimate historical connection between overarching black communal demands for civil and social rights, and black workers' agendas for fair and full employment, better wages, opportunity, justice, and respect. Liberal sociologist William Julius Wilson, for instance, has argued that "federal, state, and municipal civil rights acts were mainly due to the efforts of the black professional groups (ministers, lawyers, teachers), students, and particularly in the 1960s, sympathetic white liberals. Lower-income blacks had little involvement in civil rights politics up to the mid-1960s." Mapping the black working-class experience over time demonstrates that workers were the central element in African Americans' responses to white racial control. They formed the center of a black freedom bloc that persisted from the 1930s to the decade of the 1970s, and shaped the preeminent character, aims, and constituency of movement initiatives. In rescuing black working-class agency, one viewpoint has posited that because most black workers were excluded from conventional means of political activity and protest, they typically resorted to the "hidden transcripts" of public dissemblance, cultural rebellion, and similar "infrapolitics." Another viewpoint has highlighted black laborers' "unhidden" transcripts of interpersonal confrontation and violence with white citizens and authorities. Yet both arguments presume a black working-class politics bereft of institutional moorings. Black working-class resistance was also organized, collectively sustained, overt, and directed toward clear objectives.[9]

It encompassed issues of employment, urban policy and planning, structures of municipal governance, equal conditions of housing and education, and black representation in public office. Substandard housing, poor medical care and schooling, women's lack of household autonomy, the absence of regular neighborhood garbage pickups and other social amenities, police abuse, crowded playgrounds, political disfranchisement—these were all working-class issues, and thus arenas of mobilization. "Social wages," in the form of old age pensions, the right to unionization, guarantees of home-ownership, and a fair distribution of the nation's resources, also figured substantively in black working-class freedom agendas. Even when activists challenged segregation in its most cosmetic forms, they sought to topple a system of racial control that mandated white superiority and black subordination in all areas of public and private life. In the process, they expanded the meanings of freedom for the whole of U.S. society.

An emphasis on black worker self-organization does not negate the agency of black professionals, who pursued their interests and contributed their talents and visions to the movement, as well. But even when educators, social workers, attorneys, and other elites asserted leadership, they did so in contestation with their counterparts from the working classes, and gained legitimacy only to the extent they stood in intraracial solidarity with the grassroots majority. Attention to black class relations also reveals a Black Freedom Movement whose efforts were contested both from without and from within. Foregrounding class cleavage helps undermine popular black imaginations of an idyllic, organically unified African American urban community during the decades of Jim Crow. Such narratives of an untroubled black communal existence implicitly deny its diversity and structural fetters, and tacitly naturalize elite prerogatives within a constructed past.

Conceptually, black working-class formation offers a more comprehensive picture of the multiplicity, structure, and human agency that have shaped and reshaped the black community over time. These include the politics of capitalist economic development, in the form of depression and recovery, war production, the "runaway shop," and automation, as well as the varied processes of the state—urban renewal, spatial resettlement, public housing and social welfare, labor legislation, foreign policy, and judicial, legal, and executive action. Black working-class formation also captures the "experience-near," lived realities of the workplace. The black working class was, and is, diverse in its composition. Constituting its ranks were skilled craftsmen, trained cosmetologists, industrial operatives, domestic servants, unskilled common laborers, the "structurally unemployed," God-fearing church congregants, even petty lawbreakers and young gang members.

Its form has been fluid, uneven, and constantly becoming. During one historical period, when the contours of a black class structure were barely defined, any stably employed African American could claim respectability and elite status. As a result, the social distance between a Pullman porter and a construction laborer could be tremendous. As the Great Depression made plain, nevertheless, economic crises at other moments could reduce such distinctions to ephemera. However, as new wage-earning and professional opportunities became available after World War II, many older occupations that had typified the black middle class assumed lesser status. On closer inspection, all of the postwar black job opportunities were not what they appeared. Many clerical, sales, postal, and otherwise white-collar jobs—particularly those in which women were concentrated, and which involved routinized tasks under supervisory control—actually represented an expansion of the black working class, rather than a rapid entry into the professional strata.[10]

Black laboring people in St. Louis fought simultaneously for their racial and class interests, reinforcing the salience of each. At times, black workers were compelled to resist the racism of white workers, civic authorities, elected officials, and economic elites. Of course, the activities of the UE, the Teamsters, and local human rights and ecumenical groups demonstrated that white citizens were not monolithically racist—nor were the features of white racism undifferentiated, or unchanging. At other moments, black workers opposed the prerogatives of black professional elites, who attempted to exert stewardship and control over their activities. Their objectives, strategies, and tactics evolved, as did the social and economic geography, which shaped their conditions and racial-class identities.

Many aspects of black working-class life in St. Louis were unique. Foremost, the city's modest size contributed to remarkably dense, multiple, and simultaneous relationships within the African American community, and particularly among those active in the black public sphere. This did not, of course, guarantee unity among African Americans, and over time contention became as much a part of "community" as did consensus. Second, while the city was heavily unionized, it lacked the industrial base of cities like Chicago or Detroit. Most local mass-production industries were modest in scale, and employed relatively small workforces. Lacking a broad range of industrial labor prospects, and ritualistically excluded from skilled trade unions and commercial enterprises, the Gateway City's black working class lacked a robust, diversified character. Throughout the period from the 1930s to the 1960s, the majority of black residents, men and women alike, performed service-oriented tasks. With the exception of the World War II period, most battles for fair employment centered on the construction, retail, and banking industries central to the local economy.

Third, the scarcity of "manly" work for African Americans in St. Louis nurtured a particular emphasis on expanding black male employment. With the exception of instances like the Funsten nutpickers strike, or a few groups like the NNLC, gender equality was rarely a basis of organization among black activists. Even the CCRC, consisting almost entirely of women, issued demands for racial justice from the standpoint of being wives, mothers, sisters, and daughters, which implicitly signaled their own subordination in the public sphere, and certainly in employment. Yet women's social networks formed the bedrock of most grassroots mobilizations, and their concerns remained embedded in these struggles. Consequently, while many black activists fully accepted gendered divisions of paid labor, they fought for black women's greater range of jobs within the confines of "women's work." Thus, local employment campaigns for African American telephone operators, retail sales workers, and petty clerks were implicitly concerned with distaff opportunities. By themselves, these projects did not amount to a formally articulated, or even an organic feminism, but they nonetheless broadened black working women's options beyond domestic labor. In the case of St. Louis's public housing rent strike, working-class women articulated agendas beyond paid labor altogether; embracing their identities as full-time caretakers, they demanded the right to maintain autonomous households with respect and dignity.

St. Louis's uneven system of formal racial apartheid also shaped the rhythms of black activity. It constrained certain social opportunities available to black people in other midwestern cities, though it also enabled a range of activities that were not possible in many Jim Crow cities to the south. Consequently, at the same time that they were prohibited from many public and private spaces, and bound by constitutional law from interracial schooling and marriage, black St. Louisans were voting members of the polity. This not only gave them an important source of leverage in municipal and state affairs, but it also complicated black grassroots activism, which could be manipulated to serve the personal ambitions of would-be politicians as well as the movement. Moreover, aside from the Christian Nationalist Party in the late 1940s and early 1950s, advocates for black citizenship rarely confronted avowed white supremacists. Their main adversaries, instead, were sophisticated corporate elites and civic progressives rhetorically committed to "racial goodwill." Nonetheless, black activists faced patterns of outright racial control, such as segregated commercial accommodations, employment, and public recreation. The particularities of place, however, also forced successive waves of black leadership to deal with complex questions of urban policy and planning, social service delivery, and representation in public office.

Black working-class formation and agency in the Gateway City were unique, but not singular. Like the JOC in St. Louis, civil rights activists in Philadelphia led "Selective Patronage" campaigns in the early 1960s to open unskilled and skilled jobs for African Americans. The SCLC's "Operation Breadbasket" successfully emulated this model in Chicago, which in turn influenced efforts in numerous other cities. During the same period as concerned black St. Louis parents and clergy mobilized the strength of their numbers against the school board, black Bostonians also organized school boycotts against de facto segregation. Civil rights workers in Chicago coordinated sit-ins at the local board of education as well. Alongside the Jefferson Bank boycott, grassroots black activists in Seattle waged their own "general strike" for fair employment, open housing, and desegregated schools, while protesters in Detroit staged "freedom marches" against police brutality. Black working-class insurgents fought similar battles from Oakland to New Haven, as well as Brooklyn, where CORE organizers mobilized residents around the demand for equitable garbage collection. Examples of black working-class struggle abound in the literatures of African American urban history and Black Freedom Studies; the question is whether scholars conceptualize them explicitly as such. Ultimately, the goal of recovering social, economic, and grassroots political movements among black St. Louisans is to specify a general historical typology of black working-class formation and social movements between the Great Depression and the end of the Great Society.[11]

Black social movements provided the juncture where working-class formation and racial identities became visible, but African Americans were not just workers, nor simply movement activists. They lived in neighborhoods, paid rent or owned homes, listened to the blues, attended school and church, bought groceries, and tried to avoid running afoul of the law. Many liked to go swimming when it was hot or see the occasional movie. They were parents, siblings, husbands, wives, children, kinfolk, classmates, and friends. Their daily accommodations, as well as their moments of insurgency, matter to an overall understanding of black working-class formation. Indeed, these "everyday" activities and interests mobilized them every bit as much as workplace grievances and rituals of humiliation under Jim Crow. These everyday patterns of work and life were the crucible in which shared dispositions, mentalities, and diffuse interests and grievances were fashioned, bringing with them tendencies toward unity and fragmentation. Under certain circumstances, and at certain historical junctures, commonplace black sentiments and grievances were transformed into politicized identities, organized constituencies, and collective, programmatic action.

Notes

INTRODUCTION

1. Ken Leiser and Paul Hampel, "Group Demands That 35 Pct. of Jobs on Project Go to Minorities," *St. Louis Post-Dispatch*, July 13, 1999, 1; Alvin A. Reid, "Protesters Turning on to Highway 40," *St. Louis American*, July 15–21, 1999, 1; and Sundiata Keita Cha-Jua, "'No Piece, No Peace': Class Contradictions in the Resurging Black Freedom Movement," *Black World Today*, August 2, 1999, http://www.tbwt.com.

2. Earl Lewis, *In Their Own Interests: Race, Class, and Power in Twentieth-Century Norfolk, Virginia* (Berkeley and Los Angeles: University of California Press, 1991), 5–6. See also Joe William Trotter Jr., "African-American Workers: New Directions in U.S. Labor Historiography," *Labor History* 35 (Fall 1994): 495–523; and Kenneth W. Goings and Raymond A. Mohl, eds., *The New African American Urban History* (Thousand Oaks, Calif.: Sage, 1996). For a rich discussion of the much longer history of black labor studies pioneered by African American scholars, see Francille Rusan Wilson, *The Segregated Scholars: Black Social Scientists and the Creation of Black Labor Studies, 1890–1950* (Charlottesville: University of Virginia Press, 2006).

3. Robin D. G. Kelley, *Race Rebels: Culture, Politics, and the Black Working Class* (New York: Free Press, 1996), 4–5, 7–8; Kenneth W. Goings and Gerald L. Smith, "'Unhidden Transcripts': Memphis and African American Agency, 1862–1920," *Journal of Urban History* 21 (March 1995): 372–94; Joe William Trotter Jr., *Black Milwaukee: The Making of an Industrial Proletariat, 1915–45*, 2nd ed. (Urbana: University of Illinois Press, 2007), 62–64; Rod Bush, *We Are Not What We Seem: Black Nationalism and Class Struggle in the American Century* (New York: New York University Press, 1999), 99; Kimberley L. Phillips, *Alabama North: African-American Migrants, Community, and Working-Class Activism in Cleveland, 1915–45* (Urbana: University of Illinois Press, 1999), 11–12, 123–26; and Hayward Derrick Horton, Beverlyn Lundy Allen, Cedric Herring and Melvin E. Thomas, "Lost in the Storm: The Sociology of the Black Working Class, 1850 to 1990," *American Sociological Review* 65 (2000): 129.

4. Darlene Clark Hine, "Black Professionals and Race Consciousness: Origins of the Civil Rights Movement, 1890–1950," *Journal of American History* 89 (2003): 1279–94; Martin Summers, *Manliness and Its Discontents: The Black Middle*

Class and the Transformation of Masculinity, 1900–1930 (Chapel Hill: University of North Carolina Press, 2004); Adam Green, *Selling the Race: Culture, Community, and Black Chicago, 1940–1955* (Chicago: University of Chicago Press, 2006); Trotter, *Black Milwaukee*, 18, 32–33; Joe William Trotter, *Coal, Class, and Color: Blacks in Southern West Virginia, 1915–32* (Urbana: University of Illinois Press, 1990), 52–54, 177; Lewis, *In Their Own Interests*, 19, 63, 87; Earl Lewis, "Connecting Memory, Self, and the Power of Place in African American Urban History," in Goings and Mohl, *African American Urban History*, 127–28; Richard W. Thomas, *Life for Us Is What We Make It: Building Black Community in Detroit, 1915–1945* (Bloomington: Indiana University Press, 1992), 247–48; and Henry Louis Taylor Jr. and Song-Ho Ha, "A Unity of Opposites: The Black College-Educated Elite, Black Workers, and the Community Development Process," in *Historical Roots of the Urban Crisis: African Americans in the Industrial City, 1900–1950*, ed. Henry Louis Taylor Jr. and Walter Hill (New York: Garland, 2000), 35. Historian Kimberley L. Phillips is one scholar who has disputed the idea that black workers characteristically aligned themselves with black middle-class professionals in the interests of racial unity. See Phillips, *Alabama North*, 10–11, 266 n. 33.

5. Lewis, *In Their Own Interests*, 187; Horton et al., "Lost in the Storm"; Trotter, *Black Milwaukee*, 73–74, 82; Thomas, *Life for Us*, 46; Julian Bond, "The Politics of Civil Rights History," in *New Directions in Civil Rights Studies*, ed. Armstead L. Robinson and Patricia Sullivan (Charlottesville: University Press of Virginia, 1991), 15; Manning Marable, *Race, Reform, and Rebellion: The Second Reconstruction and Beyond in Black America, 1945–2006*, 3rd ed. (Jackson: University Press of Mississippi, 2007), 112; Nancy MacLean, *Freedom Is Not Enough: The Opening of the American Workplace* (Cambridge: Harvard University Press, 2006), 4–5, 342; and Laurie B. Green, *Battling the Plantation Mentality: Memphis and the Black Freedom Struggle* (Chapel Hill: University of North Carolina Press, 2007), 2–3. See also Jack M. Bloom, *Class, Race, and the Civil Rights Movement* (Bloomington: Indiana University Press, 1987), 171–73, 219.

6. Taylor and Ha, "A Unity of Opposites," 42; Kevin K. Gaines, *Uplifting the Race: Black Leadership, Politics, and Culture in the Twentieth Century* (Chapel Hill: University of North Carolina Press, 1996), 2–6, 129–30, 166; Mary Pattillo, *Black on the Block: The Politics of Race and Class in the City* (Chicago: University of Chicago Press, 2007), 2–3, 297; Virginia R. Boynton, "Contested Terrain: The Struggle over Gender Norms for Black Working-Class Women in Cleveland's Phillis Wheatley Association, 1920–1950," *Ohio History* 103 (1994): 5–22; Sundiata Keita Cha-Jua, *America's First Black Town: Brooklyn, Illinois, 1830–1915* (Urbana: University of Illinois Press, 2000), 198–203; and E. Franklin Frazier, *The Negro in the United States*, rev. ed. (New York: Macmillan, 1957), 298.

7. Trotter, *Black Milwaukee*, 212–13, 217; Cha-Jua, *America's First Black Town*, 183–85; Bush, *Not What We Seem*, 20–21; Antonio Gramsci, *Selections from the Prison Notebooks*, ed. Quintin Hoare and Geoffrey Nowell Smith (New York: International Publishers, 1971), 12–13; David Forgac, ed., *An Antonio Gramsci Reader: Selected Writings, 1916–1935* (New York: Schocken, 1988), 408 n. 5, 422–24; Nicos Poulantzas, *Political Power and Social Classes* (London: NLB, 1975), 138–41, 214; Stuart Hall, "Gramsci's Relevance for the Study of Race and Ethnicity," in *Stuart Hall: Critical Dialogues in Cultural Studies*, ed. David Morley and Kuan-Hsing Chen (New York: Routledge, 1996), 424. See also Martha Biondi's thesis of a "Black Popular Front." Biondi, *To Stand and Fight: The Struggle for Civil Rights in Postwar New York City* (Cambridge: Harvard University Press, 2003), 6.

8. Michael Zweig, *The Working Class Majority: America's Best Kept Secret*

(Ithaca, N.Y.: Cornell University Press, 2000), 3–4, 11–19, 28–34; Reeve Vanneman and Lynn Weber Cannon, *The American Perception of Class* (Philadelphia: Temple University Press, 1987), 230–36, 250; Jacqueline Jones, *A Social History of the Laboring Classes: From Colonial Times to the Present* (Malden, Mass.: Blackwell, 1999), 3; Evelyn Nakano Glenn and Roslyn L. Feldberg, "Degraded and Deskilled: The Proletarianization of Clerical Work," *Social Problems* 25 (October 1977): 52–64; and Andrew Levison, *The Working-Class Majority* (New York: Coward, McCann and Geoghegan, 1974), 58–61.

9. Vanneman and Cannon, *American Perception of Class*, 57–63; Zweig, *The Working Class Majority*, 20–28; E. P. Thompson, *The Making of the English Working Class* (New York: Random House, 1963); Thomas D. Boston, *Race, Class, and Conservatism* (Boston: Unwin Hyman, 1988), 9, 16–20. Ira Katznelson and Aristide Zolberg, eds., *Working-Class Formation: Nineteenth Century Patterns in Western Europe and the United States* (Princeton, N.J.: Princeton University Press, 1986); Herbert Gutman, *Power and Culture: Essays on the American Working Class*, ed. Ira Berlin (New York: New Press, 1987); and Poulantzas, *Political Power*, 99. For a riveting historical example of the dynamism of class relations, see Karl Marx, *The Eighteenth Brumaire of Louis Bonaparte* (1852; rprt New York: International Publishers, 1963).

10. Michael C. Dawson, *Black Visions: The Roots of Contemporary African-American Political Ideologies* (Chicago: University of Chicago Press, 2001), 25, 67; Hall, "Gramsci's Relevance," 436; and David Roediger, "Race and the Working-Class Past in the United States: Multiple Identities and the Future of Labor History," *International Review of Social History* 38, suppl. (1993): 127–43. See also Michael C. Dawson, *Behind the Mule: Race and Class in African-American Politics* (Princeton, N.J.: Princeton University Press, 1994); Frazier, *Negro in United States*, 282–83, 303; E. Franklin Frazier, *Black Bourgeoisie* (1957; rpt. New York: Free Press, 1990), 195–212; Vanneman and Cannon, *American Perception of Class*, 75–76, 226–30; and Pattillo, *Black on the Block*, 20–21, 116–17.

11. Vanneman and Cannon, *American Perception of Class*, 230–36, 241–42, 250; and Pattillo, *Black on the Block*, 104–6, 299.

12. Bond, "Politics of Civil Rights History," 15.

13. Zweig, *The Working Class Majority*, 39–59; and George Lipsitz, *Rainbow at Midnight: Labor and Culture in the 1940s* (Urbana: University of Illinois Press, 1994), 1–2.

14. This 1930s–1970s periodization superficially conforms to the popular thesis of the "long" Civil Rights Movement advocated by scholars like Jacquelyn Dowd Hall. Yet I am critical of the "long" movement framework's totalizing perspective, which both overstates continuity and downplays the vital discontinuities between different moments of black struggle. See Nikhil Pal Singh, *Black Is a Country: Race and the Unfinished Struggle for Democracy* (Cambridge: Harvard University Press, 2004), 5; Jacquelyn Dowd Hall, "The Long Civil Rights Movement and the Political Uses of the Past," *Journal of American History* 4 (March 2005): 1233–63; and Sundiata Keita Cha-Jua and Clarence Lang, "The 'Long Movement' as Vampire: Temporal and Spatial Fallacies in Recent Black Freedom Studies," *Journal of African American History* 92 (Spring 2007): 265–88. For a useful schema on black social movements, and a theorization of social movements more generally, see Doug McAdam, *Political Process and the Development of Black Insurgency, 1930–1970*, 2nd ed. (Chicago: University of Chicago Press, 1999); and Roberta Garner, *Contemporary Movements and Ideologies* (New York: McGraw-Hill, 1996), 11–39.

15. Peter B. Levy, *Civil War on Race Street: The Civil Rights Movement in Cambridge, Maryland* (Gainesville: University Press of Florida, 2003), 6–7. See also George Lipsitz, *A Life in the Struggle: Ivory Perry and the Culture of Opposition* (Philadelphia: Temple University Press, 1988); Yohuru Williams, *Black Politics / White Power: Civil Rights, Black Power, and the Black Panthers in New Haven* (St. James, N.Y.: Brandywine Press, 2000); Jeanne F. Theoharis and Komozi Woodard, eds., *Freedom North: Black Freedom Struggles outside the South, 1940–1980* (New York: Palgrave Macmillan, 2003); Robert O. Self, *American Babylon: Race and the Struggle for Postwar Oakland* (Princeton, N.J.: Princeton University Press, 2003); Biondi, *To Stand and Fight*; Matthew J. Countryman, *Up South: Civil Rights and Black Power in Philadelphia* (Philadelphia: University of Pennsylvania Press, 2006); and Kenneth S. Jolly, *Black Liberation in the Midwest: The Struggle in St. Louis, Missouri, 1964–1970* (New York: Routledge, 2006).

16. Josh Sides, *L.A. City Limits: African Los Angeles from the Great Depression to the Present* (Berkeley: University of California Press, 2003), 5, 9; Scott Kurashige, *The Shifting Grounds of Race: Black and Japanese Americans in the Making of Multiethnic Los Angeles* (Princeton, N.J.: Princeton University Press, 2008); Ronald H. Bayor, *Race and the Shaping of Twentieth-Century Atlanta* (Chapel Hill: University of North Carolina Press, 1996); St. Louis City Plan Commission, *History: Physical Growth of the City of St. Louis* (1969), 20; Jon C. Teaford, *Cities of the Heartland: The Rise and Fall of the Industrial Midwest* (Bloomington: Indiana University Press, 1993), 34; Ernest D. Kargau, *Mercantile, Industrial, and Professional Saint Louis* (St. Louis: Nixon-Jones Printing Company, 1902), 127–56; Robert A. Harper, "Metro East: Heavy Industry in the St. Louis Metropolitan Area," Ph.D. diss., Southern Illinois University at Carbondale, 1965, 69–82; and Colin Gordon, *Mapping Decline: St. Louis and the Fate of the American City* (Philadelphia: University of Pennsylvania Press, 2008), 8.

17. Jeffrey S. Adler, *Yankee Merchants and the Making of the Urban West: The Rise and Fall of Antebellum St. Louis* (New York: Cambridge University Press, 1991), 23–24; Gordon, *Mapping Decline*, 13; David R. Roediger, "'The So-Called Mob': Race, Class, Skill and Community in the St. Louis General Strike," in *Towards the Abolition of Whiteness: Essays on Race, Politics, and Working Class History* (London: Verso, 1994), 85–115; and Philip S. Foner, *The Great Labor Uprising of 1877* (New York: Monad Press, 1977), 157–58, 179–80.

18. Louis Gerteis, *Civil War St. Louis* (Lawrence: University Press of Kansas, 2001), 38; Christopher Phillips, *Missouri's Confederate: Claiborne Fox Jackson and the Creation of Southern Identity in the Border West* (Columbia: University of Missouri Press, 2000), 128, 292–94; Adler, *Yankee Merchants*, 121–23, 135; Richard O. Curry, ed., *Radicalism, Racism, and Party Realignment: The Border States during Reconstruction* (Baltimore: Johns Hopkins Press, 1969), xv; Rosemary Feurer, "William Sentner, the UE, and Civic Unionism," in *The CIO's Left-Led Unions*, ed. Steve Rosswurm (New Brunswick, N.J.: Rutgers University Press, 1992), 99; Frazier, *Negro in United States*, 242–43; Carl N. Degler, *Place over Time: The Continuity of Southern Distinctiveness* (Baton Rouge: Louisiana State University Press, 1977), 12–13, 27, 44, 104; and Luther Adams, "It Was North of Tennessee: African American Migration to Louisville and the Meaning of the South," *Ohio Valley History* 3 (Fall 2003): 38–39. The sharecropping system came to Missouri at the turn of the century, when the swampy southeastern region of the state—known as the "Bootheel"—was drained and became the northernmost area of the cotton-growing Mississippi Delta. See Louis Cantor, *A Prologue to the Protest Movement: The Missouri Sharecropper Roadside Demonstration of 1939* (Durham, N.C.: Duke University Press, 1969).

19. James Neal Primm, *Lion of the Valley: St. Louis, Missouri, 1764–1980*, 3rd ed. (Columbia: University of Missouri Press, 1998), 367, 393–95; Thomas M. Spencer, *The St. Louis Veiled Prophet Celebration: Power on Parade, 1877–1995* (Columbia: University of Missouri Press, 2000); Earl Black and Merle Black, *Politics and Society in the South* (Cambridge: Harvard University Press, 1987), 45; Feurer, "William Sentner," 98–99; and Rosemary Feurer, *Radical Unionism in the Midwest, 1900–1950* (Urbana: University of Illinois Press, 2006), 17.

20. William Jefferson Harrison, "The New Deal in Black St. Louis: 1932–1940," Ph.D. diss., Saint Louis University, 1976, 16; Lawrence O. Christensen, "Black St. Louis: A Study in Race Relations, 1865–1916," Ph.D. diss., University of Missouri–Columbia, 1972, 193–99; Katharine T. Corbett, "Missouri's Black History: From Colonial Times to 1970," *Gateway Heritage* 4 (Summer 1983): 22; Herman Dreer, "Negro Leadership in Saint Louis: A Study in Race Relations," Ph.D. diss., University of Chicago, 1955, 88; Leonard Curry, *The Free Black in Urban America, 1800–1850: The Shadow of the Dream* (Chicago: University of Chicago Press, 1981), 29, 34–35; Paul Dennis Brunn, "Black Workers and Social Movements of the 1930s in St. Louis," Ph.D. diss., Washington University, 1975, 87–89; Bryan M. Jack, *The St. Louis African American Community and the Exodusters* (Columbia: University of Missouri Press, 2007); and Jones, *Social History*, 91–110. See also Frazier, *Negro in United States*, 286, 289; and Charles S. Johnson, *Patterns of Negro Segregation* (New York: Harper and Brothers Publishers, 1943), 6–7, 11.

21. Trotter, *Coal, Class, and Color*, 3; George C. Wright, *Life behind a Veil: Blacks in Louisville, Kentucky, 1865–1930* (Baton Rouge: Louisiana State University Press, 1985), 192–93; V. O. Key Jr., *Southern Politics in State and Nation* (New York: Alfred A. Knopf, 1949); John H. Fenton, *Politics in the Border States: A Study of the Patterns of Political Organization and Political Change, Common to the Border States—Maryland, West Virginia, Kentucky, and Missouri* (New Orleans: Hauser Press, 1957); Degler, *Place over Time*, 18–19, 45; Black and Black, *Politics and Society*, 8; Primm, *Lion of the Valley*, 345; and E. Terrence Jones, *Fragmented by Design: Why St. Louis Has So Many Governments* (St. Louis: Palmerston and Reed, 2000), 5.

22. Lorenzo J. Greene, Gary R. Kremer, and Anthony F. Holland, *Missouri's Black Heritage* (St. Louis: Forum Press, 1980), 71, 94; Priscilla A. Dowden, "Over This Point We Are Determined to Fight: African-American Public Education and Health Care in St. Louis, Missouri, 1910–1949," Ph.D. diss., Indiana University, 1997, 5, 42; Katharine T. Corbett and Mary E. Seematter, " 'No Crystal Stair': Black St. Louis, 1920–1940," *Gateway Heritage* 16 (Fall 1995): 85; and John A. Wright, *Discovering African-American St. Louis: A Guide to Historic Sites* (St. Louis: Missouri Historical Society Press, 1994), 17.

23. Harrison, "New Deal," 4–5; Greene, Kremer, and Holland, *Missouri's Black Heritage*, 99; Christensen, "Black St. Louis," 221–22; Primm, *Lion of the Valley*, 423; and Dowden, "Over This Point," 46. See also Degler, *Place over Time*, 24, 63; Black and Black, *Politics and Society*, 3; Frazier, *Negro in United States*, 237; Wright, *Life behind a Veil*, 4–5, 76; and William H. Chafe, *Civilities and Civil Rights: Greensboro, North Carolina, and the Black Struggle for Freedom* (New York: Oxford University Press, 1981), 67–70.

24. Margaret Bush Wilson, interview by Christine Lamberson, written transcript, August 25, 2003, University Archives, Department of Special Collections, Washington University; Wright, *Life behind a Veil*, 9; Jacqueline Balk and Ari Hoogenboom, "The Origins of Border State Liberal Republicanism," in Curry, *Radicalism, Racism*, 221; Primm, *Lion of the Valley*, 345; John E. Farley, "Racial Housing Segregation in the St. Louis Area: Past, Present, and Future," in *St. Louis*

Metromorphosis: Past Trends and Future Directions, ed. Brady Baybeck and E. Terrence Jones (St. Louis: Missouri Historical Society Press, 2004), 200; Christensen, "Black St. Louis," 262–66; and Dowden, "Over This Point," 173.

25. Harrison, "New Deal," 160; Farley, "Racial Housing Segregation," 205; Jean M. White, "U.S. to Force Integrated Construction," *Washington Post*, April 2, 1966, A2; and Frazier, *Negro in United States*, 251–52. Urban historian Henry Louis Taylor, Jr. has offered a more geographically expansive view of the "borderland" that includes the "northern border states of Pennsylvania, Ohio, Indiana, Illinois and New Jersey." "Using this definition," he argues, "Cincinnati and Cairo, Illinois, would be borderland cities but not Cleveland and Chicago." Henry Louis Taylor, Jr., ed., *Race and the City: Work, Community, and Protest in Cincinnati, 1820–1970* (Urbana: University of Illinois Press, 1993), xviii n1.

26. For a substantive treatment of Black Nationalism and other black ideological traditions, see Dawson, *Black Visions*; Robert C. Smith, "Ideology as the Enduring Dilemma of Black Politics," in Georgia A. Persons, ed., *Dilemmas of Black Politics: Issues of Leadership and Strategy* (New York: HarperCollins, 1993), 200–215; and Sundiata Keita Cha-Jua, "African American Ideas" in Maryanne Cline Horowitz, ed., *New Dictionary of the History of Ideas*, Vol. 1 (New York: Scribner, 2005), 26–30.

CHAPTER ONE

1. Fenton, *Politics in Border States*, 127–29; Harrison, "New Deal," 16; Dowden, "Over This Point," 22, 75; Corbett and Seematter, "No Crystal Stair," 87; Debra Foster Greene, "'Just Enough of Everything': The St. Louis *Argus*—an African American Newspaper and Publishing Company in Its First Decade," *Business and Economic History* 4 (2006): 1–11; Daniel T. Kelleher, "The History of the St. Louis NAACP, 1914–1955," M.A. thesis, Southern Illinois University at Edwardsville, 1969; and Henry Winfield Wheeler, "History of the Saint Louis Branch of the National Association for the Advancement of Colored People," souvenir program, 44th Annual NAACP Conference, June 22–28, 1953, Missouri Historical Society Library and Research Center, hereafter referred to as MHS.

2. Brunn, "Black Workers," 110, 113, 515, 645–47; Deborah Jane Henry, "Structures of Exclusion: Black Labor and the Building Trades in St. Louis, 1917–1966," Ph.D. diss., University of Minnesota, 2002, 75; Ira De A. Reid, "A Study of the Industrial Status of Negroes in St. Louis, Missouri," Welfare Plan Committee of St. Louis and St. Louis County, Missouri, September 1, 1934, 27, Urban League of St. Louis, Records, 1910–1970, Series 4: Records of the Industrial Relations Department, Box 7, Folder 66, University Archives, Department of Special Collections, Washington University Libraries, hereafter referred to as WU; Myrna Fichtenbaum, "The Funsten Nut Strike—May, 1933," senior thesis, Department of History, St. Louis University, 1974, 13, Collection 98, Western Historical Manuscript Collection, University of Missouri–St. Louis, hereafter referred to as WHMC; and Levison, *The Working-Class Majority*, 187.

3. Joseph Heathcott, "Black Archipelago: Politics and Civic Life in the Jim Crow City," *Journal of Social History* 38 (Spring 2005): 707.

4. Doris A. Wesley and Ann Morris, eds., *Lift Every Voice and Sing: St. Louis African Americans in the Twentieth Century* (Columbia: University of Missouri Press, 1999), 3; George Lipsitz, *The Sidewalks of St. Louis: Places, People, and Politics in an American City* (Columbia: University of Missouri Press, 1991), 35–36, 68,

78–79; Corbett and Seematter, "No Crystal Stair," 86; KWMU, "The Jazz History of St. Louis," written transcripts, 1989, MHS; Wright, *African American St. Louis,* 38; John Cleophus Cotter, "The Negro in Music in Saint Louis," M.A. thesis, Washington University, 1959, 66–67; John Russell David, "Tragedy in Ragtime: Black Folktales from St. Louis," Ph.D. diss., St. Louis University, 1976, 24; and Frazier, *Negro in United States,* 237–39, 243.

5. Charles Bailey, "Symbolic Emergence of Community in an Historic Black Neighborhood: The Case of the Ville," 1975, unpublished paper, Collection 5, Folder 1, WHMC; John A. Wright Sr., *The Ville—St. Louis* (Chicago: Arcadia, 2001); Christensen, "Black St. Louis," 114–15, 126; Dowden, "Over This Point," 218–21; Afro-Americans in St. Louis, Collection 36, Folders 7, 8, and 20, WHMC; and Juliet E. K. Walker, *The History of Black Business in America: Capitalism, Race, Entrepreneurship* (New York: Macmillan, 1998), 208–9.

6. Segregation Scrapbook, MHS; Kinloch History Committee Records, Collection 151, Folders 11 and 13, WHMC; and John A. Wright Sr., *Kinloch: Missouri's First Black City* (Chicago: Arcadia, 2000). See also Andrew Wiese, *Places of Their Own: African American Suburbanization in the Twentieth Century* (Chicago: University of Chicago Press, 2004).

7. Dreer, "Negro Leadership," 96, 134, 188; Brunn, "Black Workers," 106; Reid, "Study of Industrial Status," 36, 40, Urban League of St. Louis Records of the Industrial Department, Box 7, Folder 66, WU; Afro-Americans in St. Louis Collection, Folder 14, WHMC; Dowden, "Over This Point," 312; and Christensen, "Black St. Louis," 131. See also Eric Olin Wright, *Classes* (London: Verso, 1985); Boston, *Race, Class, and Conservatism,* 12; Trotter, *Black Milwaukee,* 28, 124–25; Thomas, *Life for Us,* 14–15; Frazier, *Negro in United States,* 292–98; and Bart Landry, *The New Black Middle Class* (Berkeley and Los Angeles: University of California Press, 1987), 50–51.

8. Charles Bailey, "The Ville: A Study of a Symbolic Community in St. Louis," Ph.D. diss., Washington University, 1978; Cyprian Clamorgan, *The Colored Aristocracy of St. Louis,* ed. Julie Winch (1858; rpt. Columbia: University of Missouri Press, 1999), 46; Jervis Anderson, *A. Philip Randolph: A Biographical Portrait* (New York: Harcourt Brace Jovanovich, 1973), 160; William H. Harris, *Keeping the Faith: A. Philip Randolph, Milton P. Webster, and the Brotherhood of Sleeping Car Porters, 1925–37* (Urbana: University of Illinois Press, 1977), 15, 94; Reid, "Study of Industrial Status," 12; Frazier, *Negro in United States,* 286–90; Cha-Jua, *America's First Black Town,* 67–71; Trotter, *Black Milwaukee,* 83; Landry, *New Black Middle Class,* 29–41; and Frazier, *Black Bourgeoisie,* 92–93.

9. Wright, *The Ville—St. Louis.* See also Sharon Harley, "When Your Work Is Not Who You Are: The Development of a Working-Class Consciousness among Afro-American Women," in *"We Specialize in the Wholly Impossible": A Reader in Black Women's History,* ed. Darlene Clark Hine, Wilma King, and Linda Reed (Brooklyn: Carlson, 1995), 25–37; Frazier, *Negro in United States,* 288; and Stephanie J. Shaw, *What a Woman Ought to Be and to Do: Black Professional Women Workers during the Jim Crow Era* (Chicago: University of Chicago Press, 1996).

10. Primm, *Lion of the Valley,* 357; Gerteis, *Civil War St. Louis,* 74; and Gregory Mixon, "'Good Negro—Bad Negro': The Dynamics of Race and Class in Atlanta during the Era of the 1906 Riot," *Georgia Historical Quarterly* 81 (Fall 1997): 600.

11. Greene, Kremer, and Holland, *Missouri's Black Heritage,* 99, 115; and Dowden, "Over This Point," 165, 171.

12. Primm, *Lion of the Valley,* 411; Lana Stein, *St. Louis Politics: The Triumph of Tradition* (St. Louis: Missouri Historical Society Press, 2002), 16–17; Dreer, "Negro

Leadership," 103, 128; Christensen, "Black St. Louis," 193–95, 221–22; Harrison, "New Deal," 4–5; Dowden, "Over This Point," 257; William H. Sinkler and Sadye Coleman, "The History and Development of Homer G. Phillips Hospital," Lowe Family Papers, 1922–1970, Collection 123, Folder 1, WHMC; and David M. Grant Papers, Collection 552, Box 1, Folder 1, WHMC.

13. William Barnaby Faherty, *St. Louis—a Concise History* (St. Louis: Masonry Institute of St. Louis, 1999), 104; Brunn, "Black Workers," 169, 212–13; Primm, *Lion of the Valley*, 467; Harrison, "New Deal," 7; "50 Families Find Haven on 'Dump' on River Front," *Post-Dispatch*, July 7, 1932; Rosemary Feurer, "The Nut-pickers' Union, 1933–34: Crossing the Boundaries of Community and Workplace," in*"We Are All Leaders": The Alternative Unionism of the Early 1930s*, ed. Staughton Lynd (Urbana: University of Illinois Press, 1996), 29; Feurer, *Radical Unionism*, 32; Walker, *Black Business in America*, 209; Dowden, "Over This Point," 83–84; and Lewis, *In Their Own Interests*, 119.

14. City Plan Commission, Map of the City of St. Louis, Percent of Families on Relief as of May 1, 1934; and Home Location of Municipal Work House Cases, Admitted for Year 1932, St. Louis Public Library. See also Brunn, "Black Workers," 119, 409; and Henry, "Structures of Exclusion," 10.

15. Grant Papers, Box 2, Folder 9, and Box 1, Folder 1, WHMC.

16. Harrison, "New Deal," 19–25, 61–63; Mary Welek, "Jordan Chambers: Black Politician and Boss," *Journal of Negro History* 57 (October 1972): 353–55; and William E. Parrish, Charles T. Jones Jr., and Lawrence O. Christensen, *Missouri: The Heart of the Nation* (St. Louis: Forum Press, 1980), 305.

17. Fenton, *Politics in Border States*, 129; Primm, *Lion of the Valley*, 441–44; Stein, *St. Louis Politics*, 21–26; Lana Stein and Carol W. Kohfeld, "St. Louis's Black-White Elections: Products of Machine Factionalism and Polarization," *Urban Affairs Quarterly* 27 (December 1991): 231; Grant Papers, Box 2, Folder 9, WHMC; Harrison, "New Deal," 24; and Ernest Patterson, *Black City Politics* (New York: Dodd, Mead, 1974), 46.

18. Fenton, *Politics in Border States*, 129–37; Grant Papers, Box 1, Folder 1, and Box 2, Folder 9, WHMC; Harrison, "New Deal," 33–36, 63, 71–72; Welek, "Jordan Chambers," 356; and Earl Brown, "Negro Voters Hold Balance at Missouri Polls," *New York Herald-Tribune*, August 7, 1936.

19. Dreer, "Negro Leadership," 19–20; Fenton, *Politics in Border States*, 142; Patterson, *Black City Politics*, 10, 48; Bill Clay, *Bill Clay: A Political Voice at the Grass Roots* (St. Louis: Missouri Historical Society Press, 2004), 26, 44, 53; Robert Jacob Kerstein, "The Political Consequences of Federal Intervention: The Economic Opportunity Act and Model Cities in the City of St. Louis," Ph.D. diss., Washington University, 1975, 89; Welek, "Jordan Chambers," 366–68; and Frazier, *Black Bourgeoisie*, 108.

20. Marc W. Kruman, "Quotas for Blacks: The Public Works Administration and the Black Construction Worker," *Labor History* 16 (Winter 1975): 48; T. H. Watkins, *The Great Depression: America in the 1930s* (New York: Little, Brown, 1993), 219; Greene, Kremer, and Holland, *Missouri's Black Heritage*, 118; Henry, "Structures of Exclusion," 94–95; Cantor, *Prologue to Protest Movement*, 4; Brunn, "Black Workers," 98; and Primm, *Lion of the Valley*, 469.

21. Keith P. Griffler, *What Price Alliance? Black Radicals Confront White Labor, 1918–1938* (New York: Garland, 1995), 25, 39; Brunn, "Black Workers," 186–90, 290; Harvey Klehr, *The Heyday of American Communism: The Depression Decade* (New York: Basic Books, 1984), 324–25; and Glenda Elizabeth Gilmore, *Defying Dixie: The Radical Roots of Civil Rights, 1919–1950* (New York: Norton, 2008), 51–65.

See also Robin D. G. Kelley, *Hammer and Hoe: Alabama Communists during the Great Depression* (Chapel Hill: University of North Carolina Press, 1990); Mark Naison, *Communists in Harlem during the Depression* (New York: Grove Press, 1983); and Minkah Makalani, "For the Liberation of Black People Everywhere: The African Blood Brotherhood, Black Radicalism, and Pan-African Liberation in the New Negro Movement," Ph.D. diss., University of Illinois at Urbana-Champaign, 2004.

22. Josephine Ingram, "Hershel Walker: '60 Years of Working Class Struggle,'" and interview with Hershel Walker, both in "'A Strong Seed Planted': The Civil Rights Movement in St. Louis, 1954–1968," Oral History Collection, written transcripts, Box 2, MHS. See also Klehr, *Heyday of American Communism,* 52, 54.

23. Brunn, "Black Workers," 166–68, 173–74; interview with Walker, "Strong Seed Planted" Oral History Collection, Box 2, MHS; Klehr, *Heyday of American Communism,* 34; and Feurer, *Radical Unionism,* 33.

24. Brunn, "Black Workers," 218–25.

25. "Police Drive 3000 Led by Communists from City Hall with Tear Gas," *Post-Dispatch,* July 11, 1932, 1A; and "Police Forbid Any More Meetings of Communists Here," *Post-Dispatch,* July 12, 1932, 2A.

26. Brunn, "Black Workers," 236–44; "Directs Police to Stop Meetings of Communists," *Post-Dispatch,* July 11, 1932, 1A; Klehr, *Heyday of American Communism,* 63; and Feurer, *Radical Unionism,* 34.

27. Scott Reynolds Nelson, *Steel Drivin' Man: John Henry, the Untold Story of an American Legend* (New York: Oxford University Press, 2006), 159; and Feurer, "The Nutpickers' Union," 27–28.

28. Brunn, "Black Workers," 344–46; Dowden, "Over This Point," 95–103; and Fichtenbaum, "Funsten Nut Strike," 20–24.

29. Brunn, "Black Workers," 374; Fichtenbaum, "Funsten Nut Strike," 25–27; Philip S. Foner, *Women and the American Labor Movement: From World War I to the Present* (New York: Free Press, 1980), 271–72; and Feurer, "The Nutpickers Union," 32.

30. Feurer, *Radical Unionism,* 37; "Nut Pickers Ask Mayor to Act as Arbiter in Strike," *Post-Dispatch,* May 18, 1933; Brunn, "Black Workers," 349–50, 355; Fichtenbaum, "Funsten Nut Strike," 24–25; Foner, *Women and Labor Movement,* 272; and "Mayor's Group Takes Up Strike of Nut Pickers," *Post-Dispatch,* May 23, 1933.

31. Foner, *Women and Labor Movement,* 272–73; "Mayor Orders Inquiry in Nut Pickers' Strike," *Post-Dispatch,* May 19, 1933; Brunn, "Black Workers," 353–56; and Fichtenbaum, "Funsten Nut Strike," 33, 46–49.

32. "Mayor's Group Takes Up Strike of Nut Pickers"; and Foner, *Women and Labor Movement,* 274.

33. "Nut Pickers Ask Mayor to Act as Arbiter in Strike"; "Mayor Orders Inquiry in Nut Pickers' Strike"; and "Mayor's Arbiters Settle Strike of 1200 Nut Pickers," *Post-Dispatch,* May 24, 1933, 4A.

34. Foner, *Women and Labor Movement,* 274–75; Fichtenbaum, "Funsten Nut Strike," 34, 57; Brunn, "Black Workers," 357–62; Feurer, *Radical Unionism,* 37–38; and Beth Tompkins Bates, "A New Crowd Challenges the Agenda of the Old Guard in the NAACP, 1933–1941," *American Historical Review* 102 (April 1997): 351.

35. Bates, "New Crowd," 351.

36. Harry Haywood, *Black Bolshevik: Autobiography of an Afro-American Communist* (Chicago: Liberator Press, 1978), 343; Brunn, "Black Workers," 366–70;

Fichtenbaum, "Funsten Nut Strike," 36; Feurer, "The Nutpickers' Union," 39, 41; and "For Workers' and Farmers' Unity in Action," Statement to the Continental Congress of Missouri, July 3, 1933, Socialist Party, St. Louis and Missouri Records, Collection 90, Folder 42 (microfilm roll 5), WHMC.

37. Brunn, "Black Workers," 378, 382; Fichtenbaum, "Funsten Nut Strike," 46; and Feurer, "The Nutpickers' Union," 38–39, 42.

38. Brunn, "Black Workers," 257, 276; Klehr, Heyday of American Communism, 218; and Feurer, Radical Unionism, 59.

39. Frank R. Crosswaith, "The Negro and Socialism," Socialist Party, St. Louis and Missouri Records, Folder 81 (microfilm roll 8), WHMC; Foner, Great Labor Uprising, 170; Philip S. Foner, Organized Labor and the Black Worker, 1619–1981 (New York: International Publishers, 1981), 103; E. J. Bradley, "Some of My Early Experiences Organizing Pullman Porters in St. Louis," Socialist Party, St. Louis and Missouri Records, Folder 62 (microfilm roll 7), WHMC; Brunn, "Black Workers," 493, 496–97; Greene, Kremer, and Holland, Missouri's Black Heritage, 112; Harris, Keeping the Faith, 41–42; Anderson, A. Philip Randolph, 148–49, 175; and Paula F. Pfeffer, A. Philip Randolph, Pioneer of the Civil Rights Movement (Baton Rouge: Louisiana State University Press, 1990), 17–18.

40. Jack Santino, Miles of Smiles, Years of Struggle: Stories of Black Pullman Porters (Urbana: University of Illinois Press, 1989), 37, 43, 131; Melinda Chateauvert, Marching Together: Women of the Brotherhood of Sleeping Car Porters (Urbana: University of Illinois Press, 1998), 48–51, 69–71; Harris, Keeping the Faith, 152–53; Harrison, "New Deal," 239; Anderson, A. Philip Randolph, 224–25; Pfeffer, A. Philip Randolph, 28–29; and Manning Marable, From the Grassroots: Essays toward Afro-American Liberation (Boston: South End Press, 1980), 75.

41. Griffler, What Price Alliance? 118–19, 134–36; Cicero Alvin Hughes, "Toward a Black United Front: The National Negro Congress Movement," Ph.D. diss., Ohio University, 1982, 66–68, 75; John P. Davis, Let Us Build a National Negro Congress (Washington, D.C., 1935), 6, 12, and The Official Proceedings of the National Negro Congress (Washington, D.C., n.d.), NNC Vertical File, Archives of Labor and Urban Affairs, Wayne State University, hereafter referred to as ALUA; and Pfeffer, A. Philip Randolph, 42.

42. Dowden, "Over This Point," 78–80, 275 n. 71; Brunn, "Black Workers," 445, 448–49; Henry, "Structures of Exclusion," 100–102; Harrison, "New Deal," 229; Lester B. Granger, "Negro Workers and Recovery," Opportunity 12 (May 1934): 153; Nancy J. Weiss, The National Urban League, 1910–1940 (New York: Oxford University Press, 1974), 283–84; Feurer, "William Sentner," 97–98; and Negro Workers' Council file, Urban League of St. Louis Records of the Industrial Relations Department, Box 7, Folder 75, WU.

43. "Negro Workers' Council Bulletin," No. 11 (1936), Negro Workers' Council file, Urban League of St. Louis Records of the Industrial Relations Department, Box 7, Folder 75, WU.

44. "Workers' Council Bulletin," No. 7 (1935), Negro Workers' Council file, Urban League of St. Louis Records of the Industrial Relations Department, Box 7, Folder 75, WU; Brunn, "Black Workers," 310, 443–45; William H. Harris, The Harder We Run: Black Workers since the Civil War (New York: Oxford University Press, 1982), 110; and Henry, "Structures of Exclusion," 103–4.

45. See Bill Fletcher Jr. and Peter Agard, The Indispensable Ally: Black Workers and the Formation of the Congress of Industrial Organizations, 1934–1941 (Amherst, Mass.: William Monroe Trotter Institute for the Study of Black Culture, 1987); NNC Vertical File, ALUA; and Feurer, Radical Unionism, 23.

46. Brunn, "Black Workers," 133; Harrison, "New Deal," 207; St. Louis Housewives League Scrapbook, Collection 155, WHMC; and Colored Clerks' Circle file, Urban League of St. Louis Records of the Industrial Relations Department, Box 6, Folder 64, WU. See also Darlene Clark Hine, "African American Women and Their Communities in the Twentieth Century," *Black Women, Gender, and Families* 1 (Spring 2007): 1–23.

47. St. Louis Housewives League Scrapbook, WHMC; Wright, *The Ville—St. Louis,* 116; Grant Papers, Box 1, Folder 1, WHMC; and Dreer, "Negro Leadership," 143.

48. Kelleher, "St. Louis NAACP," 67; Lipsitz, *Sidewalks of St. Louis,* 53; Greene, Kremer, and Holland, *Missouri's Black Heritage,* 119; Wright, *The Ville—St. Louis,* 101; Dreer, "Negro Leadership," 131–32; Dowden, "Over This Point," 188–99, 233; Harrison, "New Deal," 159; Welek, "Jordan Chambers," 362; and John T. Clark, "When the Negro Resident Organizes," *Opportunity,* June 1934, 168–71, Urban League of St. Louis Records of the Industrial Relations Department, Box 7, Folder 66, WU.

49. Ernest Allen Jr., "Waiting for Tojo: The Pro-Japan Vigil of Black Missourians, 1932–1943," *Gateway Heritage* 15 (Fall 1994): 16–33; Allen, "Satokata Takahashi and the Flowering of Black Messianic Nationalism," *Black Scholar* 24 (Winter 1994): 23–42; Pacific Movement of the Eastern World file, Urban League of St. Louis Records, Series 1: Files of John T. Clark, Box 8, WU; and Dowden, "Over This Point," 107–8. At the end of 1938, planters in the "Bootheel" counties evicted more than seventeen hundred sharecroppers. Led by organizers of the Southern Tenants Farmer Union, over fifteen hundred largely black laborers encamped along the nearby highways in symbolic protest. The roadside demonstration galvanized black residents of St. Louis and South Kinloch Park, who raised money and transported provisions. See Cantor, *Prologue to Protest Movement;* Jarod Heath Roll, "Road to the Promised Land: Rural Rebellion in the New Cotton South, 1890–1945" (Ph.D. dissertation, Northwestern University, 2006); and Erik S. Gellman and Jarod H. Roll, "Owen Whitfield and the Gospel of the Working Class in New Deal America, 1936–1946," *Journal of Southern History,* Vol. 72, No. 2 (May 2006): 303–48.

50. H. Phillip Venable, "The History of Homer G. Phillips Hospital," *Journal of the National Medical Association* 53 (November 1961): 541–55, Lowe Family Papers, Folder 1, WHMC; and Grant Papers, Box 2, Folder 9, WHMC.

51. Wright, *The Ville—St. Louis,* 88.

CHAPTER TWO

1. Primm, *Lion of the Valley,* 427–29; and Cornelia F. Sexauer, "St. Louis in the 1940s–1950s: Historical Overview and Annotated Bibliography," 5–6, MHS.

2. Henry, "Structures of Exclusion," 125, 160.

3. Pfeffer, *A. Philip Randolph,* 79, 83.

4. Primm, *Lion of the Valley,* 427–29; Sexauer, "St. Louis 1940s–1950s," 5–6; Henry, "Structures of Exclusion," 125; and Feurer, *Radical Unionism,* 70–71, 143–45.

5. "Non-partisan Political Bloc, Non-violent Protesting Is Urged by Leader Randolph," *St. Louis American,* May 13, 1943, Theodore D. McNeal Scrapbook, 1941–1943, Collection 321, microfilm roll 2, WHMC; A. Philip Randolph, "Why I Would Not Stand for Re-Election for President of the National Negro Congress,"

The World Crisis and the Negro People Today (1940), NNC Vertical File, ALUA; Hughes, "Black United Front," 162–64; Herbert Garfinkel, *When Negroes March: The March on Washington Movement in the Organizational Politics for FEPC* (1959; rpt. Atheneum, 1968), 58; and Anderson, *A. Philip Randolph*, 230.

6. Andrew Edmund Kersten, *Race, Jobs, and the War: The FEPC in the Midwest, 1941–46* (Urbana: University of Illinois Press, 2000), 3, 112; Garfinkel, *When Negroes March*, 67, 71, 78; Anderson, *A. Philip Randolph*, 259; and Pfeffer, *A. Philip Randolph*, 50.

7. "Small Arms Plant Demonstration Gets Results," *American*, June 25, 1942, McNeal Scrapbook, microfilm roll 2, WHMC; Kersten, *Race, Jobs*, 116, 118; Feurer, *Radical Unionism*, 148; and Karen Tucker Anderson, "Last Hired, First Fired: Black Women Workers during World War II," *Journal of American History* 69 (June 1982): 82–97.

8. "Want Jobs in Defense Plants Here," *American*, May 14, 1942, McNeal Scrapbook, microfilm roll 2, WHMC; David Grant Papers, Box 1, Folder 1, WHMC; and Henry, "Structures of Exclusion," 136–38.

9. "'March on Washington Committee' Maps Militant Program," *St. Louis Argus*, May 29, 1942; "To Open Drive for Defense Jobs Here," *American*, June 4, 1942; "Citizens Called to Discrimination Fight," *Argus*, June 5, 1942; and "Defense Job Fight Offices Opened," *American*, June 11, 1942, McNeal Scrapbook, microfilm roll 2, WHMC.

10. See T. D. McNeal, "The March on Washington," *Argus*, May 29, June 4, and June 11, 1942, McNeal Scrapbook, microfilm roll 2, WHMC.

11. "200 Reported Out at Small Arms Plant," *Argus*, June 12, 1942; "War Plant Firings Stir Negro Protest," *Post-Dispatch*, June 16, 1942; "Protest on Firing of Negroes Planned," *St. Louis Globe-Democrat*, June 17, 1942; "Discrimination at the Small Arms Plant?" news editorial, *Post-Dispatch*, June 17, 1942; and "Negro Protest March Set at Ordnance Plant," *St. Louis Star-Times*, June 18, 1942, McNeal Scrapbook, microfilm roll 2, WHMC. See also Feurer, *Radical Unionism*, 148.

12. "Who Are the Friends of the Negro People?" circular distributed by the State Committee, Communist Party of Missouri, circa June 1942; "Training to Begin for All-Negro Ammunition Unit," *Post-Dispatch*, June 21, 1942; "Small Arms Plant Demonstration Gets Results," *American*, June 25, 1942; and "Protest Parade in St. Louis," *Pittsburgh Courier*, June 1942, McNeal Scrapbook, microfilm roll 2, WHMC. See also Lipsitz, *Rainbow at Midnight*, 195; Garfinkel, *When Negroes March*, 49, 52, 131; and Anderson, *A. Philip Randolph*, 254.

13. "Mel and Thel," *American*, June 25, 1942; and "Industrial Union Heads Ask War Jobs for Negroes," *Star-Times*, June 25, 1942, McNeal Scrapbook, microfilm roll 2, WHMC. See also Feurer, *Radical Unionism*, 180–81.

14. "Employees of Curtiss-Wright Plant Receive Praise," *American*, February 4, 1943; "Not to Let Up in Fight for Defense Jobs," *Argus*, June 26, 1942; Harold W. Ross and T. D. McNeal, open letter to "Fellow Negro Citizens," July 8, 1942; "McNeal Says Demonstrat'n Is Planned," *Argus*, August 21, 1942; and "Negroes Threaten March on Washington to Demand 'Equality' in War Effort," *Star-Times*, August 15, 1942, McNeal Scrapbook, microfilm roll 2, WHMC. See also Lipsitz, *Rainbow at Midnight*, 78; Beth Tompkins Bates, *Pullman Porters and the Rise of Protest Politics in Black America, 1925–1945* (Chapel Hill: University of North Carolina Press, 2001), 166; and Kersten, *Race, Jobs*, 117–18.

15. Garfinkel, *When Negroes March*, 82–83, 98; Anderson, *A. Philip Randolph*, 264; and Pfeffer, *A. Philip Randolph*, 51, 74.

16. "9,000 Attend Rally; to March on Plant," *Argus*, August 21, 1942; national

MOWM press release, August 17, 1942; Eardlie John, Chairman, Fair Employment Practice Committee, letter to The President of the United States, The White
House, Washington, D.C., August 16, 1942; "India and the Negro," MOWM resolution, August 1942; A. Philip Randolph and T. D. McNeal, cablegram to Mohandas K. Gandhi, Poona Jail, India, August 1942, McNeal Scrapbook, microfilm roll
2, WHMC; Kersten, *Race, Jobs*, 38; and Garfinkel, *When Negroes March*, 78, 102,
104–5.

17. "9,000 Attend Rally; to March on Plant," *Argus*, August 21, 1942; and
"Negroes Threaten March on Washington to Demand 'Equality' in War Effort,"
Star-Times, August 15, 1942, McNeal Scrapbook, microfilm roll 2, WHMC.

18. "To March on Defense Plant Excluding Race Workers," *Argus*, August 28,
1942; "March on until Victory at Home," *American*, September 3, 1942; "Negroes
March Again," *Citizens Protector*, September 3, 1942; "Negroes Stage 'March for
Jobs' to Carter Plant," *Star-Times*, August 29, 1942; "Negroes Plan March on Plant
by 10,000," *Post-Dispatch*, August 28, 1942; "400 Negroes in Protest Parade,"
Globe-Democrat, August 30, 1942; "500 March in Big Protest Parade at Defense
Plant Barring Negroes," *Courier*, September 5, 1942; "'March On' Activities
Awakening the Public," *American*, September 3, 1942; and "500 Picket St. Louis
Defense Plant to Protest Ban on Negro Workers," *Chicago Defender*, September 5,
1942, McNeal Scrapbook, microfilm roll 2, WHMC.

19. "March on Washington Meetings Attracting Larger Crowds at Y," *Ameri-
can*, September 10, 1942; St. Louis MOWM handbill, circa 1942; "Mass Prayer for
Negro Rights Sunday," *American*, October 15, 1942; and "Mass Prayer in Plaza,"
Argus, October 16, 1942, McNeal Scrapbook, microfilm roll 2, WHMC. See also
Harvard Sitkoff, "Racial Militancy and Interracial Violence in the Second World
War," *Journal of American History* 58 (December 1971): 661–81; Dominic J. Capeci
Jr., "The Lynching of Cleo Wright: Federal Protecting of Constitutional Rights
during World War II," *Journal of American History* 72 (March 1986): 859–87; and
Thomas J. Sugrue, *The Origins of the Urban Crisis: Race and Inequality in Postwar De-
troit* (Princeton, N.J.: Princeton University Press, 1996), 73–74.

20. "Soldiers Led by White Officers to Auditorium USO Refused," *American*,
July 29, 1943, McNeal Scrapbook, microfilm roll 1, WHMC; David M. Kennedy,
Freedom from Fear: The American People in Depression and War (New York: Oxford
University Press, 1999), 773; Garfinkel, *When Negroes March*, 203 n. 45; Sitkoff,
"Racial Militancy"; and Allen, "Waiting for Tojo."

21. "March on Washington Committee Outlines Plans for 1943," *American*,
January 7, 1943; St. Louis Negro Grade Teachers Association, letter to St. Louis
MOWM, March 26, 1943; T. D. McNeal, letter to Miss Beulah P. Harris, Corre-
sponding Secretary, The Booklovers Club, December 29, 1942; T. D. McNeal,
Harry Ball, Leyton Weston, letter of solicitation sent to all leading organizations,
March 25, 1943; St. Louis MOWM pamphlet, circa 1943; "Powerful Negro Politi-
cal Bloc Is Urged at Meeting," *Post-Dispatch*, May 10, 1943; "Employees of Cur-
tiss-Wright Plant Receive Praise," *American*, February 4, 1943; and "Curtiss-
Wright Employing Negro Women in Skilled Jobs," *Star-Times*, February 5, 1943,
McNeal Scrapbook, microfilm roll 2, WHMC.

22. Unknown author, undated letter to David Grant; and Floyd Bible, letter
to T. D. McNeal, May 25, 1943, McNeal Scrapbook, microfilm roll 2, WHMC; and
Kersten, *Race, Jobs*, 119.

23. Undated March on Washington summary sent to FEPC; Herman Hester,
letter to David Grant, May 27, 1943; Leyton Weston, memorandum on Meeting of
Amertorp Employes, YWCA, circa June 1943; Orden C. Oeschsli, Industrial Rela-

268 | NOTES TO PAGES 54–57

tions Manager, The Amertorp Corporation, letter to Leyton Weston, June 24, 1943; Weston, letter to Oeschsli, July 14, 1943; T. D. McNeal, letter to Mr. G. I. Barnes, General Manager, Atlas Powder Company, May 29, 1943; and "Information For Committee On Seven (7) Points To Be Discussed in Connection With Atlas Powder Company, As Set Forth In Our Letter Of May 29, 1943," St. Louis MOWM document, McNeal Scrapbook, microfilm rolls 1 and 2, WHMC.

24. Henry, "Structures of Exclusion," 140, 154; and Kersten, *Race, Jobs*, 115.

25. T. D. McNeal, Harry Ball, Leyton Weston, letter of solicitation sent to all leading organizations, March 25, 1943; St. Louis MOWM summary sent to FEPC, circa 1943; "Plan Fight for Public Utilities Jobs Here," *Argus*, January 15, 1943; Eleanor Green, Report of Application filed April 14, 1943; "The Position of the March on Washington Committee Concerning Employment of Negroes by the Southwestern Bell Telephone Company," St. Louis MOWM document, circa 1943; "Report on Initial Conference with St. Louis Public Service Company," St. Louis MOWM document, circa 1943; David M. Grant and T. D. McNeal, letter to Public Service Company, Personnel Department, March 10, 1943; and Grant and McNeal, letter to Southwestern Bell Telephone Company, Personnel Department, March 10, 1943, McNeal Scrapbook, microfilm rolls 1 and 2, WHMC. See also Venus Green, *Race on the Line: Gender, Labor, and Technology in the Bell System, 1880–1980* (Durham, N.C.: Duke University Press, 2001), 62, 134–35.

26. "Rail Hearing Killed," *Courier*, January 16, 1943; *Argus*, January 22, 1943; and A. Philip Randolph, telegrams to T. D. McNeal, January 22, 1943, McNeal Scrapbook, microfilm rolls 1 and 2, WHMC. See also Chateauvert, *Marching Together*, 117; Harris, *The Harder We Run*, 86, 118; Harrison, "New Deal," 242; and Garfinkel, *When Negroes March*, 126–27, 139.

27. "March on Washington Movement Sends Giant Protest Card," *Argus*, February 26, 1943; "March Movement to Hold Protest Mass Meeting," *Courier*, May 1, 1943; "'Victory at Home' Mass Meeting to Be at Auditorium May 9," *Argus*, April 30, 1943; "Powerful Negro Political Bloc Is Urged at Meeting," *Post-Dispatch*, May 10, 1943; "Non-partisan Political Bloc, Non-violent Protesting Is Urged by Leader Randolph," *American*, May 13, 1943; and "Randolph Advocates Solidarity," *Argus*, May 14, 1943, McNeal Scrapbook, microfilm 2, WHMC.

28. "30 at Ordnance Plant Refuse to Begin Work," *Post-Dispatch*, May 10, 1943; "30 Women at Ordnance Plant Strike," *Star-Times*, May 10, 1943; "Ordnance Plant Strike Spreads," *Globe-Democrat*, May 11, 1943; "Plant Gives Up Negro Shift, Work Resumes," *Star-Times*, May 11, 1943; Howard Woods, "Strike Called in Protest of Negro Labor," *Defender*, May 22, 1943; "Plant Starts Campaign for More Workers," *American*, May 14, 1943; and D. M. Grant, letter to U.S. Cartridge Company c/o Mr. Oliver Thornton, cc Mr. Walter Placke, May 12, 1943, McNeal Scrapbook, microfilm roll 2, WHMC. See also Feurer, *Radical Unionism*, 144, 148–49.

29. Grant, letter to U.S. Cartridge Company, May 12, 1943, McNeal Papers, microfilm roll 2, WHMC.

30. "3600 Ordnance Workers Strike; Want Negro Boss," *Post-Dispatch*, June 3, 1943; "3,600 Negroes Walk Out at Ordnance Plant," *Star-Times*, June 3, 1943; T. D. McNeal, David M. Grant, and Leyton Weston, "An Appeal From the March on Washington Committee," June 2, 1943; "To the Workers Employed in Bldg. 202," release issued by Local 825 U.E.R. & MWA-CIO, June 3, 1943; untitled St. Louis MOWM document, June 3, 1943; "1200 Negroes Return to Jobs at Ordnance Plant," *Post-Dispatch*, June 3, 1943; "Negroes Start Work Again at Ordnance Plant," *Star-Times*, June 3, 1943; "War Workers Sit-Down Laid to Failure to Advance Negroes," *Argus*, June 4, 1943; "32 Appointed Foremen at Ordnance Plant,"

Chicago Defender, June 26, 1943; "War Workers Win Decision after Strike," *Defender,* June 12, 1943; and Howard Woods, "The Lesson in Building 202," *Defender,* June 19, 1943, McNeal Scrapbook, microfilm roll 2, WHMC.

31. "M.O.W.M. to Stage March on Bell Telephone Company," *American,* May 27, 1943; "To March on Bell Building," *Argus,* June 4, 1943; written text of announcement made at leading black churches, June 6, 1943; "Widespread Support for March on Telephone Company," *American,* June 10, 1943; St. Louis MOWM, "Statement Of Facts," distributed to public at Bell Company, June 12, 1943; "Negroes March On Phone Office, Ask More Jobs," *Star-Times,* June 12, 1943; "Southwestern Bell Co. Picketed by 100 Negroes," *Post-Dispatch,* June 13, 1943; "25,000 Phone Subscribers Deserve Consideration," *American,* June 17, 1943; and Henry Winfield Wheeler, "The Dauntless 300," *American,* June 17, 1943, McNeal Scrapbook, microfilm roll 2, WHMC. See also Green, *Race on the Line,* 202–3.

32. "Typists Employed on Merit," *American,* June 17, 1943, McNeal Scrapbook, microfilm roll 2, WHMC; and Chateauvert, *Marching Together,* 118, 168.

33. "Racial Field Projects Studied," *Globe-Democrat,* April 11, 1943; National Headquarters, MOWM, "MOWM Establishes Permanent Organization," press release, July 9, 1943; March on Washington Movement, National Program of Action, August 1943 to July 31, 1944; Report of Committee on Resolutions to "We Are American—Too" Conference, circa July 1943; and "March-On-Washington Group Scores Anti-Negro Terror," *The Militant,* July 10, 1943, McNeal Scrapbook, microfilm rolls 1 and 2, WHMC. See also Garfinkel, *When Negroes March,* 135, 137.

34. "Randolph Opposes March on Capital," *Labor Action,* July 1943; National Headquarters, MOWM, notice sent to Local Units, July 20, 1943; and Harry Allen, "Unity with Labor—the Only Hope for MOW," *Labor Action,* July 1943; *American,* June 10, 1943; "Railroad Hearings Re-scheduled," editorial, *Black Worker,* July 1943; "Many Given Hopes for Jobs by Re-scheduling of R.R. Hearing," *Argus,* July 16, 1943; "Railroads Admit Guilt as FEPC Exposes Bias," *Courier,* September 25, 1943; Malcolm Ross, Chairman, President's Committee on Fair Employment Practice, Summary, Findings and Directives, November 18, 1943; Report of the FEPC Hearings and Affiliated Locals of the International Association of Railway Employees at Washington, D.C., September 15–18, 1943; "White and Negro Americans Must Unite for Victory," statement by the Executive Board, District Council No. 8, U.E.R. & MWA-CIO; "Mayor to Act on Union's Racial Amity Program," *Post-Dispatch,* July 14, 1943; "CIO Suggests Racial Relations Program," *Star-Times,* July 20, 1943; "St. Louis Needs This Committee," *Star-Times,* July 15, 1943; "Mayor Continues Plan for Better Race Relations in City," *American,* August 12, 1943; and "Don't Let It Happen in St. Louis!" *Daily Worker,* June 23, 1943, McNeal Scrapbook, microfilm rolls 1 and 2, WHMC. See also Henry Winfield Wheeler Papers, Collection 122, WHMC; Harris, *Keeping the Faith,* 76; Garfinkel, *When Negroes March,* 115–16, 127; Anderson, *A. Philip Randolph,* 173; and Pfeffer, *A. Philip Randolph,* 53–54, 62, 72, 87.

35. "Mayor Names Inter-racial Commission," *St. Louis Union Labor Advocate,* September 17, 1943; "Inter-racial Group Plans Its Program," *Defender,* September 25, 1943; "24 Negroes on St. Louis Interracial Committee," *Courier,* September 25, 1943; T. D. McNeal, letter to Hon. A. P. Kaufmann, Mayor, City of St. Louis, September 17, 1943; and Charles J. Riley, Secretary to the Mayor, City of St. Louis, letter to McNeal, September 20, 1943, McNeal Scrapbook, microfilm roll 1, WHMC.

36. Singh, *Black Is a Country,* 146–52; and Kersten, *Race, Jobs,* 50.

37. "U.S. Judge Knocks Out Differences in Pay Scale," *Argus,* August 20, 1943; *American,* August 5, 1943; "MOW Planning Mass Payment of Phone Bills in

Protest," *American*, September 2, 1943; "205 Jam Phone Co. at Once Paying Bills as Protest to Job Denials," *Argus*, September 24, 1943; "Girls Picket 'Phone Company," *American*, July 15, 1943; " 'March' Group Victory Looms," *Courier*, November 6, 1943; and St. Louis MOWM press release, December 9, 1943, McNeal Scrapbook, microfilm rolls 1 and 2, WHMC. See also *Argus*, August 6, 1943, Brotherhood of Sleeping Car Porters (BSCP) Records, Chicago Historical Society Library, hereafter referred to as CHS; and Dowden, "Over This Point," 176 n. 27.

38. "MOW Opened Jobs for 14,000," *Argus*, June 25, 1943; Wagner Electric Company employees, letter to T. D. McNeal, June 10, 1944; "1000 Face Layoffs at St. Louis Arms Plant," *Defender*, November 27, 1943; untitled letter to Nathaniel Sweets, circa December 1943; William Sentner, General Vice President, United Electrical, Radio & Machine Workers of America—CIO, District No. 8, letter to Otto Maschoff, President Local 825, U.E.R. & MWA, July 28, 1943, McNeal Scrapbook, microfilm rolls 1 and 2, WHMC.

39. "17,000 St. Louis Women Jobless as Racial Barriers Prevent Hiring," *Defender*, May 6, 1944; "Job Situation for Women Here Serious," undated St. Louis MOWM press release, circa 1944; "Randolph Warns Negroes of Post-War Unemployment," National Headquarters, MOWM, November 26, 1943; *Defender*, September 9, 1944; and Mrs. Christine Berry Morgan, letter to St. Louis MOWM, June 15, 1944, McNeal Scrapbook, microfilm roll 2, WHMC.

40. Untitled St. Louis MOWM notice, circa June 1944; "March Committee Asks Women to Fight for Jobs," *Defender*, July 21, 1944; "FEPC Hearings Here Set for August 1–2," *Globe-Democrat*, July 25, 1944; "Friend of MOW," unsigned letter to T. D. McNeal, March 16, 1944; and Arthur J. Reese, letter to St. Louis MOWM, June 15, 1944, McNeal Scrapbook, microfilm roll 2, WHMC.

41. Complaint from a General Cable Corporation employee to T. D. McNeal, June 14, 1944; "Racial Complaint against 4 More Firms Taken Up," *Post-Dispatch*, August 1, 1944; "Negroes Tell of Job Seeking at Amertorp," *Star-Times*, August 1, 1944; "Negro Hiring Practice Set by Community," *Star-Times*, August 2, 1944; "McDonnell Denies Barring Negro Workers," *Star-Times*, August 2, 1944; "Negroes Say They Sought Jobs but Were Not Hired," *Post-Dispatch*, August 2, 1944; "Employment of Negroes in War Production," *American*, September 7, 1944; "FEPC Studies Plant Cases," *Argus*, August 11, 1944; and Grant, testimony before House of Representatives, Committee on Labor, Washington, D.C., McNeal Scrapbook, microfilm roll 2, WHMC.

42. "FEPC Office Opened in Paul Brown Bldg.," *Star-Times*, October 10, 1944; "100 Complaints Filed with FEPC Here," *Globe-Democrat*, October 10, 1944; "400 Strikers Return to Liggett & Myers," *Globe-Democrat*, August 9, 1944; "90 Chippers Back on Foundry Jobs," *Star-Times*, July 24, 1944; "National Lead Strike Laid to Discrimination," *Star-Times*, July 27, 1944; "160 Negroes Strike at Titanium Plant," *Globe-Democrat*, July 28, 1944; "290 Chippers Stop Work for 5 Hours," *Globe-Democrat*, July 28, 1944; "Titanium Output Not Hurt by Strike," *Star-Times*, July 28, 1944; "Steel Chippers Again Forcing Plant to Close," *Star-Times*, August 1, 1944; "4000 Kept Idle at Steel Plant by 300 Chippers," *Post-Dispatch*, August 2, 1944; "Strike over Bias Occur at 2 Plants," *Argus*, August 3, 1944; "Granite City Steel Tie Up in 8th Day," *Star-Times*, August 4, 1944; and "End of Chippers' Strike Likely Soon," *Globe-Democrat*, August 4, 1944, McNeal Scrapbook, microfilm roll 2, WHMC. See also Brunn, "Black Workers," 675; and Kersten, *Race, Jobs*, 55.

43. "Refuse to Lift Negro Ban," *Argus*, July 30, 1943, McNeal Scrapbook, microfilm roll 1, WHMC.

44. The Comintern dissolved itself in June 1943, and by 1944 the American Communist Party ceased to exist. It was, however, reconstituted in July 1945. See Klehr, *Heyday of American Communism*, 410–11.

45. "Seek to Block Equal Rights Bill for MO.," *Defender*, February 6, 1943; "House Hearing Held on Negro Rights Bill," *Post-Dispatch*, January 28, 1943; "Postoffice Cafeteria Here Ordered to Stop Segregation of Negroes," *Post-Dispatch*, October 15, 1943; "Post Office Cafeteria Jim Crow Ordered Out," *American*, October 28, 1943; "St. Louis P.O. Defies Anti-segregation Order," *Defender*, November 27, 1943; "Bill against Race Ban," *Argus*, January 21, 1944; "Sub-committee Rejects Discrimination Clause," *Star-Times*, January 12, 1944; "Clause on Equal Rights Tentatively Agreed on by Constitution Group," *American*, January 13, 1944; "Convention Acts to 'Pull Wool over Eyes' of Negroes," *Argus*, January 21, 1944; and "Constitutional Convention Acts on Inequalities," *Argus*, May 5, 1944, McNeal Papers, microfilm rolls 1 and 2, WHMC. See also Wheeler Papers, WHMC; and Dreer, "Negro Leadership," 18.

46. Herman H. Dreer Collection, Folders 1–2, MHS; Daniel T. Kelleher, "The Case of Lloyd Lionel Gaines: The Demise of the Separate but Equal Doctrine," *Journal of Negro History* 56 (October 1971): 264–70; Dowden, "Over This Point," 202–3; and Harrison, "New Deal," 164–65.

47. "Lifting School Segregation Law Is Urged," *Star-Times*, February 16, 1944; "St. Louis U. Professor Scores Race Prejudice at Assembly," *American*, February 17, 1944; "St. Louis University to Accept Negro Students," *Defender*, May 6, 1944; "Aldermen Take Up Lunchroom Bill Dilemma," *Star-Times*, April 1, 1944; "Aldermen Get 'Hot Potato' Racial Bill," *Star-Times*, April 3, 1944; "Aldermen Pass Non–Jim Crow Bill 22 to 4," *American*, April 6, 1944; and "Millions Enfranchised by U.S. Highest Court Finding," *Argus*, April 7, 1944, McNeal Scrapbook, microfilm roll 2, WHMC. See also Dreer, "Negro Leadership," 91.

48. "ODT Lets Street Car Company Survey and Approve Private Cabs," *American*, February 3, 1944; "Discourteous Conductor-Motormen," *American*, August 24, 1944; "Gangland Rides the Street Cars," editorial, *Star-Times*, August 8, 1944; "Seek to Ease Race Tension," *Argus*, August 11, 1944; and "Racial Friction Rumors Labeled False and Absurd," *Star-Times*, July 19, 1944, McNeal Scrapbook, microfilm roll 2, WHMC.

49. "March on Washington Movement," *American*, August 26, 1943; Youth Council Order of the Eastern Star, letters to Famous-Barr Company, Scruggs-Vandervoort-Barney, Inc., and Stix Baer & Fuller Company, January 17, 1944, McNeal Scrapbook, microfilm rolls 1 and 2, WHMC.

50. "Citizens Civil Rights Committee," undated document, circa May 1944; "M.O.W. Off to Good Start," *American*, June 1, 1944, and untitled and undated draft of an article on the CCRC, circa July 1944, McNeal Scrapbook, microfilm roll 2, WHMC; and Grant Papers, Box 2, Folder 9, WHMC. See also Patricia L. Adams, "Fighting for Democracy in St. Louis: Civil Rights during World War II," *Missouri Historical Review* 80 (October 1985): 58–75.

51. H. W. Wheeler, "They Walked Past Jim Crow at Grand-Leader Lunch Counter," *American*, May 25, 1944; "The Citizens' Civil Rights Committee," *American*, June 22, 1944; and untitled and undated draft of an article on the CCRC, circa July 1944, McNeal Scrapbook, microfilm roll 2, WHMC. See also "Colored Women Crusaders Attack Downtown Dept. Store Cafeteria Discr.," *American*, June 8, 1944, BSCP records, CHS.

52. "A Jim Crow Cafeteria," *American*, August 31, 1944; Thelma Grant,

"Basement Offer Rejected; Thanks Sent to Inter-race Commission," *American*, September 7, 1944; and "Basement Cafeteria Plan Vetoed," *Argus*, September 8, 1944, McNeal Scrapbook, microfilm roll 2, WHMC.

53. Grant, "Basement Offer Rejected," *American*, McNeal Scrapbook, microfilm roll 2, WHMC; Brunn, "Black Workers," 665–66; Kersten, *Race, Jobs*, 125, 139; and Feurer, *Radical Unionism*, 187.

54. Horace R. Cayton, "NAACP-MOWM," *Pittsburgh Courier*, June 19, 1943, BSCP records, CHS. See also Garfinkel, *When Negroes March*, 134, 146, 149; John E. Means, "Fair Employment Practices Legislation and Enforcement in the United States," in *Negroes and Jobs: A Book of Readings*, ed. Louis A. Ferman, Joyce L. Kornbluh, and J. A. Miller (Ann Arbor: University of Michigan Press, 1968), 462; Anderson, *A. Philip Randolph*, 263; and Pfeffer, *A. Philip Randolph*, 64, 86.

55. Singh, *Black Is a Country*, 65; Brunn, "Black Workers," 665–66; and Sexauer, "St. Louis 1940s–1950s," 22; and Robert C. Weaver, *Negro Labor: A National Problem* (New York: Harcourt, Brace and Company, 1946), 236.

CHAPTER THREE

1. See Nelson Lichtenstein, "From Corporatism to Collective Bargaining: Organized Labor and the Eclipse of Social Democracy in the Postwar Era," in *The Rise and Fall of the New Deal Order, 1930–1980*, ed. Steve Fraser and Gary Gerstle (Princeton, N.J.: Princeton University Press, 1989), 122–52; and Lisa Granich-Kovarik, "From Picket Line to Courtroom: The 1955 St. Louis Transit Strike," *Gateway Heritage* 21 (Summer 2000): 16–27.

2. Harris, *The Harder We Run*, 138. See also Robbie Lieberman and Clarence Lang, eds., *Anticommunism and the African American Freedom Movement: "Another Side of the Story"* (New York: Palgrave Macmillan, 2009).

3. Primm, *Lion of the Valley*, 454–56; Mary Kimbrough and Margaret W. Dagen, *Victory without Violence: The First Ten Years of the St. Louis Committee of Racial Equality (CORE), 1947–1957* (Columbia: University of Missouri Press, 2000); Lipsitz, *Sidewalks of St. Louis*, 36; St. Louis City Plan Commission, *History*, 32; and Eric Sandweiss, *St. Louis: The Evolution of an American Urban Landscape* (Philadelphia: Temple University Press, 2001), 225.

4. Ernest Calloway, "The Arts of Power and the St. Louis Decision-Making Authority," address to Jewish Community Relations Centers, October 23, 1966, Ernest Calloway Papers, 1937–1983, Collection 11, Box 1, Folder 5, WHMC; Sexauer, "St. Louis 1940s–1950s," 25; U.S. Bureau of the Census, *1950 Census of Population* (Washington, D.C.: Government Printing Office, 1952); and Primm, *Lion of the Valley*, 476.

5. Kimbrough and Dagen, *Victory without Violence*, 85; Sandweiss, *St. Louis*, 233; Primm, *Lion of the Valley*, 460; "Whites Act to Retain School," *American*, August 24, 1944; "Oppose Converting School for Negroes," *Argus*, August 25, 1944; *American*, August 31, 1944; and "Cote Brilliante School Stays Shut," *Argus*, September 8, 1944, McNeal Scrapbook, microfilm roll 2, WHMC.

6. Ingo Walker and John E. Kramer, "Political Autonomy and Economic Dependence in an All-Negro Municipality," *American Journal of Economics and Sociology* 28 (July 1969): 227; Wright, *Kinloch*, 23–33; and "Kinloch Becomes Missouri's First All-Negro City," *Globe-Democrat*, August 21, 1948, Kinloch History Committee Records, Folder 11, WHMC.

7. Primm, *Lion of the Valley*, 462; Irwin Sobel, Werner Z. Hirsch, and Harry C. Harris, *The Negro in the St. Louis Economy—1954* (St. Louis: Urban League of St.

Louis, 1954), 14, 23; Lipsitz, *Life in the Struggle*, 65; Ernest Calloway, "An Introduction to St. Louis Black Politics," *Proud* magazine, June 1979, 5, Calloway Papers, Box 4, Folder 32, WHMC; and Patterson, *Black City Politics*, 54.

8. Welek, "Jordan Chambers," 366, 369; and Dreer, "Negro Leadership," 19–20.

9. U.S. Bureau of the Census, *1950 Census of Population and Housing*; Henry, "Structures of Exclusion," 179; "Through the Eyes of a Child" Oral History Project, written transcripts, MHS; Arnold Hirsch, *Making of the Second Ghetto: Race and Housing in Chicago, 1940–1960* (Chicago: University of Chicago Press, 1983); and Amy E. Hillier, "Redlining and the Home Owners' Loan Corporation," *Journal of Urban History* 29 (May 2003): 394–420.

10. U.S. Bureau of the Census, *1950 Census of Population*; U.S. Bureau of the Census, *1940 Census of the Population* (Washington, D.C.: Government Printing Office, 1943); Kersten, *Race, Jobs*, 126–28; Sobel, Hirsch, and Harris, *Negro in St. Louis Economy*, 25–28, 38; and U.S. Census, 1950.

11. U.S. Census, 1950; Sobel, Hirsch, and Harris, *Negro in St. Louis Economy*, 38–39, 46; Vanneman and Cannon, *American Perception of Class*, 232; "Girl in Search of Job Feels Pinch of Race Bias," *Argus*, July 10, 1953; and Glenn and Feldberg, "Degraded and Deskilled."

12. William L. Clay, "Anatomy of an Economic Murder: A Statistical Review of the Negro in the Saint Louis Employment Field, 1963," pamphlet, MHS, 2; and Sobel, Hirsch, and Harris, *Negro in St. Louis Economy*, 27, 79.

13. Dreer, "Negro Leadership," 13, 185; and "Through the Eyes of a Child" Oral History Project, written transcripts, MHS.

14. Dick Gregory with Robert Lipsyte, *Nigger* (New York: Washington Square Press, 1964); "Through the Eyes of a Child" Oral History Project, written transcripts, MHS; and Howard B. Woods, "Under Redevelopment," *Argus*, July 6, 1956.

15. Pfeffer, *A. Philip Randolph*, 133, 146–48; and Jack M. Bloom, *Class, Race, and the Civil Rights Movement* (Bloomington: Indiana University Press, 1987), 78–79. See also Brenda Gayle Plummer, *Rising Wind: Black Americans and Foreign Affairs, 1935–1960* (Chapel Hill: University of North Carolina Press, 1996); Mary L. Dudziak, *Cold War Civil Rights: Race and the Image of American Democracy* (Princeton, N.J.: Princeton University Press, 2000); and Thomas Bortstelmann, *The Cold War and the Color Line: American Race Relations and the Global Arena* (Cambridge: Harvard University Press, 2001).

16. William S. White, "Mississippi Bolters Seated after Fight," and "Strong-Arm Squad Halts Squabble at Convention," *New York Times*, July 14, 1948; Bloom, *Class, Race, and the Civil Rights Movement*, 74–86; Welek, "Jordan Chambers," 364–65; and St. Louis Wards Election Work Sheet, Presidential Election, 1948, Calloway Papers, Addenda, Collection 540, Box 53, Folder 640, WHMC.

17. Gerald Horne, *Black and Red: W.E.B. DuBois and the Afro-American Response to the Cold War, 1944–1963* (Albany: State University of New York Press, 1986), 45; Horne, *Communist Front? The Civil Rights Congress, 1946–56* (Rutherford, N.J.: Fairleigh Dickinson University Press, 1987), 45; and Carol Anderson, *Eyes off the Prize: The United Nations and the African American Struggle for Human Rights, 1944–1955* (New York: Cambridge University Press, 2003), 126–29. See also Manfred Berg, "Black Civil Rights and Liberal Anticommunism: The NAACP in the Early Cold War," *Journal of American History* 94 (June 2007): 75–96.

18. Harry Haywood, *Negro Liberation* (New York: International Publishers, 1948), 188; and Kelleher, "St. Louis NAACP," 106.

19. "Action Requested by Governor Requested in Killing," *Post-Dispatch*, September 24, 1946; "Killing of Negro by Patrolman to Go to Grand Jury," *Post-Dispatch*, September 26, 1946; "Ask 'Trigger' Officer's Suspension," *Argus*, October 4, 1946; "U.S. May Take Action in Wm. Howard Slaying Case," *Argus*, November 1, 1946; "N.N. Congress to Hold Wm. Howard Mass Meeting," *Argus*, November 8, 1946; "American Theater Picketed by Negroes," *Globe-Democrat*, November 18, 1946; "Picket American Theater Jim Crow," *Argus*, November 22, 1946; "Paul Robeson to Give Up Stage, Fight Race Hatred," *Post-Dispatch*, January 26, 1947; Grant Papers, Box 1, Folder 3, WHMC; *FBI Files on the National Negro Congress* (Wilmington, Del.: Scholarly Resources, 1987), microfilm reel 2; Kelleher, "St. Louis NAACP," 131; Dreer, "Negro Leadership," 155; Horne, *Communist Front?* 29; Bush, *Not What We Seem*, 128–30; and Martin Bauml Duberman, *Paul Robeson: A Biography* (New York: Ballantine, 1989), 317.

20. Kelleher, "St. Louis NAACP," 131.

21. Grant Papers, Box 1, Folders 1 and 3, WHMC; Kelleher, "St. Louis NAACP," 104; Kimbrough and Dagen, *Victory without Violence;* and Wheeler, "Saint Louis Branch."

22. Grant Papers, Boxes 1 and 2, WHMC; George Winston Cloyd Papers, 1938–1951, Box 2, Folder 14, MHS; Sobel, Hirsch, and Harris, *Negro in St. Louis Economy*, 22; and Henry, "Structures of Exclusion," 186.

23. Kelleher, "St. Louis NAACP,"104; and Joanne Grant, *Ella Baker: Freedom Bound* (New York: John Wiley and Sons, 1998), 47–49, 73–74. For a provocative discussion of how the labor-based complaints of black workers were eliminated from both the legal agenda of the NAACP and federal agencies, see Risa L. Goluboff, *The Lost Promise of Civil Rights* (Cambridge, MA: Harvard University Press, 2007).

24. Kimbrough and Dagen, *Victory without Violence*, 18, 29–30; Dreer, "Negro Leadership," 233; and Robert Bussel, "'A Trade Union Oriented War on the Slums': Harold Gibbons, Ernest Calloway, and the St. Louis Teamsters in the 1960s," *Labor History* 44 (2003): 51. See also Benjamin Cawthra, "Ernest Calloway: Labor, Civil Rights, and Black Leadership in St. Louis," *Gateway Heritage* 21 (Winter 2000–2001): 7.

25. Inge Powell Bell, *CORE and the Strategy of Nonviolence* (New York: Random House, 1968); August Meier and Elliott Rudwick, *CORE: A Study in the Civil Rights Movement, 1942–1968* (New York: Oxford University Press, 1973); Marian and Charles Oldham, interview by Ernestine Hardge, December 12, 1988, "Strong Seed Planted" Oral History Collection, written transcripts, Box 1, MHS; Kimbrough and Dagen, *Victory without Violence*, 22–26; and Michael Flug, "Organized Labor and the Civil Rights Movement of the 1960s: The Case of the Maryland Freedom Union," *Labor History* 31 (Summer 1990): 323.

26. Kimbrough and Dagen, *Victory without Violence*, 77; and Glen Jeansonne, *Gerald L. K. Smith: Minister of Hate* (New Haven: Yale University Press, 1988).

27. "Planning for an Integrated School System in St. Louis," prepared and presented by the Committee on Democratic Rights of Members, Warehouse and Distribution Workers Union, Local 688, International Brotherhood of Teamsters, circa December 1951, Cloyd Papers, Box 2, Folder 14, MHS.

28. Kimbrough and Dagen, *Victory without Violence*, 73.

29. "The Fairgrounds Park Incident: A study of the factors which resulted in the outbreak of violence at the Fairgrounds Park Swimming Pool on June 21, 1949, an account of what happened, and recommendations for corrective action," conducted for the St. Louis Council on Human Relations, St. Louis, Missouri by

George Schermer, Director, Mayor's Interracial Committee, Detroit, Michigan, July 27, 1949, 10–19, MHS; Sobel, Hirsch, and Harris, *Negro in St. Louis Economy,* 16; James Lawrence, "Trial and Error in St. Louis," January 1950, Cloyd Papers, Box 2, Folder 14, MHS; and Jeff Wiltse, *Contested Waters: A Social History of Swimming Pools in America* (Chapel Hill: University of North Carolina Press, 2007), 78–86.

30. "Through the Eyes of a Child" Oral History Project, written transcripts, MHS; Schermer, "The Fairgrounds Park Incident," MHS, 5, 20–25; and Wiltse, *Contested Waters,* 169–70.

31. Lawrence, "Trial and Error"; Grant Papers, Box 1, Folder 3, WHMC; Schermer, "The Fairgrounds Park Incident," 26–29, 31; and Wiltse, *Contested Waters,* 171–74.

32. Lawrence, "Trial and Error"; and Schermer, "The Fairgrounds Park Incident," 36.

33. Schermer, "The Fairgrounds Park Incident," 7, 36.

34. Joseph L. Ames, President, Committee of Racial Equality (CORE), letter and proposal to Joseph M. Darst, Mayor, City of St. Louis, July 22, 1949, Cloyd Papers, Box 2, Folder 5, MHS; Schermer, "The Fairgrounds Park Incident," 42–43; Kimbrough and Dagen, *Victory without Violence,* 70; and Wiltse, *Contested Waters,* 176–80. Fairgrounds Pool closed in 1956.

35. *Up To Date With CORE,* June, July, and August 1951, Cloyd Papers, Box 2, Folder 5, MHS; Kimbrough and Dagen, *Victory without Violence,* 71–72, 77; and Jeansonne, *Gerald L. K. Smith,* 84, 120–21.

36. "Attempt 'Smear' of CORE Fails," *Argus,* July 18, 1952.

37. "Tight Hold," *Time,* June 7, 1954; Horne, *Communist Front?* 65, 305–6; and William L. Patterson, ed., *We Charge Genocide* (1951; rpt. New York: International Publishers, 1970), 73. In an even bolder move in 1951, CRC national executive secretary William L. Patterson presented a petition to the United Nations General Assembly charging the United States government with the crime of genocide against the 15 million African American people within its borders, in violation of the UN's Declaration of Human Rights and its Convention for the Prevention and Punishment of Genocide. DuBois, Robeson, and Obadiah Jones were among the ninety-four black freedom activists who signed the painstakingly detailed document.

38. "Killing of Man by Officer Is Denounced at Meeting," *Post-Dispatch,* September 6, 1946; "Policeman's Indictment as Murderer Asked," *Globe-Democrat,* September 6, 1946; Boyd F. Carroll, "G.O.P. Control of the State Senate, House Is Indicated," *Globe-Democrat,* November 6, 1946; "Four Negroes Elected in Missouri," *Daily Worker,* November 8, 1946; "Proposes State Fair Employment Practices Law," *Moberly Monitor-Index,* January 15, 1947; and *FBI Files on the National Negro Congress,* microfilm reel 2.

39. Chester E. Stovall, Industrial Secretary, St. Louis Urban League, letter to Julius A. Thomas, Director of Industrial Relations, National Urban League, January 19, 1949, in John H. Bracey Jr., and August Meier, eds., *Papers of the NAACP: The NAACP and Labor, 1940–1955,* Part 13 (Bethesda, Md.: University Publications of America, 1992), microfilm reel 3; "Quality Dairy Refuses to Hire Negro Drivers," *Argus,* August 1, 1952; "Irate Citizens Cancel Quality Milk Business" and "Forget Quality Dairy," news editorial, *Argus,* August 8, 1952; and "Quality Says It Will Hire Negro Drivers," *Argus,* August 22, 1952.

40. Kersten, *Race, Jobs,* 134; National Negro Labor Council, *Let Freedom Ride the Rails* (Detroit: National Negro Labor Council, 1954), 20; Dreer, "Negro Lead-

ership," 110; Calvin Houston Stevely Jr., letter to Post Office Department Loyalty Board, August 24, 1948, and Miss Marian W. Perry, memorandum to Mr. [Roy] Wilkins and Mr. Harvey Parham, September 2, 1948, in Bracey and Meier, *Papers of the NAACP,* microfilm reel 5.

41. Kelleher, "St. Louis NAACP," 115; Horne, *Communist Front?* 304; and Feurer, *Radical Unionism,* 186.

42. Randolph, "Why I Would Not Stand," 28; Bussel, "Trade Union Oriented," 51; Harris, *The Harder We Run,* 138; Ellen W. Schrecker, "McCarthyism and the Labor Movement: The Role of the State," in Rosswurm, *CIO's Left-Led Unions,* 141; Feurer, "William Sentner," 116–17; Steven Brill, *The Teamsters* (New York: Simon and Schuster, 1978), 355, 364; Lipsitz, *Rainbow at Midnight,* 194, 203 n. 50; and Thaddeus Russell, *Out of the Jungle: Jimmy Hoffa and the Remaking of the American Working Class* (New York: Alfred A. Knopf, 2001), 59, 79.

43. C. L. R. James, "The Revolutionary Answer to the Negro Problem in the United States," in *C.L.R. James on the "Negro Question,"* ed. Scott McLemee (Jackson: University Press of Mississippi, 1996), 138–39, 145; "Initiating Sponsors, 'National Trade Union Conference for Negro Rights,'" UAW President's Office, Walter P. Reuther Papers, Collection 261, Box 348, Folder 10, ALUA; "For These Things We Fight," full text of address of William R. Hood, delivered at the Founding Convention of the National Negro Labor Council at Cincinnati, Ohio, October 27, 1951, National Negro Labor Council vertical file, African American Societies and Organizations, ALUA; and Mindy Thompson, "The National Negro Labor Council: A History," Occasional Paper No. 27, American Institute for Marxist Studies (New York, 1978), 5–6, ALUA.

44. "For These Things We Fight,"and "Work Wanted: 100,000 Jobs for Negro Workers," NNLC vertical file, ALUA; "Draft Program of Action," adopted at National Trade Union Conference for Negro Rights, Chicago, June 10–11, 1950, UAW President's Office, Reuther Papers, Collection 261, Box 348, Folder 10, ALUA; "A History of the National Negro Labor Council," NNLC Reunion booklet, June 4–5, 1993, Chris and Marti Alston Papers, Collection 1779, Box 6, Folder 6, ALUA; "Negro Unionists Hold Conference in Cincinnati," *Ford Facts,* November 10, 1951, and "For These Things We Fight," NNLC vertical file, African American Societies and Organizations, ALUA; and Thompson, "National Negro Labor Council," 8–9, 11, 28, 45.

45. "New Councils Organized," *Struggle,* Official Organ of the National Labor Council, n.d., and "For These Things We Fight," NNLC vertical file; Thompson, "National Negro Labor Council," 12, 24–25, 40; and National Negro Labor Council, "Let Freedom Crash the Gateway to the South Campaign," circa 1954–55, Nat Ganley Papers, Series 1, Collection 320, Box 6, File 41, ALUA. See also Ingram, "Hershel Walker," and interview of Hershel Walker, both in "Strong Seed Planted" Oral History Collection, written transcripts, Box 2, MHS.

46. Thompson, "National Negro Labor Council," 17, 39; and "Brownell Adds to Our Country's Shame," statement by National Negro Labor Council, circa 1956, NNLC vertical file, ALUA; and "Mass Picket before Sears Store Saturday," *Argus,* March 20, 1953.

47. "Labor Council Fails to Get Support of NAACP; Subversive Charge Leveled," *Argus,* June 5, 1953; and Harris, *The Harder We Run,* 139–40. See also Thompson, "National Negro Labor Council," 14, 30, 34–35; UAW-CIO press release, October 22, 1951, NNLC vertical file; William H. Oliver, codirector, Fair Practices and Anti-Discrimination Department, UAW-CIO, letter to Jack Conway, October 30, 1952; and Oliver, letter to all UAW international union officers, exec-

utive board members, department heads, and advisory council members on antidiscrimination, January 23, 1952, Donald Montgomery Papers, Collection 36, Box 25, Folder 10, ALUA.

48. Red Davis, quoted in Rose Feuer, ed., "The St. Louis Labor History Tour," 37, MHS; and interview with Hershel Walker, "Strong Seed Planted" Oral History Collection, written transcripts, Box 2, MHS.

49. Ibid.

50. "First Drivers of Busses and Streetcars Accepted," *Argus,* April 24, 1953; interview with Hershel Walker, "Strong Seed Planted" Oral History Collection, written transcripts, Box 2, MHS; Thompson, "National Negro Labor Council," 42, 69, 72; "A History of the National Negro Labor Council," NNLC Reunion booklet, June 4–5, 1993, Alston Papers, Box 6, File 6, ALUA; and "Brownell Adds to Our Country's Shame," NNLC vertical file, ALUA.

51. Harris, *The Harder We Run,* 127, 133; and Means, "Fair Employment Practices," 464.

52. AFL-CIO, "1955 Convention Resolution on Civil Rights," publication No. 8, Ganley Papers, Series 1, Box 6, File 39; and NNLC, "An Open Letter to the AFL and CIO: The Only Road to Labor Unity: The Only Road to Labor Unity Is Equality and Democracy for All!" Ganley Papers, Series 1, Box 6, File 41. ALUA. See also Harris, *The Harder We Run,* 140–41; Anderson, *A. Philip Randolph,* 297; and Pfeffer, *A. Philip Randolph,* 207–8.

53. Thompson, "National Negro Labor Council," 73, 75; "Red Inquiry to Reach into Local Community," *Argus,* June 1, 1956; "Labor Council Once Rejected by NAACP Here," *Argus,* June 8, 1956; Committee on Un-American Activities, United States House of Representatives, *Investigation of Communist Activities in the St. Louis, MO., Area* (Washington, D.C.: Government Printing Office, 1956); Horne, *Black and Red,* 212–18; and Horne, *Communist Front?* 114–15, 304, 308.

54. Pettis Perry, "The Third Annual Convention of the National Negro Labor Council," *Political Affairs* 3 (February 1954): 1–8, NNLC vertical file, ALUA. See also Haywood, *Black Bolshevik,* 601, 603, 618; Feurer, "William Sentner," 116–17; Klehr, *Heyday of American Communism,* 327, 332, 336, 343; and Horne, *Communist Front?* 65.

55. "Brownell Adds to Our Country's Shame," NNLC vertical file, ALUA; and Sidney R. Redmond, "The Board of Aldermen and Civil Rights," *Argus,* June 29, 1956.

56. Jeansonne, *Gerald L. K. Smith,* 100.

CHAPTER FOUR

1. Ernest Calloway, "St. Louis Black Politics"; Dreer, "Negro Leadership," 129, 222; "Moberly School Trial to Be Held Monday," *Argus,* August 17, 1956; "Moberly Case in U.S. Court Here," *Argus,* August 24, 1956; "CORE Lists 19 Eating Places," *Argus,* June 5, 1953; "Movies Here Hold Color Line," *Argus,* October 9, 1953; and Dreer, "Negro Leadership," 8.

2. Harris, *The Harder We Run,* 143–45; Grant, *Ella Baker,* 101; and Jo Ann Gibson Robinson, *The Montgomery Bus Boycott and the Women Who Started It* (1987; rpt. Knoxville: University of Tennessee Press, 1996), 54. See also Peniel E. Joseph, "Waiting till the Midnight Hour: Reconceptualizing the Heroic Period of the Civil Rights Movement," *Souls,* Vol. 2, No. 2 (Spring 2000): 6–17.

3. A similar battle around a proposed new St. Louis charter had occurred in

1950, though with far less intensity. See Robert H. Salisbury, "The Dynamics of Reform: Charter Politics in St. Louis," *Midwest Journal of Political Science* 5 (August 1961): 260–75. See also Clarence Lang, "Civil Rights versus 'Civic Progress': The St. Louis NAACP and the City Charter Fight, 1956–1957," *Journal of Urban History* 34 (May 2008): 609–38.

4. "Admiral Jimcrow Mars Y Excursion," and "Some More Dodging," news editorial, *Argus*, July 20, 1956; "The Highland Half-Loaf," news editorial, *Argus*, June 1, 1956; "Forest Park Highlands Partly Lowers Racial Bar," and "Retrenchment by Area Cafes," *Argus*, June 8, 1956; Dreer, "Negro Leadership," 10; and "Pope Quits," and "Harry Pope's Resignation," news editorial, *Argus*, April 13, 1956.

5. "Two Named to Top City Government Positions," and "Two Appointments," news editorial, *Argus*, May 4, 1956; "George Draper Named Assistant Atty. General," *Argus*, July 13, 1956; "Race Council Sponsors FEP," *Argus*, May 25, 1956; "FEP Bills for City Voted Out of Committee," *Argus*, June 29, 1956; "City Gets Fair Job Ordinance," and "Well Done," news editorial, *Argus*, July 6, 1956; and Sidney R. Redmond, "City FEP Law," *Argus*, August 10, 1956. See also Means, "Fair Employment Practices,"469, 473, 494, and Herbert Hill, "Twenty Years of State Fair Employment Practices Commissions: A Critical Analysis with Recommendations," both in Ferman, Kornbluh, and Miller, *Negroes and Jobs*, 497, 500.

6. Sexauer, "St. Louis 1940s–1950s," 31–32; Ernest Calloway, "The Time of the St. Louis Black Renaissance," *American*, June 12, 1980, Calloway Papers, Box 4, Folder 46, WHMC; Frankie Muse Freeman with Candace O'Connor, *A Song of Faith and Hope: The Life of Frankie Muse Freeman* (St. Louis: Missouri Historical Society Press, 2003), 53–55; and "Two Named to Top City Government Positions," *Argus*, May 4, 1956.

7. Calloway, "St. Louis Black Renaissance"; Calloway, "St. Louis Black Politics"; "Registration Drive On," *Argus*, June 8, 1956; and "Registration Adds 9000 to Voter Rolls," *Argus*, June 22, 1956; Lipsitz, *Life in the Struggle*, 66; Stein, *St. Louis Politics*, 69; and Clay, *Bill Clay*, 89, 95.

8. "List of Donors to Montgomery Fund Posted," *Argus*, April 13, 1956, "3 Cities Locked in Bus Boycott throughout Dixie," *Argus*, June 15, 1956, and "Negroes Weigh Boycott of Fla. Merchants," *Argus*, July 6, 1956, DeVerne Calloway, *St. Louis NAACP—1956, 1957, 1958: Clippings and Documents Concerning the St. Louis NAACP and Ernest Calloway*, 1989, MHS; "Wheeler May File Suit on Official," *Argus*, November 6, 1953; Kelleher, "St. Louis NAACP," 133–35; Dreer, "Negro Leadership," 267–68; and Clay, *Bill Clay*, 15–17. See also Mamie Till-Mobley and Christopher Benson, *Death of Innocence: The Story of the Hate Crime That Changed America* (New York: Random House, 2003).

9. "Robeson Began Crusade Here; Bigot Probe Likely," *Argus*, June 15, 1956. "Ernest Calloway Named to Run for NAACP Head," *Argus*, November 11, 1955; "Calloway Releases Full Scale Program for NAACP," *Argus*, November 18, 1955; "NAACP Encroachment," news editorial, *Argus*, November 4, 1955; and "Calloway Wins NAACP Election with Harmony," *Argus*, December 1955, Calloway, *St. Louis NAACP*, MHS.

10. Calloway Papers, Boxes 1 and 2, WHMC; Cawthra, "Ernest Calloway," 6; Bussel, "Trade Union Oriented," 51–52; and Lon W. Smith, "An Experiment in Trade Union Democracy: Harold Gibbons and the Formation of Teamsters Local 688, 1937–1957," Ph.D. diss., Illinois State University, 1993, 174–75, 234.

11. "An Economic Description of Teamsters Local 688," n.d., Calloway Pa-

pers, Addenda, Collection 550, Box 5, Folder 40, WHMC; Cawthra, "Ernest Calloway," 8; Brill, *The Teamsters*, 356–57, 359; Smith, "Trade Union Democracy," 139–40, 157–63; Levison, *The Working-Class Majority*, 196; and Russell, *Out of the Jungle*, 60, 105, 118.

12. Calloway Papers, Box 4, Folder 46, WHMC; Bussel, "Trade Union Oriented," 52–54; Smith, "Trade Union Democracy," 172, 198 n. 88; and Feurer, *Radical Unionism*, 231.

13. "Registration Drive On," *Argus*, June 8, 1956; "Registration Adds 9000 to Voter Rolls," *Argus*, June 22, 1956; Lipsitz, *Life in the Struggle*, 68; "NAACP Achieves Highest Membership Peak in 6 Yrs.," *Argus*, May 11, 1956; Marisa Chappell, Jenny Hutchinson, and Brian Ward, "'Dress modestly, neatly . . . as if you were going to church,'" in *Gender and the Civil Rights Movement*, ed. Peter J. Ling and Sharon Monteith (New Brunswick, N.J.: Rutgers University Press, 1999), 77, 83, 89; and Belinda Robnett, "African-American Women in the Civil Rights Movement, 1954–1965: Gender, Leadership, and Micromobilization," *American Journal of Sociology* 101 (May 1996): 1661–93.

14. Sobel, Hirsch, and Harris, *Negro in St. Louis Economy*, 55; "Ora Lee Malone, Organized Labor," *Proud* magazine, March–April 1975, MHS; "100 Service Car Drivers Join NAACP as Group," *Argus*, April 20, 1956; "Freedom Circle Expands among Area Social Clubs during NAACP Campaign," *Argus*, April 27, 1956; "NAACP Reports 2200 Members in Campaign," *Argus*, April 27, 1956; "Teacher-Nurse Division Leads in NAACP Campaign," *Argus*, April 20, 1956; and "Final Weeks in NAACP Drive," *Argus*, May 25, 1956.

15. Ernest Calloway, "Planning for a New Offensive on the Local Civil Rights Front," speech at Pine Street YMCA, January 3, 1956, Calloway Papers, Box 1, Folder 4, WHMC; Jon C. Teaford, *The Twentieth-Century American City*, 2nd ed. (Baltimore: Johns Hopkins University Press, 1993), 120; Primm, *Lion of the Valley*, 459–60; Joseph Heathcott and Maire Agnes Murphy, "Corridors of Flight, Zones of Renewal: Industry, Planning, and Policy in the Making of Metropolitan St. Louis, 1940–1980," *Journal of Urban History* 31 (January 2005): 157; and St. Louis City Plan Commission, *History*, 34–35. See also Charles E. Connerly, *"The Most Segregated City in America": City Planning and Civil Rights in Birmingham, 1920–1980* (Charlottesville: University of Virginia Press, 2005).

16. MacLean, *Freedom Is Not Enough*, 31; Civic Progress, Inc. Records, 1953–1979, Collection 153, WHMC; Stein, *St. Louis Politics*, 87–95, 247; and Jones, *Fragmented by Design*, 22–23.

17. Civic Progress Records, WHMC; "Opposition Grows to Plaza Bonds," *Argus*, September 11, 1953; "Aldermen to Get Plaza Bond Issue Resolution," and "We Have Waited in Vain," news editorial, *Argus*, September 25, 1953; "Protest Vote Given in 4 Wards," and "Under the Surface," news editorial, *Argus*, October 2, 1953; Primm, *Lion of the Valley*, 460, 468; Stein, *St. Louis Politics*, 97; and Henry, "Structures of Exclusion," 184, 197 fn 239.

18. Civic Progress Records, WHMC; St. Louis Bond Issues Collection, 1955–1962, MHS; *Poor's Register of Corporations, Directors, and Executives—1953* (New York: Standard and Poor's Corporation, 1953); and Teaford, *Twentieth-Century American City*, 119.

19. Salisbury, "The Dynamics of Reform," 262–63; Heathcott and Murphy, "Corridors of Flight," 161; Calloway Papers, Box 1, Folder 4, WHMC; St. Louis Bond Issues Collection, MHS; "Two Named to Top City Government Positions," *Argus*, May 4, 1956; Primm, *Lion of the Valley*, 466; "Citizens Group Urges Election of Freeholders," *Argus*, April 20, 1956; "Freeholder Group Starts on Charter," *Ar-*

gus, May 18, 1956; St. Louis City Charter Collection, MHS; Kerstein, "Political Consequences," 88–89; and Jones, *Fragmented by Design,* 13, 21.

20. Grant Papers, Box 2, Folder 9, WHMC; "Citizens' OK Grant, Broussard as Freeholders," *Argus,* April 13, 1956; and "Freeholders Face Issues," *Argus,* May 11, 1956.

21. "Challenge to the Freeholders," news editorial, *Argus,* May 11, 1956; Calloway, *St. Louis NAACP,* MHS; St. Louis City Charter Collection, MHS; "Mayor Opposed to Changing Form of Gov't," *Argus,* August 3, 1956; "New Charter Retains Same Basic Form," *Argus,* August 10, 1956; and Stein, *St. Louis Politics,* 105–6.

22. Calloway Papers, Box 3, Folder 22, WHMC.

23. Grant Papers, Box 2, Folder 9, WHMC; St. Louis City Charter Collection, MHS; and Calloway Papers, Box 1, Folder 4, WHMC.

24. St. Louis City Charter Collection, MHS; Calloway Papers, Box 4, Folder 46, and Box 1, Folder 4, WHMC; and Clay, *Bill Clay,* 18.

25. Calloway Papers, Addenda, Box 4, Folder 91, WHMC.

26. Calloway Papers, Box 3, Folder 22, WHMC; Calloway Papers, Addenda, Box 4, Folder 91, WHMC; Calloway Papers, Box 1, Folder 4, WHMC; Bussel, "Trade Union Oriented," 52; Brill, *The Teamsters,* 364–65; Smith, "Trade Union Democracy," 224–30; Russell, *Out of the Jungle,* 171, 176, 214; and "Mr. Calloway and the NAACP," news editorial, *Argus,* July 5, 1957, and "Aldermen and Teamsters vs. The City," news editorial, *Globe-Democrat,* June 23, 1957, Calloway, *St. Louis NAACP,* MHS. See also Frazier, *Black Bourgeoisie,* 126, 146–49.

27. Mixon, "Good Negro—Bad Negro," 594, 596, 600; Gaines, *Uplifting the Race;* and Lynn Weber Cannon, "Trends in Class Identification among Black Americans from 1952 to 1978," *Social Science Quarterly* 65 (March 1984): 112–26.

28. See Gaines, *Uplifting the Race;* and Georgina Hickey, "From Auburn Avenue to Buttermilk Bottom: Class and Community Dynamics among Atlanta's Blacks," in Taylor and Hill, *Historical Roots,* 118.

29. Lance Hill, *The Deacons for Defense: Armed Resistance and the Civil Rights Movement* (Chapel Hill: University of North Carolina Press, 2004), 14; St. Louis City Charter Collection, MHS; Calloway Papers, Box 4, Folder 46, and St. Louis Wards Election Work Sheet, Special Election, New Municipal Charter, August 6, 1957, Calloway Papers, Addenda, Box 53, Folder 640, WHMC; and Clay, *Bill Clay,* 19.

30. Ernest Calloway, "New Job Opportunities Must Be Our First Line of Attack," statement before the Job Opportunities Council of the St. Louis NAACP, Pine Street YMCA, August 26, 1957, Calloway Papers, Box 1, Folder 4, WHMC; interview with William L. Clay, "Strong Seed Planted" Oral History Collection, written transcripts, Box 1, MHS; and Calloway, "The Time of the St. Louis Black Renaissance, Part 2," *American,* June 19, 1980, Calloway Papers, Box 4, Folder 46, WHMC.

31. Calloway, "New Job Opportunities"; Calloway, "The Time of the St. Louis Black Renaissance, Part 3: The Battle for Black Sales Personnel," *American,* June 26, 1980, Box 4, Folder 46, WHMC; Atty. Margaret Bush Wilson, "Negroes Must Eat Too! (and Not Just Stew): The A&P Story," St. Louis NAACP Job Opportunities Council pamphlet, Calloway Papers, Box 2, Folder 12, WHMC; and Sobel, Hirsch, and Harris, *Negro in St. Louis Economy,* 28, 30–31, MHS.

32. Calloway, "New Job Opportunities."

33. Calloway, "St. Louis Black Renaissance, Part 3"; and Wilson, "Negroes Must Eat Too!"

34. Calloway, "St. Louis Black Renaissance, Part 3"; and Meier and Rudwick, *CORE,* 93.

35. Calloway, "St. Louis Black Renaissance, Part 3"; Meier and Rudwick, *CORE*, 62; and Kimbrough and Dagen, *Victory without Violence*, 76.

36. Kimbrough and Dagen, *Victory without Violence*, 90; Meier and Rudwick, *CORE*, 63, 71, 73–74, 83; and Calloway, "St. Louis Black Renaissance, Part 3."

37. Dreer, "Negro Leadership," 23, 44, 135.

38. Calloway Papers, Boxes 1 and 4, WHMC; interview with Clay, " 'Strong Seed Planted" Oral History Collection, written transcripts, Box 1, MHS; "A Report of the St. Louis NAACP's Job Opportunities Council for 1958," *St. Louis NAACP Citizen*, January 1959, in Bracey and Meier, *Papers of the NAACP:* Branch Department Files, Series C, microfilm reel 4; and Meier and Rudwick, *CORE*, 93.

39. Ernest Calloway, "On Famous Barr Department Store: The Value of the Disciplined Consumer Dollar in the Fight for Jobs," August 17, 1958, Calloway Papers, Box 1, Folder 4, WHMC.

40. Calloway, "St. Louis Black Renaissance, Part 3."

41. Interview with Clay, "Strong Seed Planted" Oral History Collection, written transcripts, Box 1, MHS; and Meier and Rudwick, *CORE*, 93–95.

42. "Downtown Scruggs Target of Pickets," *Post-Dispatch*, August 14, 1960, *Negro Scrapbook*, vol. 1, MHS; "Calloway Releases Full Scale Program for NAACP," *Argus*, November 18, 1955, Calloway, *St. Louis NAACP*, MHS; interview with Clay, "Strong Seed Planted" Oral History Collection, written transcripts, Box 1, MHS; Clay, *Bill Clay*, 58–60, 75; and Patterson, *Black City Politics*, 31–32.

43. Interview with Clay, "Strong Seed Planted" Oral History Collection, written transcripts, Box 1, MHS; Meier and Rudwick, *CORE*, 93–95; and Kimbrough and Dagen, *Victory without Violence*, 90.

44. Ernest Calloway, "The Time of the St. Louis Black Renaissance, Part 5: Electing the 1st Black State Senator and Issuing a Black Political Manifesto in 1960," *American*, July 10, 1980, Calloway Papers, Box 4, Folder 46, WHMC; Freeman, *Song of Faith*, 68–69; Clay, *Bill Clay*, 72; and Patterson, *Black City Politics*, 165–67.

45. Ernest Calloway, "Hicks Becomes the First Negro Elected to Ed Board," *NAACP Citizen*, June 1959, Calloway, *St. Louis NAACP*, MHS; and Calloway, "The Time of the St. Louis Black Renaissance, Part 4: Electing First Black to School Board," *American*, July 3, 1980, Calloway Papers, Box 4, Folder 46, WHMC.

46. Calloway, "St. Louis Black Renaissance, Part 4"; Calloway, "Hicks First Negro Elected"; and Calloway, "Jim Hurt's Victory Climaxes 35 Year Struggle," *Citizen-Crusader*, April 14, 1961, Calloway, *St. Louis NAACP*, MHS.

47. Ernest Calloway, "Victory Gives St. Louis Six Negro Aldermen," *NAACP Citizen*, June 1959; Calloway, *St. Louis NAACP*, MHS; Calloway, "St. Louis Black Renaissance, Part 5"; Sidney R. Redmond, "Seventh Senatorial District," *Argus*, July 13, 1956; and Sidney R. Redmond, "Fifth Senatorial District," *Argus*, July 27, 1956.

48. "7th Senatorial Race Looms as Political Test," *Argus*, July 20, 1956; Calloway, "St. Louis Black Renaissance, Part 5"; McNeal for Senator Headquarters, press release, February 3, 1960, "Members of Volunteer Telephone Corp for T. D. McNeal Tea," *St. Louis Crusader*, n.d.; and Citizens Committee for the Election of T. D. McNeal to the Missouri Senate, campaign brochure, Calloway Papers, Box 2, Folder 21, WHMC.

49. Calloway, "St. Louis Black Renaissance, Part 5"; and "McNeal Wins, Is First Negro Elected to Missouri Senate," *Post-Dispatch*, November 10, 1960, Negro Scrapbook, vol. 1, MHS.

50. Calloway Papers, Box 2, Folder 17, and Box 3, Folder 24; and "Calloway Accused of Soft Approach," *St. Louis Defender*, August 21, 1963, Calloway Papers,

Box 6, Folder 58, WHMC. See also Clay, *Bill Clay*, 73, 80–83; Brill, *The Teamsters*, 366–67; Russell, *Out of the Jungle*, 194, 199; and Smith, "Trade Union Democracy," 234–44.

51. P. I. Ward, "Alderman Clay Ignores Tactics of Opponents," *Crusader*, July 22, 1960, 14, and "Facts about the Record of Ald. William L. Clay," n.d., Calloway Papers, Box 3, Folder 24, WHMC.

52. See Clay, *Bill Clay*, 69, 73, 98–100; Patterson, *Black City Politics*, 38, 42 n. 18; and Stein, *St. Louis Politics*, 79–80.

53. Calloway, "Victory Gives St. Louis Six Negro Aldermen"; and Calloway, "St. Louis Black Renaissance, Part 5."

54. Ernest Calloway, "The Time Is Now," *New Citizen*, March 17, 1961, Calloway Papers, Box 4, Folder 32, WHMC; and Cawthra, "Ernest Calloway," 12.

55. Calloway Papers, Boxes 1 and 4, WHMC; and Stein, *St. Louis Politics*, 130.

56. James C. Millstone, "Citizens Debate Hot Issue," *Post-Dispatch*, January 24, 1960, Negro Scrapbook, vol. 1, MHS; "Overflow! Public Accommodations Hearing Continues Tonight," and Al Sonnenschein, "For Anti-bias Bill When U.S. Supreme Court Says Proceed," *Claytonian-Tribune*, January 18, 1960, Race Relations Collection, Box 1, MHS; Ernest Calloway, "It Finally Came to Pass: Board of Aldermen Adopts First Major Civil Rights Ordinance," *New Citizen*, May 26, 1961, Calloway Papers, Box 4, Folder 32, WHMC; Meier and Rudwick, *CORE*, 109; Stein, *St. Louis Politics*, 127, 130; Aldon D. Morris, *The Origins of the Civil Rights Movement: Black Communities Organizing for Change* (New York: Free Press, 1984), 188–89, 197–215; and Clayborne Carson, *In Struggle: SNCC and the Black Awakening of the 1960s* (Cambridge: Harvard University Press, 1981), 9–18.

57. Ernest Calloway, "The Time of the St. Louis Black Renaissance, Part 6: Aldermanic Body Adopts First Major Civil Rights Ordinance in St. Louis," *American*, July 17, 1980, Calloway Papers, Box 4, Folder 46, WHMC; Calloway, "St. Louis Mayoralty Elections; A Reform Period Closes," *FOCUS/Midwest*, May 1965, Calloway Papers, Box 4, Folder 32; Stein, *St. Louis Politics*, 114, 116–17; and "Anti-bias Bill Is Approved by Aldermen," *Globe-Democrat*, May 20, 1961, Negro Scrapbook, vol. 1, MHS. The Board of Aldermen passed an FEPC amendment the following year that covered private businesses.

58. "Tucker Names Stovall Welfare Director in Historic Move," *Globe-Democrat*, September 20, 1961, Negro Scrapbook, vol. 2, MHS; and Ernest Calloway, "The Political Impact of the Appointment of Chester Stovall as Welfare Director," *New Citizen*, September 29, 1961, Calloway, *St. Louis NAACP*, MHS.

59. Calloway, "St. Louis Black Renaissance, Part 2"; St. Louis NAACP and Citizens Assembly for a Representative Legislative Body, brochure, circa 1957, and Calloway, letter to Board of Freeholders, February 12, 1957, Calloway Papers, Box 3, Folder 22, WHMC; and Calloway, "Why We Are in Opposition to the Proposed New City Charter," July 30, 1957, Calloway Papers, Box 1, Folder 4, WHMC. See also Ernest Calloway, "The Negro Social and Economic Thrust," *Missouri Teamster*, December 20, 1963, Calloway Papers Addenda, Box 4, Folder 108, WHMC.

CHAPTER FIVE

1. "J. W. Chambers Funeral Will Be Wednesday," *Post-Dispatch*, August 12, 1962, and "Jordan W. Chambers Funeral Is Wednesday," *Globe-Democrat*, August

13, 1962, Negro Scrapbook, vol. 2. MHS. See also Ernest Calloway, "The Last Days of a Patriarch: Jordan Chambers," *Proud* magazine, June 1979, MHS; Howard B. Woods, "Pay Final Tribute to Political Leader," *Argus*, August 17, 1962; Michael Johns, *Moment of Grace: The American City in the 1950s* (Berkeley and Los Angeles: University of California Press, 2003), 83; Ernest Calloway, "The Community That Worked to Save a Dying City," *New Citizen*, March 23, 1962, and Calloway, "100,000 Negro Voters Make up Political Power Corridor," *New Citizen*, June 22, 1962, Calloway Papers, Box 4, Folder 32, WHMC; and League of Women Voters of St. Louis, "Background Material on New Bond Issue Proposals," and Mrs. John W. Seddon, "St. Louis Looks Ahead . . .Time for League Stand on Bond Issues," *League Reporter*, September 1961, St. Louis Bond Issues Collection, MHS.

2. Ray J. Noonan, "Role of the Negro in Local Politics," *Globe-Democrat*, May 11, 1963, Negro Scrapbook, vol. 2, MHS; and Calloway, "St. Louis Black Politics"; interview with DeVerne Calloway, December 5, 1988, "Strong Seed Planted" Oral History Collection, written transcripts, Box 1, MHS; Clay, *Bill Clay*, 95; and Patterson, *Black City Politics*, 39.

3. Henry, "Structures of Exclusion," 227, 250; William K. Wyant Jr., "Churches of St. Louis Area Have Fought Bias for Years, Aren't Satisfied with Results," *Post-Dispatch*, May 28, 1963, and Michael Dixon, "Civil Rights Groups in This Area Have Grown in Last Two Years," *Post-Dispatch*, August 1965, Negro Scrapbook, vol. 2, MHS; and Clay, *Bill Clay*, 62. See also Martin Luther King Jr., "Letter from Birmingham City Jail," April 16, 1963, in *The Eyes on the Prize Civil Rights Reader: Documents, Speeches, and Firsthand Accounts from the Black Freedom Struggle, 1954–1990*, ed. Clayborne Carson, David J. Garrow, Gerald Gill, Vincent Harding, and Darlene Clark Hine (New York: Penguin, 1991), 153–58.

4. Dawson, *Behind the Mule*, 97; and Stein, *St. Louis Politics*, 128–29.

5. James Boggs, *The American Revolution: Pages from a Negro Worker's Notebook* (New York: Monthly Review Press, 1963), 85; Clarence J. Munford, *Production Relations, Class, and Black Liberation: A Marxist Perspective in Afro-American Studies* (Amsterdam: B. R. Gruner, 1978), 69–71; Calloway, "The NAACP and the Crisis on the Civil Rights Front," Calloway Papers, Box 1, Folder 4, WHMC; Bush, *Not What We Seem*, 65, 155; Sidney M. Willhelm, *Who Needs the Negro?* (Cambridge: Schenkman, 1970), 136; David M. Gordon, "Capitalist Development and the History of American Cities," in *Marxism and the Metropolis: New Perspectives in Urban Political Economy*, ed. William K. Tabb and Larry Sawers, 2nd ed. (New York: Oxford University Press, 1984), 39–47; and Mercantile and Manufacturing Scrapbook, vols. 3–5, MHS.

6. Civic Progress Records, WHMC; City Plan Commission, "A Study of Space Use in the St. Louis Central Business District" (March 1958), Downtown St. Louis, Inc., Records Addenda, 1928–1978, Collection 703, Box 1, Folder 7, WHMC; Mercantile and Manufacturing Scrapbook, vols. 3–5, MHS; Ernest Calloway, "The Nature and Flow of Economic Power: The How and Who of the City's Inner Power Core, and Its Effects," *Missouri Teamster*, November 1, 1963, Calloway Papers, Addenda, Box 4, Folder 108, WHMC; and Heathcott and Murphy, "Corridors of Flight," 166–67.

7. Henry, "Structures of Exclusion," 184, 239, 250; "Plaza Apartments Have 'Safeguards,'" *Argus*, June 1, 1956; Stein, *St. Louis Politics*, 97; Primm, *Lion of the Valley*, 457, 470; Mercantile and Manufacturing Scrapbook, vols. 3–5, MHS; and Calloway, "Nature and Flow."

8. Calloway Papers, Box 1, Folder 7, and Calloway Papers, Addenda, Box 53,

Folder 643, WHMC; Jones, *Fragmented by Design*, 83–84; and Gordon, *Mapping Decline*, 46–49.

9. Clay, "Anatomy of Economic Murder," 7, 23, MHS; Henry, "Structures of Exclusion," 229–30; "C. of C. to Meet on Negro Plea to End Job Bias," *Post-Dispatch*, July 5, 1963, Calloway Papers, Box 6, Folder 58, WHMC; Dick Gregory, *From the Back of the Bus*, ed. Bob Orben (New York: E. P. Dutton, 1962), 59; Ernest Calloway, "The Ultimate Conquest of Negro Economic Inequality," remarks before St. Louis Chapter of the Frontiers International, December 10, 1963, Calloway Papers, Box 1, Folder 5, WHMC; Metropolitan St. Louis Division, Negro American Labor Council, press release, June 5, 1963, Calloway Papers, Box 2, Folder 14, WHMC; Sobel, Hirsch, and Harris, *Negro in St. Louis Economy*, 30–31, 80; and Clay, *Bill Clay*, 249.

10. Robert Jackson, "Furthers Negro Cause Quietly," *Globe-Democrat*, November 12–13, 1963, Negro Scrapbook, vol. 2, MHS; Clay, "Anatomy of Economic Murder," 1–2, MHS; Mercantile and Manufacturing Scrapbook, vol. 3, MHS; and "Says U.S. Jobs Open to Negroes If They're Ready," *Globe-Democrat*, April 7, 1963, and "Negroes File $10 Million Suit against MoPac," *Globe-Democrat*, August 2, 1963, Negro Scrapbook, vol. 1, MHS.

11. Calloway, "The NAACP and New Frontiers," Calloway Papers, Box 1, Folder 4, WHMC; AFL-CIO Industrial Union Department, "Statement on Civil Rights," March 15, 1956, Ganley Papers, Series 1, Box 6, File 40, ALUA; Mercantile and Manufacturing Scrapbook, vol. 3, MHS; Robert Jackson, "Negro Leaders Call Hadley Technical 'Second-Class' School," *Globe-Democrat*, 4–5 May 1963; "First Negro Designated Here for Carpenter Apprenticeship," *Post-Dispatch*, April 6, 1962, "Hill Tells Rally School Board System Is Rotten," *Argus*, September 6, 1963, and Kenneth Jacobson, "N.A.A.C.P. Chooses St. Louis for Drive to Obtain Skilled Jobs," *Post-Dispatch*, April 1, 1962, Negro Scrapbook, vol. 2, MHS; and Patterson, *Black City Politics*, 38; and Henry, "Structures of Exclusion," 189.

12. Clay, "Anatomy of Economic Murder," 9–18, 24, MHS; Calloway, "Nature and Flow"; and Calloway, "The Campaign to Up-Grade Negroes at Southwestern Bell Telephone Co.," report to a special meeting of the St. Louis Division, NALC on the Southwestern Bell Telephone Project, Dining Car Employees Hall, July 6, 1963, Calloway Papers, Box 1, Folder 5, WHMC.

13. Clay, "Anatomy of Economic Murder," 3, 8, 27; Calloway, "Negro Social and Economic Thrust"; and Calloway, "New Job Opportunities."

14. "N.A.A.C.P. Survey Puts Jobs as Top Problem Here," *Post-Dispatch*, July 24, 1960, Negro Scrapbook, vol. 1, MHS; Haywood, *Black Bolshevik*, 667 n. 8; Calloway, "Negro Social and Economic Thrust"; Anderson, *A. Philip Randolph*, 298–99, 319–20; Pfeffer, *A. Philip Randolph*, 21, 206; and Marable, *From the Grassroots*, 83.

15. Henry, "Structures of Exclusion," 245; and "Labor Council Establishes Black Groups for Crusade," *American*, July 5, 1963, Calloway Papers, Box 6, Folder 58, WHMC.

16. "Negro Labor Council Views Job Training," *Argus*, August 23, 1963; and Metropolitan St. Louis Division, NALC, press release, June 5, 1963, and Metropolitan St. Louis Division, NALC, press release, August 1, 1963, Calloway Papers, Box 2, Folder 14, WHMC.

17. Metropolitan St. Louis Division, NALC, press releases, July 8, July 12, and August 1, 1963, Calloway Papers, Box 2, Folder 14; Calloway, "Campaign to Up-Grade Negroes"; and Calloway, "Nature and Flow." See also "Labor Group

to Use All Force in Securing Jobs for Negroes," *American,* July 11, 1963, Calloway Papers, Box 6, Folder 58, WHMC.

18. Calloway, "Campaign to Up-Grade Negroes"; and Metropolitan St. Louis Division, NALC, press releases, July 8 and July 12, 1963, Calloway Papers, Box 2, Folder 14. WHMC; Metropolitan St. Louis Division, NALC, press release, July 19, 1963, Calloway Papers, Box 2, Folder 14; "Negro Council Drops Phone Firm Picketing Plans," *Globe-Democrat,* July 17, 1963; and "Council Calls Off Pickets, Tells of Gains," *Argus,* July 19, 1963, Calloway Papers, Box 6, Folder 58, WHMC.

19. "Labor Council Cracks Phone Co. Crafts," *Argus,* August 9, 1963; "C. of C. to Meet on Negro Plea to End Job Bias"; "Calloway Accused of Soft Approach," *Defender,* August 21, 1963; and "Why Did Ernest Calloway Back Down?" *St. Louis Defender,* July 17, 1963, Calloway Papers, Box 6, Folder 58, WHMC. See also Anderson, *A. Philip Randolph,* 306; and Pfeffer, *A. Philip Randolph,* 235–39.

20. St. Louis Division, NALC, press release, October 6, 1963; G. Newton Cox, Coca-Cola Bottling Co. of St. Louis, letter to Mr. Ernest Calloway, October 25, 1963; Edward J. Fitzgerald, president, Canada Dry Bottling Company of St. Louis, Inc., letter to Mr. Ernest Calloway, President, St. Louis NALC, October 29, 1963; and A. F. Oberbeck, President, Vess Bottling Company of St. Louis, letter to Mr. Ernest Calloway, November 4, 1963, Calloway Papers, Box 2, Folder 14, WHMC.

21. Job Opportunities Committee, St. Louis Metropolitan Council of NAACP Branches, "Lever Brothers, U.S.A.," fact sheet; "Metropolitan St. Louis NAACP's Project on Fair Employment at Lever Bros. Plant Located in the St. Louis Area," April 1964; JOC, St. Louis Metropolitan Council of NAACP Branches, "Brief Outline of a Series of Proposals by the St. Louis Metropolitan Council of NAACP Branches to the Management of the Lever Brothers Plant in the St. Louis Area on the Matter of a Fair Employment Program (Proposed April 7, 1964)"; NAACP Council of the St. Louis Metropolitan Area, press release, April 16, 1964; and JOC, NAACP Council of the St. Louis Metropolitan Area, leaflet, April 1964, Calloway Papers, Box 1, Folder 10, WHMC. See also Ernest Calloway, "The Lever Brothers Campaign: Its Background and Thrust," report to the Metropolitan St. Louis NAACP Council on Progress of Job Drive at Lever Brothers, April 25, 1964, Calloway Papers, Box 1, Folder 5, WHMC.

22. "Extends Lever Brothers Detergent and Selective Buying Drive to 10-State Area," *Truth* (United Freedom Front of St. Louis), Calloway Papers, Box 4, Folder 45, WHMC.

23. William K. Wyant Jr., "Negroes Constitute Two-Thirds of Jobless in City and County Despite Removal of Barriers," *Post-Dispatch,* June 12, 1963, and Jackson, "Furthers Negro Cause Quietly"; and Calloway, "Ultimate Conquest."

24. Stein, *St. Louis Politics,* 96; Primm, *Lion of the Valley,* 462, 466, 468; Henry, "Structures of Exclusion," 185, 201; and "In Support of the Mill Creek Massive Slum Clearance Program," Ernest Calloway, statement before the Housing and Land Clearance Committee of the St. Louis Board of Aldermen, Kiel Auditorium, March 17, 1958, Calloway Papers, Box 1, Folder 4, WHMC.

25. Dreer, "Negro Leadership," 259; Sobel, Hirsch, and Harris, *Negro in St. Louis Economy,* 16; Sidney R. Redmond, "Public Housing Policies Need to Be Changed," *Argus,* July 20, 1956; Stein, *St. Louis Politics,* 96; and Primm, *Lion of the Valley,* 461.

26. "Through the Eyes of a Child" Oral History Project, written transcripts,

MHS; Stein, *St. Louis Politics*, 85–86, 95–97; Primm, *Lion of the Valley*, 463, 496–97; St. Louis City Plan Commission, *History*, 34–35; Lee Rainwater, *Behind Ghetto Walls: Black Family Life in a Federal Slum* (Chicago: Aldine, 1970); Naomi W. Lede, *A Statistical Profile of the Negro in St. Louis: Research Report of the Urban League of St. Louis* (St. Louis: Urban League of St. Louis, 1965), 65–66, and "Through the Eyes of a Child," Oral History Project, written transcripts, MHS. See also Joseph Heathcott, "The City Remade: Public Housing and the Urban Landscape in St. Louis, 1900–1960," Ph.D. diss., Indiana University, 2002, 444.

27. Dreer, "Negro Leadership," 151–53; Lede, *Statistical Profile*, 9–10, 43–44; Primm, *Lion of the Valley*, 485–89; Stein, *St. Louis Politics*, 129, 141. See also "95% of State's Negro Students Desegregated, Survey Shows," *Post-Dispatch*, June 7, 1959, "The Negro Population in St. Louis," *Post-Dispatch*, June 5, 1961, and "Negroes in City Move West Rapidly, Survey Shows," *Globe-Democrat*, March 16, 1961, Negro Scrapbook, vol. 1, MHS.

28. Dreer, "Negro Leadership," 73–74; Howard B. Woods, "Under Redevelopment," *Argus*, July 6, 1956; Sobel, Hirsch, and Harris, *Negro in St. Louis Economy*, 16; Lede, *Statistical Profile*, 24; Lipsitz, *Life in the Struggle*, 68; and Primm, *Lion of the Valley*, 468.

29. "Negro Families Have Moved into 10 Cities in the County," *Post-Dispatch*, November 10, 1963, "Jennings to Act on Stoning of Negroes' Home," *Post-Dispatch*, January 2, 1964, and Richard Jacobs, "Nights of Terror Follow Move by Negroes into Jennings Home," *Post-Dispatch*, January 5, 1964, Negro Scrapbook, vol. 2, MHS; and Robert J. Byrne, "Freedom of Residence Idea Gets Boost," *St. Louis Review*, November 9, 1962, Freedom of Residence, Greater St. Louis Committee, Records, 1962–1969, Collection 438, Folder 23, WHMC.

30. "A Wall of Opportunity," news editorial, *Post-Dispatch*, November 13, 1962; "Prominent St. Louisans in Group Working to End Housing Bias," *Post-Dispatch*, August 19, 1962; and Byrne, "Freedom of Residence."

31. "Prominent St. Louisans in Group Working to End Housing Bias," *Post-Dispatch*, August 19, 1962; "Negro Families Have Moved into 10 Cities in the County," *Post-Dispatch*, November 10, 1963, Negro Scrapbook, vol. 2, MHS; and Byrne, "Freedom of Residence."

32. Anderson, *A. Philip Randolph*, 323; and Pfeffer, *A. Philip Randolph*, 180; Willhelm, *Who Needs the Negro?* 90; "95% of State's Negro Students Desegregated, Survey Shows," Negro Scrapbook, vol. 1; and Naomi W. Lede, *De Facto School Segregation in St. Louis*, 22–23, MHS.

33. Lede, *De Facto School Segregation*, 43–44, 50, MHS; "Rights Group to Study Pupil Complaints Here," *Globe-Democrat*, February 19, 1960, Negro Scrapbook, vol. 1. MHS; Jeanne Theoharis, "'I'd Rather Go to School in the South': How Boston's School Desegregation Complicates the Civil Rights Paradigm," in Theoharis and Woodard, *Freedom North*, 134; and Willhelm, *Who Needs the Negro?* 92.

34. Lede, *De Facto School Segregation*, 37–38, MHS; and "Negroes Consider Legal Action on School Policy," *Globe-Democrat*, July 27–28, 1963, and Buddy Lonesome, "NAACP Asks End of School Bias in Federal Law Suit Filed Here," *Argus*, August 30, 1963, Negro Scrapbook, vol. 2, MHS.

35. Lede, *De Facto School Segregation*, 37–38, MHS; "Hickey Report Disappoints 2 Integrationists," *Globe-Democrat*, July 25, 1963, Negro Scrapbook, vol. 1, MHS; "Police Reserve to Stand by as Negroes Protest Here," *Post-Dispatch*, June 20, 1963, and Lonesome, "NAACP Asks End"; and Meier and Rudwick, *CORE*, 246.

36. Interview of Jerome Williams, "Strong Seed Planted" Oral History Collection, written transcripts, Box 2, MHS; and William K. Wyant, "Churches of St. Louis," and "Police Reserve to Stand by as Negroes Protest Here," *Post-Dispatch,* June 20, 1963, Negro Scrapbook, vol. 2, MHS.

37. "Protest Rally Small, Orderly," *Globe-Democrat,* June 21, 1963, Negro Scrapbook, vol. 2, MHS.

38. "Protest Rally Small, Orderly," "Negroes Consider Legal Action on School Policy," *Globe-Democrat,* July 27–28, 1963; and "NAACP Prepares School Suit Here," *Globe-Democrat,* July 27, 1963, Negro Scrapbook, vol. 2, MHS.

39. "School Demonstration Scheduled for September 1," *Argus,* August 16, 1963; "NAACP Says Politics in Withdrawal," *Argus,* August 30, 1963; Buddy Lonesome, "Grass Roots Show Lack of Knowledge," *Argus,* August 30, 1963; and "Hill Tells Rally School Board System Is Rotten," *Argus,* September 6, 1963, Negro Scrapbook, vol. 2, MHS. See also Theoharis, "'I'd Rather Go to School,'" 135.

40. "Negroes Picket in Kottmeyer's Office Against Add-on Rooms," *Post-Dispatch,* February 3, 1964; and "NAACP Demands Kottmeyer's Ouster, Special Board Meeting," *Post-Dispatch,* February 4, 1964, Negro Scrapbook, vol. 2, MHS.

41. "Hicks Opposes Negro Attack on School Tax," *Post-Dispatch,* January 25, 1964, Negro Scrapbook, vol. 2, MHS.

42. "22,313 Police Checks Yield 122 Weapons," *Globe-Democrat,* June 30, 1961, and "Weiss Raps Police Auto Search Tactic," *Globe-Democrat,* June 30, 1961, Calloway Papers, Box 2, Folder 13, WHMC; Lipsitz, *Life in the Struggle,* 70; and Clay, *Bill Clay,* 62.

43. The indignity prompted Clay to introduce an ordinance in the Board of Aldermen prohibiting the release of police records to the general public, except in cases when convictions followed arrests. M. Leon Bohanon, Executive Director, Urban League of St. Louis, letter to Col. H. Sam Priest, President, Board of Police Commissioners, December 13, 1961, and William L. Clay, Alderman, press release, September 18, 1962, Calloway Papers, Box 2, Folder 13, WHMC; and "Disrupting Racial Harmony," St. Louis Argus Publishing Company, United Negro Citizens, paid advertisement, *Globe-Democrat,* September 29, 1960, Negro Scrapbook, vol. 1, MHS. See also Clay, *Bill Clay,* 62–64.

44. Margaret Bush Wilson, President, St. Louis Branch NAACP, press release, May 15, 1962; Norman R. Seay, Chairman, Special Committee on Police Affairs, NAACP, statement and fact sheet on segregation and discrimination against Negroes in the St. Louis Police Department, May 5, 1962; "NAACP Charges Bias in Jobs by Police Dept.," *Globe-Democrat,* March 6, 1962; and "Police Force Accused of Lag in Ending Bias," *Post-Dispatch,* March 6, 1962, Calloway Papers Box 2, Folder 13, WHMC.

45. Wilson, NAACP press release, May 15, 1962; Ernest Calloway, "The Fine Arts of Obscuring a Public Issue," *New Citizen,* May 18, 1962; "Police Picketed, Board Denies Discrimination," *Post-Dispatch,* May 13, 1962; "A Disgraceful Performance," news editorial, *Globe-Democrat,* May 14, 1962; and "N.A.A.C.P. Invites Politicians to Hear Charges against Police," *Post-Dispatch,* May 16, 1962, Calloway Papers, Box 2, Folder 13, WHMC.

46. "4 Gas Bombs Hurled into Negro Crowd," *Globe-Democrat,* July 7, 1964, Negro Scrapbook, vol. 2, MHS. See also the Kerner Commission's *Report of the National Advisory Commission on Civil Disorders* (Washington, D.C.: Government Printing Office, 1968).

47. Kinloch History Committee Records, Folders 6 and 7, WHMC; and

"Aged Couple Flees Home to Avert Flames," *Globe-Democrat*, September 26, 1962, Negro Scrapbook, vol. 2, MHS.

48. Lede, *De Facto School Segregation*, 67.

49. "Through the Eyes of a Child" Oral History Project, written transcripts, MHS. See also Peter L. Goldman's four-part series on the Nation of Islam, published in the *Globe-Democrat* in early January 1962, Negro Scrapbook, vol. 2, MHS.

50. Peter Goldman, "Black Muslims Fail to Flourish Here," *Globe-Democrat*, January 2, 1962; Goldman, "Racial Harmony Here Stunts Growth of Muslims," *Globe-Democrat*, January 3, 1962; and "Black Muslim Inroads Here Called Slight," *Post-Dispatch*, August 14, 1962, Negro Scrapbook, vol. 2, MHS.

51. Goldman, "Attitudes of Negro Leaders Vary on Black Muslims," *Globe-Democrat*, January 5, 1962; "Black Muslim Leader Says 'Rule' of Whites Is Coming to an End," *Globe-Democrat*, August 13, 1962; "2000 Hear Black Muslim Chief Predict End of White Race's Rule," *Post-Dispatch*, August 13, 1962; Robert H. Collins, "Black Muslims Fail to Gain Members Here," *Post-Dispatch*, June 2, 1963; "Black Muslims Draw 3000 to Kiel Rally," *Argus*, August 17, 1962; and "Malcolm X Explains Muslim Objectives," *Globe-Democrat*, April 12, 1963, Negro Scrapbook, Vols. 1–2, MHS.

52. Malcolm X, "Message to the Grassroots," in *Malcolm X Speaks*, ed. George Breitman (New York: Ballantine, 1973), 1–16.

53. Jackson, "Furthers Negro Cause Quietly"; and Timothy J. Hogan, "Rev. King Praises Integration Here," *Globe-Democrat*, May 29, 1963, Negro Scrapbook, vol. 2, MHS.

54. Granich-Kovarik, "Picket Line to Courtroom," 17–20; Hillier, "Redlining," 413; and Primm, *Lion of the Valley*, 478.

CHAPTER SIX

1. Meier and Rudwick, *CORE*, 224; "200 St. Louisans Go to Washington March," *Globe-Democrat*, August 28, 1963, Negro Scrapbook, vol. 2, MHS; "St. Louis Has 300 at March," *Argus*, August 30, 1963; Anderson, *A. Philip Randolph*, 324; and Pfeffer, *A. Philip Randolph*, 246.

2. Meier and Rudwick, *CORE*, 93–95, 131–35; and "3 St. Louis Freedom Riders Jailed at Jackson, Miss., in Airport Test," *Post-Dispatch*, June 8, 1961, and "4 Freedom Riders Return from South," *Globe-Democrat*, July 18, 1961, Negro Scrapbook, vol. 1, MHS.

3. Bell, *CORE*, 17; and Meier and Rudwick, *CORE*, 124, 148, 237.

4. Meier and Rudwick, *CORE*, 190, 229.

5. Ibid., 151; Marvin Rich, "Civil Rights Strategy after the March," *New Politics* 2 (Fall 1963): 43–52; Lipsitz, *Life in the Struggle*, 57–61, 69–70. The quote is also from Lipsitz, 63.

6. Florence Shinkle, "Climbing toward Equality? Percy Green Predicts That Activism Will Rise Again," *Post-Dispatch*, March 8, 1992, 12; and interview with Percy Green, "Strong Seed Planted" Oral History Collection, written transcripts, Box 1, MHS. See also Gerald J. Meyer, "Percy Green's Tactic: Stir Public Outrage," *Post-Dispatch*, July 12, 1970, Negro Scrapbook, vol. 3, MHS.

7. Interview with Green, "Strong Seed Planted" Oral History Collection, written transcripts, Box 1, MHS.

8. Ibid.

9. Meier and Rudwick, *CORE,* 194.

10. Interview with Green, "Strong Seed Planted" Oral History Collection, written transcripts, Box 1, MHS.

11. Ibid.; and David Benjamin Oppenheimer, "The Story of *Green v. McDonnell Douglas,*" in *Employment Discrimination Stories,* ed. Joel William Friedman (New York: Foundation Press, 2006), 16.

12. Bell, *CORE,* 59–61.

13. "Leader of CORE Drive on Banks Says Race Fight Is Really a War," *Post-Dispatch,* Negro Scrapbook, vol. 2. MHS.

14. Interview with Green, "Strong Seed Planted" Oral History Collection, written transcripts, Box 1; and Munro Roberts III, "Racial Fight Replaces Religion for Rebellious Gene Tournour," *Globe-Democrat,* November 16–17, 1963, Negro Scrapbook, vol. 2, MHS.

15. "Negroes Constitute Two-Thirds of Jobless in City and County Despite Removal of Barriers," *Post-Dispatch,* June 12, 1963, Negro Scrapbook, vol. 2; interview with DeVerne Calloway, "Strong Seed Planted" Oral History Collection, written transcripts, Box 1; and "Through the Eyes of a Child" Oral History Project, written transcripts, MHS.

16. "1,200 March on Capital to Protest Civil Rights Failure," *Argus,* August 16, 1963.

17. "Leader of CORE Drive on Banks Says Race Fight Is Really a War," and Roberts, "Racial Fight Replaces Religion"; "Negroes Pray for Jobs in Demonstration at Banks," *Globe-Democrat,* August 15, 1963; and "Eastside Protests Mount!" *Argus,* August 16, 1963, Negro Scrapbook, vol. 2. MHS. See also Meier and Rudwick, *CORE,* 236.

18. "Showdown Nears on CORE Job Fight Ultimatum," *Argus,* August 30, 1963, and "Leader of CORE Drive on Banks Says Race Fight Is Really a War," Negro Scrapbook, vol. 2, MHS; and Patterson, *Black City Politics,* 92.

19. "Firms Here Tell CORE Job Quota Demands Will Be Turned Down," *Globe-Democrat,* August 28, 1963, Negro Scrapbook, vol. 2, MHS.

20. "Seven Banks Adopt 10-Point Job Equality Program for Negroes," *Globe-Democrat,* August 30, 1963, Negro Scrapbook, vol. 2, MHS. See also Gina L. Henderson, "The Civil Rights Movement in St. Louis, 1954–1970: A Sociohistorical Perspective," senior thesis, Washington University, 1980, 39, WHMC; and Clay, *Bill Clay,* 115.

21. "9 Leaders of Bank Demonstration Arrested for Contempt of Court," *Globe-Democrat,* September 2, 1963, Negro Scrapbook, vol. 2, MHS; and Virginia Brodine, "The Strange Case of the Jefferson Bank vs. CORE," *FOCUS/Midwest,* 1964, 13.

22. Clay, *Bill Clay,* 109; and Brodine, "Strange Case," 12.

23. "9 Leaders of Bank Demonstration Arrested for Contempt of Court," Negro Scrapbook, vol. 2, MHS; Brodine, "Strange Case," 14; and Clay, *Bill Clay,* 111.

24. "15 Convictions in Protests at Bank Upheld, Four Reversed," *Post-Dispatch,* January 15, 1964, and Roberts, "Racial Fight Replaces Religion"; and Patterson, *Black City Politics,* 104, 111, 157.

25. Denny Walsh, "Inside CORE" series, *Globe-Democrat,* December 27, 1963–January 7, 1964, Negro Scrapbook, vol. 2, MHS; Brodine, "Strange Case," 24; and Meier and Rudwick, *CORE,* 227.

26. Curtis Stadtfeld, "Two Aldermen, House Member Arrested at Jefferson

Bank," *Post-Dispatch*, October 12, 1963, Negro Scrapbook, vol. 2, MHS; and Clay, *Bill Clay*, 113.

27. "Review of Cases of 19 Convicted Demonstrators Being Sought," *Post-Dispatch*, October 29, 1963, and "Text of Judge Scott's Pre-sentence Statement," *Globe-Democrat*, October 25, 1963, Negro Scrapbook, vol. 2, MHS; and Meier and Rudwick, *CORE*, 233–34.

28. "Ministers Urge Buying Boycott Nov. 14 and 15 in Bias Protest," *Post-Dispatch*, October 30, 1963, and "CORE Petitions Supreme Court to Release 15," *Post-Dispatch*, January 23, 1964, Negro Scrapbook, vol. 2, MHS; and Brodine, "Strange Case," 15.

29. "Tucker Urges Ban on Disorder and Asks Bank to Observe Pact," *Post-Dispatch*, October 29, 1963, Negro Scrapbook, vol. 2, MHS; and Patterson, *Black City Politics*, 110.

30. Henderson, "Civil Rights Movement," 39; and "Ministers Urge Buying Boycott Nov. 14 and 15 in Bias Protest," and "Review of Cases of 19 Convicted Demonstrators Being Sought," Negro Scrapbook, vol. 2, MHS. See also Patterson, *Black City Politics*, 168–70.

31. "8 Spend Night in City Hall in 'Jim Crow' Bank Demonstration," Negro Scrapbook, vol. 2, MHS; and Patterson, *Black City Politics*, 169.

32. "Review of Cases of 19 Convicted Demonstrators Being Sought," Negro Scrapbook, vol. 2, MHS; and Brodine, "Strange Case," 24.

33. "Ministers Urge Buying Boycott Nov. 14 and 15 in Bias Protest," and "Review of Cases Of 19 Convicted Demonstrators Being Sought," Negro Scrapbook, vol. 2, MHS; and Brodine, "Strange Case," 15.

34. "Minister Group Opens Drive to Halt Buying as Rights Protest," *Post-Dispatch*, November 14, 1963, Negro Scrapbook, vol. 2, MHS.

35. "19 Are Freed on Bail Bonds in Race Case," *Post-Dispatch*, November 1, 1963, Negro Scrapbook, vol. 2, MHS.

36. "Few Groups Back Holiday Buying Boycott," *Post-Dispatch*, November 21, 1963, Negro Scrapbook, vol. 2, MHS.

37. Interview with Jerome Williams, "Strong Seed Planted" Oral History Collection, written transcripts, Box 2, MHS; Richard Jacobs, "The Rev. Amos Ryce Proves an Enigma for Some in Civil Rights Movement," *Post-Dispatch*, March 4, 1964, Negro Scrapbook, vol. 2, MHS; and Patterson, *Black City Politics*, 110. See also Chappell, Hutchinson, and Ward, "Dress Modestly."

38. Boggs, *The American Revolution*, 83; "CORE's Tactics Criticised by NAACP Leader," *Globe-Democrat*, November 7, 1963, and "Review of Cases of 19 Convicted Demonstrators Being Sought," Negro Scrapbook, vol. 2, MHS; "CORE Made Error in Violating Order, Sen. McNeal Asserts," *Globe-Democrat*, October 21, 1963; and Meier and Rudwick, *CORE*, 230–32.

39. Calloway, "The NAACP and New Frontiers," and Ernest Calloway, "Some Working Lessons from the CORE-Jefferson Bank Controversy," comments before the St. Louis Division of the NALC, Dining Car Employees Hall, October 27, 1963, Calloway Papers, Box 1, Folders 4–5, WHMC. See also Patterson, *Black City Politics*, 118; and Levy, *Civil War*, 92–102.

40. Calloway, "Some Working Lessons."

41. Calloway, "Ultimate Conquest."

42. Walsh, "Inside CORE."

43. "Two Arrested for Blocking Door to Office at City Hall," *Post-Dispatch*,

November 12, 1963, Negro Scrapbook, vol. 2, MHS; and Meier and Rudwick, *CORE*, 233–34.

44. Calloway Papers, Addenda, Box 46, Folders 520 and 525; Jim Miller, "Jack Dwyer, White Boss of All-Negro 4th Ward Reaches Out for Control of Entire Negro Area," *Defender*, October 1, 1963, Calloway Papers, Box 2, Folder 18, WHMC; Cawthra, "Ernest Calloway," 14; and Clay, *Bill Clay*, 80, 91.

45. Walsh, "Inside CORE," "Few Groups Back Holiday Buying Boycott," and "11 Choose Jail over Probation in Bias Protest," *Post-Dispatch*, December 18, 1963, Negro Scrapbook, vol. 2, MHS; Meier and Rudwick, *CORE*, 233–34; and Lipsitz, *Life in the Struggle*, 77–80.

46. Jackson, "Furthers Negro Cause Quietly"; and Walsh, "Inside CORE"; and Patterson, *Black City Politics*, 112.

47. Walsh, "Inside CORE."

48. See Kenneth O'Reilly, *"Racial Matters": The FBI's Secret File on Black America, 1960–1972* (New York: Free Press, 1989); "State Agency Studies Charge of Job Bias at Jefferson Bank," *Post-Dispatch*, December 19, 1963; "22 Protesters in CORE Group in Court after Holiday in Jail," *Post-Dispatch*, January 2, 1964; "Jail Won't Block Drive to Win Equality, Alderman Clay Says," *Post-Dispatch*, January 14, 1964; and "15 CORE Leaders Go Back to Jail As Appeals Court Upholds Scott," *Globe-Democrat*, January 16, 1964, Negro Scrapbook, vol. 2, MHS.

49. "15 Convictions in Protests at Bank Upheld, Four Reversed," *Post-Dispatch*, January 15, 1964; "60 Supporters Circle City Jail and Sing to Clay," *Post-Dispatch*, January 19, 1964; "15 Who Lost Appeal in Bank Protests Plan Further Pleas," *Globe-Democrat*, January 16, 1964; "CORE Will Ask State Supreme Court Monday to Release 15," *Post-Dispatch*, January 17, 1964; "CORE Petitions Supreme Court to Release 15," *Post-Dispatch*, January 23, 1964; and "Writs Denied, CORE Lawyers Meet on Action to Release 15," *Post-Dispatch*, February 1, 1964, Negro Scrapbook, vol. 2, MHS. See also Clay, *Bill Clay*, 24, 33, 117.

50. "CORE Will Ask State Supreme Court Monday to Release 15," Negro Scrapbook, vol. 2, MHS; and Clay, *Bill Clay*, 121–22.

51. "Writs Denied, CORE Lawyers Meet on Action to Release 15"; "86 Arrested, Balk at Release, in CORE Protest," *Globe-Democrat*, February 15, 1964; and "84 Arrested as Police Halt Racial March to Johnson's Hotel," *Post-Dispatch*, February 16, 1964, Negro Scrapbook, vol. 2, MHS. See also Henderson, "Civil Rights Movement," 44–45.

52. "Mrs. Freeman Named to U.S. Rights Group," *Globe-Democrat*, March 2, 1964, Negro Scrapbook, vol. 1, MHS; interview with Frankie M. Freeman, "Strong Seed Planted" Oral History Collection, written transcripts, Box 1. MHS; and Freeman, *Song of Faith*, 86–88.

53. Meier and Rudwick, *CORE*, 312; Patterson, *Black City Politics*, 111; and Joseph Schuster, "The Warrior," *Riverfront Times*, October 19–25, 1988, 8.

54. Calloway, "St. Louis Black Politics," and "The Powerful 26th Ward Regular Democratic Organization Announced Its Endorsement," n.d., Calloway Papers, Box 2, Folder 17, WHMC; and Stephen Darst and Ray J. Noonan, "Political Overtones in CORE Action," *Globe-Democrat*, November 16, 1963, Calloway Papers, Addenda, Box 46, Folder 520, WHMC. See also Patterson, *Black City Politics*, 185, 201–2, 219; and Clay, *Bill Clay*, 270.

55. "The Strange Political Marriage between Mo. Segregationists and St. Louis 'Militants,'" *Truth* (United Freedom Front of St. Louis), May 1964, Cal-

loway Papers, Box 4, Folder 45, WHMC; Clay, *Bill Clay*, 131–32; and Patterson, *Black City Politics*, 225–26.

56. Ernest Calloway, "How to Unite Negroes through Massive Division," *Truth*, March–April 1964, Calloway Papers, Box 4, Folder 45, WHMC.

57. Calloway Papers, Addenda, Box 46, File 525, WHMC; Manuel Chait, "St. Louis NAACP Drifts Aimlessly, State Officer Says; Blames Leaders," *Post-Dispatch*, December 3, 1964, Negro Scrapbook, vol. 2, MHS; and "2 Strategists Fail in Bid for NAACP Board," *Argus*, March 5, 1965, 4A.

58. "2 Strategists Fail in Bid for NAACP Board."

59. "Henry Winfield Wheeler Succumbs after Illness," and "Henry Wheeler's Contribution," editorial, *Argus*, June 5, 1964; and "Memorial to Mr. Wheeler Is Sunday at St. Paul," *Argus*, June 12, 1964.

60. "Memorial to Mr. Wheeler Is Sunday at St. Paul," *Argus*, June 12, 1964; Calloway, "Unions—Instrument of Counter-Pressure," *Missouri Teamster*, December 6, 1963, Calloway Papers, Addenda, Box 4, Folder 108, WHMC. See also "Stores Report 32 Pct. Rise in Employment of Negroes Here," *Post-Dispatch*, July 14, 1964; Richard Jacobs, "Negro Leaders Call Advances Here Limited in Last 2 Years," *Post-Dispatch*, August 2, 1965; Ted Schafers, "Washington Eyes Progress of Negro Job-Training Here," *Globe-Democrat*, September 25–26, 1965; and E. F. Porter Jr., "Despite Nonbias, Few Negroes Are Building Trade Apprentices," *Post-Dispatch*, October 10, 1965, Negro Scrapbook, vol. 2, MHS.

61. "Ex-CORE Head Calls Job Bias Serious Here," *Globe-Democrat*, August 28, 1964, Negro Scrapbook, vol. 2, MHS.

62. "Two CORE Members Climb Arch Leg and Refuse Appeals to Come Down," *Post-Dispatch*, July 14, 1964; "CORE Member Gets 30 Days, Is Fined $250 for Climbing Arch," *Post-Dispatch*, July 15, 1964; and "Arch Climber Gets 30 Days, Fined $250," *Globe-Democrat*, July 16, 1964, Negro Scrapbook, vol. 2, MHS. See also Lipsitz, *Life in the Struggle*, 84–85; Robert J. Moore Jr., "Showdown under the Arch: The Construction Trades and the First 'Pattern or Practice' Equal Employment Opportunity Suit, 1966," *Gateway Heritage* 15 (1994–95): 30–43; Thomas J. Sugrue, "Affirmative Action from Below: Civil Rights, the Building Trades, and the Politics of Racial Equality in the Urban North, 1945–1969," *Journal of American History* 91 (2004): 145–73; Flug, "Organized Labor," 325; and MacLean, *Freedom Is Not Enough*, 92. See also Brian Purnell, "'Drive Awhile for Freedom': Brooklyn CORE's 1964 Stall-in and Public Discourses on Protest Violence," in *Groundwork: Local Black Freedom Movements in America*, ed. Jeanne Theoharis and Komozi Woodard (New York: New York University Press, 2005), 45–75.

63. James C. Millstone, "Arch Symbolizes Hope in St. Louis," *New York Times*, January 6, 1964, 92; and Donald Janson, "Arch in St. Louis Inching Skyward," *New York Times*, August 30, 1964, 73.

CHAPTER SEVEN

1. Calloway, "St. Louis Mayoralty Elections"; Kerstein, "Political Consequences," 95–96, 260–61; Clay, *Bill Clay*, 145; and Patterson, *Black City Politics*, 228.

2. "'Savages in Jungle' Author Slated for Top Position If Tucker Loses," *Argus*, March 5, 1965; Buddy Lonesome, "Says Cervantes Runs Cabs with Racist Policies," *Argus*, February 5, 1965; "We Ask Again, Where Does He Stand?" news editorial, *Argus*, March 5, 1965; "William L. Clay Named to Head New Commit-

tee on Negro Jobs," *Post-Dispatch,* August 27, 1965; and "Mayor, Negro Leaders Review Race Program," *Post-Dispatch,* August 26, 1965, Negro Scrapbook, vol. 2, MHS. See also Clay, *Bill Clay,* 147.

3. "William L. Clay Named to Head New Committee on Negro Jobs," and "Cervantes Asks Time on Negro Problems," *Globe-Democrat,* August 27, 1965, Negro Scrapbook, vol. 2, MHS; Clay, *Bill Clay,* 148–49; and Patterson, *Black City Politics,* 233–34.

4. Jacobs, "Negro Leaders"; interview with Ivory Perry, "Strong Seed Planted" Oral History Collection, written transcripts, Box 1, MHS; and Clay, *Bill Clay,* 122, 125–26.

5. Willhelm, *Who Needs the Negro?* 258; and Ernest Calloway, "By Statistics, City Could Become Riot Leader," *Missouri Teamster,* January 5, 1968, Calloway Papers, Addenda, Box 5, Folder 128, WHMC. See also Clay, *Bill Clay,* 102; Patterson, *Black City Politics,* 202; Gordon, *Mapping Decline,* 23; Roger Yockey, "Fight to End St. Louis Area Job Bias Making Headway," *Globe-Democrat,* July 1, 1968; Al Delugach, "Area Has Nation's Worst Case of Negro Joblessness," *Globe-Democrat,* February 14, 1968; Delugach, "'Hard-Core Jobless' Term Fits Many Negroes," *Globe-Democrat,* February 15, 1968; "Negro Steamfitters at Busch Brewery," *Post-Dispatch,* July 25, 1968; and "Negro Opportunities Called Few in County," *Post-Dispatch,* January 15, 1970, Negro Scrapbook, vol. 3, MHS.

6. Henry, "Structures of Exclusion," iv, 168, 210; Philip C. Hauck, "The St. Louis Blues: Will They Ever Finish That Gateway Arch?" *Wall Street Journal,* July 14, 1967, 1; John Herbers, "U.S. Court Weighs 'Gateway' Tie-Up," *New York Times,* February 4, 1966, 16; Herbers, "U.S. Sues Unions to Halt Job Bias," *New York Times,* February 5, 1966, 1; "Sam Sharpens Teeth to Bite Craft Unions," *New York Amsterdam News,* May 28, 1966, 12; Moore, "Showdown under the Arch," 30–31; and MacLean, *Freedom Is Not Enough,* 92–93.

7. Jacobs, "Negro Leaders"; Calloway, "By Statistics"; and Lede, *De Facto School Segregation,* 61.

8. Calloway Papers, Addenda, Box 5, Folders 128 and 139, WHMC; and Gordon, *Mapping Decline,* 102.

9. James C. Millstone, "St. Louis Housing Suit Has Striking Parallels with Dred Scott Case," *Post-Dispatch,* December 10, 1967, and Al Delugach, "Efforts to Find Housing Outside Negro Ghetto Hit Stone Wall," *Globe-Democrat,* September 7, 1967, Freedom of Residence Committee Records, Folder 27, WHMC; and Timothy Bleck, "Pair 'Just Wanted a House'; Issue Has Gone to High Court," *Post-Dispatch,* October 29, 1967, Race Relations Collection, Box 1, File 3, MHS.

10. *United States v. City of Black Jack, Missouri,* 508 F.2d 1179 (8th Cir. 1974).

11. Teaford, *Twentieth-Century American City,* 125; "Negro Opportunities Called Few in County," Negro Scrapbook, vol. 3, MHS; and Timothy Bleck, "Rap Brown Urges E. St. Louisans to Get Arms," and "Negroes Invade Police Station, Press Offices," *Post-Dispatch,* September 11, 1967, Negro Scrapbook, vol. 2, MHS. See also Edward C. Burks, "2 East St. Louis Negroes Hurt by Firebomb as Unrest Goes On," *New York Times,* September 13, 1967, 32; and Jones, *Fragmented by Design,* 28.

12. Calloway, "By Statistics"; Timothy Bleck, "Panel Members Tell Why Riots Were Averted Here," *Post-Dispatch,* January 18, 1968; and "St. Louisans Join in Tribute," *Post-Dispatch,* April 9, 1968, Negro Scrapbook, vol. 3, MHS. See also interviews with Freeman and Perry, "Strong Seed Planted" Oral History Collection, written transcripts, Box 1, MHS; and Timothy Bleck, "Poverty, Decay Hand-in-

Hand on Thomas Street," *Post-Dispatch*, supl. *Everyday Magazine*, September 7, 1967, 3.

13. Kerstein, "Political Consequences," 37–38, 134, 143; and Lede, *De Facto School Segregation*, 61.

14. Lede, *De Facto School Segregation*, 61; Kerstein, "Political Consequences," 132, 137, 167, 175, 179; and Ernest Calloway, "Creative Self-Determinism," *St. Louis Sentinel*, August 23, 1969, Calloway Papers, Addenda, Box 5, Folder 139, WHMC.

15. Kerstein, "Political Consequences," 143–44, 222–24.

16. Benjamin Looker, *"Point from Which Creation Begins": The Black Artists' Group of St. Louis* (St. Louis: Missouri Historical Society Press, 2004), 42–43; Jolly, *Black Liberation*, 68; and Lipsitz, *Life in the Struggle*, 173–79. See also Lisa Gayle Hazirjian, "Combating NEED: Urban Conflict and the Transformation of the War on Poverty and the African American Freedom Struggle in Rocky Mount, North Carolina," *Journal of Urban History* 34 (May 2008): 639–64.

17. Cawthra, "Ernest Calloway," 14; Bussel, "Trade Union Oriented," 53–57; Marable, *Race, Reform, and Rebellion*, 114; Brill, *The Teamsters*, 357, 375, 377; Lipsitz, *Rainbow at Midnight*, 5; Jones, *Fragmented by Design*, 114; and Anderson, *A. Philip Randolph*, 309–10, 312.

18. George Morrison, "Ghetto Area Group Flexing Its Muscle," *Globe-Democrat*, September 16, 1968, Negro Scrapbook, vol. 3, MHS.

19. "CORE May End Protests Here If Disorders Occur Again," *Post-Dispatch*, September 29, 1966, Negro Scrapbook, vol. 2, MHS.

20. Jolly, *Black Liberation*, 42, 52–59; Patterson, *Black City Politics*, 238–39, 242–45; Timothy Bleck, "Negro Unity as Hard to Attain as Equality," *Post-Dispatch*, September 20, 1968, 1B; Kerstein, "Political Consequences," 137; Meier and Rudwick, *CORE*, 369–70; Henderson, "Civil Rights Movement," 53–57; and "CORE Charter Bars Whites," *Globe-Democrat*, September 17, 1968, Negro Scrapbook, vol. 3, MHS.

21. "New Civil Rights Group Formed Here," *Defender*, February 3, 1965, Calloway Papers, Box 3, Folder 23, WHMC; Lang, "Between Civil Rights and Black Power in the Gateway City," 725–54; Flug, "Organized Labor," 330; and Patterson, *Black City Politics*, 130.

22. MacLean, *Freedom Is Not Enough*, 8–9; Green, *Battling the Plantation Mentality*, 258; Percy Green, taped interview with the author, August 20, 1997; interview with Green, "Strong Seed Planted" Oral History Collection, written transcripts, Box 1, MHS; and Action Council to Improve Opportunities for Negroes circular, April 20, 1965, in author's possession.

23. Bleck, "Negro Unity"; Lang, "Between Civil Rights," 733–34; and Lede, *De Facto School Segregation*, 67. See also Daniel Patrick Moynihan, *The Negro Family: The Case for National Action* (Washington, D.C.: U.S. Department of Labor, 1965); Rhonda Y. Williams, *The Politics of Public Housing: Black Women's Struggles against Urban Inequality* (New York: Oxford University Press, 2004); and Steve Estes, *I Am a Man! Race, Manhood, and the Civil Rights Movement* (Chapel Hill: University of North Carolina Press, 2005), 108, 119.

24. "ACTION Leaders Here Jailed in Telephone Co. Demonstration," *Argus*, June 11, 1965, 1A; "Local Civil Rights Groups Feud over Negro Job Progress at Phone Co.," *Argus*, April 30, 1965, 1A; and "Dispute Runs on Phone Co.'s Hiring Policy," *Argus*, May 7, 1965, 1A.

25. "McDonnell Wins Percy Green Suit," *Post-Dispatch*, September 26, 1970,

Percy Green Papers, WHMC; and "ACTION Hits 'Mac' with Bias Charge," *Argus,* July 9, 1965, 1A.

26. "4 Arrested in Deflating of Bread Truck Tires," *Post-Dispatch,* June 18, 1967; Buddy Lonesome, "Youth—Handcuffed—Shot to Death by a Policeman Here," and "A Shocking Incident," news editorial, *Argus,* June 18, 1965, 1A and 2B; Buddy Lonesome, "Rights Groups Oppose Cop Slaying of Handcuffed Youth," *Argus,* June 25, 1965, 1A; "Any More John Bircher??" news editorial, *Argus,* June 25, 1965, 2B; "Policeman Shoots Youth," *Argus,* September 10, 1965, 1A; and "In White America," news editorial, *Argus,* June 25, 1965, 2B. See also "Crash Program on Negro Jobs Proposed Here," *Post-Dispatch,* August 19, 1965; and "65 Leaders Ask City to Ease Racial Tensions," *Globe-Democrat,* August 21–22, 1965, Negro Scrapbook, vol. 2, MHS.

27. Spencer, *St. Louis Veiled Prophet,* 126–30; Helen Dudar, "A Virgin Cult in St. Louis," *FOCUS/Midwest,* June 1962, 22–23; "ACTION Group Obstructs Veiled Prophet Spectacle," *Argus,* October 8, 1965, 1A; "Police Bar Protesters at Auditorium," *Post-Dispatch,* October 7, 1967; and Monte Reel, "ACTION, Known for Its Original Acts of Civil Disobedience, Plans a Reunion," *Post-Dispatch,* August 9, 1999, D1.

28. Eugene B. Redmond, *Drumvoices: The Mission of Afro-American Poetry, a Critical History* (Garden City, N.Y.: Anchor, 1976), 300–301; Waldo E. Martin Jr., *No Coward Soldiers: Black Cultural Politics and Postwar America* (Cambridge: Harvard University Press, 2005), 26–30; and Garner, *Contemporary Movements and Ideologies,* 16–17.

29. "Luther Mitchell: Builder of Black Culture," *Proud* magazine, January 1970, 7; Looker, *Point from Which Creation Begins,* 26–27, 46; Redmond, *Drumvoices,* 350; and James Edward Smethurst, *The Black Arts Movement: Literary Nationalism in the 1960s and 1970s* (Chapel Hill: University of North Carolina Press, 2005), 213.

30. Timothy Bleck, "Militants' Goal: Black Self-Determination by Any Means Possible," *Post-Dispatch,* September 16, 1968, 1B. See also James Boggs, *Racism and the Class Struggle: Further Pages from a Black Worker's Notebook* (New York: Monthly Review Press, 1970); Robert L. Allen, *Black Awakening in Capitalist America: An Analytic History* (1969; rpt. Trenton, N.J.: Africa World Press, 1990), 5; and Robert Blauner, "Internal Colonialism and Ghetto Revolt," *Social Problems* 16 (Spring 1969): 393–408.

31. Estes, *I Am a Man!* 124–25; and Clarence Lang, "'Forward Still!': The Development of Black Radical Insurgency in St. Louis, 1940–1990," M.A. thesis, Southern Illinois University at Edwardsville, 1997.

32. Lang, "Forward Still!" 113.

33. Ibid.; "GI Refuses to Shave: Gets 3 Years Hard Labor," *Jet,* December 3, 1970, 52; and Thomas A. Johnson, "Negro Veteran Is Confused and Bitter," *New York Times,* July 29, 1968, 14.

34. Komozi Woodard, *A Nation within a Nation: Amiri Baraka (LeRoi Jones) and Black Power Politics* (Chapel Hill: University of North Carolina Press, 1999), 7; James A. Geschwender, *Class, Race, and Worker Insurgency: The League of Revolutionary Black Workers* (New York: Cambridge University Press, 1977); Charles E. Jones, ed., *The Black Panther Party Reconsidered* (Baltimore: Black Classic Press, 1998); and Scot Brown, *Fighting for US: Maulana Karenga, the US Organization, and Black Cultural Nationalism* (New York: New York University Press, 2003). See also Stokely Carmichael and Charles V. Hamilton, *Black Power: The*

Politics of Liberation in America (New York: Vintage, 1967); and Dean E. Robinson, *Black Nationalism in American Politics and Thought* (New York: Cambridge University Press, 2001).

35. Jolly, *Black Liberation*, 120; Looker, *Point from Which Creation Begins*, 85–87; Bussel, "Trade Union Oriented," 57; "The Black Collegians," *Post-Dispatch*, December 8, 1968, "Negro Church Group Sets Parley Here," *Globe-Democrat*, September 26–27, 1968, and "Negro Churchmen Called Weak," *Post-Dispatch*, October 31, 1968, Negro Scrapbook, vol. 3, MHS. See also S. E. Anderson, "Black Students: Racial Consciousness and the Class Struggle, 1960–1976," *Black Scholar*, vol. 8, (January–February 1977): 35–43; and Angela D. Dillard, *Faith in the City: Preaching Radical Social Change in Detroit* (Ann Arbor: University of Michigan Press, 2007), 287–95.

36. Jolly, *Black Liberation*, 120; Bleck, "Militants' Goal," 1B, 4D; and Pfeffer, *A. Philip Randolph*, 276.

37. Kerstein, "Political Consequences," 261; William L. Clay, *Just Permanent Interests: Black Americans in Congress, 1870–1991* (New York: Amistad Press, 1992), 102; Jack Flach, "Negroes Plan Drive to Get Congress Seat," *Globe-Democrat*, February 1, 1967, "Negro Leaders Agree on Plan for New District," *Globe-Democrat*, February 14, 1967, and "Plan for Negro Congressional District Here Is Ordered Drawn," *Post-Dispatch*, February 5, 1967, Negro Scrapbook, vol. 2, MHS; Patterson, *Black City Politics*, 2; and Clay, *Bill Clay*, 155.

38. Jack Flach, "Negro Democrats May Vote GOP in First District," *Globe-Democrat*, June 21, 1968; and Al Delugach and Mel Luna, "Negro Publishers' Meeting with Politicians Falls Short," *Globe-Democrat*, May 7, 1968, Negro Scrapbook, vol. 3, MHS. See also Cawthra, "Ernest Calloway," 14; Calloway, "St. Louis Black Politics"; and Clay, *Bill Clay*, 157–58, 165–66.

39. "New Blood—Perhaps a Landmark," *Globe-Democrat*, August 8, 1968; Louis J. Rose, "Howard Defeats Kinney in State Senate Race," *Post-Dispatch*, August 7, 1968; and Robert Blanchard, "Kinney Defeat Is Birth of New Era," *Globe-Democrat*, August 8, 1968, Negro Scrapbook, vol. 3, MHS. See also Bleck, "Militants' Goal"; "9 Black St. Louis Candidates Win State House Seats," *Jet*, November 21, 1968, 19; and Clay, *Just Permanent Interests*, 108–22.

40. Johnson, "Negro Veteran"; and Jon Dressel, "Poor Marchers Bring Spirit of Brotherhood," *Globe Democrat*, May 21, 1968, Al Delugach, "Departing Marchers Laud City's Hospitality," *Globe-Democrat*, May 22, 1968, and "Poor Marchers Leave City," *Post-Dispatch*, May 21, 1968, Negro Scrapbook, vol. 3, MHS.

41. Looker, *Point from Which Creation Begins*, 15, 42–43, 96; Jolly, *Black Liberation*, 88–89, 95; Bleck, "Militants' Goal"; Redmond, *Drumvoices*, 398, 400; Smethurst, *The Black Arts Movement*, 221–22; and George Lipsitz, "Like a Weed in a Vacant Lot: The Black Artists Group in St. Louis," in *Decomposition: Post-Disciplinary Performance*, ed. Sue-Ellen Case, Philip Brett, and Susan Leigh Foster (Bloomington: Indiana University Press, 2000), 50–61.

42. Timothy Bleck, "Black Liberators Represent Type of Militancy Unknown in St. Louis before This Summer," *Post-Dispatch*, September 17, 1968, Negro Scrapbook, vol. 3, MHS; Harold R. Piety, "Revolution Comes to East St. Louis," *FOCUS/Midwest*, 1968, 13–15; Carson, *In Struggle*, 290; Jolly, *Black Liberation*, 63–64, 72; Looker, *Point from Which Creation Begins*, 41–44; James Forman, *The Making of Black Revolutionaries* (1972; rpt. Seattle: University of Washington Press, 1997), 460; Michael Watson and Betty J. Lee, "Cairo," *Proud* magazine, October

1971, 17, MHS; J. Anthony Lukas, "Bad Day at Cairo, Ill.," *New York Times Magazine*, February 21, 1971, 78; and Charles E. Koen, *The Cairo Story: And the Roundup of Black Leadership* (Cairo, Ill.: Koen Press, n.d.), 55–56.

43. Bleck, "Black Liberators"; interview with Charles Koen, the Freelance Archive, Series 111, Box 1, Folder 40, WU; and Jolly, *Black Liberation*, 75, 163. See also See also William B. Helmreich, *The Black Crusaders: A Case Study of a Black Militant Organization* (New York: Harper and Row, 1973), 174; and Helmreich, "The Black Liberators: A Historical Perspective," in Judson L. Jeffries, ed., *Black Power in the Belly of the Beast* (Urbana: University of Illinois Press, 2006), 281–95.

44. Timothy Bleck, "Negro Militants Make Proposal to Businessmen," *Post-Dispatch*, August 23, 1968; "Police Investigate Negro Group's 'Protection' Plan," *Globe-Democrat*, August 24–25, 1968; Bleck, "Black Liberators"; "Powell Calls for Negro 'Green Power,'" *Post-Dispatch*, August 19, 1968; and Larry Fields, "200 Hear Adam Clayton Powell in Racially-Toned Talk at Kiel," *Globe-Democrat*, August 19, 1968, Negro Scrapbook, vol. 3, MHS. See also interview with Koen, the Freelance Archive, WU.

45. Jolly, *Black Liberation*, 77–84, 105–6; Helmreich, "The Black Liberators," 292; Donald E. Franklin, "Carmichael Urges Negro Unity," *Post-Dispatch*, August 30, 1968, Bleck, "Black Liberators," and "New Negro Group Presents 15 Demands to Cervantes," *Post-Dispatch*, May 2, 1968, Negro Scrapbook, vol. 3, MHS. See also Looker, *Point from Which Creation Begins*, 81; and Lipsitz, "Like a Weed," 54–55.

46. "Attempt to Forestall Black Sundays Fails," *Post-Dispatch*, June 14, 1969; and "3 Negroes Arrested in Church Protests," *Globe-Democrat*, June 16, 1969; and "3 Black Militants Arrested in Church Confrontations," *Post-Dispatch*, June 16, 1969, Negro Scrapbook, vol. 3, MHS. See also Robert S. Lecky and H. Elliott Wrights, eds., *Black Manifesto: Religion, Racism, and Reparations* (New York: Sheed and Ward, 1969); Forman, *Making of Black Revolutionaries*, 543–50; and Lang, "Between Civil Rights," 742.

47. "Aldermen Adopt Resolution Asking Quick Police Aid," *Globe-Democrat*, June 13, 1969; "3 Black Militants Arrested in Church Confrontations," *Post-Dispatch*, June 16, 1969; and "Militants Burn Restraining Order," *Globe-Democrat*, June 23, 1969, Negro Scrapbook, vol. 3, MHS. By the spring of 1971, James Forman reported that the BEDC had received $306,000 since beginning the national campaign around the "Black Manifesto." See "'Reparation' Cash Totals $306,000; Says Manifesto Strengthened Black Clerics," *Jet*, May 27, 1971, 17.

48. Clay, *Just Permanent Interests*, 175–76; "Baptist Ministers Union Condemns 'Unholy Acts,'" *Globe-Democrat*, July 13, 1969; "2 Members of ACTION Arrested at Church," *Globe-Democrat*, August 24, 1970; and "Black Protest at Church," *Post-Dispatch*, September 14, 1970, Negro Scrapbook, vol. 3, MHS.

49. Lang, "Between Civil Rights," 743; Green Papers, WHMC; Testimony of Mr. Mango Ali, Mr. Ernest Dean, Mr. Percy Green, and Mr. Eugene Hamilton, *Hearing Before the United States Commission on Civil Rights: Hearing Held in St. Louis, Missouri, January 14–17, 1970* (Washington, D.C.: Government Printing Office, 1971), 106; and Freeman, *Song of Faith*, 128–31.

50. Green Papers, WHMC.

51. Lang, "Betweeen Civil Rights," 740.

52. "HDC Asks Writ to End 9-Day Sit-in at Office," *Globe-Democrat*, August 23, 1967; "Women Face Forcible Removal in HDC Sit-In," *Globe-Democrat*, August 25, 1967; "Tenants Picket Public Housing Agency Offices," *Post-Dispatch*, Novem-

ber 8, 1967; and Al Delugach, "Public Housing Tenants to Continue Picketing," *Globe-Democrat*, November 9, 1967, Negro Scrapbook, vol. 2, MHS.

53. "200 Negroes March on City Hall," *Post-Dispatch*, May 13, 1968; "1000 Tenants Open Rent Strike," *Post-Dispatch*, February 3, 1969; and Richard Krantz, "Leader of Housing Strike Tells of Tenants' Plight," *Globe-Democrat*, n.d., Negro Scrapbook, vol. 3, MHS. See also interview with Loretta Hall, "Strong Seed Planted" Oral History Collection, written transcripts, Box 1, MHS; and Johnson, "Negro Veteran," 14.

54. Ibid.

55. Calloway, "Creative Self-Determinism"; Calloway, "Public Housing in St. Louis," *Sentinel*, February 21, 1970; and Harold J. Gibbons, "The Poor Must Find Dignity, Security in Housing," *Missouri Teamster*, September 19, 1969, Calloway Papers, Addenda, Box 5, Folder 139, WHMC. See also Lipsitz, *Life in the Struggle*, 148; and Bussel, "Trade Union Oriented," 59.

56. Bussel, "Trade Union Oriented"; "Gibbons, Rent Strikes Propose Housing Coalition," *Post-Dispatch*, October 10, 1969, Calloway Papers, Addenda, Box 5, Folder 139, WHMC; Harry B. Wilson Jr., "Stalemate in Public Housing Crisis," *Globe-Democrat*, August 29, 1969, Negro Scrapbook, vol. 3, MHS; and Kerstein, "Political Consequences," 162.

57. "Gibbons, Rent Strikes Propose Housing Coalition," *Post-Dispatch*, October 10, 1969; and Ernest Calloway, "The Evolution of a New Public Housing Concept," *Missouri Teamster*, October 1968, Calloway Papers, Addenda, Box 5, Folder 139, WHMC.

58. Lipsitz, *Life in the Struggle*, 148; Looker, *Point from Which Creation Begins*, 82–84; Marsha Canfield, "Coalition Formed; Rent Strike End Seems Near," *Globe-Democrat*, October 11, 1969, and Ernest Calloway, "A Small October Revolution," *St. Louis Sentinel*, November 8, 1969, Calloway Papers, Addenda, Box 5, Folder 139, WHMC. See also Bussel, "Trade Union Oriented," 49, 60–61.

59. See Countryman, *Up South*; Williams, *Black Politics / White Power*; and Willams, *The Politics of Public Housing*.

60. Willhelm, *Who Needs the Negro?* 189.

CHAPTER EIGHT

1. Levison, *The Working-Class Majority*, 262; Landry, *New Black Middle Class*, 70, 85–86; Morton G. Wenger, "State Responses to Afro-American Rebellion: Internal Neo-colonialism and the Rise of a New Black Petite Bourgeoisie," *Insurgent Sociologist* 10 (Fall 1980): 62–63, 69–71; Munford, *Production Relations*, 53, 61; Robert C. Smith, *We Have No Leaders: African Americans in the Post-Civil Rights Era* (Albany: State University of New York Press, 1996), 33; and Allen, *Black Awakening*, 125–26; and *Boston, Race, Class, and Conservatism*, 41–45.

2. Wenger, "State Responses," 61; and Richard Child Hill, "Race, Class and the State: The Metropolitan Enclave System in the United States," *Insurgent Sociologist* 10 (Fall 1980): 50.

3. Timothy Bleck, "Police, Militants Here in Open Confrontation," *Post-Dispatch*, September 15, 1968, 1B; "Brostron Denies Truce with Black Liberators," *Globe-Democrat*, November 18, 1968; and "Lucas Police Station Fired On after Black Liberator's Arrest," *Post-Dispatch*, November 16, 1968, Negro Scrapbook, vol. 3, MHS.

4. "Testifies He Saw Officer Fire On Liberator Office," *Post-Dispatch*, October 18, 1968; "21 Black Militants Arrested in Terrorism" and "Stop Guerrilla War in St. Louis!" news editorial, *Globe-Democrat*, September 6, 1968; "Long Indorses Crackdown on Black Militant Groups," *Post-Dispatch*, September 6, 1968; and "Battle of Police, Militants Subsides into Verbal Feud," *Globe-Democrat*, September 7–8, 1968, Negro Scrapbook, vol. 3, MHS.

5. "Battle of Police, Militants Subsides into Verbal Feud"; "Two Top Black Power Leaders Fined $500 Each as Result of Rally," *Post-Dispatch*, September 9, 1968; "Four Are Fined for Inflammatory Remarks Here," *Globe-Democrat*, September 10 1968; and "Arrested for Speaking?" news editorial, *Post-Dispatch*, July 10, 1968, Negro Scrapbook, vol. 3, MHS.

6. Jolly, *Black Liberation*, 163–69; Helmreich, "The Black Liberators," 283; and Bleck, "Negro Unity." See also "Mayor for Outsiders in Inquiry," *Post-Dispatch*, September 16, 1968; "Black Liberators Submit Reports to Police Inspector's Office," *Post-Dispatch*, September 27, 1968; "Protest at Home of Mayor," *Post-Dispatch*, September 14, 1968; "ACLU to Sue Police Department," *Post-Dispatch*, September 13, 1968; and Bleck, "Black Liberators."

7. "Mayor for Outsiders in Inquiry"; "St. Louis Suspends Cops for 'Overreaction,'" *Jet*, October 3, 1968, 7; and "6 Black Power Leaders Acquitted in Rally Case," *Globe-Democrat*, April 29, 1969, "Brostron Denies Truce with Black Liberators"; "Lucas Police Station Fired On after Black Liberator's Arrest"; and Timothy Bleck, "Liberators Profess Interest in Politics," *Post-Dispatch*, November 20, 1968, Negro Scrapbook, vol. 3, MHS.

8. Samuel F. Yette, *The Choice: The Issue of Black Survival in America* (1971; rpt. Silver Spring, Md.: Cottage Books, 1982), 32–34, 268–71; Gerald D. McKnight, *The Last Crusade: Martin Luther King, Jr., the FBI, and the Poor People's Campaign* (Boulder, Colo.: Westview Press, 1998), 86; and Allen, *Black Awakening*, 196–208.

9. Yette, *The Choice*, 167, 222–23; and Sundiata Keita Cha-Jua and Clarence Lang, "Providence, Patriarchy, Pathology: Louis Farrakhan's Rise and Decline," *New Politics* 6 (Winter 1997): 52.

10. "The Real Martin Luther King," news editorial, *Globe-Democrat*, March 30–31, 1968, 2C; Nicholas M. Horrock, "Report by a Missouri Man Suggests Plotters Sought Murder of Dr. King," *New York Times*, July 26, 1978, 1A; and McKnight, *The Last Crusade*, 60–62. See also Ward Churchill and Jim Vander Wall, *The COINTELPRO Papers: Documents from the FBI's Secret Wars against Domestic Dissent in the United States* (Boston: South End Press, 1990), n. 351.

11. *COINTELPRO: The Counter-Intelligence Program of the FBI* (Wilmington, Del.: Scholarly Resources, 1978), microfilm reels 1 and 2; and "Raid on Militants Criticized," *Post-Dispatch*, January 30, 1970, and Charles Edward W. O'Brien, "Militants Tied to Extortion Plot," *Globe-Democrat*, June 26, 1969, Negro Scrapbook, vol. 3, MHS.

12. Charles J. Oswald, "Arms Cache Seized at Militants' Office," *Globe-Democrat*, January 30, 1970, Negro Scrapbook, vol. 3, MHS; and McKnight, *The Last Crusade*, 8, 86.

13. *COINTELPRO*, microfilm reel 2; Jake McCarthy, "Sad Story of Jimmy Rollins," *Post-Dispatch*, December 19, 1975, 3A, Green Papers, WHMC; "Liberators, SNCC Form an Alliance," *Post-Dispatch*, November 9, 1968, and "Two Black Liberators Indicted in Assault Case," *Globe-Democrat*, November 20, 1968, Negro Scrapbook, vol. 3, MHS; Lukas, "Bad Day at Cairo," 86; Koen, *The Cairo Story*, 60; "Koen Begins 6 Month Term in St. Louis Jail," *Jet*, August 12, 1971, 9;

and "Rev. Koen Paroled from St. Louis, Mo., Workhouse," *Jet*, October 14, 1971, 57.

14. *COINTELPRO*, microfilm reel 3; and Schuster, "The Warrior," 9. The actual text of the phony letter later appeared in a series of *Post-Dispatch* articles following the public disclosure of COINTEL activities in 1975. See Martha Shirk, "False Letter Used by FBI to Defile St. Louisan," *Post-Dispatch*, November 19, 1975, 1; and Robert Adams, "FBI Tactics Likened to Those of Russia," *Post-Dispatch*, November 19, 19, 1975, 1, Green Papers, WHMC.

15. *COINTELPRO*, microfilm reel 3; and Marable, *Race, Reform, and Rebellion*, 132–34.

16. Neil R. McMillen, *The Citizens' Council: Organized Resistance to the Second Reconstruction, 1954–64* (Urbana: University of Illinois Press, 1971), 150 n. 50; Dean Kotlowski, "Black Power—Nixon Style: The Nixon Administration and Minority Business Enterprise," *Business History Review* 72 (Autumn 1998): 413; and Kenneth D. Durr, *Behind the Backlash: White Working-Class Politics in Baltimore, 1940–1980* (Chapel Hill: University of North Carolina Press, 2003), 33–52, 120. See also Jonathan Rieder, "The Rise of the 'Silent Majority,'" in Fraser and Gerstle, *Rise and Fall*, 243–68.

17. Matthew D. Lassiter, *The Silent Majority: Suburban Politics in the Sunbelt South* (Princeton, N.J.: Princeton University Press, 2006), 15; Gordon, *Mapping Decline*, 51; Levy, *Civil War*, 92–94, 152–55; *Durr, Behind the Backlash*, 130, 144–45; and Donald T. Critchlow, *Phyllis Schlafly and Grassroots Conservatism: A Woman's Crusade* (Princeton, N.J.: Princeton University Press, 2005), 109.

18. Jefferson Cowie, "Nixon's Class Struggle: Romancing the New Right Worker, 1969–1973," *Labor History* 43 (2002): 257, 281–82; Bussel, "Trade Union Oriented," 63–64; and Kotlowski, "Black Power—Nixon Style," 421.

19. Lassiter, *The Silent Majority*, 227; MacLean, *Freedom Is Not Enough*, 95–102; Cowie, "Nixon's Class Struggle," 258, 263, 274; Joshua B. Freeman, "Hardhats: Construction Workers, Manliness, and the 1970 Pro-war Demonstrations," *Journal of Social History* 26 (Summer 1993): 725, 733–36; and Lang, "Between Civil Rights," 743.

20. James W. Naughton, "U.S. Will Extend Minority Job Aid," *New York Times*, September 30, 1969, 1; and Marsha Canfield, "Agency Makes St. Louis Plan Mandatory," *Globe-Democrat*, n.d., Negro Scrapbook, vol. 3, MHS.

21. Cowie, "Nixon's Class Struggle," 264; "100,000 May Take Part in Parade of 'Hard Hats,'" *Post-Dispatch*, June 7, 1970, 1A; and "Some Violence at March Backing War," *Post-Dispatch*, June 8, 1970, 1A.

22. National Socialist White People's Party flyer, 1969, Race Relations Collection, Box 1, File 4, MHS; and Robert H. Collins, "Anti-Negro Leaflets on South Side," *Post-Dispatch*, December 3, 1969, Negro Scrapbook, vol. 3, MHS.

23. McMillen, *The Citizens' Council*, 150 n. 50; St. Louis Neighborhoods Collection, MHS; Bussel, "Trade Union Oriented," 65; Russell, *Out of the Jungle*, 223–24; and Brill, *The Teamsters*, 380–83.

24. Pfeffer, *A. Philip Randolph*, 286–87, 290; Estes, *I Am a Man!* 122–23; McKnight, *The Last Crusade*, 14–19, 92; Clay, *Bill Clay*, 133, 135; "Will Missouri Fail Again? A Frank View of Gov. Hearnes' Position on Title 19," *FOCUS/Midwest*, 1967, 11; and "2 Men Paid by HDC Assigned to Support Busch Boycott," *Globe-Democrat*, December 7, 1970, Les Pearson, "HDC Orders Trainee Plan Shake-Up," *Globe-Democrat*, December 10, 1970, Dennis J. McCarthy, "Stores Threatened in

Busch Boycott," *Globe-Democrat*, December 9, 1970, and "FBI Inquiry Asked in HDC Fund Use" and "St. Louis Job-Training Swindle," news editorial, *Globe-Democrat*, December 8, 1970, Negro Scrapbook, vol. 3, MHS.

25. Teaford, *Twentieth-Century American City*, 125; Bussel, "Trade Union Oriented," 61–62; and Kerstein, "Political Consequences," 189–92, 212, 251, 260.

26. Kerstein, "Political Consequences," 137; and Calloway, "Creative Self-Determinism."

27. Yette, *The Choice*, 37; Melvin Small, *The Presidency of Richard Nixon* (Lawrence: University Press of Kansas, 1999), 188–89; Hill, "Race, Class and State," 50; Walker, *Black Business in America*, 267–70, 276–77, 312; and Robert E. Weems Jr., and Lewis A. Randolph, "The National Response to Richard M. Nixon's Black Capitalism Initiative: The Success of Domestic Détente," *Journal of Black Studies* 32 (September 2001): 67.

28. Allen, *Black Awakening*, 23, 70; Clay, *Bill Clay*, 219; and Jolly, *Black Liberation*, 131–36. See also "$30,000 Grant to St. Louis U. for Negroes," *Globe-Democrat*, August 16, 1968; Curt Matthews, "Black Capitalism Seeks Niche Business World for Negro," *Post-Dispatch*, March 3, 1969; and Bleck, "Negro Unity."

29. "Negro Business Drive Gets a Financial Lift," *Globe-Democrat*, September 25, 1968; Mel Luna, "SBA to Open Offices in Ghetto Here," *Globe-Democrat*, September 24, 1968; "Move to Promote Negro Businesses," *Globe-Democrat*, October 24, 1968; "Negro Buys White-Owned Firm," *Globe-Democrat*, October 12–13, 1968; Curt Matthews, "Problems for Black Capitalism: Financing, Out-of-Ghetto Sites," *Post-Dispatch*, March 4, 1969; "City's Largest Negro-Owned Firm to Open," *Post-Dispatch*, March 12, 1969; and "Grandel Square Loan by Gen. American," *Post-Dispatch*, August 26, 1968, Negro Scrapbook, vol. 3, MHS.

30. Mel Luna, "2 Grants Spur Program for Negro Firms," *Globe-Democrat*, January 4–5, 1969; "$130,000 for Black Capitalism," *Post-Dispatch*, January 28, 1970; Matthews, "Black Capitalism Seeks Niche Business World for Negro"; "Blacks Form Building Group," *Globe-Democrat*, July 10, 1970; "All-Black Construction Group Formed to Increase Negro Jobs," *Post-Dispatch*, July 9, 1970; Mel Luna, "New Motto of Militant Leaders—Build, Baby, Build," *Globe-Democrat*, December 30, 1968; and "McDonnell Douglas Names Job Opportunity Director," *Post-Dispatch*, April 29, 1970, Negro Scrapbook, vol. 3, MHS. See also Jolly, *Black Liberation*, 131–36; and Walker, *Black Business in America*, 332.

31. Matthews, "Black Capitalism Seeks Niche Business World for Negro"; Timothy Bleck, "Mid-City Community Congress Seeks Power for Poor in Ghetto," *Post-Dispatch*, August 6, 1968; Mel Luna, "Negro-White Partnership in Ghetto Emerges," *Globe-Democrat*, August 24–25, 1968; "'Buy Black' Campaign Starting," *Globe-Democrat*, July 20–21, 1968; and Luna, "New Motto of Militant Leaders—Build, Baby, Build," Negro Scrapbook, vol. 3, MHS. See also Kotlowski, "Black Power—Nixon Style," 415; Walker, *Black Business in America*, 333; Meier and Rudwick, *CORE*, 420–23; "CORE Seeks $10 Million for Black Business Venture," *Jet*, November 14, 1968, 50; Jolly, *Black Liberation*, 49, 137–38; Allen, *Black Awakening*, 48; and Robert L. Joiner, "Militants' Aim: Better West End," *Post-Dispatch*, November 2, 1971, 3A.

32. Kotlowski, "Black Power—Nixon Style," 435–39, 445; Weems and Randolph, "The National Response to Richard M. Nixon's Black Capitalism Initiative," 265; "Businessmen Meet Nixon; Get $50 Million in Contracts Promised," *Jet*, August 6, 1970, 20–22; Gerald Meyer, "Black Owned Firms Not Eager to Win

Special SBA Contracts," *Post-Dispatch*, August 13, 1970, and Meyer, "Minority Business Aids Win Few Friends Here," *Post-Dispatch*, February 9, 1971, Negro Scrapbook, vol. 3, MHS.

33. George Morrison, "Black Capitalism Here Is Myth, Study Shows," *Globe-Democrat*, June 28–29, 1969; Gerald Meyer, "Capital Shortage Slows Black Business Growth," *Post-Dispatch*, February 10, 1971; and Curt Matthews, "Problems for Black Capitalism: Financing, Out-of-Ghetto Sites," *Post-Dispatch*, March 4, 4, 1969, Negro Scrapbook, vol. 3, MHS. See also Walker, *Black Business in America*, 268–69.

34. Morrison, "Black Capitalism," and Matthews, "Black Capitalism Seeks Niche Business World for Negro," Negro Scrapbook, vol. 3, MHS; and Walker, *Black Business in America*, 342, 345.

35. Matthews, "Black Capitalism Seeks Niche Business World for Negro," Negro Scrapbook, vol. 3, MHS; Looker, *Point from Which Creation Begins*, 56, 130–31; Lipsitz, "Like a Weed," 57; Munford, *Production Relations*, 55, 60; Allen, *Black Awakening*, 190, 226–27; Hill, "Race, Class and State," 50; and Kotlowski, "Black Power—Nixon Style," 441.

36. Allen, *Black Awakening*, 233.

37. Walker, *Black Business in America*, 285; Cha-Jua and Lang, "Providence, Patriarchy, Pathology," 53; Leonard N. Moore, *Carl B. Stokes and the Rise of Black Political Power* (Urbana: University of Illinois Press, 2002), 56; Smith, *We Have No Leaders*, 33, 106, 115–17; Calloway, "St. Louis Black Politics"; Clay, *Bill Clay*, 196; and Clay, *Just Permanent Interests*, 102.

38. Clay, *Just Permanent Interests*, 139–47, 181; and Smith, *We Have No Leaders*, 34, 107.

39. William L. Clay, "Emerging New Black Politics," *Black World*, October 1972, 33–34; Clay, *Bill Clay*, 189, 191, 205; and Clay, *Just Permanent Interests*, 323–31. Prompted by his conviction in a 1967 civil contempt of court case, the U.S. House of Representatives had stripped Powell of his committee chairmanship and denied him his seat.

40. Marable, *Race, Reform, and Rebellion*, 112–35; Woodard, *Nation within a Nation*, 185, 196–99; Clay, *Just Permanent Interests*, 202–11; Smith, *We Have No Leaders*, 43, 53–54, 113; and Imamu Amiri Baraka, "Toward the Creation of Political Institutions for All African Peoples," *Black World*, October 1972, 65, 71.

41. Smith, *We Have No Leaders*, 71–72, 123; Hill, *The Deacons for Defense*, 15; Donald Tapperson, "City's Blacks Staying Away from Polls," *Post-Dispatch*, April 18, 1971, Negro Scrapbook, vol. 3, MHS; and Ernest Calloway, "School Board Elections Illustrate Decline of St. Louis Black Politics," *Missouri Teamster*, May 18, 1979, Calloway Papers, Box 3, Folder 28, WHMC. See also Adolph Reed Jr., *Stirrings in the Jug: Black Politics in the Post-segregation Era* (Minneapolis: University of Minnesota Press, 1999), 18.

42. Anderson, *A. Philip Randolph*, 342; Robert Adams, "Blacks in St. Louis Area Still Lag in Well-Paying Jobs," *Post-Dispatch*, June 25, 1972, 12A; "15-Month-Long Boycott of Krey Products Lifted," *Globe-Democrat*, August 22–23, 1970, and "United Black Alliance Ends Krey Packing Co. Boycott," *Post-Dispatch*, August 22, 1970, Negro Scrapbook, vol. 3, MHS. See also "The Program of the CBTU," Ora Lee Malone Research Papers, 1940–1990, Collection 670, Box 2, Folder 5, WHMC; and Foner, *Organized Labor*, 432–33.

43. "St. Louis Women's Labor Conference: Suggested Resolutions," November 17, 1973, and Coalition of Labor Union Women, "Statement of

Purpose/Structure and Guidelines," adopted March 23–24, 1974, Ora Lee Malone Papers, Collection 383, WHMC. See also Foner, *Women and Labor Movement*, 507–8, 516.

44. "Gooey Protest at Bell Brings Arrest for 2," *Globe-Democrat*, July 8, 1970; "Protesters Arrested at UE," *Post-Dispatch*, May 28, 1975; "Gas Repair Jobs Halted by ACTION," *Post-Dispatch*, July 24, 1974, 3C; "Laclede Accuses ACTION of Threats," *Post-Dispatch*, July 26, 1974; and "Percy Green and ACTION Decorate Laclede Gas," *Evening Whirl*, August 7, 1973, Green Papers, WHMC; and Green, interview with author.

45. Lang, "Between Civil Rights," 743.

46. "McDonnell to Keep Hiring Plan Secret," *Post-Dispatch*, February 13, 1970; "4 Charged with Trespassing," *Globe-Democrat*, March 19, 1970; "ACTION's Tet Offenses," ACTION press statement, May 24, 1971; "2 Charged in McDonnell Protest," *Globe-Democrat*, May 30, 1974; "2 Seized in Building," *Post-Dispatch*, May 11, 1974; "ACTION Members Invade McDonnell's," *American*, June 6, 1974; and "Testimony on McDonnell Policy," *Post-Dispatch*, August 6, 1970, Green Papers, WHMC. See also Meyer, "Percy Green's Tactic."

47. Oppenheimer, "Story of *Green*," 29–30, 35; Rudolph Alexander Jr., "A Mountain Too High: African Americans and Employment Discrimination," *African American Research Perspectives* 9 (Winter 2003): 33–37; and Schuster, "The Warrior," 9.

48. Smith, *We Have No Leaders*, 75.

49. Landry, *New Black Middle Class*, 120; Allen, *Black Awakening*, 14–18; Walker, *Black Business in America*, 364; Weems and Randolph, "The National Response to Richard M. Nixon's Black Capitalism Initiative," 66; Woodard, *Nation within a Nation*, 203; and Smith, *We Have No Leaders*, 122.

50. Landry, *New Black Middle Class*, 194–96, 210; and Marable, *Race, Reform, and Rebellion*, 149–84.

51. Allen, *Black Awakening*, 26; Munford, *Production Relations*, 62; and Carter Smith, "Laclede Minority Hiring Plan," *Post-Dispatch*, September 1, 1976, 3A, Green Papers, WHMC. See also William Julius Wilson, *The Declining Significance of Race: Blacks and Changing American Institutions*, 2nd ed. (Chicago: University of Chicago Press, 1980), 21, 135–36, 178.

CONCLUSION

1. Gordon, *Mapping Decline*, 10; Ernest Calloway, "'80 Census Will Show Black Urban Enclaves' Changing Character," *Missouri Teamster*, April 20, 1979, Calloway Papers, Box 3, Folder 28, WHMC; and Robert L. Joiner, "St. Louis Ranked 2nd Most Depressed City in New Study," *Post-Dispatch*, July 8, 1980, 4A.

2. "David M. Grant Dies at 82; Lawyer Active in Civil Rights," *Globe-Democrat*, August 13, 1985; "E. Calloway Dies; Labor Activist," *Post-Dispatch*, January 4, 1990; and Ingram, "Hershel Walker," "Strong Seed Planted" Oral History Collection, written transcripts, Box 2, MHS.

3. MacLean, *Freedom Is Not Enough*, 291; Primm, *Lion of the Valley*, 515; and Stein, *St. Louis Politics*, 227–40.

4. Reed, *Stirrings in the Jug*, 79–116; "Racial Split in a Primary Disturbs Core of St. Louis," *New York Times*, March 10, 1997; and Stein, *St. Louis Politics*, 227–40.

5. Theodore D. McNeal Jr., "Where Are the Construction Jobs for African-

Americans?" *Post-Dispatch*, January 21, 2002, B7; Ralph Blumenthal and Robert D. McFadden, "Bush Sees Long Recovery for New Orleans; 30,000 Troops in Largest U.S. Relief Effort," A1, and Felicity Barringer and Jere Longman, "Owners Take Up Arms as Looters Press Their Advantage," *New York Times*, September 1, 2005, A14; David Gonzalez, "From Margins of Society to Center of the Tragedy" and Joseph B. Treaster and Deborah Sontag, "Despair and Lawlessness Grip New Orleans as Thousands Remain Stranded in Squalor," *New York Times*, September 2, 2005, A1; and Todd S. Purdum, "Across U.S., Outrage at Response," *New York Times*, September 3, 2005, A1.

   6. John M. Broder, "Amid Criticism of Federal Efforts, Charges of Racism Are Lodged," *New York Times*, September 5, 2005, A10; Susan Saulny, "Newcomer Is Struggling to Lead a City in Ruins," *New York Times*, September 3, 2005, A7; Manley Elliott Banks II, "A Changing Electorate in a Majority Black City: The Emergence of a Neo-conservative Black Urban Regime in Contemporary Atlanta," *Journal of Urban Affairs* 22 (2000): 265–78; and John Arena, "Race and Hegemony: The Neoliberal Transformation of the Black Urban Regime and Working-Class Resistance," *American Behavioral Scientist* 47 (2003): 352–80.

   7. Horton et al., "Lost in the Storm," 128; Adolph Reed Jr., "The Underclass as Myth and Symbol: The Poverty of Discourse about Poverty," *Radical America* 24 (1990): 21–40. See also *The Underclass: Hearing before the Joint Economic Committee, Congress of the United States, One Hundred First Congress, First Session, May 25, 1989* (Washington, D.C.: Government Printing Office, 1989).

   8. Reed, *Stirrings in the Jug*, 117–59; Calloway, "'80 Census"; Ernest Calloway, "Black Underclass Needs 'Selfhood' Revolution," *Missouri Teamster*, May 19, 1978, Calloway Papers, Box 3, Folder 28, WHMC; William Julius Wilson, *The Truly Disadvantaged: The Inner City, the Underclass, and Public Policy* (Chicago: University of Chicago Press, 1987), 3–19; and Singh, *Black Is a Country*, 9–10.

   9. Wilson, *The Declining Significance of Race*, 135; Robin D. G. Kelley, "'We Are Not What We Seem': Rethinking Black Working-Class Opposition in the Jim Crow South," *Journal of American History* 80 (1993): 75–112; and Goings and Smith, "Unhidden Transcripts."

   10. Landry, *New Black Middle Class*, 116–19.

   11. MacLean, *Freedom Is Not Enough*, 104; and Brian Purnell, "'Taxation without Sanitation Is Tyranny': Civil Rights Struggles over Garbage Collection in Brooklyn, New York during the Fall of 1962," *Afro-Americans in New York Life and History* 31 (July 2007): 61–88. See also Green, *Battling the Plantation Mentality*, 280.

Index